Palestinian Village Histories

Stanford Studies in Middle Eastern and Islamic Societies and Cultures

Palestinian Village Histories

GEOGRAPHIES OF THE DISPLACED

Rochelle A. Davis

Stanford University Press
Stanford, California

Stanford University Press
Stanford, California

Printed in the United States of America on acid-free, archival-quality paper

Library of Congress Cataloging-in-Publication Data

Davis, Rochelle.
  Palestinian village histories : geographies of the displaced / Rochelle A. Davis.
    p. cm.--(Stanford studies in Middle Eastern and Islamic societies and cultures)
  Includes bibliographical references and index.
  ISBN 978-0-8047-7312-6 (cloth : alk. paper)--ISBN 978-0-8047-7313-3 (pbk. : alk. paper)
  1. Palestinian Arabs--Historiography. 2. Palestine--History, Local. 3. Villages--Palestine--Historiography. I. Title. II. Series: Stanford studies in Middle Eastern and Islamic societies and cultures.
  DS113.6.D38 2011
  956.940072--dc22   2010032339

Typeset by Bruce Lundquist in 10/14 Minion

To my parents and my nephew Evan Goodwin (1984–2004)

CONTENTS

LIST OF ILLUSTRATIONS

NOTE ON TRANSLATIONS AND TRANSLITERATIONS

I have chosen to write this book in a style that contributes to the scholarly literature but that can be read by scholars and nonscholars alike. My goal is to communicate what is contained in the village books, especially to those who cannot find them or read them. Thus I have minimized my use of Arabic transliterations of words, and for those that I have used, definitions are provided the first time they appear in the text.

That said, because of the topic, the Arabic names of people and places appear frequently. I have used a modified system of transliterating Arabic to English according to the *International Journal of Middle East Studies* and eliminating the diacriticals and long vowel markers. I have chosen to skip the diacriticals to avoid all of the dots and lines that are irrelevant to the reader who does not know Arabic. Diacritical marks make it easy to turn English back into Arabic script, and I recognize that I have now made that task more difficult. On occasion I have chosen to transcribe a more colloquial pronunciation of a name instead of using the Modern Standard Arabic, so occasionally an "ee" is used instead of an "i." But in general I have transliterated the *ta marbuta* as "a" and not as "eh" or "ah," at least in part because Palestinians vary in their pronunciation of that letter as well. I have used standard conventions to render the letters ayn (') and hamza ('). In choosing the transliterations of village names, I have referred to the spellings used in *All That Remains* (published by the Institute of Palestine Studies and edited by Walid Khalidi) and by PalestineRemembered.com. For the sake of clarity, I have chosen the English spellings of the refugee camp names used by the United Nations Relief and Works Administration, which administers services in the camps; these spellings do not follow my transliteration system. If the Arab authors cited are published in English, I use the spellings they used for their names in their texts (for example, Constantine Zurayk and Sarif Kanaana), but transliterated their Arabic works according to the modified IJMES system (Zurayq and Kana'ana). The unique Palestinian family names were sometimes challenging to transliterate into English, and those who want to reconstruct them back into Arabic may also face some difficulty. Because in most Arabic texts the short vowels are not marked, some family and place names are my educated guesses. For example, I initially transliterated the Arabic name S-m-r-y-n as Samarayn. Despite asking every Palestinian I knew, it was not until I met Ghalib Sumrayn that I learned the correct vowels. I hope that I have been right more often than not, and that those who have been misrepresented by my transliterating hand will be forgiving.

ACKNOWLEDGEMENTS

Because my project on Palestinian villages began as a side interest while I was doing research on Palestinian narratives of life before 1948, the research for and writing of this book have taken place over the course of more than ten years. I try here to acknowledge some of the debts I owe, though I am bound to have inadvertently left out people I should have thanked. Errors remain my own.

The village book authors in Jordan, Syria, Lebanon, and Palestine/Israel made this research a stimulating and pleasurable process. They explained their writing and research techniques to me and shared their perspectives on writing history. They told me about the sensitive and at times painful subject of the community's reception of their work. I hope that both those I interviewed and those I did not will see my commentaries on their books as those of an engaged reader, one who sees history through eyes both similar to and different from theirs. Countless numbers of their families and friends unearthed their books, introduced me to the authors, and provided me with tea and coffee and rides home. I am grateful for their cooperation and generosity.

Institutional support made this book possible in many ways: from the men and women who have cleaned my offices, to the librarians who have hunted down books, to the granting agencies that have given me research funds. I was affiliated at different stages of this research with the Institute for Jerusalem Studies in Ramallah and the Center for Strategic Studies at the University of Jordan. While I was a postdoctoral fellow at Stanford University, I received an Andrew W. Mellon grant for research leave from teaching. A National Endowment for the Humanities fellowship received through the American Center of Oriental Research (ACOR) provided me with essential research time in Jordan. Grants from Georgetown University's School of Foreign Service and Graduate School and a Sultanate of Oman Faculty Research Grant from Georgetown's Center for Contemporary Arab Studies (CCAS), funded through the Oman Program Endowment to the CCAS, allowed me to take numerous research trips. I am grateful for the support of the library staff at the University of Jordan and its microfilm room; the library and photocopy staff at the Abdul Hameed Shoman Library in Amman; the staffs of al-Jana—the Arab Resource Center for Popular Arts in Beirut—and Dar al-Shajara in Damascus; the library staff of the Institute for Palestine Studies in Beirut, headed by the wonderful Mona Nsouli; Middle East librarian Brenda Bickett at Georgetown University; and the InterLibrary Loan staff at Georgetown University. The editorial staff of Stanford University Press have been a pleasure to work with and improved my writing.

In Jordan, long-time acquaintance Bilal al-Hijjawi was fearless in tracking down village book authors and in finding their homes amid the unmarked streets of Amman. The staff of ACOR—Nisreen Abu al-Shaykh; Mohammed, Sa'ed, and Abed Adawi; Humi Ayoubi; Pierre and Patricia Bikai; Samya Kafafi; Kathy Nimry; Barbara Porter; and Chris Tuttle—deserve my professional and personal thanks for their support over the years. In Syria, Sulayman al-Dabbagh, Ayman Qasim, Ghassan al-Shihabi, Muhammad Jalbout, Mai al-Shihabi, Nahed al-Shihabi, and Omar Shanbour shared their ideas with me; arranged meetings; found useful books, videos, and DVDs; and made my research possible and enjoyable, for which I am particularly indebted to them. The young men and women of al-Shajara and Samed put up with me wandering in and out of their work spaces and asking them all sorts of unexpected questions. Others in Lebanon, Palestine, Jordan, and the United States kindly assisted me with this project, including Saqr Abu Fakher, Moataz al-Dajani, 'Uthman Hasan and his son (of the Chicago Qalunya community), and Abu Qusay al-Najjar. Saleh Abdel Jawad, professor of political science at Birzeit University, gave generously of his time, his library, and the correspondence on the village books sent to him as director of the Center for Research and Documentation of Palestinian Society (CRDPS) at Birzeit University. He is a walking compendium of the village books and of the issues the CRDPS faced in publishing them. My research assistants over the years at Georgetown University—Ziad Abu-Rish, Adam Coogle, Dahlia Elzein, Andrew Farrand, Elizabeth Grasmeder, David Greenhaulgh, Hammad Hammad, Nehad Khader, Ava Leone, Megan Schudde, Omar Shakir, Dina Takruri, Alissa Walter, and Mat Zalk—put up with some incredibly tedious but useful tasks, and they have my gratitude for their perseverance and dedication. The faculty and staff at CCAS have become my friends and colleagues and their spirit and dedication make it a wonderful place to work.

Many individuals have been crucial to the process of conceptualizing and writing this book. I owe an intellectual and inspirational debt to Salim Tamari, who has been my mentor and friend for many years. His scholarly guidance, encouragement, and support have meant a great deal to me. Kimberly Katz, as both friend and colleague, has been unstintingly selfless in her continuous encouragement and intelligent and detailed comments on drafts, and she has made my writing better. My colleagues Fida Adely and Melissa Fisher have provided invaluable support and intellectual input, from talking through ideas to reading drafts. Because of them I have enjoyed the process of writing this book. I benefited from numerous conversations early on with Andrew Shryock and Rosemary Sayigh about oral histories and written texts. Drafts of a chapter were read by Lila Abu-Lughod and Ahmad Sa'di. I must thank Joseph Sassoon for his gentle assistance in reading chapters, for helping with translations from Arabic and Hebrew, and for his attention to detail. The manuscript benefited enormously from the comments of two anonymous reviewers, who have my gratitude.

Others have facilitated my research in numerous ways and discussed intellectual subjects with me, to my great benefit: Suad al-Amiry, Kara Cooney, Sharif Elmusa, Brien Garnand, Issam Nassar, Sherene Seikaly, Lucia Volk, and Dan Walsh (curator of the Palestine Poster Project Archive). My gratitude also goes to Jomana Amara, who generously expanded my collection of village books by opening her own bookshelves to me; to Noor Hasan, for her meals and unending sweetness; to Kholoud Hussein, for her hard work transcribing and her wry humor; to Mahmoud Zeidan of Sifsaf, for his always interesting conversations; to Muhammad Zeidan of al-Reineh near Nazareth, for his inspiring work at the Arab Association for Human Rights; and Areej Sabbagh-Khouri and her family, for their passion and belief. Kenneth Herbst has been generous in too many ways to enumerate. I am delighted to have as my friends Sulayman al-Dabbagh and Ayman Qasim, whom I admire for their dedication and honesty. My Arabic teachers in Egypt, Jordan, and Michigan helped me become fluent, but the ones who taught me the most beautiful and expressive Arabic were Marcel Khalifa, Mahmud Darwish, Shaykh Imam, and Ahmad Fu'ad Nagm.

The companionship, discussions, and abodes of many friends provided me with homes away from home: Anna Newman and Mueen Ghani (in Menlo

Park, California; Mazen Daqqaq and Tania Attiya and their little Ahlam, who arrived during the writing of this book, and Sufian al-Hijjawi, who left us much too soon (in Amman); Yaser Rawashdeh and his wonderful family (in Shobak, Jordan); and the Griffins (in New York and Lyme, Connecticut). Friends have been great supporters and welcome distractions throughout this long process: Robin Bhatty (for those three hours), Ahmad Dallal, Vickie Langohr, Noureddine Jebnoun, Kimberly Katz, Laurie King, Armand Lione, Anna Newman, and Nadya Sbaiti. Nick Griffin has encouraged many adventures, taught me to love the water, and helped me to know what is important. Finally, the support and love of my family have allowed me the privilege of choosing my life's profession: Mom and Bob; Dad and Fifi; Mark, Ellie, and LiAnna; Andrea, Lindsay, and Evan; Melinda, Brian, Brett, and Chelsea; and Kevin, Kjersten, Dustin, Kane, and Chase. My grandmothers, Martha Canterbury Davis (1903–1995) and Anne Pommeroy Orlowski (1911–1990), enriched my childhood with spirited stories of Colorado homesteading and racy San Francisco city living, and formed my early fascination with everyday life.

PREFACE

More than 120 *village memorial books*, about the more than four hundred Palestinian villages that were depopulated and largely destroyed in the 1948 Arab-Israeli War, have been published.[1] Compiled as documentary histories and based on the accounts of those who remember their villages, they are presented as dossiers of evidence that these villages existed and were more than just "a place once on a map."[2]

This book examines one facet of what it means to be a Palestinian refugee by examining how the villages and their histories are part of people's lives today. Based in multisited research work, this book explores the roles that the village has played in people's lives since the 1948 War. My sources are diverse: I collected village books in the West Bank, Gaza, Lebanon, and Israel; and conducted ethnographic research and collected more village books in Jordan and Syria. My research traces how people have conceived of the textual representation of their villages in book form, from the perspectives of both the authors writing village books and the audiences reading them, and it examines the types of knowledge these books engender and what representing that part of their history means to the Palestinians.

Why do Palestinians write these village books? In cataloguing, describing, creating, and narrating their histories, the authors of village books seek to pass on information about their villages and their values to coming generations. Some books were written by older men who grew up in the village and felt that recording their family and village history was their nationalistic duty. A few books were composed by young female social activists who sought to transform their communities through connections to their heritage. The majority of authors, middle-aged men, were born in their villages but left as children and wrote these books to ensure that their children and grandchildren will know the villages as they did.

The authors have conceived of their books as histories, often in a very local, familial, and documentary sense, borne out of their desire to record for their descendants the lives, the land, and the village culture that were lost in 1948. To record that past, they have turned to the older people who remember the village and have, most often, reconstructed a collectively held vision of what village life was like. My ethnographic research revealed the ruptures and disagreements that were sparked within the refugee communities over how their histories were presented in the village books, which provoked strong reactions from readers and calls for public apologies, reprints, and second editions.

As they constructed these texts, the authors embedded their narratives within that of the Palestinian national struggle for political rights and for a Palestinian state. The rise of these local histories, which began to appear only in the 1980s, paralleled the waning of pan-Arabism and the end of the armed struggle of the PLO following its exile in Tunis in 1982. Palestinians' interest in recording these local histories shifts the struggle of ordinary Palestinians from focusing on a distant (and now largely discredited) leadership to attending to their own voices, stories, perspectives, and histories. As Ted Swedenburg discusses in his article on the Palestinian peasant as national signifier, the *fallah* (peasant) has always carried multiple meanings as resistor to the specific form of Israeli settler-colonialism as well as maintainer of customs that "secure a national culture's timeless character."[3] But the village books allow the former peasants themselves to valorize their contributions to the national history of Palestinians, thus contributing to the development of the nationalist discourse that asserts a Palestinian presence on the land that is rooted in the histories of peoples' everyday lives.

The codification of this local history in the village books finds different expressions when used by Palestinian communities in commemorative events such as marches of return, plays about village life, and school assignments that concern pre-1948 Palestinian history. By analyzing the content of the books and their stories, accounts, and portrayals of Palestinian life before 1948, we can understand which subjects and events contemporary Palestinians want to include in their history and keep alive to define who they are. I also read the village books to see how the dominance of certain stories and perspectives marks the influences of various powers in both the past and the present: the dominance of men as the voices of village history, the carryover of certain class and family hierarchies into the diaspora and the elimination of others, the re-creation among the younger generations of a particular vision of village life that romanticizes and glorifies the village, and the role of the village history in creating a land-based Palestinian identity. These books of local history also allow authors to write over or silence other narratives and subjects, which I attempt to unearth and comment on throughout. I conclude by examining how Palestinians connect across the geographies of dispossession that have characterized their contemporary lives, using the social structures of the village, family relations, and new technologies.

Because a clear historiographical picture of pre-1948 village history has not yet developed, my contribution seeks to raise awareness of issues related to the writing of history, the ways in which peasant history is recorded in the absence of written sources, refugee understandings of home, the pull of local and familial concerns, the attraction of memory, the forces that silence and repress, and ways of commemorating the past. These local histories are shifting away from oral narratives and toward written forms, and away from familial knowledge and toward public spheres; my analyses therefore focus on these transitions in terms of inspiration, publication, content, narrative form, authority, and reception during the embryonic creation of a genre of local history. My suppositions and surmising here are meant to contribute to long-standing discussions of these issues and, hopefully, to generate new ideas. Given the difficulties in understanding the context of the production of the village books in all of the places in which they are produced and how they are received by the village communities in the diaspora and in the West Bank, Gaza, and Israel, and given the difficulties in dating the writing of these publications, I am reluctant to make definitive declarations. To use the words with which Ijzim village book author Marwan al-Madi closes his book, "I am aware that the information I was able to collect remains fragmentary [. . .], therefore I ask that people [. . .] write to me and provide me with missing information that they have so that I can include it [in the next work]."[4]

MY OWN GEOGRAPHIES AND POSITIONALITY

I have been collecting Palestinian village books off and on since 1990, when I found the first two village books in the Birzeit University series, with their distinctive black and red covers, in an east Jerusalem bookstore on Salah al-din Street. I struggled through reading them, because of their mix of Modern

Standard and colloquial Arabic, but also because I was only in my third year of Arabic study. When I lived in Jerusalem in 1995, Sahira Dirbas gave me her 1993 book on Salama village and I pored over it, loving its bricolage of photos from the village, reproductions of a diary, and astute summarizing of village life. During this time, through edifying conversations with Susan Slyomovics while she was conducting research for her book *The Object of Memory: Arab and Jew Narrate the Palestinian village*, on the once Palestinian and now Israeli village of 'Ayn Hawd/Ein Houd, I also began to understand the scope of village books as local productions on a national scale. While in Jordan in 1998, I found that the Abdul Hameed Shoman Library in Amman had a collection of thirty or so village books. Hooked on their stories of village life, in 2002 I began in earnest to pursue research on the village books. I now have in my collection more than 112 books on destroyed villages (and know of 10 more that I do not have), more than 30 on Palestinian cities, and 40 or more books that are histories of still extant villages in Israel/Palestine, Jordan, Syria, and Lebanon. To complement the textual material I work with, I began ethnographic research in 2005, and interviews with village book authors took me to Jordan, Lebanon, and Syria, where I lived for almost eight months spread over multiple years.

My position as an American researcher figured at all times into this research—a result of the world we have created. My American passport allowed me to travel easily to all of the places where Palestinians live today, something that a Palestinian (even with an American passport) might find challenging. I lived in Egypt while studying Arabic for three years in the late 1980s and 1990s, while a university student (undergraduate and graduate), and I spent four years in Jordan—in Amman, Irbid, and in a village in the south—living, studying, conducting research, and volunteering in grassroots social development organizations. I also spent more than three years living in the West Bank, where I began my first research project, collecting oral histories of Palestinians who lived in Jerusalem before 1948.

Although I am fluent in Arabic, both written and spoken, and speak a Palestinian dialect almost without an accent, my Americanness informed all of my interactions with Palestinians and Arabs, whether living among them or interviewing them. At the most basic level this meant they knew that the stories they were telling me were for consumption by others, by people outside of their communities. Rhoda Kanaaneh, who grew up as a Palestinian-American inside Israel and writes about Palestinian-Israelis, found that "people were aware that my narrative about them would eventually travel in global circuits—circuits that have not been too kind to them."[5] At the outset of interviews, often my interviewees would give me lectures about American foreign policy and the history of Palestine. Because I am an educated, white American, I would be told to make sure that my people understood how Palestinians (and Jordanians, Lebanese, and Syrians) viewed these subjects. I was seen as the conduit for telling their stories and having their perspectives reach America—both its people and its halls of political decision making.

I am grateful for these interactions because they provided the opportunity for people to tell me what concerned them and not just to answer my questions. I understand these interactions partly as their speaking to someone who represents the power of the United States. On a more methodological level, these interactions allowed for a situation in which not all of the questions were driven by me and in which people could tell me in their own language what they thought about my country and my government. These opporotunities allowed them to see that I wanted to hear their perspectives as individuals and as Palestinians. I always listened (although sometimes with an eye on the diminishing time left on the recorder), and often responded with my own perspectives. I was always honest with them about my work and background, forthcoming about my position, and forthright about what I believe. I saw them as colleagues, and argued with them over ideas, their opinions, and mine, and expressed myself freely. I mention this here because researchers are often either seen to be passive absorbers of information or, worse, accused of hiding information about ourselves in order to get what we need or want from informants. I did neither. I also took time and made the effort to engage with scholars and communities in the Arab world, presenting my research in Arabic in public talks and written publications, which has been possible thanks to my wonderful colleagues there.

Beyond my Americanness, I engendered no small amount of consternation among many people because of my name. Was I Jewish? I would explain that I spent every Sunday morning of the first eighteen years of my life going to a very warm, open, progressive Christian church in my small hometown in northern California, a church that gave me a sense of community, an anchor for my family, and a humanist perspective. Because Protestants do not wear crosses with the same vigor as Arab Christians who are Catholic and Orthodox, I did not wear the outward symbols of Christians that my interviewees knew. One author of a village book in Jordan (may God be generous to him) even came to see me a week after I interviewed him to ask me "*mitakdeh innik mish yahudiyya?*" [Are you sure you're not Jewish?]. The Palestinians in Jordan were unique both in this suspicion of me and in the religious conservatism of some of the older male authors. I found that it was only they who would not shake my hand (or any other woman's hand), following a newfangled trend of religious conservatism that encourages people to avoid any physical contact between the sexes outside of the family. They did, however, invite me into their homes; answer my questions; ply me with tea, coffee, fruit, and nuts; and share their trials and successes as authors. Their religiosity in no way impacted our intellectual exchange.

Palestinians living in Lebanon, the West Bank, Israel, and Syria did not share these ultraconservative norms or have as many suspicions about me. I remember a slight trepidation when going to interview an author on my very first visit to one of Lebanon's refugee camps. The posters of Palestinian and Lebanese martyrs, new and old, hung from the walls, and children's kite strings were braided into the thick masses of electrical wires strung in the tiny, dark alleys. I had just finished reading the author's book the night before and had noted that the introduction was written by the general secretary of the Islamic Jihad in Lebanon. I had grown accustomed to Jordan's social religious conservatism; now I contemplated how a particular political-religious bent in Lebanon might affect this elderly author's perception of me. At the end of our very warm interview, he walked me out to the main street, his arm linked in mine, patted my hand, and invited me to come back to visit again. He was not conservative in the ways I had come to expect when living in Jordan. I continue to exchange greetings with him via a female mutual acquaintance in the camp.

One of the advantages of doing research over a long period is the ability to witness change. In my interactions with Palestinian people in the late 1990s and early 2000s, I found that the verbal dressing down of American foreign policy was always prefaced or followed by "but we have no problems with the American people." Following the increased violence in Palestine/Israel and the isolation of Palestinians on the world stage, the complete lack of U.S. initiatives to address Palestinian issues, the U.S. invasion of Iraq in 2003, and the 2004 re-election of George W. Bush as president of the United States, these pro forma denials of anger toward the American people diminished. People saw the complicity of the American population in the dispiriting policies of the United States and made sure I knew it. Whereas many of them live in autocratic regimes in which they have no say in politics or are from a politically disenfranchised minority, they saw me as coming from a country that touts itself around the world as the greatest democracy. In their minds, so many years of U.S. citizens voting for presidents and congresses who clearly have failing relations with and policies toward the Middle East signals to Middle Easterners that the policies that Americans have been exporting to the world are what the American people are choosing. Needless to say, we had many interesting discussions. I must be sure to emphasize, however, that despite their attacks on America's foreign policy and on the American people's fairly silent complicity with it, the Arabs and Palestinians with whom I interacted as interviewees and colleagues were unfailingly kind and generous to me.

My own history has taken me across borders and into cultures, religions, and languages in ways that are informed by the global pressures and forces of politics, patriotism, class, race, gender, fear, and belief. When I was a child, my two grandmothers told me stories of their lives that fascinated me. One homesteaded in southern Colorado in the early 1900s, made butter, cut hay, and put up jam each summer; the other was a working-class San Franciscan who lifeguarded at Seal Point, painted her nails red, and smoked Camel cigarettes. They both gifted me with the love of stories and everyday life, which I brought to this study of Palestinian village history. This book is my attempt to explore what the living memory and recorded history of the Palestinian geography of dispossession that took shape in the twentieth century means for Palestinians today.

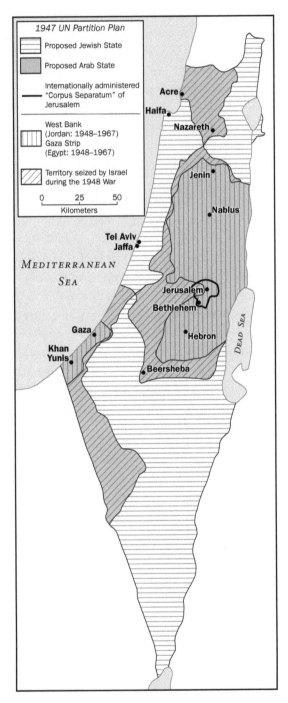

Map 1 British Mandate Palestine with the borders of the 1947 UN Partition Plan and the 1949 Armistice Agreements. Created by Chris Robinson based on UN maps.

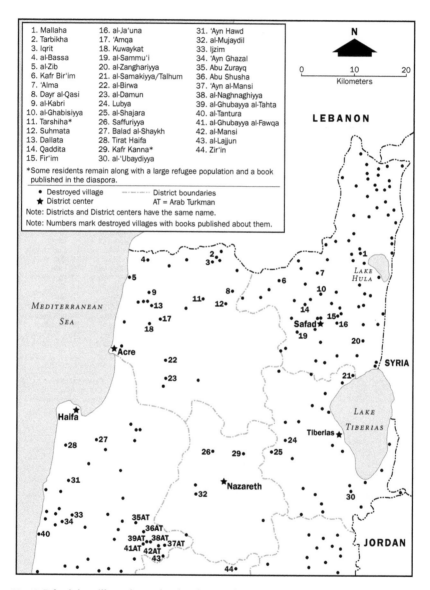

1. Mallaha	16. al-Ja'una	31. 'Ayn Hawd
2. Tarbikha	17. 'Amqa	32. al-Mujaydil
3. Iqrit	18. Kuwaykat	33. Ijzim
4. al-Bassa	19. al-Sammu'i	34. 'Ayn Ghazal
5. al-Zib	20. al-Zanghariyya	35. Abu Zurayq
6. Kafr Bir'im	21. al-Samakiyya/Talhum	36. Abu Shusha
7. 'Alma	22. al-Birwa	37. 'Ayn al-Mansi
8. Dayr al-Qasi	23. al-Damun	38. al-Naghnaghiyya
9. al-Kabri	24. Lubya	39. al-Ghubayya al-Tahta
10. al-Ghabisiyya	25. al-Shajara	40. al-Tantura
11. Tarshiha*	26. Saffuriyya	41. al-Ghubayya al-Fawqa
12. Suhmata	27. Balad al-Shaykh	42. al-Mansi
13. Dallata	28. Tirat Haifa	43. al-Lajjun
14. Qaddita	29. Kafr Kanna*	44. Zir'in
15. Fir'im	30. al-'Ubaydiyya	

*Some residents remain along with a large refugee population and a book
published in the diaspora.

- • Destroyed village   - - - - - District boundaries
- ★ District center   AT = Arab Turkman

Note: Districts and District centers have the same name.

Note: Numbers mark destroyed villages with books published about them.

N

0   10   20
Kilometers

LEBANON

MEDITERRANEAN
SEA

LAKE
HULA

Safad★

SYRIA

Acre

Haifa

LAKE
TIBERIAS

Tiberias★

Nazareth

JORDAN

Map 2 Palestinian villages depopulated or destroyed 1948–1967 (**North**). Created by Chris
Robinson. Based on work published in *All That Remains* (Institute for Palestine Studies, 1992).

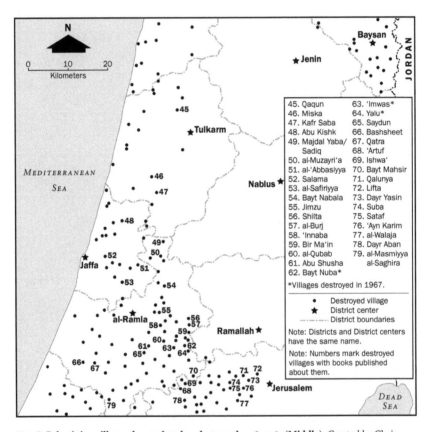

N

0   10   20
Kilometers

MEDITERRANEAN
SEA

Baysan ★

★ Jenin

★ Tulkarm

●45

●46
●47

Nablus ★

●48

49●
50●

★   ●52
Jaffa   ●51

●53   ●54

●55
al-Ramla ★   ●56
58●   ●57
         59●
60●   ●62   Ramallah ★
61● 63● ●64
65●
66●
67   70
        ●69   71 ●72
        68●   ●74 ●73
79●   78● ●75 ●76   ★ Jerusalem
         ●77

DEAD
SEA

JORDAN

45. Qaqun	63. 'Imwas*
46. Miska	64. Yalu*
47. Kafr Saba	65. Saydun
48. Abu Kishk	66. Bashsheet
49. Majdal Yaba/	67. Qatra
Sadiq	68. 'Artuf
50. al-Muzayri'a	69. Ishwa'
51. al-'Abbasiyya	70. Bayt Mahsir
52. Salama	71. Qalunya
53. al-Safiriyya	72. Lifta
54. Bayt Nabala	73. Dayr Yasin
55. Jimzu	74. Suba
56. Shilta	75. Sataf
57. al-Burj	76. 'Ayn Karim
58. 'Innaba	77. al-Walaja
59. Bir Ma'in	78. Dayr Aban
60. al-Qubab	79. al-Masmiyya
61. Abu Shusha	al-Saghira
62. Bayt Nuba*	

*Villages destroyed in 1967.

●	Destroyed village
★	District center
---·---·---	District boundaries

Note: Districts and District centers
have the same name.

Note: Numbers mark destroyed
villages with books published
about them.

Map 3 Palestinian villages depopulated or destroyed 1948–1967 (**Middle**). Created by Chris
Robinson. Based on work published in *All That Remains* (Institute for Palestine Studies, 1992).

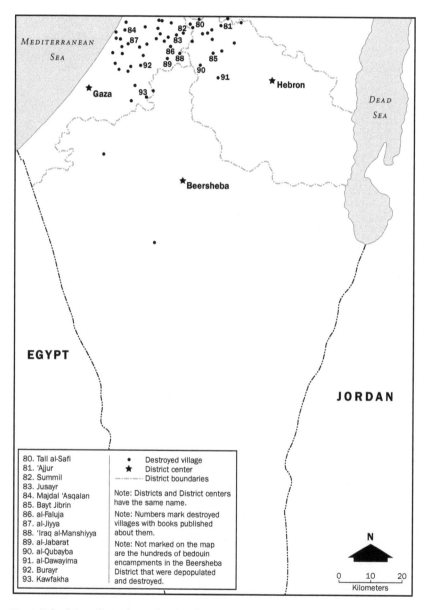

Map 4 Palestinian villages depopulated or destroyed 1948–1967 (South). Created by Chris Robinson. Based on work published in *All That Remains* (Institute for Palestine Studies, 1992).

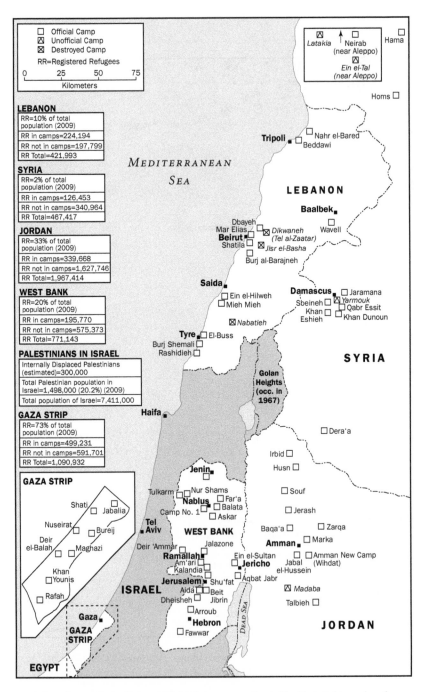

Map 5 Locations and populations of Palestinians, 2009. Created by Chris Robinson based on UNRWA maps and data.

Palestinian Village Histories

1 GEOGRAPHIES OF DISPOSSESSION

Jordan, the West Bank, and Israel: 2004

I am looking for the Palestinian villages of Bayt Mahsir and Suba, which were physically destroyed and emptied of their residents in the 1948 Arab-Israeli War,[1] in which the state of Israel was created. I have been told that a few of the houses and recognizable landmarks remain. The villagers of Suba and Bayt Mahsir have written four *village books* that record the pre-1948 history of life in these villages. In the books, the authors describe the villages in ways that are meaningful to them today: the location of the villages; the livelihoods of their inhabitants; and their agricultural practices, historic sites, natural resources, family genealogies, folklore traditions, and cultural customs. The books also include long documentary sections of wedding songs, maps of the village lands and houses, reproductions of Ottoman and British Mandate era documents, and photographs of the village then and now.

I find and interview the authors of the two books about Suba village: Ibrahim 'Awadallah, a refugee living in Jordan who self-published his book in 1996; and Muhammad Sa'id Rumman, whose carefully detailed, historically sourced 331-page book appeared in print in 2000 in the West Bank.[2] Rumman's book has a striking cover of glossy contemporary photographs of the archeological ruins (a Crusader castle) at the heart of the village.[3] The two books about the village of Bayt Mahsir are from refugees living in Jordan; one was written in calligraphic longhand and published in al-Baq'a refugee camp in 1988, the second was published in 2002.[4] These books inform me that the villages have been largely destroyed, and replaced by two Israeli towns: Bayt Mahsir is now named Beit Meir and is a religious moshav (cooperative farm), and Suba has become Kibbutz Tzova.

I locate contemporary maps of the areas west of Jerusalem and discover that Kibbutz Tzova/Suba and Beit Meir/Bayt Mahsir are located in the Martyrs' Forest (Ya'ar HaKdoshim). Established by the Jewish National Fund (JNF) in 1951, the Martyrs' Forest commemorates the six million European Jews who died in the Holocaust.[5] The JNF map of the Martyrs' Forest shows the commemorative locations, along with picnic areas, biking paths, archaeological sites, and the Israeli towns that have been built there.[6] The geography is such that without knowledge of the Palestinian villages' existence in the past it would be impossible to know that they were once here.

As I continue to research other Palestinian villages, the palimpsests of twentieth century geography reveal the layers of destruction, renaming, and rebuilding that have taken place in Palestine/Israel and that connect around the globe. Saffuriya, once the largest village in the Nazareth district, was depopulated in July of 1948 and completely destroyed; today it hosts an archeological park for the ancient Roman and Jewish town of Tzippori, as well as a JNF forest commemorating Guatemalan independence on September 15, 1821.[7] The small Palestinian village of Biriya, near the city of Safad, was emptied on May 2, 1948, and is now enveloped in the Israeli Biriya National Forest, part of which was renamed in 2007 in honor of Coretta Scott King, the widow of American civil rights leader Martin Luther King Jr.[8] Twentieth-century maps of Palestine from the 1940s show hundreds of villages, along with cities, towns, kibbutzim, and moshavim. Today the maps of Israel reveal a new geography of Israeli towns, farms, fields, factories, water parks, and universities replacing the majority of Palestinian villages that used to be within its borders.[9]

The geographies of dispossession that accompany and contextualize these names in the twenty-first century cross global and historical lines; render subjects that provoke deep emotions, historical victories, and injustices; and engender no easy mapping process. I am keenly aware that mentioning commemorations of the Jewish victims of the Holocaust and destroyed Palestinian villages in the same paragraph, not to mention opening a book with such a vignette, places the subject of this book—Palestinian refugees—and me and my scholarship in the unenviable position of being "controversial," as if talking about these subjects itself is problematic. My point is not to engender controversy, but rather to show the dispossessions of the twentieth century, the victims of which cross many geographical borders. I tread lightly here, with the intent to focus on the devastating effects on people of ideologies, state policies, and armed movements. My point is not to compare suffering, provoke comparisons, or invoke blame. It is to understand how we record history, make sense of our pasts, and map the geographies of the displaced in our world today. It is also to show how we reconnect across our geographies as we take active roles in the present and create new futures.

.   .   .

Suba, Saffuriyya, Bayt Mahsir, Biriya—their stories illustrate how throughout Israel the more than four hundred Palestinian villages that were conquered and depopulated in the 1948 War have been renamed and put to different uses; most of their houses have been destroyed or taken over, their terraces left to disintegrate, their mosques and churches put to other uses, and their cemeteries plowed under and planted over.[10] Palestinians have carried these village and city names (not to mention their memories, hopes, tragedies, and possessions) with them into the diaspora. Despite the destruction of the physical landscape, the village names continue to be part of Palestinians' everyday lives, evoking memories of the past.[11] In the act of recalling and commemorating their villages and cities, Palestinians have also re-placed these names into their current landscapes.

Today, driving up the main road of Jabal al-Mareekh (Mars Mountain), one of the seven "mountains" of Amman, the capital city of Jordan, shopfront signs announce "al-Sarees for Electronics" and "the 'Aykirmawi Grocery." In Yarmouk refugee camp in Damascus, Syria, people buy the latest fashions on Lubya Street, gold on Safad Street, and the best fruits and vegetables on Palestine Street, and they live in the Tarsheeha or Saffuriyya neighborhood. In the Ein el-Hilweh refugee camp in southern Lebanon, every morning children pour into to the Faluja and Qibya elementary schools. If you did not know that al-Sarees, 'Ayn Karim, Lubya, Tarsheeha, Saffuriyya, Faluja, and Qibya were Palestinian villages, you would not be aware of the geography of dispossession mapped into the contemporary fabric of the Palestinian diaspora. Unlike in other parts of these countries, where the streets are named after famous people or historical events and the shops are named after owners or adjectives that describe their contents, in Palestinian communities it is not uncommon to find shops and streets named after the Palestinian villages and cities that were emptied and destroyed in the 1948 War.

In this geography of dispossession, names and references from the past, seen and spoken with regularity, visibly and verbally landmark daily life. These names commemorate the Palestine that is their history, what they knew and what was lost in 1948; using the names for new places in the diaspora thus becomes an embodied and communal act of remembering. In telling people where you bought your refrigerator, explaining where you live, or walking your daughter to school, you are not only recalling the places of the past, but you are also investing them with new meanings and associations in the present. Even as they serve as reminders of the general Palestinian dispossession of 1948, these names also reference new associations and stories tied to life in the diaspora.

This book chronicles the geographies of dispossession in modern Palestinians' lives by analyzing how Palestinians in the diaspora maintain their knowledge of pre-1948 Palestine by transforming stories, documents, and family experiences into formal histories for their communities. These histories take on many different forms, expressing the intertwined generational, gendered, and embodied knowledge of the past and the roles that knowledge plays in the present. I focus on the transformational processes that are taking place primarily in Palestinian written compositions of local history—village books—because these works reflect on the past from the perspective of everyday life, which itself reflects the larger social, political, cultural, and natural environment.[12]

Written by Palestinians displaced from their homes who today live in Lebanon, Syria, Jordan, the West Bank, Gaza, and Israel, these village books chronicle everyday life in the village before 1948 from the perspective of the refugees; they also provide firsthand accounts of the events of the 1948 War and, on occasion, information on the refugee community in the diaspora. The detailed and local subject matter and perspectives expressed in the village books allow us to understand how people's lives are enmeshed within political, social, economic, and religious relations. "It is in daily experience, in the settings of ordinary desire and the trials of making it through, that the given power relations are contested or secured, in an always-incomplete process of negotiation, which is rarely unambiguously 'lost' or 'won.'"[13] As products that reflect everyday life, the books form a major body of historical and social knowledge on village life that is entering the public sphere when the only other sources for such knowledge—those who lived in the village—are dying. They are evidence of the active concern and efforts of Palestinians to record and preserve the histories of village life.

This book examines local Palestinian understandings and consumptions of these histories within the larger historical and political contexts of their production. The goal is to analyze how village histories are written, recorded, and relived, and the roles that Palestinian conceptions of the past play in contemporary life. In this context I also discuss other commemorative activities—local museums, celebrations, village days, marches of return, school assignments, and Web sites, among others—that urge people to remember and celebrate elements of local history and communal life that both fill in and fall outside of the larger frameworks of Palestinian national history and politics. I focus on the activities of non-elite actors—neither the politically powerful nor the globalized professionals. Although the authors, school teachers, and civil servants who write the village books and design the commemorative activities I describe form an educated local elite, they remain enmeshed in and an inextricable part of their small communities. Thus, by exploring these myriad sources from different locations and in different media, this book provides everyday views of Palestinians on their own histories and on what they want to accomplish by producing books and events that propagate those histories.

Despite being *about* history, this book is not intended as a book *of* history. Instead, it describes and analyzes Palestinians' conceptions of their own histories and the role those histories play—in oral, visual, performative, and especially written forms—in their lives today. Neither is it a strict work of historiography, for in this book I use anthropological theories and methods to communicate the contexts and environments in which information about the Palestinian past is produced, made public, and consumed. I weave into the book and into my analysis the interviews with authors and the ethnographic fieldwork that I conducted in Jordan, Syria, Lebanon, and the West Bank. Understanding the intentions and interests of authors in writing about the past allows me to explicate the ways that history is conceived of and portrayed by individuals. Through the interviews and through living among a community of village-book readers I was provided with the opportunity to explore the local forces that constrict and restrict certain subject matter and encourage engagement with other subjects, the influence of gendered concerns on representation, and the roles that living memory and written books play in Palestinian communities.

WRITING PALESTINIAN HISTORY AND THE *NAKBA* OF THE 1948 WAR

Dr. Haidar 'Abd al-Shafi (1919–2007), Gaza, June 1998: "It is difficult to forget the years of the Catastrophe, 1947–1950, when Palestinians lost three quarters of their homeland and when half their society was expelled by force and terror to become homeless refugees."

Reuters, July 22, 2009, "Israel bans use of Palestinian term nakba *in textbooks"*

The Palestinian village books describe life before the 1948 War in the villages that had been within the borders and jurisdiction of British Mandatory Palestine (often referred to as historic Palestine). In these books and in other forums, Palestinians often portray their history according to how others have made decisions about their fate. Prior to Western colonial rule in the form of the British military occupation that began in December 1917, geographic Palestine had been part of the Ottoman Empire for more than four hundred years. During this period, the inhabitants formed their local leadership; lived under a variety of regimes, such as Jazzar Pasha's rule of Acre and the surrounding lands; revolted against oppressive rulers; and experienced invasions, such as that of Ibrahim Pasha from Egypt, which occupied Palestine from 1831 to 1839. These people, regardless of how they thought of themselves, were drafted to fight in the Ottoman army, participated in the Arab revolt against the Ottoman Empire during World War I, and suffered from, died in, and survived the epidemics and famines that accompanied the war. The major markers of late-Ottoman-period Palestinian history appear in stories, in family histories and migrations, and in recollections of village life in the village books.

When the lands of the former Ottoman Empire were divided following World War I, the European imperial powers divided up control of the Levant, and the British Mandate over Palestine began in 1922.[14] The division of these lands roughly followed the outlines of the British and French Sykes-Picot agreement, imposed against the wishes of the population, who desired self-rule and independence in one form or another.[15] The British Mandate marked a period, from 1922 to 1948, that witnessed economic and administrative growth, large Jewish immigration to Palestine, and political repression of the indigenous population. During this time, the percentage of the Jewish population in Palestine went from 11 percent to 33 percent; they came to own nearly 8 percent of the land and they created separate social and political institutions for the Jewish community.[16] At the end of this period, the British government turned to the newly formed United Nations to provide a solution for the end of its era of colonial rule over Palestine.

On November 29, 1947, the United Nations General Assembly passed Resolution 181, which contained a plan to partition Palestine into Arab and Jewish states, with an international zone (called a *corpus separatum*) for the "holy areas" in Jerusalem and Bethlehem, to be administered by the UN (see Map 1). The Arab state, which never came to fruition, was to have a population of 725,000 Arabs and 10,000 Jews on some 43 percent of the land of Palestine. The Jewish state was to have a Jewish population of 498,000 and an Arab population of 407,000 on 56 percent of the land. The population of the International Zone was to be 105,000 Arabs and 100,000 Jewish inhabitants.[17] Communal fighting through this period until the armistice agreements were signed in late 1949 resulted in the expanded borders of the Jewish state, declared to be the state of Israel on May 15, 1948, and the expulsion or flight of the majority of the Arabs living within its borders.[18] From this point until 1967, Israel existed in some 78 percent of historic Palestine; the rest—the West Bank and Gaza—was under Jordanian and Egyptian rule, respectively.

Twentieth-century Palestinian scholars and writers center their history around this war and consider the dispersion of the population—*al-nakba*, "the catastrophe"—to be the seminal event that marked and defined their contemporary existence.[19] The *nakba* refers to the entirety of the events of this period: the 1948 War, the creation of the state of Israel on the lands of historic Palestine and the resulting displacement of half of the 1.5 million members of its Palestinian Arab population, the destruction of more than four hundred villages (see Maps 2–4),[20] the depopulation of Palestinians from cities—Acre, Haifa, Safad, Tiberius, Beersheba, Jaffa, and Baysan—and the expulsion of tens of thousands of Bedouin from the Galilee, the Baysan area, the coastal plains, and the Negev.[21]

It is estimated that, in total, more than 750,000 Palestinians were given refuge in the surrounding countries—Lebanon, Syria, Jordan (which soon annexed the West Bank), Egypt, and the Gaza Strip—and another 45,000 became internally displaced persons (IDPs) inside Israel.[22] Approximately one hundred villages and two towns remained that had at least partial Arab populations within the Israeli state, and a few of the cities—Haifa, Jaffa, and Acre—also retained a small measure of their Arab populations. Jerusalem was divided into Israeli and Jordanian sides.[23] In certain districts, such as Ramla, Jaffa, Haifa, and Baysan, and the parts of Tulkarm, Gaza, and Jerusalem districts that fell under Israeli control, almost all of the villages were depopulated, and then destroyed in part or in total. Those displaced from the villages made up half of the total number of refugees.[24]

Refugee camps became, and remain, a hallmark of Palestinian existence in the diaspora. Based on models developed during and after World War II, the camps were first run by international organizations such as the American Friends Service Committee and the International Committee for the Red Cross.[25] In 1949 the United Nations founded the United Nations Relief and Works Administration for Palestinian Refugees, or UNRWA, which in May of 1950 helped establish the refugee camps (see Map 5). They also took over providing aid, primary health care, and primary and vocational (and in some cases secondary) education services, mandates it continues to administer to this day. Over time the refugees built up the camps—which often were located on the outskirts of major towns or cities in Jordan, the West Bank, Gaza, Lebanon, and Syria—into thriving and crowded neighborhoods. But the majority of refugees did not end up in the camps; the first statistics in 1953 placed camp residents at 34.6 percent of the total number of refugees.[26] Most refugees from Palestinian cities managed to find places of refuge outside of camps and were later joined by upwardly mobile village refugees, particularly in Jordan and the West Bank, where they were given Jordanian citizenship. The Palestinian refugees in Syria do not have Syrian passports, or the right to vote, but they do have access to work, education, and most other services and rights of Syrian citizens of the state.[27] In Lebanon, the Palestinian refugees have been prohibited from jobs protected by trade unions (which are almost all of the white-collar, skilled-labor positions, such as those in medicine, law, education, engineering, and so on), and thus work in low-paying, unskilled labor, or for UN or international groups. They are basically treated according to the laws governing foreigners, with various variations over the course of the sixty years since they were displaced.[28] The refugees in Gaza, who were initially under the Egyptian administration (1948–1967), then under Israeli occupation (1967–2005), and are now under the Palestinian Authority and the Hamas-led government (2005–present), once lived in a functioning society.[29] Today, in 2010, they have been under an international and Israeli blockade for three years and are unable to leave, and some 80 to 90 percent of the 1.4 million inhabitants are receiving food and other basic living assistance. Thus, to speak of Palestinian refugees is to describe a population formed by the 1948 War that shares sentiments and national aspirations but does not share many contemporary experiences, for a variety of reasons.

Despite the 1948 War, half of the Palestinian population remained in their home villages and cities, but the *nakba* transformed their worlds as well. The fabric of Palestinian society was destroyed; borders were placed where none had existed before, severing business and trade relations and breaking up families and social relations. The 125,000 Palestinians who found themselves within the Israeli state borders became citizens of a state whose founders had evicted their families, neighbors, and compatriots. They were also subject to a new governmental structure and to a new status as minorities. In the West Bank and the Gaza Strip, the refugees placed disproportionate burdens on the society members who remained in their homes and on the land—burdens to provide and care for the refugees in their communities.[30] Because the *nakba* was such a formative element of Palestinian history and because there has not yet been an accepted solution to the continuing conflict, the *nakba* remains part of the consciousness of Palestinians, a shared experience that binds them together and that has become part of their common history and a marker of contemporary Palestinian identity.

The 418 villages that were emptied during the fighting between 1947 and 1949 were absorbed geographically into the new Israeli state. The state's policy during and after the 1948 War was to destroy the houses in the villages so that people would not be encouraged to return.[31] In the process, some 70 percent of these villages were completely destroyed, and another 22 percent were left with only a few houses or religious places standing.[32] Thus, almost all of the physical places that these books describe no longer exist or lie in ruins.[33] Although the villages are largely absent from the physical landscape, the village books commemorate, memorialize, and document the lives of their inhabitants and the villages, creating a published collective record of information that was once available only through separate documents, photographs, statistics, stories, and songs.

REPRESENTING THE PAST—TWENTIETH-CENTURY PALESTINIAN HISTORY

In analyzing the production of village books and commemorative events, this book addresses Palestinians' keen awareness of what is at stake in the narration of their local and national history, and examines the inclusion and exclusion of certain information, narrators, families, events, and stories. The village book authors engage with Western and Zionist narratives of progress and development, which are so well refined in colonial and modernist arguments.[34] The Zionist movement—a Jewish nationalist political movement based in biblical beliefs—adopted much of the same colonial rhetoric. To the Zionist visionaries, leaders, and believers, Palestine was a barren and deserted land inhabited by uncivilized, penurious, and backward souls, while

the Zionist project was creative, forward looking, and enlightened. In justify-
ing the Zionist project, one author described in the following language the
dichotomy that these views created:

> On one side the Arab community was characterized by a rigid, centuries'-old
> class system based on clannish separatism, at the head of which was a small
> group of land-owning families, while the majority of the population comprised
> the fellahin and the urban workers, who were illiterate, poor and in a perpetual
> state of indebtedness. The Jews on the other hand, predominantly European in
> characters, were dynamic, educated and modern.[35]

Such a conceptual division, echoed in British, French, Spanish, Dutch, Bel-
gian, and Portuguese colonial visions, made it possible to think of the people
living in Palestine, both the indigenous and settlers, as two distinct and un-
integratable groups whose very characters were at odds with each other. This
way of thinking created a dynamic of separation and superiority—embodied
in so many other colonial projects in North Africa, Latin America, sub-Saha-
ran Africa, the Indian subcontinent, and Southeast Asia—that was imbibed
by both those in power and those who were colonized.[36]

The early Zionist movement, based as it was in Europe, adopted many of
the colonial ways of looking down on Arabs, which also shaped Zionist settlers' attitudes toward the indigenous Arab Jews in the region (known today
as Mizrahim).[37] In the 1950s and 1960s, the Arab Jews who had come to Israel
were perceived as an internal other—one that needed to be civilized and made
to be like the Ashkenazi or European Jews.[38] The process of turning Arab Jews
into Israelis involved decoupling them from their culture and language, a
process that identified their Arabness as something they shared with Israel's
enemy. Thus colonial perceptions of the Middle East informed the perspectives of Europeans (both Christians and Jews) toward the cultures and peoples
of the region and set up divisions that still exist today.

Palestinians existed within and reacted against these portrayals of themselves (and continue to do so today). And even if they acknowledged the poverty
of village life in the first half of the twentieth century—as Palestine emerged
out of the tyranny of World War I and the devastation of mass starvation and
disease—they refused the colonial notion that others were more deserving of
the land than those who already lived on it. 'Awni 'Abd al-Hadi, secretary of the
Palestinian Istiqlal (Independence) Party, said in a 1935 discussion with Haim
Kalvarisky,[39] "There can be no conciliation between Jews who desire Palestine as

a Jewish country.... In Palestine ... for thousands of years, Arabs have existed. They have lived poorly, it is true, but they have lived.... We are not against Jews because they are Jews. Your living must not prevent us from living."[40] With the rise of nationalist movements in the late nineteenth century, Palestinians began producing newspaper articles, books, papers, speeches for the local populace and for the international community, popular songs, poetry, and art that asserted their Palestinianness and their indigenous right to the land.[41]

Palestinian nationalism has been expressed through many different elements, yet because they do not have a state, Palestinians have not had available to them the hegemonic state powers outlined in the work of scholars of nationalism.[42] Inside Israel, the West Bank, and Gaza as well as in the diaspora, the political actors have never consistently been able to establish a military, control borders, issue money, decide on school curricula, establish and run museums and other cultural institutions, control media, and create and run other bodies that define state sovereignty.[43] In some places (Jordan, 1968–1970; Lebanon, 1969–1982; and the West Bank and Gaza, 1994–present), the Palestinian nationalist movements had more power to take on pseudo state roles; for example, in some of these places, during those periods they were able to patrol spaces, make decisions, decide on educational curricula, and issue stamps, among other things. But for most of the sixty years since 1948, expressions of Palestinian nationalism have been embodied through nonstate channels: in the rise of national resistance movements and military groups; in cultural groups that have kept alive Palestinian handicrafts, dance, and music; in visual productions such as posters, films, and art; in the issuing of leaflets during the first Intifada; in demonstrations; in commemorative events such as visits to cemeteries; in the rise of publishing houses; and in the production of plays, ceremonies, and books, among other activities that straddle clear divisions between state body and civil society.[44] Because of this history, Palestinians embed their lives, work, and culture, as is evident throughout the book, within the frameworks of Palestinian nationalism and the struggle for political and civil rights.

Even if they were not taking an active role in defining themselves as Palestinians, they are defined as such by others—host country populations, governments, and global regimes—with all that follows.[45] The specter of Palestinian national loss and the nonexistence of a Palestinian state is never absent from even the most mundane experiences. Palestinians are defined by their lack of citizenship in the host countries of Lebanon and Syria; by their lack of inclusion, despite being citizens, in Israel because they are not Jewish; by their existence in the West Bank under military occupation; by their lives in Gaza, which are fatally circumscribed by Israeli and Egyptian policies and international indifference; or by their diasporic places of birth, which mark them as other, into families that are Palestinian.[46]

The bitter humor of one Palestinian on a border illustrates this world in which they live. Standing in the foreigner line to leave Lebanon, a trim older man behind me had a cedar tree on his travel documents, a clear sign of being Lebanese. Another man said to him, "You're Lebanese. You don't have to stand in this line." "No," the man replied, "I'm Palestinian." We all recognized what this meant: he had been allowed by the Lebanese to get a travel document that then allowed him, after submitting special visa requests, to travel to countries that accept this document. To the murmurs of sympathy uttered by those in the line he responded drolly, "It's only bad for the first sixty years and then you get used to it." Palestinians—dispersed, stateless, and often without the rights of citizens—are subjected to state powers that treat them as outsiders and foreign bodies (even when they are citizens of a country). Within this environment, they struggle against state powers to maintain their own nationalism, identifications, discourses, and narratives through which they define their Palestinianness. One way to understand this Palestinianness, which I attempt in this book, is to use the lens of everyday life and its expressions to understand what being Palestinian means today.

VILLAGE HISTORY AND REPRESENTATION

Today, more than sixty years after their displacement from their villages in 1948, Palestinian village book authors assert that it is their right to represent themselves as Palestinians, as a people, and as a nation. Barbara Parmenter sees this interplay of experience and rhetorical narrative as a key part of the Israeli-Palestinian conflict:

> Zionists came to Palestine with a land rhetoric already at hand, and sought to replace its overworked words with the unarticulated, unquestioned bonds that grow from experience. In attempting to do this, they have in many ways forced Palestinian writers to move in the opposite direction—to create a persuasive and encompassing rhetoric as a replacement for experience over which they have lost control.[47]

But the struggle over representation is not a uniformly national one; the village books also engage the local Palestinian and village communities in debates over the representation of the village and its people. Because the village books do not speak for any kind of "official" history, they are subject to intense scrutiny within Palestinian communities both during the writing process and after publication. As these textual and visual productions become a body of knowledge more accessible to many, they also become more contested and contestable within the village communities themselves. I explore the production of these local historical texts by investigating the oral and written sources that authors turn to in writing these histories, the narrative methods they use, and the authors' methods of collecting sources. Throughout the book I describe engagement with these texts by readers, who respond to the books in various, oftentimes unpredictable ways.

This book explores how these populations relate to that past—in other words, how Palestinian refugees today write a history of a place they may never have seen or lived in, one with no written sources to discover, and with a living population that provides multiple perspectives on and individual memories of that place, and a strong nationalist narrative about the importance of Palestine. This moment presents a unique opportunity to capture expressions about the past. Following the signing of the (now largely defunct) Oslo Accords by Israelis and Palestinians in 1993, the death of longtime leader of the Palestinian Liberation Organization Yasir Arafat in 2004, the continued Israeli occupation of the West Bank and the Gaza Strip, the weakening of longtime Palestinian political movements, and the rise of Islamic resistance movements, Palestinians in the diaspora feel further than ever from a political settlement that would include them in any meaningful way. As refugee Palestinians, they want recognition of their right of return, and of their emotional and national attachments to historic Palestine. At the same time, those who remember the villages and cities of historic Palestine constitute an ever-dwindling segment of the population. Therefore, in this book I capture a moment of transition as Palestinians are pushing to make public their knowledge of the past as a part of their identity and as a historical rights discourse, and to transform knowledge and memory in various ways into written and visual forms. In short, this book is an effort to discern how history is written.

HISTORY, ANTHROPOLOGY, AND HISTORIOGRAPHY

The village books position themselves as histories, but struggle, as do all historical texts, with what history means. As scholars and as language users, we are constricted by the linguistic ambiguity in the English word *history*. The difficulty in talking about how we understand what history is, and how it represents the past, is inherent in language. As noted African historian Elizabeth Tonkin states, "In more than one language, the same word—in English it is 'history'—has to stand both for 'the past,' history-as-lived, and 'representation of pastness,' history-as-recorded."[48] In Arabic, the same is true: "before the late 19th century, *ta'rikh* seems to refer only to a kind of writing or knowledge, but in modern Arabic *ta'rikh* (like English *history*, German *Gechichte*, etc.) is equivocal, comprising both events *per se* and the verbal representation of these events."[49]

Related to the linguistic unraveling that scholars have undertaken with the word *history*, the conceptual understanding of history has occupied the forefront of intellectual discussions about knowledge itself.[50] The discipline of anthropology has participated in these discussions by redefining how we think about human behavior and meaning within the culture concept—the hallmark of cultural anthropological research. Anthropologist Clifford Geertz changed the dominant intellectual discussion of culture by shifting the debate to thinking about representation, both by others and by anthropologists themselves.[51] He described his own understanding in a now-famous reference to webs of meaning: "Believing, with Max Weber, that man is an animal suspended in webs of significance he himself has spun, I take culture to be those webs, and the analysis of it to be therefore not an experimental science in search of law but an interpretative one in search of meaning."[52] This shift to interpreting representations—as understood through both the actors' and the observers' lenses—characterizes much of contemporary anthropology, sociology, history, and other fields in the social sciences and humanities.

Literary criticism has long embraced, and even now normalized, the importance of analyzing the meaning-making power of knowledge via narrative production. Postmodern literary scholar Edward Said believed that historical action is accessible only through historical representations that "are embedded first in the language and then in the culture, institutions, and political ambience of the representer. [. . .] We must be prepared to accept the fact that a representation is *eo ipso* implicated, intertwined, embedded, interwoven with a great many other things besides the "truth," which is itself a representation."[53] If we accept the primacy of historical representation as a force of history, then understanding the past cannot be based on some abstract recording of events but must be seen through the filters of language, sentiment, and cultural and political assumptions that exist within individuals and communal selves and are embedded in the very processes of composing history. Anthropologist Michael Kenny, in his study of memory, expresses this analytical perspective in a different way: "It is necessary to also recognize that in certain respects the past is up for grabs. It is really the *meaning* of the past that is of issue."[54]

This concern with meaning has engendered a bifurcated understanding of the historical subject: meaning is dictated not only by the events or actions or speech of actors, witnesses, chroniclers, scholars, journalists, and others, but also by the representation of the events, actions, and speech produced by those actors. Anthropology has particularly embraced the meaning-making aspects undertaken in representations. The seminal volume *Writing Culture* explores how anthropologists' ethnographies are contingent on the forces and structures in which the anthropologists live and work, a concern for context that most anthropologists would argue applies to all disciplines.[55]

Despite this interest in the multiple forces of representation, the authors of *Writing Culture* present their ideas within older conceptions about what constitutes culture. In response, Lila Abu-Lughod injects the theoretical and practical concerns of feminist theories (among others) into her "Writing Against Culture." In that article she expresses fears that the idea of a "culture," which anthropologists wrote about until the 1980s, suggests one homogenous culture that characterizes a place or a people. She argues instead for ethnographies of the particular, of the everyday, which are "useful because they work against the assumption of boundedness, not to mention the idealism . . . of the culture concept."[56] She writes,

> the particulars suggest that others live as we perceive ourselves living, not as robots programmed with "cultural" rules, but as people going through life agonizing over decisions, making mistakes, trying to make themselves look good, enduring tragedies and personal losses, enjoying others, and finding moments of happiness.[57]

Her point pushes us to move from a sense of "us and them" (as objects, and different) to a sense of "we" (all of us as subjects that share a common humanness). This sense of "we" dominates anthropological studies today, even as anthropologists document, chart, and analyze how different we are. This underlying sense of shared human culture is in contrast to how governments, militaries, and other exclusionary groups (and scholars who work in their interests) frame their views of people and their use of the "culture" concept.

Anthropologists have also altered the focus of their research and writing by shifting the field from charting "slice of time" cultural explications to work that incorporates historical context (change over time) and includes analyses of class, power, and gender.[58] Gerald Sider argues that the social relations and daily life charted in anthropologists' research "delineate terrains of struggle over the ways local inequalities are formed, made materially consequential, and reproduced." At the same time, Sider believes that our analyses must address "the characteristic ways in which localized systems of opposition to larger systems of inequality take shape simultaneously separate from, in alliance with, and in opposition to larger systems of domination and exploitation."[59] This concern with multiple systems and powers characterizes anthropologists' work in the present. Although they retain their focus on the concrete expressions of living in the world, they contextualize them within the local and global spheres in which they exist, and they analyze the political, social, and economic forces that affect culture, society, and human existence.

This concern with context and power has also affected how anthropologists engage with what is the hallmark of the discipline of anthropology: its position of extolling the necessity of understanding others' perspectives. New theorists and perspectives have pushed anthropologists to consider that such a position needs only to be made conscious and to be acknowledged from a position of power and when considering those in weaker positions. In other words, powerful actors ensure by force or coercive actions that their perspectives are always considered, while weaker actors struggle to present their perspectives. Thus, anthropology has been influenced by the addition of Gramscian notions of hegemony and Foucauldian ideas of power to understand the production of knowledge: the ability to generate information and, with it, as Hayden White describes, the ability to make the "real" become "true."[60] Theoretical works of the last forty years have pushed scholars to see power as no longer merely the domain of the state, and to see that control is enforced in many ways beyond repressive laws and apparatuses.[61] Scholars have explored how power exists in the relations of everyday life: embodied, expressed, negotiated, ignored, and resisted through the social roles we play, and through the political environments in which we live.[62] This way of viewing the world suggests that the world should be understood in relational terms rather than in isolationist conceptions of static entities, and that "power cannot somehow be stripped away from social relations or discursive forms to expose the essence at the core."[63] This intellectual trend has pushed us to explain the historicity of what we call history, of why certain narratives dominate at certain times despite the existence of other sources, counterarguments, and other narratives. My analysis of the village books, memory, and commemorations of the past addresses these issues of power and meaning from different angles: as Palestinians' efforts to write their history in the face of dominant Zionist narratives; as Palestinian men's authoritative perspectives within dominant definitions of what constitutes history; as attempts at the ascendancy of certain families within local social structures; and as the pervasive and silencing presence of certain social values.

This understanding of history, as contingent on narrators, perspectives, and power, pulls in two directions how we grapple with history as a subject of inquiry. As a tool of analysis, this way of thinking encourages scholars to analyze the historical narratives and to recognize the hegemonic power of those who write "history" and can turn their understanding of events into a "history" (in other words, those who can represent those events as authoritative and definitive). This process of transforming the past into one discursively unified account is, for many modern anthropologists and historians, of as much interest as the occurrence of the events themselves.[64] At the same time, this analytical turn has encouraged scholars to construct narratives as historians and anthropologists with awareness of the hegemonic discourses and the representation of materials, which are rooted in the norms and powers of their time. Penelope Papailias' study of personal archives and the production of knowledge in modern Greece reveals the value in unearthing the ways in which events are inexorably embedded within narrative structures, cognitive frameworks, and social structures.[65]

Raphael Samuel best articulates the shift away from the important-men-doing-important-things type of history in his *Theatres of Memory*. He takes as his starting point the idea that history is "a social form of knowledge: the work, in any given instance, of a thousand different hands." He believes that "if this is true, the point of address in any discussion of historiography should not be the work of the individual scholar, nor yet rival schools of interpretation, but rather the ensemble of activities and practices in which ideas of history are embedded or a dialectic of past-present relations is rehearsed."[66] This idea of how to understand history—attributable not just to individual source bias or rival interpretations but instead to a confluence of composition, actions, and understandings—forms the basis of how I approach the reading, analyzing, and contextualizing of Palestinian village books.

If the writing of history relies on the context of knowledge production, Palestinian authors are in a unique position to provide the perspectives of stateless, marginal populations. In our contemporary world of powerful state governments, Palestinians as uprooted refugees or occupied populations or minority citizens are not only minorities in the countries where they live; they are also seen as stateless, and thus are pathologized as abnormal in the global political system.[67] The ongoing existence of Palestinian refugees in the diaspora who continue to think of themselves as Palestinians and who hold tight to the past is often labeled by political commentators and analysts as a "problem," not because these refugees were uprooted but rather because they have not accepted the status quo and given up that past and integrated into their host countries as others have in order to make their "problem" go away.[68] Palestinian refugees, of course, do not see themselves as the "problem," but rather point to global forces, international political regimes, the Arab states, Israel, and their own political leadership as reasons for their continuing dispossession and lack of citizenship, and the absence of their presence in the international state system.

WRITING HISTORIES OF DISPOSSESSION AND DESTRUCTION

Palestinians' conceptions of place and history oppose but do not necessarily negate Zionist ideas about this same land, Israel, which Zionists see as a homeland and staging ground for the history of the Jewish people. What Palestinians struggle against is the right of Jews to form a state that excludes Palestinians from their lands, livelihoods, and rights. The historical view of the Israeli state, fueled by modern national ideology, has sought to understand the history of the land primarily through times and events relevant to ancient Jewish life.[69] As Meron Benvenisti, Nadia Abu El-Haj, and Ted Swedenburg explore, the narratives of Zionism and the Israeli state seek not only to assert their own conception of the history of the land, but also to deny a history to a Palestinian Palestine.[70] Consequently, the destruction of pre-1948 Palestinian places and ways of life has been accomplished by more than just bulldozers and dynamite. "One need only read Israeli textbooks or see albums with 'before and after' photos—the Land before 1948 and today," writes Benvenisti, an Israeli political scientist, "to realize how close we are to the point when the vanished Arab landscape will be considered just a piece of Arab propaganda, a fabrication aimed at the destruction of Israel through incitement of 'The Return.'"[71] It is not just the eviction of half of the Palestinians in 1948 that allows for this transformation; it is also the destruction of Palestinians' physical presence and the renaming of what remains that allows their historical presence to be written over, ignored, and forgotten.

For Palestinians, the destruction they experienced in 1948 has resulted in continuous assertions in writing, oral accounts, and everyday conversations of their indigenous presence on the land; of their connections to the surrounding cultures and heritages; and of their long history and ties to the land of Palestine as the land of their ancestors.[72] Palestinians' understanding of their places and their past is also cast with a political and national character—to record their lives as part of Palestinian history, to remember when all of Palestine was one geographic entity, and to register a community that existed prior to its destruction. In this final sense, Palestinian efforts to recall and record the past echo closely the same sentiments of Eastern European Jews, who sought through memorial books, oral history collections, and museums to record life as it had been before their communities were wiped out in the Holocaust.[73] Palestinian efforts, however, exist in a much different post-destruction environment than post-Holocaust recollections.

The post-Holocaust European Jewish population was almost decimated due to the Nazi anti-Semitic campaigns that killed six million European Jews; destroyed their homes, villages, and lives; and created a Jewish refugee community. In many cases, the Jewish refugees did not want to or were unable to return to the countries that had been part of the Nazi regime or to the populations who were complicit with it. Thus, many could not rebuild their lives in those countries following the massacres, deportations, and pogroms that had taken place in Germany, Poland, Romania, Hungary, Austria, Czechoslovakia, Greece, Italy, Bulgaria, Lithuania, Latvia, Ukraine, and western Russia.[74] Their categorization as Jews rather than as Germans, Poles, or Latvians, at the hands of the Nazis weakened their nationalist sentiments toward the states of their citizenship and urged them to feel part of a rising sense of a Jewish nation or to become citizens of the states of their exile. The killing and death of more than two-thirds of the Jewish population of Europe indelibly marks European and Jewish self-identification in the twentieth and twenty-first centuries. The survivors were forced to seek new lives elsewhere, in Israel, the United States, Canada, South America, England, and beyond.

Multiple dispossessions and destructions mark the recent history of Palestinians and Israelis. The Israeli state discourse emphasizes European anti-Semitism as the main impetus behind the Zionist movement, and behind the

Holocaust that destroyed the majority of European Jews and their communities. Since Israel was established, the state has continued to emphasize its connection to Europe while largely ignoring the dispossession of the large number of Mizrahi Jews from Arab and Muslim countries following Israel's creation.[75] These Jews from Morocco, Tunisia, Algeria, Libya, Egypt, Yemen, Syria, Lebanon, Iraq, Iran, Turkey, and Central Asia added to the long-standing small communities of Palestinian Jews and earlier Mizrahi immigrants (who made up half of the population of Israel until the 1990s.)[76] Following the creation of Israel, most Arab states implemented a variety of oppressive and restrictive polices toward their Jewish citizens, which pushed large numbers of Jews to leave.[77] Many of these countries put severe restrictions on Jews who chose to leave in terms of how much property and money they could take with them or sell.[78] Israel absorbed these dispossessed populations and, as described earlier, Israeli policies and the dominant Ashkenazi social and cultural norms were held up as standards to which they should aspire in order to be "modern" citizens of Israel. Many Mizrahim held onto their language and culture, particularly in private; through immigration they experienced not just a geographical displacement but also a dispossession of their communal culture and language. Younger generations, however, eagerly sought to assimilate to what the dominant culture defined as being "Israeli."

GEOGRAPHIES OF DISPOSSESSION

In this complicated history of the twentieth century, the dispossessions I describe mark not only physical displacement but also its effects on social, cultural, linguistic, religious, and other elements of people's lives. *Geographies* refers not only to the geographic relocation of people but also to the creation of spaces and forums in which they reconstitute their communities and memories. Thus these geographies of dispossession and the re-placing of people and sites result in an arresting similarity of narratives and activities in terms of space, temporality, and form.

The recording of these dispossessions has been taken up by a number of uprooted and destroyed communities that have written books about their former villages, cities, and lives. Armenians, Jewish communities from Eastern Europe, Palestinians, and most recently Bosnians have all embraced this method of preserving a lost past for the former residents.[79] The primary motive behind such books is to document what was destroyed and to record the stories and memories of the residents about their houses, lands, and religious institutions, as well as social relations and major events. Jack Kugelmass and Jonathan Boyarin's volume *From a Ruined Garden: The Memorial Books of Polish Jewry* details these memorial (*yizkor*) books), which reveal the "traditions and transformations that marked everyday life in the shtetl" and include maps, names of the dead, stories, and architecture.[80] In her innovative, multisited ethnography of the destroyed Palestinian village of Ein Houd ('Ayn Hawd), now the Israeli artists' village of Ein Hod, Susan Slyomovics provides background on the genre of memorial books and shows how the few Palestinian village books that she studied are part of this memorial book tradition.[81]

Although the Palestinians' books do indeed fit into this genre, I have chosen to call them village books instead of memorial books.[82] In my reading of these Palestinian village books I have found that they share many similarities with the other memorial books, including subject matter, emotion and sentiments expressed, and a focus on places and lives lost in the past. I found no evidence, however, that Palestinians ever knew about or had any contact with these other books or read the languages in which they were written (Armenian, Hebrew, Yiddish, Polish, English, and so on). None of these books are cited in the bibliographies of the Palestinian village books, and no one I interviewed mentioned having knowledge of these books. Additionally, given the multitude of books in Arabic on Arab and Islamic history to which the village books bear a resemblance, I believe there are compelling reasons to think that Palestinian authors had their own cultural sources to inspire them, in terms of both subject matter and style.

Palestinians have struggled for the UN-backed right to return to their homes and for international recognition of their situation. Like the European Jewish refugee community, Palestinians have been indelibly marked by their experiences of displacement, violence, and exile.[83] Palestinians were exiled from their lands, and some were killed or otherwise died, but it is the displacement of more than half of the total Palestinian population that marks Palestinians' concurrent and contemporary sense of self-definition. By the time of their displacement in 1948, Palestinians had constructed a shared sense of national collectiveness based on the geographic borders of British Mandate Palestine, a national movement that was anticolonial and anti-Zionist, and one that espoused an Arab Palestinian state within those borders.[84] This sense of nation was not destroyed by their exile from their land, by their residence in other countries or under Israeli rule, or by the destruction of their local communities. Palestinians today still share a national sentiment that ties them to the land of historic Palestine. Most recently this sense of nation has been injected with an exclusivist religious sentiment that places Palestine (and by extension the people who live in it) within the purview of Islam as the dominant identifying force, thus privileging Muslim claims and Muslims themselves over the more inclusive nationalism of earlier times.[85]

These village books occupy a quickly changing niche in contemporary Palestinian life. Older Palestinians still form a cultural and historical resource for information about the past as they tell their histories, stories, and memories to the next generations. As of this writing, however, sixty plus years after the depopulation and destruction of the villages, few people are still alive who remember life in the pre-1948 villages. The village books, which first appeared as printed publications in the mid-1980s, take these oral accounts and personal memories and distill them into written histories with the intent that they will be a source for Palestinians to learn about the lives of their predecessors and ancestors and about rural Palestine during their times.

This book analyzes the content of the village books and the role they play in contemporary Palestinian history-writing, and explains their importance in contemporary Palestinian culture and society. As an account of how Palestinians are composing their histories of life before 1948, this book seeks to understand and address the meanings of these histories as composed in the village books, the forms that history-writing takes, the sources it uses, and the role that the history of village life plays in the lives of Palestinians today. It does not set out to write that history; rather, it is a study of those who do write village history. Studying these books when the authors are still alive and when the books are circulating in society gives us the opportunity to explore the local context of history production. *Palestinian Village Histories* examines the process of writing history and not just the reading of the finished product; it considers the choices that authors make, the reactions of readers, and the social, political, and cultural forces and influences that inform style, narrative form, and content. All of these elements offer insight into how these texts shape the subjects and narrative styles that constitute history for Palestinians—the sources that are used and how the past is recorded and presented in written form. Within their authors' communities, during the writing process and after publication, these books are subject to intense scrutiny that illuminates what is at stake in the narration of history, and the inclusion and exclusion of certain people, events, stories, and information. These memorializations of the village and its past constitute a significant element of Palestinian identity and express Palestinians views about the past, the present, and the future. Whereas my book reflects on the construction of history, it is also an ethnography of local and national identity as communicated and negotiated in the Palestinian communities and in textual form.

In similar situations in other parts of the world, historians are left with only official records to construct the past, resulting in serious gaps in understanding the perspectives and issues of importance to rural populations. The historiographical study presented in this book, however, is not simply a history of life before 1948; rather, it explores the new means and methods that Palestinians have chosen *in the present* to compose their history in forms that have meaning in their communities, culture, and varying political circumstances. Through textual analysis of the narratives and sources used in the village books, it provides a detailed understanding of what constitutes history and historical sources (both oral and written) for Palestinian authors. At the same time, it investigates the corresponding communal responses to these textualizations of memory. Rather than take a more traditional approach that examines the finished product, this book draws on an interdisciplinary approach that combines the historical methodology of textual analysis with the anthropological methods of interviews, local ethnography, and narrative analysis. My analysis thus explicates the processes of *writing* history—evaluating sources, choosing subjects, and creating historical texts—and *reading* history—through understanding the incorporation of these texts into communal life.

NOSTALGIA AND THE PAST

The issue of nostalgia inevitably arises when the topic of writing about a past is raised. Palestinians' sense of the injustice and violence done to them in removing them from their homeland fuels the desire to maintain a memory of what was lost. In addition, the past—what was and what happened—remains a central part of the continuing political debate around the right of return, the delineation of borders, and the desire for apologies. Although it is easy to attribute Palestinians' feelings to a nostalgic longing for the long-absent past and their lost lands, the present also plays a role. Their families' experiences of the destruction, upheaval, and exile in 1948 and their continuing poverty, absence of rights, and for many, lack of citizenship within the countries in which they were born and raised informs their perspectives on the past.

Despite the influence of the poverty of refugee life, village book authors also recognize the influence of idealization and nostalgia that Palestinians, both young and old, attach to the stories of the past. One village book author described to me:

> This new generation thinks that we were all kings back then. They don't know that all the people were essentially shepherds, and there weren't any bathrooms or bedrooms. But they don't want to hear this—they want me to paint an image of our poor modest village to be that of something recent and modern. They don't want to accept the fact that we were riding donkeys and walking around barefoot.[86]

That said, for many refugees, life in their villages, no matter how difficult, was far superior to the life they had to lead in the camps after 1948. One man comments in the village book, "By God, even when we were beggars when we were in Palestine, our lives were better than they are now."[87] The oral testimonies relied on in the composition of the village books are from men and women who had lived agrarian lifestyles and were suddenly made landless and forced to depend on charity and their relatives to survive, and to find low-paying jobs in other Arab countries. For many, the past was indeed preferable. In the refugee camps, villagers found their farming skills worthless, and they were forced to live with people they didn't know in crowded, unsanitary camps and to depend on others, in particular the United Nations, for their day-to-day survival.[88] The city refugees lost property, businesses, and wealth in addition to their family, social, and economic networks and capital.[89] Given the poverty and lack of access to farmland that came with their displacement, they have a tendency to look back on the past as a cornucopia of natural abundance. Umm Jamal, returning to visit her village after forty years remarked that

> we owned 200–300 dunums of land in the village [of 'Allar] and life was prosperous. We never needed even straw from outside. There were lots of springs! The spring of Umm al-Hasan, the spring of Umm al-Sa'd, the spring of Umm Nuh, the spring of al-'Uyun, and the spring of Umm al-'Uyun. The waters would gush forth and never let up. Our village provided water for, if I remember correctly, Bethlehem and Bayt Jala. We used to plant everything on our village lands, all the way up to the ruins of Tannour: eggplant, pomegranates, cucumbers, and green beans. We never ever had to buy so much as a tomato or lentils or barley.[90]

Remembering the abundance of the village and the products of the lost land characterizes many of the descriptions of older people recalling the past.

The original meaning of the word *nostalgia* is perhaps closer to the way Palestinians recall the past than the current use of the word in English today. Nostalgia is "pseudo Greek" and was coined in 1688 by a Swiss doctor, Johannes Hofer, to describe "the sad mood originating from the desire for return to one's native land."[91] A medical term, it spread quickly in Europe to describe an extant mental phenomenon that also afflicted the bodies of the "various displaced people of the seventeenth century."[92] Svetlana Boym charts the association between the affliction of nostalgia and the strength of national spirit in that "nothing compared to the return to the motherland believed to be the best remedy for nostalgia."[93] Although return may be the desired solution, given the changes that have taken place in the intervening years, Palestinians know that the land has changed. A poem in one of the village books opens in free verse and expresses the desire of the poet to hold on to the past.

> I haven't visited my village [*baladi*] since I left its land. Longing still grows inside me every day, pulling me to it. I still ask those who come from there about the playgrounds of youth and the land of dreams. I learn from them that the land has become desolate, the gardens withered and the landmarks have changed. These verses are an attempt to express the feelings of those visitors who choke themselves in the bitterness of the encounter.[94]

His poem then switches to a *qasida*, a highly structured poetic literary form, in order to express these sentiments in a way that makes sense to Arab readers. This expression of longing for a place the author once knew (but resides in no longer and has no access to) also typifies how we think of nostalgia, as "a wistful yearning for the past."[95]

Today scholars posit that understanding nostalgia is more a way of making sense of the present rather than pointing to the original association to displacement from a physical space, or to our more colloquial use of longing for some aspect of the past. Kathleen Stewart emphasizes the meaning-making properties of nostalgia in an uncertain present: "In positing a 'once was' in relation to a 'now' it creates a frame for meaning, a means of dramatizing aspects of an increasingly fluid and unnamed social life."[96] I argue here that we must understand how people see their past in order to know how they conceive of their lives and of their place in the world today. If we see Palestinian accounts of pre-1948 village life as reflecting the richness of a life lived rather than the poverty of a life observed, the unique elements of the lived experiences can be read for what they are rather than for what we think they should be. It is this spirit of understanding how Palestinians understand, write about, and pass on their conceptions of the Palestinian past that this book adopts.

.   .   .

The following chapters discuss how the histories that are written in these village books reflect Palestinians' varying perceptions of what constitutes the subjects that should be included in a history and the sources that can tell those subjects. Generally speaking, in these books history is an account of family names and origins. It is detailed descriptions of the land, from the springs and wells to the caves, orchards, and Roman ruins. It is also a record of the homes and schools they built, the foods they ate, they ways they made their living, the relationships they had with other villagers, and their wedding and funeral customs. History is also framed as the responsibility of the older generations to make sure that it is indeed recorded. Most important, for all of these books history is about transferring knowledge about the village to those who never lived in or saw the village. And along with the transfer of that knowledge comes the push for the diaspora generations to feel connected to the village, to share the sentiments of love and longing for that land and for that past. By explicating the knowledge of and feelings about what it means to be from a certain Palestinian village, the authors advocate in the village books for history's role in helping the diaspora generations maintain their identity as villagers and as Palestinians.

2 VILLAGE BOOKS: LOCAL HISTORIES, NATIONAL STRUGGLES

Salama, Palestine: 1948
   Birzeit, West Bank: 1986
   Amman, Jordan: 1990
   Haifa, Israel: 1993
Kfar Shalem, Israel: 2007

On December 25, 2007, the Israeli police evicted thirty families from their homes in Kfar Shalem, after a long legal battle. Over the years the government had sold the land to various private developers as part of a gentrification scheme in this poor, largely Mizrahi Jewish neighborhood of Tel Aviv. The evictions of these families from Kfar Shalem had been taking place since the 1980s, although the previous families had all been provided with compensation or new housing. This last group of people, whose families had lived there for more than half a century, also asserted their right to compensation or alternative housing, because they had been settled there by the government and had paid rent to the government housing company, Amidar. The authorities maintained that they were squatters and therefore, after the court decided in the government's favor, evicted the families and denied them compensation.

All of the evicted were Jews of Yemeni descent who, according to one journalist, had been settled "on the lands of what had been the hostile Arab village of Salama; Israeli forces had conquered the area in order to stop Arab sniper fire at the Jewish neighborhoods of Yad Eliyahu, Ezra and HaTikva. The new Jewish neighborhood was named Kfar Shalem."[1] According to one man, Avi Harayti, a thirty-two-year-old father of three children, "Ben Gurion put my wife's grandfather and grandmother here."[2] The story of Kfar Shalem reveals some of the ways in which the state managed land and settled the influx of immigrants and refugees in the early years; by putting the newcomers in the homes of those whom it had driven out or who had fled, the state was able to absorb large populations.[3] After the war ended, in 1949, the land of the Palestinian refugees was taken over as Israeli state property, per the Absentees'

Property Law of 5710/1950, under the jurisdiction of the Custodian of Absentee Property.[4] According to this law, the lands were administered or owned by various government institutions that collected rent from the tenants. The issue under contention in the evictions in Kfar Shalem was that the government maintained that the land was owned by a British citizen whereas the residents maintained that they had contracts with the government and had been paying rent to government bodies. Dudi Balasi, whose family came from Yemen and was settled there, said, "I have been paying rent to the Amidar government housing agency for many years—even though in 2002 [I now hear that] this very property was sold to Mrs. Efrati [the developer]. So why did they take money from me?"[5]

Ironically, proving that Palestinians once owned this land might help the case of the Yemeni Jews who are being evicted as squatters. According to journalist Meron Rapoport, "The contracts the heads of the families signed with the Custodian of Absentee Property testify that the Jewish Agency sent them to Salameh [sic] after they had emigrated from Yemen. The documents also indicate that they moved into the abandoned Arab house legally and with permission."[6] If this is the case, then the families are entitled to compensation and alternative government housing. One activist involved offered that the Yemeni Jews of Kfar Shalem could talk to those Palestinians from Salama village who previously had been dispossessed: "Will they speak with former Salama residents to ask them for copies of their deeds to the land, so that they can prove to the government that the land is actually Absentee and not privately owned? Will this make their situation even more provocative, to bring in land issues of Palestinians in order to prove the Israeli state wrong in its judicial decisions?"[7]

Sahira Dirbas's book on the destroyed village of Salama, published in 1993 in Israel, might have been of help in this case. In her book she reproduces sixty-six British Mandate–era land documents from the village, all registering land being bought and sold in the 1940s by Salama's Palestinian Arab residents—almost seven thousand people. After the extensive fighting that engulfed Jaffa and the surrounding villages at the end of April 1948, most of Salama's residents fled, ending up, finally, in Jordan and what became the West Bank. Dirbas notes that due to mortar attacks during the war and urban development after, "almost nothing of the village remains today except for a few houses, coffee shops, the Sayyidna Salama mosque, and the cemeteries which the governmental company Halamish has turned into high rise buildings, erasing most indications of their existence."[8] She chronicles this latest eviction of Palestinians from Salama in 1993 (the dead interred in the cemetery) as symbolic of how the lives, history, and heritage of the Salama is being covered over—destruction through construction. She includes photographs of the cemetery site as the Halamish company set up work, their "no trespassing" sign, and five articles on the subject from the Arabic and English press.

In the context of the Palestinians' dispossession, the Palestinian village books serve as dossiers of evidence: land records, genealogies, photographs, and stories all aimed toward showing the villagers' relationship to the places in the village and thus toward proving their existence on the land, and therefore their history, even though they are no longer there and the village no longer exists. Yet given the local audiences, the Palestinian village books function, most importantly, as individual efforts to record the villages' histories— defined not only in terms of archaeology and geography but also in terms of the experiences of the villagers themselves as told to and recounted by the authors. Through the books the villages become a past to be captured and maintained in textual form through stories, maps, photographs, family trees, and poems, all of which seek to retain the history of the people who lived there, a past to be transferred on to the coming generations. Examining the content, composition, and publication of the village books, the reasons why authors say they write them, and the historical context behind the appearance of the books in the 1980s provides us with the opportunity to understand the public nature of Palestinian history, and the various political powers and identities in which Palestinians have invested their voices in the recent past.

VILLAGE BOOKS: LOCAL HISTORIES

In the rest of this chapter I examine three books about the village of Salama to focus on the issues that surround the production of the village books as texts. By explaining and interpreting these three books within the processes of publication and distribution, I address more broadly some of the stylistic and practical considerations that are part of the visual and material composition, organization, authorship, printing, and distribution of the village books. All but three of the 112 village books I studied were published in the Arab world, and all are written in Arabic.[9] These three village books on Salama represent many of the tropes, debates, and historical trends that are common in the production of local history and allow us to use them as a base from which to explore the diversity and variety in the decentralized production of village books.

Published in 1993, Sahira Dirbas's book is the third in her series, "A Homeland Refusing to be Forgotten" (*Watan 'asi 'ala al-nisyan*). A descendant of Tirat Haifa villagers, she was born in the 1960s and raised in Haifa, Israel. Her first book, on her natal village, she researched, composed, and published in 1991, and her second, on the village of al-Birwa in the Galilee, she published in 1992. Dirbas composes her books as "studies that turn the memory of the villagers into written words, to be documentary evidence in the hands of the villagers and the coming generations, reaching them here in the country and in the diaspora."[10] She organized the Salama book around the following subjects: location; residents and families; the cultural, social, and architectural history; folklore; national struggle; and maps and land documents. She conducted twelve interviews with former village residents (three women and nine men). Her other books were similarly organized, researched, and composed. Dirbas's book on Salama, however, is the third book on Salama; two earlier books on Salama were produced, one in the West Bank and one in Jordan.[11]

A number of Palestinian villages (sixteen are represented in my collection of village books) enjoy this wealth of multiple publications. In addition to the three books on Salama, there are two books each on 'Innaba, 'Imwas,[12] Bayt Mahsir, 'Ayn Karim, Suba, al-Duwayma, al-Zanghariyya, al-'Abbasiyya, al-Faluja, and 'Arab al-Turkmen of Marj bin 'Amir; three books on Qalunya, Lifta, and Majdal 'Asqalan; four on Saffuriyya; and five on Tirat Haifa. As Dirbas's case illustrates, the refugees were scattered in multiple countries and not always able to communicate with one another. She cites only one of the two earlier books published on the village: the one published in the West Bank appears in her bibliography, the one published in Jordan does not. As an Israeli citizen, Dirbas would not have been able to travel to Jordan prior to the peace agreement between Jordan and Israel that was signed in 1994, and the trade in books back and forth was (and continues to be) extremely limited.

The first book on Salama was published in 1986 by the Birzeit University's Center for Research and Documentation of Palestinian Society (CRDPS) in a series on the destroyed villages in Palestine. Under the leadership of Sharif Kanaana, an accomplished folklorist, CRDPS envisioned the memorial books as a project that would profile six representative villages from all of historic Palestine whose residents would be interviewed and provide the content for the books.[13] This series was pioneering in its vision and scope. Up to this point, only two other village books had been published. The books on the villages of 'Ajjur by Muhammad Abu 'Abd al-Hadi Fadda and al-Duwaymeh by Musa 'Abd al-Salam Hadeem both appeared in Jordan in 1985.[14]

The Birzeit project was set within the national context of the Palestinian *nakba* of 1948: "The series *The Destroyed Palestinian Villages* is a collection of ethnographic snapshots of the Palestinian villages as they were in the 1940s of this century before they were destroyed between 1948 and 1950."[15] In the beginning this group included Kanaana, five other researchers, a typist, and a mapmaker, and they began work in 1985. The authors of these books, unlike the authors of most of the other village books, were not from the villages where they collected the oral histories.[16] Under Kanaana, the series expanded and at least thirteen books were published.[17] A second group in the series was produced under the supervision of the new head of CRDPS, Saleh Abdel Jawad; it differs significantly in that these books were written by former villagers and edited by the CRDPS staff.

The Birzeit project was framed to look systematically at selected villages from among the destroyed villages throughout Palestine. Each book in the first group follows the same format. The first chapter describes "the popular history of the village" (*al-tarikh al-sha'bi lil-qarya*), including the location of the village and the other villages or towns that border it. The remaining chapters are titled "Clans and Families," "The Village in the 1940s," and "Politics, Wars, and Exile." Although methodologically these books are collections of oral histories, the interviewers who gathered the information are absent from the text and their questions have been removed. Almost all of the information in the books comes from stories the authors collected that are attributed to specific narrators. In scrupulous adherence to the standards of oral history brought to the project by Kanaana, the authors transcribe each story in the dialect of the villagers. Almost all the other village books in my collection (a notable exception is Iyad Shaheen's *Bashsheet*, published in 2002) reconfigure the stories and quotations into Modern Standard Arabic (*fusha*). For example, in the Birzeit village book for al-Faluja, the modern standard Arabic *hadha* (meaning "this") is written as it is spoken ("hada"), and for the Bedouin village of Miska, *hadha* is transcribed as *they* say it ("hah-tha").[18] Such ways of writing and recording provide both the historian and the reader with a close understanding of the original sources, the language of the time, and the ways of narrating stories that are lost when the language is transformed into Modern Standard Arabic. When transcribed in the colloquial language, these stories remain as they were originally told (minus the questions and context) and can be easily retold in oral form. When I asked the authors I interviewed why they took the stories they heard and changed them from the colloquial language into Modern Standard Arabic, they remarked that this is the way Arabic is written. Modern Standard Arabic is also a sign of education and sophistication, and a world that the authors, as authors, not as folklorists, feel they are part of. This use of colloquial language, this quoting of the exact words of those interviewed, and the attribution of information to named individuals make this first group of the Birzeit books unique, and creates a certain number of problems as well.

According to 'Abd al-'Aziz Saqr when I interviewed him in Jordan, the Birzeit book on Salama was what prompted him to write and publish his own village book, *Salama al-basila: Basalat balda Filastiniyya* (Brave Salama: The heroism of a Palestinian village). Saqr's book is carefully organized and written. He recounts the history, background, political activities, economic developments, and social worlds of the village in 174 packed pages divided into nine chapters. Saqr's facility in knowing the details as well as the breadth of information about the village is a result of his own past: he was twenty-four in 1948 and already a lawyer at that time, as well as a founding partner in a weaving company and a member of one of the major families in the village. He was active in local politics and a fighter with the committee for the village defense. Given this background, his book differs dramatically from the Birzeit and Dirbas books, which were based on interviews with village refugees living in the West Bank.

Saqr's book presents his material about the history of the village in the way that many villagers recognize as the proper way to render historical information *in writing*. Thus, after opening with an introduction that explains why he wrote the book, followed by a very simple map placing the village in historic Palestine, Saqr addresses the various beliefs and claims about the person after whom the village was likely named. He evaluates the different claims and then weighs in decisively that the only possible option is Salama bin Hashim, one of the companions of the Prophet Muhammad who was part of the conquest in 14 AH (635 CE) of the Levant, where he was killed in the Battle of al-Sifr. Saqr then details some of the medieval Muslim history related to the village and to the building of the Sayyidna Salama mosque in the early nineteenth century. In contrast, the Birzeit book presents the same information as "the story that the villagers believe about the name of the village, one that they retell as a real historical event that happened in the village, is of a martyr during the Islamic conquest named Salama who fought with the companions of the Prophet."[19]

It then tells three different versions of the story in colloquial Arabic. Saqr, however, chooses to evaluate and make a judgment on which story about the village name is true, as a historian might. These contrasting styles stem not only from a desire by the Birzeit book authors to present the villagers' ways of telling the origin story, but also from Saqr's concern that there be a verified history to the village that can be traced back accurately.

With the village origin stories thus anchored to historical events, Saqr then adds in the more recent history of the village. In the beginning of the 1800s, waves of people came and built up the village. Saqr provides an idea of the population numbers and economic activities. He tells how the families that populated the village between 1810 and 1850 came from Palestinian villages as well as from Egypt, as did his family. These families partitioned the village's land into four sections, which were divided (or rotated) among the people. Those who became part of the village after this period did not have land rights or, alternatively, had to purchase land or inherit it. Saqr thus explains the origin of the village, the socioeconomic divisions of the village families on the basis of their history in the village, and the dominance of certain families. He also tells the story of the most prominent building in the village—the Sayyidna Salama mosque. The mosque, which is still standing, figures as a symbol that all the villagers can identify with because it connects the name of the village to its origin and carries that story into the present.

But the most dominant and detailed part of Saqr's book on Salama is the seventy pages on the politics and events that took place during the British Mandate and the fighting that occurred during the 1948 War. The Birzeit book, by contrast, has sixteen pages on politics and the war, and Dirbas's book has twenty-seven pages on politics and the war, including multiple pages of newspaper articles. Saqr's book, unlike the other two, however, does not have a bibliography. When I interviewed Saqr, I asked him about the sources that informed his writing. I had been surprised that he did not cite any in his very detailed text. He replied that he had lived in the village and therefore knew it. His experience was particularly evident in the wealth of detailed information about the struggle and fighting that took place before and during the 1948 War. This perspective on the village is rare, and Saqr represents a small group of village book authors who were adults or nearly adults when they left the village; their own experience therefore forms their conception of the village.[20]

The vast majority of the village books were authored by men, many of whom took up writing after they retired from teaching. Only three women, among them Sahira Dirbas, authored books. The earliest village book authored by a woman was penned by 'Alya' Khatib. *'Arab al-Turkuman: Abna' marj ibn 'amir* (The Turkmen Arabs: Sons of Marj ibn 'Amir) was originally written as her master's thesis in social history in 1982 in Jordan. It is one of the first projects of its kind, although she did not publish it until 1987. Khatib's impressive work consists of 120 interviews she conducted with men and women, and reproductions of seventy documents, to tell the origins of this settled Bedouin tribe and its history in the area. Kawthar al-Amir wrote *Likay la tansi hafidati al-Burj* (So my granddaughter doesn't forget al-Burj) in a question and answer format, as a conversation between her and her granddaughter Bahiyya. This short book published in 2002 is innovatively styled for children, the descendants of the village who do not know about the village. The author was clearly angered by the outbreak of the al-Aqsa Intifada. Parts of the sixty-four-page book shift from being about the village to describing the violence in the West Bank and Gaza, and to glorifying the armed struggle and those killed in it.

Most village books explain how the author went about collecting information on the village. The Birzeit book on Salama explicitly discusses the methodology its authors employed: "We collected the information in this monograph from the people of Salama located in the Ramallah area during the months of February and March 1985. We found them to be very cooperative, honest, and generous, which greatly aided our tasks and encouraged us to continue with this project despite all of the difficulties."[21] As do the other village book authors, they express their gratitude for the cooperation of the community, acknowledging both how crucial to the project the villagers were and how potentially painful it was for people to talk about these subjects. They modestly acknowledge the potential weaknesses of their efforts: "in spite of the cooperation and generosity of the villagers—there are undoubtedly gaps and mistakes and missing information. We apologize for this and hope that those who notice mistakes or absences in this material will provide us with the correct information so that we can add it in future printings."[22] This invitation for the community to respond suggests some of the collaborative nature of conducting research for these books. Other village book authors have included their postal addresses and telephone numbers so they can be easily contacted with such information.

And readers did indeed respond. Letters sent to the CRDPS reveal the depth at which the books resonated with readers and how seriously they took the authors' calls for corrections. Although I did not have access to the

CRDPS's records from the time of the publication of the Salama book, the second CRDPS director, Salih 'Abd al-Jawad, kindly shared with me material from subsequent correspondence. Readers sent in numerous letters of praise. For example: "Greetings to you for the rare treasure that you published—the book on the village of Zir'in. I devoured in one sitting. It made me return to the past, to the time I lived in my village of Zir'in with its people, fields, harvests, houses, and struggle." Another man wrote from Irbid, Jordan, saying how pleased he was to get a copy of the book on the village of Lubya: "these books are needed and important for the Palestinian people because the Zionist occupation destroyed so many villages and if books about them aren't written then many people will forget."

More commonly people sent in corrections and additions that they thought needed to be made and added to the books. The CRDPS's director wrote back to someone in al-Wihdat camp in Amman, Jordan, saying, "we look forward to receiving at your earliest convenience the material you refer to so that we can use it in preparing the second edition of the book, which we promise we will produce as soon as the copies from the first printing are distributed."[23] The Birzeit series did actually reprint a number of the books, although I am not aware to what extent they made significant changes. Only two authors that I know of produced second editions of their books, significantly modified with new information.[24] One author was the head of a village *diwan* (association) and used new computer technology to produce a much more stylish format and included more photographs and charts. For most authors, because they financed their own publication, the issue of reprinting was one of major effort, distribution, and monetary consequences. With most print runs at five hundred or a thousand books, many had numerous copies of their books left and did not have the resources to rewrite, edit, and then reprint them. What a number of authors did instead was print out a list of corrections on a single sheet of paper and staple it onto the back cover of the remaining books. These corrections were largely just typos, but a few included missing or misspelled family names.

A letter to the CRDPS from 'Abdallah 'Awda, the author of a village book about the extant village of al-Kababeer, published in 1980, praises the Birzeit book on Tirat Haifa. 'Awda was pleased to read the book because Tirat Haifa had a close relationship with his own village and the Tirat Haifa book quotes his work. He mentions that he is unable to find another copy of the book in any of the Arab bookstores where he lives in Haifa, and he hopes that they can provide him with one.[25] This request for more copies (which was probably the most common type of correspondence that CRDPS received) reveals one of the major issues that authors face in writing their books—that of printing, publication, and distribution.

PUBLISHING VILLAGE BOOKS

Village books are most often published and distributed under individual initiative and financing, but a number of institutional structures also participate. The processes involved in producing village books include village societies and associations (including *diwans*), publishing houses, printing presses, and research institutes. The Birzeit University project started by Sharif Kanaana was significantly altered by new director Saleh Abdel Jawad.[26] Under his leadership, CRDPS began to publish books written by authors from the villages rather than authoring books from oral histories that the CRDPS staff had collected. In the new series, Abdel Jawad himself edited and worked closely with the authors to create longer and more comprehensive books.[27] Another project in Gaza conducted by the National Center for Studies and Documentation, published at least four books in the late 1990s and early 2000s.[28]

Saqr's book on Salama illustrates how the village societies play a role in distributing the village books. Many villages (and large families) have founded *diwans,* as described by Susan Slyomovics and Anne Marie Baylouni.[29] Twenty of the village books mention these societies that exist in the West Bank and Jordan. Saqr's book on Salama is given to each person who joins the association in Amman, thus ensuring its distribution to many people, especially all those in Jordan who are from the village.[30] At least ten of the books have been published with the name or logo of the village association on the cover and are given to members when they join. The publication of two other books was funded by family-specific diwans rather than village-specific associations. Thus, at least in Jordan, by selling or giving the books to members, the associations advocate that their members should have the information about the village that appears in the books.

The most common way of publishing the village books, however, is for the author to pay for a book to be printed and then distribute it himself or herself. Publishing in the Arab world differs significantly from publishing in Europe and North America. There are three primary actors in the process: the printing press, the publishing house, and the bookstore. The printing press (*matba'a*) produces the books. The press may only print the camera-ready copy given to it, but it more likely also helps to design the cover, create the layout, and format maps, charts, and other images. Once the book is printed, however, the press doesn't distribute, market, or otherwise have much to do with the books it publishes.

Some publishing houses (*dur nashr*) publish village books, although many first-time and amateur authors find it difficult to get their works accepted by well-established publishing houses. Like their counterparts in other parts of the world, the well-known publishing houses in the Arab world have an editorial staff and both accept manuscripts submitted to them and search out manuscripts. Dar al-Shajara is the only extant publishing house that has produced numerous village books. Located in a refugee camp in Damascus, it had published eighteen village books by 2008, along with books on many other subjects. It functions both as a publishing house with an editorial component and as a commercial publishing house that will format and publish the book of any author who pays for it. The director of Dar al-Shajara described for me their editorial and publishing policies. For the village books, authors are given two options. The first option is for the author to submit the book manuscript to the press to be read by the main editor, who then offers suggestions for changes. If the author chooses to accept these suggestions, the press then adopts the manuscript and pays to publish and market it. The second option is for the author to pay for the publication of the book without any editorial process; the publishing house creates the layout and cover design, and serves as a contractor with the printer.

Distribution is another issue that authors struggle with. In the Arab world, bookstores (*maktabat*) sell books from a variety of publishing houses and self-published books. They acquire their stock in numerous ways: an independent distributor may come around with some books from which the bookstore owner will select, the bookstore owner may go to the publishing houses, publishing house representatives may visit stores with their books, owners may go to warehouses of books to select the titles they wish to have in their store, or individual authors may bring around their books. Some stores, particularly those near universities and religious institutions, are known for carrying certain subjects and genres, and some personalize their services and seek out the books that customers request. Many authors complained to me about bookstore owners, whom they had a difficult time getting any money from for selling their books. Large publishing houses have a store (or stores) where they sell their books (but not books published by other publishing houses). Be-

cause the vast majority of the village books are self-published, they are therefore self-distributed; most commonly the authors give away or sell the books
to people who come to their homes.

Given that in all of the Arab countries, publishing and distributing books
is fundamentally a decentralized process, it is never easy to find and purchase a book. There is no centralized database of books in print or even Web-
sites like Amazon or Alibris or Bookfinder on which to search for books.
To publish a book in Jordan today, one submits a request for an accession
number, which puts the book on record, and copies of the book are held in
the National Archive. Lebanon, Syria, the West Bank, Gaza, and Israel have
all lessened their censorship restrictions and thus village books are published
and distributed without recourse to governmental authority, and no records
or copies are held in any one location in the country. A person looking for a
book on a particular village could likely find it by asking the older and more
prominent people from the village. In almost all of the countries where village books are produced, the authors also give copies to public and private
libraries and archives. So, for someone like me who has not been living in
these communities for all of my life and who does not know people from
each village, collecting the village books has involved spending a great deal
of time going to bookstores, libraries, and village associations. In my interviews with authors, with the exception of those whose books were distributed by the village associations, many of them expressed unhappiness about
their efforts to get their books into the hands of the villagers. Most of them
ended up distributing them for free, which placed a not-insignificant financial burden on the authors and sometimes made them feel that people did
not value their work.[31]

DOSSIERS OF EVIDENCE

All of the village books include photographs, maps, documents, and other
items of significance, which are woven throughout or appended at the end, and
in some cases these constitute a good portion of the total book.[32] Almost all of
them (80 percent) have photographs of modern subjects—the villages, people,
dress, and so on—and almost half have pre-1948 photos of the villages, their
residents, or both. Many of the books reproduce official documents; more
than half of them contain British Mandate tax receipts, identity cards, animal
enumeration bills, membership cards for sports clubs, tithe receipts, birth certificates, licenses to grow tobacco and to drive, marriage certificates, passports,

report cards, and land documents. Given the central concerns of Palestinian refugees about land, it is not surprising that more than a third of the books contain reproductions of land documents from the Ottoman and British Mandate periods that show land sales and purchases, or even the entire registry of the village lands created as part of the British cadastral land surveys.[33]

The Birzeit and Dirbas books on Salama are among the richest in terms of the diversity and detail of the material they contain. They reveal a village that was tied into the systems of law and governance established by the British, and into the structures and activities of the Palestinian national movement. They include reproductions of British Mandate government documents that were part of being a citizen of Palestine and evidence of how people's lives were regulated by the state: British Mandate of Palestine passports; an official driver's license; and the block plan map and index for Salama (in English, Arabic, and Hebrew). The villagers' Palestinian nationalist activities are documented in copies of articles from the Arabic newspaper *Filastin* from 1945 to 1947 in which the village was mentioned, particularly during the major clash with Jews that occurred in 1947,[34] and a request dated April 10, 1948 (on letterhead paper with a stamp), from the leadership of the "mid-western sector," asking for free transport back and forth from Salama to Jaffa for the activist Tawfiq Abu Zayid.[35] In her book, Dirbas reproduces sixty-six land registration certificates from the British Mandate period—more land registration forms than are in any other village book that I have seen.

Many of the documents contained in the Birzeit and Dirbas books on Salama come from the family of Mustafa Abu Nijim, who was co-owner of the Salama Bus and Cars Companies (among other business ventures). Dirbas uses the Salama Cars Company's map of the bus routes for the cover of her book; it makes an arresting illustration of the connections between the cities (Jaffa, Ramla, and Lydda), the nearby villages (Salama, Khayriyya, Saqiya, Kafr 'Ana, al-'Abbasiyya, and so on), the German Templar settlement (Wilhelma), and the Jewish settlements (HaTikva, Tel Litwinsky, Ramat Gan, Petah Tikva, and so forth).[36] She also includes the Salama Bus Company's timetable. The Birzeit book reproduces a Salama Bus Company ticket and the cover of the contract and rules for the establishment of Salama Cars Company, Ltd. These printed materials also reveal the relationships that the village had with the nearby urban centers. The Salama Cars Company's advertisements were designed and printed by United Artists Advertisements in Jerusalem, and the founding contract was printed by the Commercial Press in Jaffa.[37]

Abu Nijim's connections to the urban elite, the British Mandate authorities, and the Palestinian nationalist leadership are illustrated in the myriad documents and photographs he collected in his lifetime; they also reveal the deep connections he maintained in Salama, and his dedication to developing the village. A formal, printed card invites the receiver to attend a lunch at the house of Mustafa Abu Nijim in 1945 to honor the outgoing British Mandate District Commissioner Ihsan Hashim. Abu Nijim not only was a prominent businessman but also was politically active. He was a member of the Futuwwa, a Palestinian nationalist group formed to organize young men and provide them with limited military training.[38] Multiple pages of Abu Nijim's daily diary, reproduced in his own handwriting, from 1947 to 1948 are included in each book; they give an idea of the activities he was part of in Salama (and beyond) and of the events happening in the country.

The diary pages reproduced in the Dirbas and Birzeit books provide us (perhaps inadvertently) with a glimpse into the economic life and social history of Palestine in the late 1940s. Abu Nijim wrote his daily entries in a commercially produced daily agenda book that has advertisements from major manufacturers and businesses at the bottom of each dated page. For example:

The Arab Company for Knitting of Textiles and Socks Ltd. Jaffa–Tel Aviv Street, Jaffa P.O. Box 319.

Furniture Showroom owned by 'Ali al-Dabbagh and partners. Jaffa, al-Mahatta Street, Telephone 653. Largest Arab factory for modern furniture.

Al-Tahir Brothers Library. P.O. Box 134, Jaffa, Telephone 261. The largest warehouse in Palestine for Arabic books and school books and supplies for offices and schools.

The advertisements also reveal the role of importing and exporting, and Palestine's relations with nearby countries as part of the economics of the time:

Hajjaj Company, Jaffa P.O. Box 4020, Telephone 1217. Producer and source of citrus and all kinds of vegetables and fruits, fresh and dried. Contractor for packaging and exporting oranges by sea and to the Middle East.

The Sa'diyya Bookstore, Jaffa. Telephone 1255. The most recent scientific and literary books, stationary supplies of all types, and Palestinian, Syrian, Lebanese, and Egyptian newspapers and magazines.

Refreshments for all tastes and environments: Cola, Champagne, Sherry Cider, Tutti Frutti. In the San Pierre warehouse, Picot Street, Beirut. Telephone 97–55.

Other advertisements appealed to the reader's sense of what it means to be modern in terms of products, services, and entertainment:

> Boliphoto. Jerusalem. Jaffa Street, in the former Municipality Building, in the direction of Barclay's Bank. The most modern artistic photographic techniques and seller of all photography needs.

> To the elegant smoker: we offer you Dunhill, the premier English lighters. Jordan Arab Agency. Telephone 896, Jaffa, Post Building, P.O. Box 268.

> Edward Restaurant—Cafe—Bar. Haifa, Muluk Street, Carmelite Building, Telephone 4056.

Many of these advertisements were infused with a Palestinian nationalist spirit, which can be seen in the highlighting of their Arabness. The publisher also placed words of advice and nationalist duty on the pages that did not have advertisements:

> Grow . . . don't cut. The life of the country and its beauty and wealth is in its trees and forests. Plant more trees.

> The Arab Doctor in Palestine—outstanding in his profession, devoted to his duty, never exploits anyone. So why deal with doctors who exploit you and suck your blood?

> Support all of the nationalist projects aiming to save the lands of the homeland and prevent their loss to the invading enemies.[39]

The preponderance of material from the collection of Mustafa Abu Nijim influences our perspective on the village. Because of his careful archiving of all parts of his life, we have incredible access on subjects and information related to him. However, although this material is rich and unique, it also gives the reader a skewed perspective on Salama, and leaves a rather large gap in knowledge about subjects not related to the Abu Nijim family.

Saqr's book presents a somewhat different perspective—that of the younger generation that came of age in the village in the 1940s and that of a different family—although Saqr too was invested in the nearby urban, educated lifestyle. He has paragraphs describing the Salama Bus and Cars Companies, the Modern Arab Dairy Company, the Salama Company for Spinning and Weaving (which he was part of), the Salama Trading Company. None of these, except for the Bus and Cars Companies, are mentioned in the other books. Saqr describes the village's numerous economic activities in addition to agriculture: leather dyeing, two grain mills, trucking, and water storage and distribution. He also does a more complete job of documenting the families of the village, which he had more access to than the other authors given his role as the founder of the village association in Jordan in 1978. In total, thirty-eight pages of his book are devoted to the families that made up Salama, their origins, and graphic representations of some of the family trees. Saqr's fourth chapter focuses on customs and traditions (religious and secular), education and schools in the village, the various organizations in the village (such as the Arab Workers Association, the Salama Sports Club, and the Najjada and Futuwwa political associations), and the Village Council and its elected representatives.

THE CHANGING VILLAGE

The descriptions, documents, and photographs in the village books reveal the transitions that took place in villages in the twentieth century. Many of the pre-1948 photographs in the Salama books are credited to Mustafa Abu Nijim, who owned a camera.[40] The types of photos that Abu Nijim took do not exist in any of the other village books. Whereas the other books contain formal portraits of individuals or photos of the village taken by professional photographers, Abu Nijim's photos are those of a villager taking photos of his own village and therefore capture very different subjects. The informal, intimate details of village life emerge: four men smile broadly while balancing on the edge of the water storage facility that was installed by the Salama Land Investment Company to provide water to the village; a crooked photo shows the Salama soccer team posing in their striped jerseys; the Hajj Juma'a Brass Band from Jaffa serenades a groom at his wedding; and village women walk along the path to get water from the well with large pottery jars balanced on their heads. Four members of the Futuwwa group, of whom Abu Nijim was one, pose for the camera while at the Royal Agricultural Association in Cairo on February 16, 1946. These are not the folkloric photos of people posed (or interpreted) as biblical vignettes that are so typical from that time. (Postcards of Palestinian villagers harvesting wheat or barley and labeled as the biblical story of Ruth and Boas in the fields was a common one).[41] Because these photos were taken by someone from the village, most of the people in them—men and women— are named. Abu Nijim's photos show us the villagers, aware of the camera and representing both significant and everyday events in their lives.

These photographs capture more than just a particular moment or person; when we view them alongside the textual descriptions of social customs and traditions, we see the changes that took place in technology, beliefs, and clothing, in particular. For example, photos from the late 1920s and early 1930s of women carrying jars on their heads on the way to the spring contrast sharply with photos from the 1940s of two new water storage facilities and pumps. Many of the photos of men from the 1930s show them wearing either urban dress (suits and ties) or village dress, which consists of a belted *qumbaz* and suit jacket.[42] In all of these pictures, the men's heads are covered with either a *tarboush* (fez) or a *kufiya* (headscarf) with *'iqal* (rope holder); none of the Arab men wear western-style hats (although a German in one picture wears a fedora). Mustafa Abu Nijim, who appears in at least four of the pictures, wears village dress in the formal studio portraits (with his father and brother in one and with his son and his assistant in another). He appears in a military uniform and a suit in others while in Cairo for the Futuwwa group meeting in 1947. These pictures illustrate how people fluidly integrated and switched among the clothing styles relevant to their context, from the village formal peasant wear to the urban suits and military dress.

The customs and folklore discussed in the village books also reveal the various ways that class, gender, modernity, and education were played out and changed over time. Three of the photos in the Salama books are from weddings. Two of them show grooms sitting on chairs, with male guests around them. The third photo, from the 1940s, was taken from a distance and shows the backs of men and women outside some buildings. The caption on the photo reads, "The wedding procession passing through Farhana street in Salama. In the background is the second story of the house of Muhammad Hussein of the Fallahin family and next to it the guesthouse of the Ramadan family."[43] Dirbas describes these weddings:

> The wedding party begins at the groom's house when the guests and the groom's family head to the bride's house to fetch her. The women sing and ululate and the men dance and sing the *sahjeh*. They circle the village from the Salama mosque to the square in the middle of town and then to the groom's house.
>
> The *sahjeh* is organized by the balladeers [*hadda'un*], the most famous of whom was Rajih al-Salfeeti, repeating poems and songs in praise of the bride, groom, and the people of the village. In the midst of them, a masked gypsy woman entertainer dances,[44] and around them the women stand in a circle where they sing and dance the *huwaydla* [a type of song], and ululate.
>
> At night they bring a band to play [. . .] along with the gypsy women entertainers and they dance until the early hours of the morning. These

festivities last for a week. The women sing songs about the couple, often praising the groom and his family. [...]

> You, golden youth, we follow your good reputation in every village.
> Oh you, golden one, we follow your reputation in all of the country.
> Bring them, Abu Fulan, by sword or rifle, to take their women.
> Give them, Abu Fulan, a sword or rifle, to take their girls.

Sometimes, however, if the groom had professed his love to one of the women but had betrayed her and married someone else, the songs would slander him. [...]

> Village son, you're the one who every day adopts the new thing. Because you are depriving me of my lover, you will be deprived of enjoyment. Every day, my cousin, wearing the *kufiya* and *'iqal*, you deprive me of what belongs to me. You then will be deprived of pleasure. [...]

At the end of every wedding, a member of the groom's family climbs to the roof of a house and calls all of the villagers to come eat, saying, "There's plenty of sustenance for those who are hungry. We are providing the food, but the sin is your own [if you don't come]."[45]

The popular and locally specific wedding traditions documented and detailed in the Salama books appear in almost all of the village books. The book on Sataf by Muhammad al-Fatayani has six pages of wedding songs, Hani al-Hindi's book on al-Qubab contains fourteen pages of wedding songs and descriptions, and Qasim al-Ramahi includes thirty-eight pages of customs and songs from the wedding traditions in al-Muzayri'a village. The Salama village books provide a glimpse into how popular social traditions coexisted with the class conscious activities of wealthier villagers who linked themselves to more staid and formal, perhaps even urban, practices. For example, Dirbas includes the printed wedding invitation (albeit a simple card) of Mustafa Abu Nijim:

To the Esteemed and Revered _____ :

I am honored to invite you to attend the wedding party of our son, Mustafa 'Abd al-Qadir Abu Nijim, on Sunday, the 16th of November 1932, at our premises in Salama village. Our pleasure will be fulfilled with the distinction of your company.

—Al-Shaykh 'Abd al-Qadir Abu Nijim[46]

Unlike the more traditional wedding, to which people would have been invited via oral invitation and which lasted for days, this wedding party is on only one day. This invitation indicates a literate and formal village culture marked by both class and prestige, and also one that went beyond the bounds of the village, because they had to have the financial wherewithal and knowledge to go to Jaffa to print the cards, as well as associates from outside the village to invite to the wedding.

Documents like this detail more than just changing traditions; they also mark the shifting landscapes of patronage, class, and social position. According to Salim Tamari, the modifications to land-owning laws and educational institutions created numerous opportunities for the village elite. "Influential village patriarchs who succeeded in consolidating large estates for themselves after the dissolution of the *musha'* system [shared rotating possession of agricultural plots] would soon send a few of their capable sons or relatives to establish themselves in the regional center or acquire a public post themselves."[47] The family history of Mustafa Abu Nijim evidences that they played the role of village patrons. A handwritten but formal invitation to Abu Nijim from the Athletic Committee of the Salama Youth Club notes that the football match between the Salama club and the Arab Club of Qalqilya on Sunday, April 7, 1946, at 2:30 in the afternoon will be held under his patronage. It concludes, "May you remain a treasure for the country and help for all athletes."[48] That he was the patron of the Salama club indicates both the respect he received in the community and his financial support for the club, and communicates ideas about prestige that existed within the literate upper classes of village society.

Other material in the village books reveals similar shifts in access to services, beliefs, and class ideas about propriety. A picture of a boy sitting backward on a mule is captioned with "It is thought that this picture was taken on June 14, 1932, and it shows the way paralysis was treated in children. It was believed that this act, along with the family distributing food to other children and the poor, would cure him."[49] This alternative to treating physical illness biomedically also appears on two pages on health in the Birzeit book on Salama that describe the common ailments in the village, their treatment, traditional medicine, and spells and magic. They also include names of doctors who came to the village, and the hospitals in Jaffa to which villagers went. One of Saqr's objections to the Birzeit book was these kinds of details. He said, "[the woman interviewed] talked about how people were treated with traditional medicine and magic. Even if she lived these things, she didn't represent the experiences of the villagers."[50] Saqr dismissed the idea that an illiterate woman who hung onto traditional ways of dealing with illness should be empowered to provide a perspective on this practice in the village. As we can see in other parts of his book, he portrays the village as taking part in the economic development of the country and as engaged with modernity, and he suggests that the country's demise is brought about by overreliance on traditional social structures and ways of thinking and behaving.

Finally, the photos and documents included in these books on Salama reveal the changing village landscape and population. Pictures of the remaining sites in the village from the 1980s and 1990s combined with pictures from before 1948 show how basic urban architectural styles entered the village vernacular, and that two-story houses of concrete block (rather than stone) still exist today. Three pictures from 1993 of the village coffee shops reveal what had existed and how it has changed: the café of Abu Usba', above which was the youth club; the Hafiz café, which was situated between Ibn Nassar's barbershop and the butcher, Mahmoud al-Zaghloul; and the al-Kamoudi café, which has become a synagogue.[51] The final pages of Saqr's book detail the process by which the Salama villagers in Jordan established a village association (*Rabitat Ahali Salama*), which was formally recognized by the Jordanian government in 1977. Saqr then details the association's founders and their extensive activities (and reproduces the association's founding documents). This association also plays a role in documenting village society and history for its members by publishing and distributing Saqr's village book. (In 2004, membership in the village association, which included a copy of the book, cost two Jordanian dinars (US$3). Documenting life before 1948 and distributing it to villagers today underpins the authors' work.

THE PALESTINIAN NATIONAL STRUGGLE, LOCAL HISTORY, AND THE VILLAGE BOOKS

In an attempt to answer the question of why the village books started appearing only in the 1980s, thirty years after the destruction and depopulation of the villages, we must place in a larger context the shifts in how Palestinian history has been written by Palestinians (and others). In many ways, these shifts in historiographical subjects and material reflect the varying dependence on and relevance of the national struggle and national leadership in Palestinians' lives. Historiographical texts reveal how Palestinian history has largely been told through metanarratives of the past that mark the guideposts of modern

Palestinian life within a Palestinian nationalist narrative. The metanarratives of Palestinian history and their political struggle have contained Palestinian expression within larger structures of political identity and within certain historical contexts. These structures, which are concerned with politics and one unified narrative, have sidelined local Palestinian stories, histories, and subjects. More recently, Palestinians have used those frameworks to assert their own experiences and interpretations of the past, filling in details of or even challenging the historical record, and shifting Palestinian historiography from one of metanarratives to one of social and cultural histories of everyday life.

The Palestinian metanarratives rely on certain dates that signal the collective meanings that have been given to the 1917 Balfour Declaration,[52] the imposition of the British Mandate over Palestine (1920–1948), the advent of the Zionist movement, the 1936–1939 Palestinian revolt, the *nakba* of 1948,[53] the 1967 Arab-Israeli War, the 1982 Israeli invasion of Lebanon, the ousting of the Palestinian Liberation Organization (PLO) from Lebanon, the Sabra and Shatila massacre in 1982, and more. Although the conceptual process of understanding this history focuses on Palestinian involvement in these largely political events, the metanarratives tend to give primacy to the powers and forces that undermined Palestinian aspirations and actions, forces that were at different times British, Zionist, Palestinian, Israeli, and American. These metanarratives echo the development of Palestinians' struggle as they assert that they want to be seen as both Arabs *and* Palestinians rather than as non-Jews, as the statistics have so often referred to them, or as the "existing non-Jewish communities in Palestine," as they are referred to in the Balfour Declaration.

Saqr relies on these chronological guideposts in organizing the seventy-page second section of his village book on Salama. He frames each chapter chronologically, from the Balfour Declaration through the *nakba*, and after setting up the major political events of the period, he immediately plunges into the ways the villagers of Salama participated in and were affected by the events. He opens the section, however, by cautioning the reader that in mentioning the political situation in Palestine he is not intending the section to be a comprehensive historical discussion, for such a text would need volumes, many of which have already been written by others. He provides his summary of history, he says, in order to make the events that took place in Salama make sense in the larger context.[54]

As metanarratives, the discussion of these events creates frames in which to understand history within the greater political and national narrative of dispossession and struggle. Examining the political frameworks embraced by Palestinians thus reveals the evolving history of the Palestinian struggle and how Palestinians express themselves. They are frameworks of collective struggle, Arab nationalism, and sacrifice. Laleh Khalili, in her insightful study *Heroes and Martyrs of Palestine*, describes how the chronicling of these events connects individuals to collective commemorative practices that are part of a process to "represent, reinterpret, and remember the national past in an ongoing and dynamic way and in doing so, set the stage for crafting future strategies."[55] In contrast, very few personal stories, autobiographies, or memoirs were published by Palestinians in Arabic until the later part of the 1960s. Poverty, lack of employment, absence of a politically active or representative body, low levels of literacy, and the scattered population all made it difficult for Palestinians to form a sense of individual self beyond their loss.[56]

Examining Palestinian historiography after the 1948 War up to the present allows us to see how the ways in which Palestinians have chosen to write their histories have changed, and mirrors the evolving political contexts in which Palestinians have lived. Authors in the 1930s and 1940s wrote books about local subjects, as Tarif Khalidi discusses in his essay on Palestinian historiography. For example, ʿArif al-ʿArif's *Tarikh Ghazza* (The history of Gaza) and Ihsan al-Nimr's *Tarikh Jabal Nablus wal-Balqaʾ* (The history of Nablus and the Balqa) are all narrated in the local history tradition. "Seen as a whole," Khalidi writes, "their histories constitute a kind of land survey where the authors seek to repeople the terrain with the thick presence of ancestors, as if in response to the continuing obliteration of Palestine by Zionist settlements." He concludes his discussion on these early works with the comment, "this massive Arab historical existence on the land of Palestine was a means of forging a sense of national unity."[57] Following the 1948 War, writers examined the causes of their losses and possible solutions. Initially, those struggling for an Arab Palestinian state invested their voices in Arab nationalism, believing that these political movements would save them and provide them with a homeland.[58]

Intellectuals writing about Palestinian history have expressed these beliefs within their analyses, and many of those active on the subject have embraced Arab unity and the Arab states as the means to achieve the liberation of Palestine. Qustantin Zurayq, who wrote and published the influential *Maʿna al-nakba* (The meaning of the catastrophe) in 1948, was a prominent proponent of the need for internal reform and national Arab unity. He and others expressed disappointment with the inactivity of the Arab states, both in general and around Palestine specifically. Students of his at the American University in Beirut—most prominently George Habash, a Palestinian refugee from al-Lyd who was studying medicine—adapted these ideas into a political movement called the Arab Nationalists Movement (ANM, *Harakat al-Qawmiyyin al-'Arab*).[59] Pursued by the various Arab regimes they threatened, this now defunct movement spawned increasingly activist and communist-socialist-oriented political movements throughout the Arab world. Arab nationalism, embraced rhetorically by Egypt's president Gamal Abdel Nasser as well as by the founders of the Ba'th party, began to wane as a viable political ideology in the 1960s with, among other events, the dissolution of the United Arab Republic of Syria and Egypt, which had lasted a mere three years (1958–1961).

The evident ineffectualness of Arab nationalist rhetoric to liberate Palestine resulted in Palestinians creating Palestinian nationalist movements by which they aimed to liberate Palestine themselves. Political scientist Yezid Sayigh has written a definitive and comprehensive account of this transformation in his *Armed Struggle and the Search for State*. These movements incorporated the word *Palestine* into their names and put the platform of Palestine front and center. Thus the 1960s witnessed the rise of Fatah (the reverse acronym for *harakat al-tahrir al-watani al-filastin* (the Movement for the National Liberation of Palestine), the Palestine Liberation Front, and the Popular Front for the Liberation of Palestine, among others. Sayigh quotes an anonymous Fatah leader as saying in a 1968 press conference, "it was necessary to extricate the Palestinian from the grasp of Arab patronage, party feuds, and Arab regional designs, and to return him to his natural place as a human being who has lost his land and must strive to recover it. . . . This is why [Fateh] has raised these slogans: unity of Palestinian effort, rejection of Arab patronage, independent Palestinian will. [. . .]"[60]

These revolutionary movements formed a variety of nonstate alliances, engaged in direct military assaults on Israel, challenged Arab regimes, and united themselves as the PLO. They came to prominence after the 1967 War, in which the Arab regimes were seen as entirely impotent in the fight against Israel. The 1968 Battle of Karameh in the Jordan Valley pitted the PLO fighters and the Jordanian army against the Israeli Defense Forces, who had invaded Jordan to attack the town of Karameh. This event catapulted the Palestinian liberation movements into the spotlight, and the *fida'iyeen* (fighters) became heroes. Their most daring and debilitating action came in 1969–1970, in the civil war between the PLO and the Jordanian government, which resulted in the PLO being expelled from Jordan. Per the Cairo Accords of 1969, the PLO had limited autonomy in the Palestinian refugee camps in Lebanon and built up a significant resistance movement that lasted through (and participated in) the Lebanese civil war, until the PLO was ousted from Lebanon in 1982.

With the rise of these Palestine-focused nationalist and militant movements of the 1960s, the way Palestinians envisioned their situation was fundamentally transformed.[61] Laleh Khalili cogently charts how Palestinians developed narratives of heroism and sacrifice for the nation to accompany the rise of the PLO and other resistance movements' activities in Jordan and Lebanon. Khalili details how the rhetoric at this time was about concepts—sacrifice, struggle, and heroism—and fighters and martyrs embodied those descriptions. She notes, however, that individuals, their stories, and local or village identities were subsumed into the greater national movement. "While various political factions created many holidays and produced numerous symbolic events, their efforts at recording ordinary refugees' memories were at best dismal."[62] Palestinians invested their voices in these movements, which spoke as a national bloc, as advocates for the Palestinian cause.

With the 1982 Israeli invasion of Beirut, the PLO was driven out of Lebanon and took up residence in Tunisia. For the first time the Palestinian leadership—and the structures of military resistance that had developed since 1948—was no longer connected geographically to a border with Israel-Palestine. Confrontations between the armed wings of the groups that made up the PLO and Israel were impossible from 1,500 miles (2,300 kilometers) away. The appearance of the first of the village books in 1985 is concurrent with this significant juncture in the Palestinian struggle. At the same time, the Israelis seized the entire archive of the PLO's Palestine Research Center in Beirut,[63] which signaled to many Palestinians that the documentation of their history that they had amassed was no longer in their hands. The first Intifada, in the West Bank and Gaza, which began in late 1987, also reflects this shift toward the local in the form of the popular, grassroots struggle. For many Palestinians, the secret Oslo Accords signed by the PLO and the Israeli government in 1993 revealed that the PLO's interest was its own survival rather than representing the Palestinian people, particularly those Palestinians in the diaspora (and inside Israel).

For many Palestinians, these events indicated that the Palestinian political leadership no longer figured as the sole form of struggle to achieve their rights and preserve their history. Instead, Palestinians turned to local and personal resources: memories, personal records, and documents held within their own families and communities. The sudden flourishing of the village books in the later 1980s reflects this fundamental shift in where Palestinians are investing their voices. No longer are they relying on a distant and compromised PLO leadership to represent and define them; rather, they are creating elaborate dossiers in the form of village books to tell who they were, who they are today, and why their histories are important.

In the context of these many forces, Palestinians continue in earnest those projects that are under their own individual and communal control. The village books are also projects that the educated, respectable man can adopt when not able or willing to fight. They shift the meaning of "struggle" from carrying arms and fighting to writing, and they allow Palestinians to take control of their own histories and representation.

Salim Tamari argues that this type of localism is also a reaction to the dominance of urban centers over villages, which had characterized Palestinian social and political history during much of the twentieth century. He describes

> the emergence of a small-town milieu as a backdrop to a reactive ideology of particularistic localism and a more recent ideology of religious triumphalism. This religious ideology emerged after the military encirclement of the PLO in Lebanon in the 1980s, and since then it has begun to replace the tradition of urban liberalism that emerged with the Ottoman reforms and during the British Mandate period, and the secular nationalism that marked Palestinian and Arab political culture for most of the twentieth century."[64]

Other factors affecting the rise of texts about life before 1948 include the trend toward autobiographies and memoirs in world literature, and new theoretical interests that focus on the importance of everyday life issues, subaltern history, and oral histories as historical sources.[65] Academic and theoretical perspectives that promote "history from the bottom up" have focused not only on Palestinians as a disenfranchised group, but also on marginalized sections within Palestinian society.[66] These academic, social, and political impulses have enabled the production of texts authored by people who are not from the Palestinian intellectual and political elite, particularly villagers and women, who were not represented in earlier historical literature describing life before 1948. Thus the emerging texts and stories reveal new facets of Palestinian society, as well as enrich the past through their individual contributions to the historical record.

These productions by individuals, nongovernmental organizations, and publishing houses give voice to Palestinians' own stories in the face of being ignored by their chosen political representatives in the PLO as well as by the international community. The Palestinian village books publicly acclaim who Palestinians are and what lands and properties were theirs, and affirm the need to document and remember for present and future generations. Of course Palestinians have previously told their memories of pre-1948 village life to family, friends, and even oral historians.[67] In the composition and publication of the village books, however, Palestinian narratives are being elicited, heard, collected, and published in public forms both for people from the village and for outsiders, thus expressing a collective notion of a particular way of understanding the village's past, with one eye toward the present and the other toward the future. Village book authors cite different reasons for why they write the village books: those who remember the villages are passing away, and the new generations of Palestinians do not personally know their villages. The next section focuses on the communal concern about passing on the intimate knowledge of village life to children and grandchildren.

THE PURPOSE OF HISTORY: TO REMEMBER FOR THE FUTURE

The changing relationship of Palestinians to their struggle and to national leadership over the sixty years since they were displaced has meant that Palestinians have aligned with a variety of political movements through which to express themselves. The appearance of the village books in the 1980s manifests how Palestinians have shifted where they invest their voices and who represents them, but the village books also reflect the generational shifts taking place among Palestinians. With the rise in the 1960s of the Resistance movements, which mobilized many people born after 1948 or raised in the diaspora, people realized how little the new generations knew about pre-1948 Palestine compared to the older generations. Ribhi 'Alyan wrote in his book about Yalu, published in 1988, "The idea was born in me to write this book from the beginning of the 1970s, when the new generation of those from Yalu were coming of age, and who knew nothing of the village."[68] Almost all of the authors of the village books express that this is what pushes them to write: the desire to pass on knowledge to the coming generations and to preserve the past for the future.

The range of subjects addressed in the village books reveals the authors' intentions to preserve the breadth of the Palestinians' geohistorical, socioeconomic, and familial and cultural experiences. To do that, they write about physical space, social worlds, family relations, economic activities, and cultural practices. The books' creators explain the reasons behind their production, focusing on their concern for legacy and heritage, as well as for creating a collective nationalist history. But the authors and compilers of the village books tackle these needs in order to register their history and position their works to serve as educational material for their children and grandchildren, and more generally as a way to ensure that knowledge of the village is preserved for future generations. The following examples, gleaned from both the village books themselves and from interviews with the authors, depict the authors' stated reasons for writing their books and for choosing the materials they included.[69]

Two goals are evident: first, to make the village history available to everyone in a printed text; and second, to express the villagers' sentiments toward and emotional attachment to their emptied and destroyed village. Deeb Kan'aan, for example, writes, "The object of this book is for readers to know Ishwa', the land and the people, before the *nakba* in 1948."[70] And the four authors of a book on al-Walaja state, "We have undertaken to prepare a book about al-Walaja that will remain a landmark, in which we have placed valuable information about our village. This book will serve as a resource [*marja'*] for our children in the present and future."[71] In an interview with Ibrahim 'Awadallah, author of one of the village books on Suba who was living in Jordan, he told me:

> The new generations are scattered in various countries—Jordan, Saudi Arabia, Palestine, America—and no one knows each other. The people who live in America can go and visit Palestine and then they come tell us about it, while those of us here in Jordan are fifty kilometers away and cannot reach it or see it. So I wanted our children to know about the village. I wanted each house to have a book about their village to remember it and be able to read about it.[72]

And in Lebanon, author Hussein al-Lubani told me, "My book is nothing more than a document I have put in the hands of the people of my village so that they can benefit from it and enjoy and remember that there was once a village on a map named Damun that existed, that had a particular character, and its own flesh and blood[. . . .] So that Damun won't be forgotten."[73] Historians write history to study change over time and not to record events for the sake of the future per se. So, in effect, the village book authors document what existed previously, precisely because it has changed. Their compilations of documents, the oral histories and stories they collect, and the maps they create are based on their own conceptions of writing history and can serve as material for historical research.

As these examples illustrate, the explicitly stated goal of these books and their authors is to pass on knowledge of the village, of its land, and of the greater Palestinian homeland. The authors make clear that they feel that having this information includes or implies a dual set of rights and responsibilities. The older generations have the duty and the responsibility to undertake these memory projects, whereas the younger generations possess the right and responsibility to want to know this information. These sentiments appear in the memorial book for the village of Suhmata, whose authors have positioned knowing names as part of the village's heritage and the duty of all villagers. The following composition entitled "So That We Don't Forget," from the book, is in the form of a "call" and "response":

> *Call (ancestors' words to their descendants)*: Suhmata is your village, a dear portion of your homeland; all of its land is ours, we inherited it from our fathers, who inherited it from our grandfathers. . . . Our bequest to our children and grandchildren and the generations that follow us: "Remember your homeland, do not forget your village. . . . We have put before you the names of the village lands, part by part, the names of the springs and valleys, the names of the pools and wells, the names of the fruit trees and other trees, the names of the seasonal crops, and we give you the responsibility, this charge, to you, the children and grandchildren, who are the trustees. . . .

> *Response (answer of the descendants to the bequest of the ancestors)*: We will retain the names and places, defend our rights, and maintain the land and stone, the crops and trees. We will maintain the bequest and fulfill our responsibility, cooperating with all who are sincere, for however long it takes, and despite the hardships and difficulties to liberate Suhmata and Palestine.[74]

This call-and-response section conveys the bequest of the village—even though the village itself no longer exists—from the elders who lived in it prior to 1948, to their children, reinforcing to them that the village and its lands are their birthright and their legacy. The ancestors hand down not a physical bequest but a particular knowledge, and they admonish their descendants to remember the village, the names of the springs, the wells, the crops, and the village lands. The text calls on the younger generations to learn these names and thus to know the village and the location of these places, despite their absence from the contemporary landscape and despite the removal of the villagers and their descendants from that land. The composition in the Suhmata village book—which was published inside Israel where the now-destroyed village is located—functions as a plea to both young and old. It is a call to young people to know their past and respect their history, to receive the teaching and knowledge of their elders, and to continue to fight and believe that Suhmata and Palestine can be returned. It is a call to the older generation, whose members remember their lives in their village, to ensure that their heritage and legacy are maintained. This composition urges young and old to struggle against the geography of dispossession by remembering, and to fight against their physical remove from the land, which challenges their ability to remember and learn about the places that were so meaningful to them in the past.

The Suhmata book, like a number of the other Palestinian village books published in Israel, reflects a very different lived reality and relationship to the village than the books written in the diaspora. The Suhmata book's authors are among those Palestinians who were internally displaced persons (IDPs) in 1948 and stayed within the borders of what became Israel but were not allowed to live in their own village, which was subsequently destroyed. They call themselves the *muhajjarin* (the "forcibly removed"] whereas the Israeli state refers to them as "present absentees" (*hadirin gha'ibin* in Arabic, *nokhehim nifkadim* in Hebrew), in reference to the Absentees' Property Law of 5710/1950.[75] Israeli law categorized all those not living in their homes in May of 1948 as "absent," thus granting itself permission to confiscate their homes, lands, and properties. Primarily this action was aimed at preventing the return of Palestinians who were outside the borders of the state. However, according to Wakim and Beidas, the United Nations Relief and Works Agency estimated in 1950 that this group included some 46,000 of the 156,000 Palestinians still living in Israel who were granted Israeli citizenship.[76] For nineteen years after the creation of the Israeli state, until 1966, Palestinians living inside Israel were subject to military rule, which required them to obtain travel permits to move outside of their place of residence.[77] Although they usually lived near their former villages, these Palestinians were prevented from returning to live in those villages or even to visit them (or their ruins). Once a year, on Israeli Independence Day, Palestinians were legally permitted to visit their former villages, which in the 1970s and 1980s became collective gatherings, as chronicled in Michel Khleifi's film *Ma'loul Celebrates Its Destruction* (*Ma'loul tahtafil bidimariha*). More recently, visiting has been made easier, and individuals return to visit and clean up cemeteries and holy places, and to eat the fruits and plants that still grow on the land.[78] Groups such as the Association for the Defense of the Rights of the Internally Displaced Persons in Israel (*Jama'iyat al-difa' 'an huquq al-muhajjarin*) host yearly "Marches of Return," and Zochrot organizes regular trips to the destroyed villages and erects commemorative signs there.[79]

Whereas the displaced villagers living within Israel can return to visit their villages, those across borders, in Jordan, Syria, and Lebanon, for the most part cannot. However, in the diaspora, particularly in the camps, the villagers create public performances and other events that connect people collectively to their villages. In Yarmouk Camp in Damascus, Syria, and in schools in Ein el-Hilweh Camp in Lebanon, in 2008, those commemorating the sixtieth anniversary of the *nakba* witnessed day-time school productions and evening get-togethers of villagers celebrating their histories, the villages, and who they are as Palestinians. In one such celebration, the villagers (now urban refugees) listened to recitations of poetry, children dressed in traditional clothes performed dances, and older men stood on stage and handed the keys of their houses to their grandsons.

Regardless of whether their village is nearby or across borders, people place the obligation for providing knowledge of the village on the older people, the ones who lived in and knew the village and Palestine. Older people's roles include writing books, speaking publicly, giving interviews to the press or to those collecting oral histories, and helping with their grandchildren's school assignments. People I spoke with felt that if they did not pass on what they knew of the village to the younger generations, they would be seen first and foremost as shirking their responsibilities as Palestinians, and then as failing to provide a heritage and ancestry to their descendants. The author of the Ishwa' village book explains:

> It is the right of the generation that was born outside of the homeland to request from those who lived in it [. . .] and who knew the ways of life there, to put the truth between their hands so that the young generation can be clear about the situation. So that they can take up the cause of their lost rights and stolen homeland. They have inherited a heavy burden and a great responsibility. If they want to unencumber themselves and achieve what the previous generation was unable to do, they need to be armed with, among other things, knowledge and wisdom.[80]

This encouragement for one generation to remember and recall and the next generations to listen and learn is articulated in part because Palestinians, both young and old, feel that Palestinians are losing this history and that information is not being passed down. During my experiences living with Palestinians in Jordan, Palestine, and Syria, I heard young people complaining that their elder relatives did not tell them about their lives prior to 1948. Young people wanted to know this information, and interviews that I conducted with Palestinian Jerusalemites who left the city in 1948 often became collective affairs, with younger family members coming into the room as the interviews progressed, joining me in asking questions of their older relatives, prompting the interviewee to tell certain stories, and reacting to new ones.

When older Palestinians are called on by younger generations to recount their experiences, they respond with stories that contain many moments of both personal grief and collective anguish as painful emotions over the loss of family members and their uprooting from the land are dredged up. For those who are unable or unwilling to relive these moments, the village books conveniently serve a purpose. Author Ghalib Sumrayn answered my question about who responded more to his book, the older people or the younger, by saying that the older people told him, "you relieved us, because so many members in the family say to us older folk, tell us the stories of the past, but we don't want to, so now we say, take the book and read it."[81] Others, like older people everywhere, expressed their dismay over the lack of interest of the younger generations, saying that they are concerned only with making money and music videos. Sumrayn continued, "At least half of the new generation, they read and ask questions, but the rest care more about Haifa [Wehbe, a popular singer], television, and dancing. These young people don't want to know these things about the village."[82]

· · ·

The village books, unlike the metahistorical history texts, focus on recreating village life in ways that chronicle the social fabric of everyday life. They focus on the mundane as well as the political—on harvest practices, wedding songs, children's games, the names of village fighters in the 1936–1939 revolt—and their narratives consider everyday life and the meaning of what was lost by the Palestinian national body politic. In contrast to the metanarratives of modern Palestinian history, the village books offer a local and detailed account of village life that describes the events as well as the suffering and struggles of the villagers against Zionism and British colonial rule. At the same time, the authors of the village books celebrate and detail village life, dedicating themselves to explaining the village's ways of life, customs, traditions, and landscapes for future generations.

Palestinian political struggles invite us to contextualize the appearance and flourishing of the village books within this larger political movement in which Palestinians are involved. In this movement, initially the local was eschewed for Arab nationalist and Palestinian nationalist frameworks; but by the 1980s, as these nationalist frameworks failed to continue the struggle or represent all Palestinians, they began to voice their own individual and local understandings of themselves and their identities as Palestinians outside of political resistance.[83]

Although the event-based and political narrative history provides the framework for many of the village books, their general content reflects their authors' willingness to acknowledge Palestinian nationalist concerns (less so Arab nationalism) as a way to emphasize that they, this small group of villagers, still exist. Therefore they record in painstaking detail and publish, at much personal expense, their books detailing village life, its people, and the material and social practices that were meaningful to them. The authors of the village books package what they present as a testament of the villagers' survival, and as a chronicle and catalogue of what was lost to local communities that were part of the Palestinian national fabric that was ripped apart in 1948.

Perhaps the appearance of the village books in the 1980s, and their detailed construction of village history, can be read as part of a struggle over political authority. Once governed by village elites and landowners, villagers became refugees who were used and empowered by various political movements and leaders. In the 1990s, the PLO anchored itself in the West Bank and Gaza and abandoned the Palestinians in the diaspora and in Israel. In light of this political absence, the village books signify a shift by Palestinians to new ways of producing Palestinian-ness, and the authority of individuals to represent who Palestinians are today.

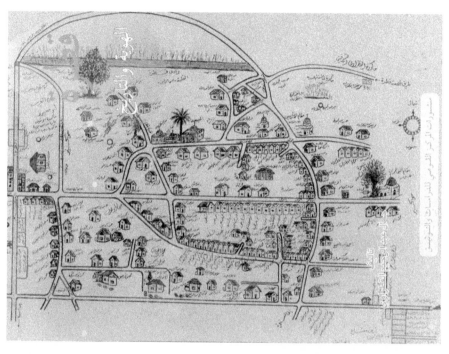

Figure 1 Cover of the village book for Qatra (al-Ramla district) with a hand drawn map of the built up part of the village. Along with the houses labeled with family names, the map includes the school, mosque, shrines, and major geographic landmarks. Book by Jamal 'Abd al-Rahim al-Qatrawi. Reproduced with permission of the al-Markaz al-Qawmi lil-Dirasaat wal-Tawthiq (National Center for Studies and Documentation, Gaza).

الحاج عبد المجيد العلي

كويكات

لبنان

كويكات ● عكا

القدس ●

أحد شرايين فلسطين

كويكات ●

عكا ●

قضاء عكا

أحد بيوت القرية

Figure 2 Cover of the village book for Kuwaykat (Acre district). It shows a map of historic Palestine and the location of the village, an outline of the Acre District borders and the village, a photograph of a village home today, and the stamp from 1941 of the village *mukhtar*, Khalil Ibrahim al-ʿAli. Book by al-Hajj ʿAbd al-Majid al-ʿAli and reproduced with his permission (Lebanon).

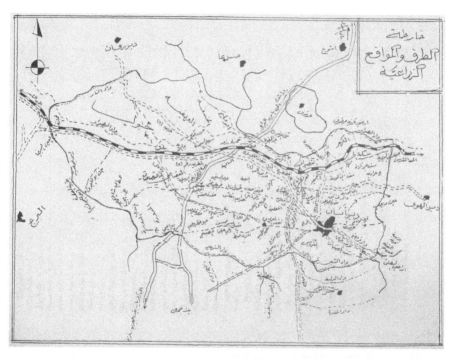

Figure 3 Map of "Roads and Agricultural Sites" in Dayr Aban (Jerusalem District). Within the village borders, this map shows all of the named places for crops and farming that defined the physical landscape of the village. In addition to train tracks, roads, and built-up area of the village (the filled in area), the map also shows the surrounding villages of Dayr Rafat, Sara'a, Ishwa', 'Artuf, Dayr al-Hawa, Jarash, and al-Burayj. Reproduced with permission of village book author 'Abd al-'Aziz Abu Hadba (West Bank).

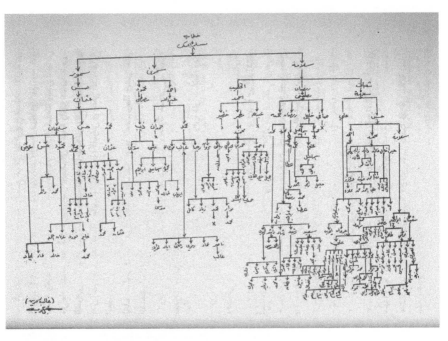

Figure 4 Family tree from Qalunya village book (Jerusalem District). This family tree from the Khitab family charts more than eight generations of male descendants from their original ancestor. It also shows the genealogical connection of three of the village families in the third generation: Salama, Sumrayn, and Sumur. The author of the village book for Qalunya, Ghalib Muhammad Sumrayn, is the seventh generation. Reprinted with the author's permission (Jordan).

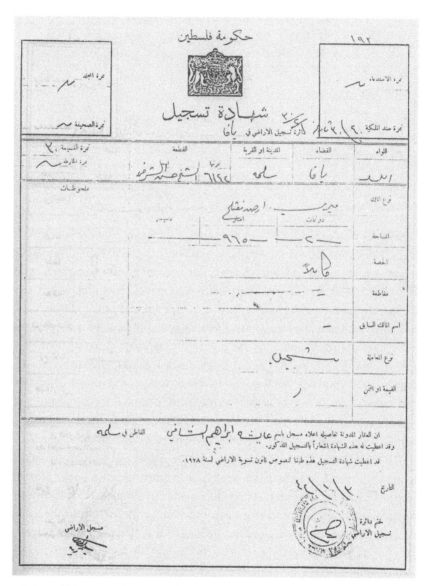

Figure 5 **British Mandate Land Registration Document.** The document shows the registration of 2 dunum, 965 meters, of agricultural land by 'A'isha Ibrahim al-Shafi of Salama in the District of Jaffa in 1942. Reprinted from the Salama village book with permission of author Sahira Dirbas (Israel).

3 VILLAGE HISTORY AND VILLAGE VALUES

Damascus, Syria: 2008

In 2008, as part of the sixtieth anniversary of the *nakba*, the Palestinian villages (and cities) were the centerpiece of school assignments in a Damascus
refugee camp that sought to teach the children about Palestine in general and
about their individual origins specifically. One school assignment asked students from ages seven to ten to write a four-page report on their village. They
had to write about the location of the village and place it on a map, draw
the village's borders, and label the natural topographic elements (canyons,
springs, mountains, valleys) and the significant archaeological sites (including mosques, churches, the Roman-era wells, citadels, and so on). They also
had to draw one of those sites, list the village's most famous foods and a recipe,
record the names of the martyrs from the village, identify the most famous
battles, and draw a picture of the dress of men and women of the village.

The knowledge the students needed for the report was a mixture of both
familial knowledge and book knowledge, so neither reference books nor the
students' families alone would allow the students to complete the assignment.
Their families (grandparents or great-grandparents) could tell them about the
different features of the villages, but because this information exists in people's minds as a lived, spatial experience (meaning they saw these features and
walked among them), the children had to transfer their grandparents' verbal
accounts into two-dimensional representations on paper. Their elders who
were women could also tell them about or even show them village dresses,
and cook for them the village foods, because these continued to be part of
their everyday lives or had become popularized as folklore. For the most part,
however, other kinds of information, such as famous battles and lists of village

martyrs and visual representations of archaeological sites and village boundaries, had to be found outside the family, in books written about the villages
specifically and about Palestine in general. It thus became a challenge for these
students to complete the assignment—partly because refugees did not necessarily have access to reference books, and partly because the students might not
have had relatives old enough to remember some of this information.

The Internet served as a reference for those without access to books.
Although home Internet access in Syria is very limited, people could go to
the many Internet shops and find online generic pictures of the men's and
women's clothing and the geographic information requested in the assignment. Ahmad, whose charitable shop sells Palestinian nationalist items such
as flag bracelets, olive-wood plaques of Palestine, embroidered dresses, and
T-shirts, said the kids would ask him for help with this project. He would
do a Google search in Arabic on the Internet, and then decide, on the basis
of what came up, which sites were best for particular information. "People
do not know much of this information," he said when I asked. "Instead, they
have to find it in outside sources." He reported that he usually turned to an
impressively large and comprehensive Arabic and English Web site called Pal-
estineRemembered.com, which has a page with multiple links for each village. This Web site, originally built around the contents of the book *All That
Remains*, which describes in detail all of the destroyed villages,[1] also provides
various forums where villagers may input their own stories, upload photos,
assert their sentiments, and make connections across cyberspace.[2]

For this school assignment, it was not enough to know one's family stories
and to be familiar with the collectively held sense of the village's ethos and
values. In addition, the children and adults needed to find the kind of information about their family's place of origin to set within a scientific, fact-based
framework (geography, visual representations, and statistics) that would be
contained in a history book about a place. This assignment made people—
both children and adults—think about their villages and reconsider what
they, as Palestinians, were supposed to know about them.

That is, the assignment pointed out to people a sensitive subject—
what they did not know about their villages, and the inadequacies of their
family-based knowledge of the villages for understanding Palestinian history in general, as was expected of their children in school-based learning.
For children who have never seen or visited their families' former villages,
the village is being positioned in school as an origin and as geographical and

cultural information that children can write reports on to turn in for school assignments. This type of information falls outside of how the families and the former villagers pass on information to each other about the village. Instead, they conceive of the village as an origin, to be sure, and for those individuals who remember the village, that understanding of origin comes with foundational values about what it means to be from that village and to be Palestinian and Arab, including knowledge of the genealogies of the families of the village. None of this information about values, however, was required of the children for their school assignment. As this story of children writing about their village origins illustrates, different sources of information on their villages are still available. But as the older people who remember the villages pass away, this lived, experiential knowledge about the village goes with them. With the passage of time, both the sources and type of village history that children learn is shifting to book and Internet-based knowledge.

Much of the information the children were to report on is contained in the village books, with their mixture of family, communal, and traditional historical information. The director of a local publishing house whom I talked to has published more than fifteen books on Palestinian villages and numerous others on Palestinian culture and history. Children lucky enough to have available to them a book written about their family's village could turn to this book to find maps of the village, lists of the natural and archeological sites, pictures of the old buildings and the clothing, names of the martyrs, lists of the fruits and vegetables and other crops grown, and the village's history. The director told me that people who came to him felt ashamed that they did not know the information their children were asking about for their school project. He described how parents bought (or borrowed) the village books so they could help their children and be a source of information for them.

The village books do not claim to be history books in the professional sense. Although the authors draw on well-known Palestinian history texts to support their portrayal of the villages and although they see themselves contributing to the body of knowledge about the villages specifically and about Palestine in general, at the same time they write these books to help the local community retain and maintain their connection to the village in terms of both knowledge and sentiment. They provide a didactic forum in which this information about origin, anchored in both family and village, is presented and recorded. As is discussed throughout this chapter and in the other chapters of this book, village book authors draw on a number of sources—both written and oral—to construct their detailed texts on the village. This combination of both traditional scholarly material on the village (population, land ownership, size of built space, and so on) and information meant to educate the reader about village life creates books that, in addition to their documentary elements, reveal the concerns of the diaspora community about representation, continuity, and accuracy. As such, the village books contain "facts" like those presented in modern history texts, such as the geographic location of the village, statistics, and etymological information about the village's name; but they also embody the desire of the villagers to communicate a specific local way of being by focusing on collectively held values, family genealogies, and origin stories. Together this material makes up what the authors envision as comprehensive village histories that carry forward and transfer to others what it means to be from the village.

WRITTEN SOURCES OF PALESTINIAN HISTORY

As the school assignment illustrates, people who want to learn about their villages turn to a number of sources. The Palestinian village books also reference an impressive contingent of formal history books about Palestine, including books that document pre-1948 Palestine. These books provide specific information about the villages—primarily geography, historical references to the village, and Ottoman and British Mandate statistics, but they offer little about villagers and their lives. Because the vast majority of the village book authors do not see themselves as professional historians, they cite from this well-known canon of Palestinian secondary historical sources not only to evidence for their readers their knowledge of the subject and thus their qualifications to write within the larger context of Palestinian history, but also to situate the village within the larger context of historic Palestine and the catastrophe of 1948.

Citations of well-known Palestinian-authored books appear in all of the 112 village books' footnotes and bibliographies. Only one source appears in all of them: Mustafa Murad al-Dabbagh's ten-volume opus *Biladuna Filastin* (Our country Palestine). These volumes briefly mention each Palestinian village, noting its location in relation to the nearby cities, its topography, and the amount of land and number of inhabitants as recorded in British Mandate statistics, as well as the origin of its name; the mention of the village in any ancient, classical, Jewish, Christian, or Muslim sources; and any nearby Jewish settlements resulting from the rise of the Zionist movement in the 1880s through the 1950s.

The entries on each village comprise a page or two at most and serve an ency-clopedic function by providing basic information without many details, much to the dismay of village book authors. Al-Dabbagh's work is a massive collec-tion of previously documented information about Palestine; it is impressive in the sheer breadth of the area it covers and in the author's commitment to col-lecting and publishing the book.[3]

The next most popular source for village book authors is *al-Mawsu'a al-Filastiniya* (The Palestinian encyclopedia),[4] which provides information similar to that found in *Our Country Palestine*, although in a different format. Also commonly cited is a 1992 publication of the Institute for Palestine Stud-ies (IPS), *All That Remains* (which has been translated into Arabic as *Kayy la nansa*, which means "So that we don't forget"), which catalogues each vil-lage that was destroyed, drawing on such sources as British Mandate statistics, travelers' accounts, contemporary visits by researchers, and photographs. *All That Remains* is by far the most comprehensive and detailed of these three sources of historical information on the villages, due to the impressive work of its many researchers and writers.[5] Because it is based entirely on textual sources, it does not provide information on the social history, on the villagers and their customs and ways of life, or on the details of the village landscape. It relies on government documents and statistics to provide population num-bers and statistics on land ownership by religion. Unfortunately, it is not well-distributed in Arabic (or English) in Jordan, Lebanon, and Syria.[6]

The village books depend on these well-known and comprehensive schol-arly books of Palestinian history for both information and status. Many au-thors take excerpts from al-Dabbagh's *Our Country Palestine* and *The Palestin-ian Encyclopedia* for their geographical descriptions of the villages, which in many books make up the opening lines or paragraphs of the first chapter. Other authors rely on al-Dabbagh only for the information from the prehistoric, an-cient, and classical periods, which are not part of the villagers' direct experience or family stories. By citing these published histories as sources of information about their village, the authors tie themselves and the village to that history and land within a larger conception of the geographic entity of Palestine.

Village book authors lament, however, that these encyclopedic, well-known, and well-respected sources provide only limited information about the individual villages. Ibrahim 'Awadallah, the author of one of the village books about Suba discussed in Chapter Two, told me that "for written sources, I turned to the books about Palestine. [...] I read these books and they always write in a general way about Palestinian history. I couldn't find a book that has written more than one line about Suba."[7] When I asked Ghalib Sumrayn about the sources he used for writing his book on the village of Qalunya, he remarked that in addition to oral sources he also used "written sources. First the history book series by Mustafa Murad al-Dabbagh, and the second source, the works of the writer 'Arif al-'Arif." As I pursued the subject with him further, he said, "I know the Palestinian historical writers [and] I use their books as references . . . but when Mustafa al-Dabbagh wrote about Qalunya, he only wrote a few lines. . . . I read many books that mentioned my village, but they never wrote more than ten lines. [. . .] They wrote in general about all the villages, but I wrote *specifically* about my village."[8] By citing al-Dabbagh and al-'Arif both in his bibliography and to me in the interview, Sumrayn showed that he had read the standard texts and relied on them, despite the fact that they say little about his village. He tied his work to these texts as works of history, thereby giving credibility to his own text.

Such large, collective histories such as those already mentioned, as well as 'Abd al-Wahhab al-Kayyali's *Tarikh Filastin al-Hadith* (published in English as *Palestine: A Modern History*) and 'Arif al-'Arif's *Nakbat Filastin wal-Firdaws al-Mafqud* (The catastrophe of Palestine and the lost paradise), have contributed to the development of a written history that prioritizes the political events that resulted in the 1948 War and the loss of Palestine.[9] These meta-narratives of Palestinian history create a vision of the past that consists of dates and politically meaningful events made numerical, depersonalized, and generalized, and that invests the events with meaning relative to the nation and land of Palestine. The historiography of these texts reveals Palestinian conceptions of the consequences of the 1948 War as conceived by an intellectual, social, and political elite. Salim Tamari has pointed out in various contexts that these perspectives suffer from an absence of normalcy: the narrator assumes that the "normal" is known and taken for granted, and therefore does not need to be recalled.[10] Elided in these accounts is Palestinian society—the everyday lives of the people; the significance of the places they lived, worked, farmed, harvested, grazed, and traveled across; their complex communal relations, intimate social and family lives, and economic processes; and the myriad other details of existence that are not part of this type of history-writing.

By including this social history, the authors of the village books add qualitatively different information and perspectives to the corpus of books that seek to communicate Palestinian history within a Palestinian national narrative. Comparing the entry on Qalunya in al-Dabbagh's *Our Country Palestine* with the information rendered in Ghalib Sumrayn's village book reveals the different approaches to historical information pursued by al-Dabbagh and the authors of other, similar encyclopedias and histories of Palestine. Qalunya appears in al-Dabbagh's volume on Jerusalem, where he notes that the village lies five miles northwest of Jerusalem on the road to Jaffa, with al-Qastal the nearest village. Qalunya, al-Dabbagh tells us, was most likely built in 81 CE on the remains of the Canaanite settlement of Mosa and was known during the rule of Roman leader Titus as Colonia Amassa, from which the name Qalunya is derived. Jumping to the late Ottoman period, he states that two modern Jewish settlements were established nearby, one in 1894 called Motza, which was destroyed in 1929 and rebuilt in 1930.[11] A second Jewish settlement, named Mevaseret Yerushalayim, was established in 1956 on the remnants of Qalunya. In addition to providing the land statistics from 1922, 1931, and 1945, al-Dabbagh mentions that the highest class in the school in 1942–1943 was third grade. Completing this description, he mentions that the village was destroyed in 1948 and its inhabitants scattered.[12]

This example of al-Dabbagh's entry for a village shows why his work constitutes such a valuable source for the village books. In addition to gleaning the archaeological history of the villages from English language sources, for each village he presents the available British Mandate statistics for land, population, and education, including the percentages of village land that were owned by Arabs, Jews, and the state; the village population by religion and sex; how many dunums of land were planted with olive trees; and the names of the surrounding villages. He does not include any previously unpublished information, nor any original documents. But for most Palestinians, British Mandate sources and archaeological reports are not easily accessible, nor are they published in Arabic; thus al-Dabbagh's series offers this information to Arabic readers.

Although they are valuable for the reasons noted here, al-Dabbagh's entries on villages also show why the villages' inhabitants would also find his accounts lacking. Missing is any sense of the people of the village, the village space, its social history, and the sentiments of those who lived and worked and married and raised children in the village. Ghalib Sumrayn's 343-page book on Qalunya, by comparison, includes the following subjects (as listed in the table of contents): the village's landscape, landmarks, neighborhoods, and land; its history, roots, and families; Qalunya village and the Jews; fighting for the village; education in Qalunya; marriage and love; popular medicine and treatment; and folklore and traditions (songs, rites of passage, children's games, and so on). He incorporates maps of the village, including one of the built-up area, marking each house and listing its head of household, as well as the school, the grain mill, and other significant sites.

As this example illustrates, although the authors of village books frequently cite al-Dabbagh and the *Palestinian Encyclopdia*, they use little information about the villages from them. The value of the village books as histories lies in their ability to broaden our understanding of the Palestinian past in two ways: the content of these books contributes to and builds up Palestinian collective history; at the same time, the village books undo the tightly controlled Palestinian historical narrative by chronicling the individual idiosyncrasies of each village's history. The village books both enrich and challenge the homogenizing, broadly framed national histories that have so long dominated Palestinian historiography.

Because so many of the village books are written by older men, their content reflects the interests of this generation and gender in terms of the portrayal of the village and the presentation of what material should be known and what emotions should be felt. If we investigate the books from this angle, we see not just lists of places, genealogical family trees, and descriptions of weddings, but also the communication of an ethos. As the rest of this chapter explores, the village books are didactic communal histories and impart what it means *to be* from a particular village. The authors construct their narratives as stories in order to instruct readers, and in order to be understood as offering a collective history that presents the values, morals, and characteristics of the village within its distinctive physical space.

BOOKS OF VILLAGE VALUES

Village books contain more than the straightforward documentation of village life. In the types of stories they tell and in the ways they are told, the books communicate a history of being—of what it means to be from a certain village and to be Palestinian and Arab. These ways of being are embedded within certain mores, values, and standards that influence authors' choices of source, content, narration, and narrative styles. Certain types of narratives are told in the books—narratives, even tropes, that reflect more than just how the villagers want to remember themselves, but also the values they hold to be important. They convey a sort of utopian but not incorrect vision of what was important, rather than an event-based history.[13]

At their heart, the village books contain descriptions and stories that express the shared values that dominated village life; they present a unified community that bestowed honor on its guests and showed generosity to all. Some authors express these values in a straightforward manner:

> The village of al-Walaja, whose inhabitants, since days of old, have been known for their pleasantness, courage, and generosity, are the ones who raised the slogan of cooperation [al-ta'wun], known as assistance [al-'awna]. They would fly to help each other in building, harvesting, and planting, in times of happiness and sadness. They are the ones who refuse to accept humiliation and enmity, who preserve the dignity of each individual, and who rush to their aid if faced with harm from a nearby village. In our village, the guest was pleased, and always found welcome and kindness, with young and old competing to honor him.[14]

The village is portrayed as a collectivity that comes together in times of need. This concept of al-'awna appears in numerous books as the ideal of communal conduct, and it is what made individual and family life possible given the unpredictable nature of village life in the nineteenth and early twentieth centuries.

Village values, particularly nationalist ones, are communicated through stories told about places in the village (such as caves, wells, trees, or public buildings). The stories then segue into conclusions or morals that exemplify the village's values, such as generosity and unity, which are also tied to and contextualized within nationalist sentiments in the pre-1948 struggle against Zionism.[15] In the village book about Qalunya, the author's account of the different wells of the village informs the reader where each well was located and who owned it, and also provides a location to which to anchor a story about one of the ways the villagers aided each other in times of difficulty.

> Because of the springs in our village, people didn't [need to] dig private wells in the courtyards of their homes. But there still were a number of privately dug wells in the village. The most renowned of these was the well of Isma'il Khalil Ramadan that was in the center of the courtyard of the tens of rooms he owned. He offered this well to the people of the village during the days when the Jews of the settlements of Motza and Erza besieged the village.[16] He offered a great service, providing necessary water to the families when it was impossible for the

women to go either to the upper or lower springs where they would be targets for the Jewish snipers.[17]

This account tells readers about the villagers' sharing of resources, their commitment to collectively held values, and how in a time of crisis they (through the actions of one man) placed collective needs before individual interests. The struggle of the villagers to survive the attacks on them by the Zionist forces frames the story, as it does the entire book. Not anchored to a specific date or incident, however, the story, is presented as a basic element of life in the village leading up to the villagers' dispossession and exile.

Village book authors use stories to communicate how individuals represented values such as honesty, generosity, and manliness (or failed to embody them). Telling stories as a way to impart lessons and morals exists in many places, societies, and eras. Such stories serve as part of a shared cultural narrative trope to impart values and enforce collective understanding of the social norms, to judge individual behavior, and to warn and teach others. Liisa Malkki's work on Hutu refugees in Tanzania portrays the refugees' understanding of the past recast in narrative through "fundamentally moral terms."[18] In addressing narrative structures, Andrew Shryock analyzes Jordanian Bedouin accounts of "how it used to be," to illustrate how norms and values were commonly expressed through poems and stories, and that the passing on of information is embedded within larger meaning systems.[19] The Palestinian village books transfer the purpose of oral narratives into their written narratives and content. For example, in the village book about Abu Kishk, one man tells the story of the village's relations with the village of Kafr Thulth.

One time dar Abu Kishk [the Abu Kishk family] ran out of wheat. [They arranged with] Dar Hilal [the Hilal family] to send fifteen camels and money to Qalqilya to get the wheat. So the camel drivers set out to get the wheat from a man named Farha who was the wealthiest of Dar Hilal. But he refused to give them the wheat. His relatives became upset with him. Dar Abu Kishk had sent gold to him, but he would not load up the wheat. So the camel drivers left with the camels. Who saw them but someone called al-Hassan from Dar Shraym [the Shraym family] from the village of Khirbat Kafr Thulth. He came across all of these camels and asked what was going on. They said, "By God, Farha will not give us the wheat". So this man, Mahmoud al-Hassan, went to Dar Shraym and loaded the camels. He wouldn't take any money but said instead, give my regards to the elders [mashayikh] of Abu Kishk.[20]

This story celebrates the actions of one man and indicts another man because of his dishonesty. Judiciously, it is noted, however, that the dishonest man's relatives expressed their dissent over his actions; the story critiques only one man and not his family or village. This story, then, is not just a story of how the villagers managed to get wheat; it also contains within it the norms of behavior and the values that the villagers held in esteem, and demonstrates their ability to censure an individual and evoke these norms in order to achieve their ends.

These stories also portray the values of the villagers not only to indict individual actions but also to show the defense of those Palestinian values in the face of the British colonial authority. In a village book about al-Shajara, Rasmiya Muhammad al-Salih recounts a story that she heard from Qasim al-Khatib from Faradiya village about al-Shajara's reputation for generosity. That the story was originally told by someone not from the village but is about its good reputation evidences the importance of the values of generosity and nationalist activism among Palestinian villagers in general. It tells of a time during the British Mandate period when the customs police searched people and fined them for smoking locally grown Arabic tobacco in order to get them to smoke government-regulated (and taxed) cigarettes. In this story, the customs police officers are Palestinian employees of the British Mandate authority.

> One day the customs policemen came to al-Shajara, to the house of Ahmad al-'Ali, who took them to the guesthouse of their neighbor, Yusif al-Hassan of the al-Khutba' *hamula* [clan]. While sitting in the guesthouse, the customs policemen went through the offered cigarettes and fined Yusif one Palestinian pound (PP) and three lira for having nongovernmentally regulated cigarettes. Ahmad told his father what happened and that they had potentially lost a neighbor's friendship to this situation. So his father came and said to the police, "Here, take one PP from me and one from my son and smoke from my cigarettes." After that, Yusif stood up and said to the policemen, "We are not going to serve you lunch." The customs police left rather annoyed and continued on to Tamra village, where they went to the *mukhtar*'s [mayor's] guesthouse complaining that they had not received lunch at al-Shajara village. Qasim al-Khatib from Faradiya village was also there. The *mukhtar* was surprised and said, "The people of al-Shajara are known for their generosity; it is impossible that they would let anyone go without feeding them." So the customs police told the story of what happened, and the *mukhtar* got angry. He threw them out, saying, "Heaven help you! Nor

will you put a morsel of my food in your mouths either. I swear to God the people of al-Shajara are generous."[21]

When the customs police tried to exploit this concern with being generous toward guests by saying that the al-Shajara villagers had not taken care of them, the Tamra *mukhtar* managed to get them to admit to why they had not been served, and he sided clearly with the al-Shajara villagers as he too refused to feed them. Ultimately the story reveals the al-Shajara and Tamra villagers' loyalty to one another, their unwillingness to offer their typical generosity when one of them is badly treated by the policemen who are their guests, and their strong nationalist sentiments about sticking together and defying the demands of the British Mandate authority. Indeed, authors of village books retell these stories to illustrate the actions and behaviors of the people (both good and bad) with seemingly little interest in the historical information contained within the stories. In the case of the contraband cigarettes, the author of the book does not comment on the fact that the British Mandate was regulating what cigarettes people were smoking, or that they were fining people for breaking the law; rather, the story centers on how the (Palestinian) customs policemen broke social customs and insulted people, and on how the villagers banded together and defied the authority with dignity.[22]

Village values are narrated through direct statements about those values as well as through individual stories about personal and collective experiences and known events. These multiple forms of narrating history communicate collectively held ideas and social norms by directly addressing values and by including individual stories that may have other subjects or goals. Ultimately, regardless of how these stories are told, they communicate people's awareness of what it meant to be a Palestinian villager before the *nakba*, the collective values they held, and how they expressed those values. The authors' concern in portraying collectively held village values in narratives of village life centers on the way things ideally should have been. The author of the village book on Ijzim portrays the villagers as Palestinians cooperating with one another against colonial forces: "Just as the people of the country were united in the struggle against the Ottoman Empire, the British Mandate, and Zionist settlement, so also were the efforts of the villagers and their leaders unified in their struggle from the time that the British stepped onto the land of Palestine, and toward the Turkification policies before that."[23] Despite this statement about unity, Ijzim hosted—like other Palestinian villages, indeed like communities everywhere—struggles over power, loyalty, and political alliances. As Ylana Miller and Efrat Ben-Ze'ev have shown, the villagers fiercely contested their say and representation in local government, and both the British and the Zionists influenced these struggles and were especially keen to exploit them.[24] These events told in oral histories and historical documents reveal the family conflicts that occurred in the attempts to gain control of the leadership of the village, as well as stories of one man's collaboration with the Zionist movement. None of this appears in the Ijzim village book.

One explanation for the elision of negative historical events is an author's concern for an individual's behaviors and the reputation of that person's family. When I asked 'Abd al-'Aziz Saqr about land in his village of Salama, he said that indeed Jews had owned some land in the village. They had purchased it not from a villager, he said, but instead from "someone from the Abu Khadra family from Jaffa, and they established a settlement [on it]." Having read the book closely, I followed up: "I don't think you wrote the family name of Abu Khadra in the book. You just wrote 'one of Jaffa's citizens.'" Saqr replied, "I didn't want to cause problems. I'm telling you the truth. It's not right what he did, but the family is patriotic, and they are good people. So if a member of this family sold his piece of land, I can't write and mention his name or say the Abu Khadra family, because if I do that, I will offend all Abu Khadra family members."[25] Authors' unwillingness to cause problems or offend others reveals the strength of communal responsibility and the fear of negative repercussions that they take into consideration in publishing these local histories. Such concerns illustrate the contemporary force of village values that pushes authors to suppress information. In other words, avoiding mentioning names, refraining from stating negative things about individuals, and being aware of the repercussions for their families, as Saqr has expressed, can be seen as ways of respecting the village values of unity and generosity. Thus, by eliding bad or negative comments about individuals, the authors are also adhering to the village values of not sowing enmity and bad will among the villagers. This fear of tainting the family or of repercussions to the family due to the actions of one individual undoubtedly plays a role, as we have seen, in what gets told (or not) and how it is told.

At the same time, negative stories about village behaviors may also provide an opportunity for authors to illustrate village values and thus fulfill the didactic purpose of the books. Saqr described a feud between two families in the village that began in the early 1940s. According to Saqr's story, two men (Khalil

'Abd al-Hadi and Shahada 'Ali Salih) playing cards in a café got into a fight and Khalil hit Shahada with a chair. Taking this as a great insult, Shahada got ahold of a pistol and waited for Khalil to return from his work one day and shot and killed him. Then someone from Khalil's family attacked someone from the 'Ali Salih family (whose mother happened to be Khalil's sister), and then the 'Ali Salih family attacked Khalil's family and killed one and injured another. Multiple interventions finally resulted in the end of the feud. The resolution was spurred on by the increasing violence between Arabs and Jews and by Zionist attacks on the village, which created the need for the villagers to come together.[26] In my interview with Saqr I expressed my surprise that he would include such a negative story, and I asked if the Salama citizens were upset by its appearance in the book. He replied,

> No, because it was real and they know it. But I wrote it to show how much we were a forgiving people, and how they forgot the hatred and revenge and how they supported each other to face the enemy. It shows how they came together to fight the enemy despite the bad blood between them. And also because today's young people wanted to know how their parents and grandparents were noble and well-mannered, and how they forgot their hatred between each other and turned to the real enemy.[27]

By including this story in his book, Saqr took what was a negative incident in the village and turned it into an instructive incident to illustrate how the villagers could put their conflicts behind them and unite.

One letter from the director of Birzeit University's Center for Research and Documentation of Palestinian Society (CRDPS) illustrates how he handled a situation in which a person had written to complain about the way the families were represented in one of the CRDPS village books. Saleh Abdel Jawad, the director, replied:

> Regarding your critique of the way some of the families were portrayed in the book, it is my belief that such matters are unimportant in relation to the work that eternalizes the village. . . . It is extremely unfortunate that the competition among and the grudges held by the families in your village caused many problems in the past, and we hope that the new generations can get beyond the differences of the past.

The communication of village values occurs not just in the content of the books but also in the contemporary negotiation of those values in the community.

The CRDPS director takes the letter writer to task for arguing about an element of village families and suggests that the values of today require them instead to get beyond the way things were handled in the past.

The general books of Palestinian history communicate the larger narratives of what it means to be Palestinian whereas the village books dedicate themselves to illustrating village life, including what it means to be from a particular village defined by a set of highly esteemed values that are communicated both directly and through stories. By focusing specifically on village values, authors promote a vision of the village that centers on unity and cooperation, ignores individual missteps and negative behaviors, and is set within the context of the Palestinian national struggle.

WRITING FAMILY GENEALOGIES

The village book authors envision family histories as crucial to the histories of the villages, so they anchor the village to family origins that connect to Arab, Muslim, regional, ancient, local, and foreign origins. Almost every book devotes some space to representing the families, tribes, clan relations, and origins in written or visual form, or both. The books can be characterized either by the incredible detail of genealogical information—taking up one-third of the book or more—or in a few cases by the total opposite—the noticeable absence of this information. The weight given to these genealogies in the majority of the village books reflects that this knowledge figures as an essential component of the cultural memory that Palestinians maintain. Family identification also connects Palestinians' understanding of the past to the larger sense of Arabness that most Palestinians identify with and that is often rendered in genealogical terms.

The types of genealogical information represented in the village books varies from lists of family names to drawings of family trees to long descriptive accounts of family origins, ancestors, and descendants. For example, the Qalunya village book by Ghalib Sumrayn, written and published in Jordan, includes fifty-seven pages of descriptive family genealogies spanning a period of 100 years. In contrast, the Qalunya book by 'Othman Muhammad Hassan, written and published in Chicago, summarizes the village families in two pages of text with a one-page diagram of the four *hamulas* (clans) of the village.[28] In large part, how much family information is published depends on the authors' access to people from the various families who can provide that information. In the original Birzeit University series on the destroyed villages, chapter two of each book is dedicated to the "clans and families" (al-hama'il wa-al-'a'ilat) and contains extensive family trees. The other books in the Birzeit series also contain that information, although not necessarily in a dedicated chapter.

Both family and clan identities continue to be used by Palestinians in the present as ways of understanding their relations, writing history, and categorizing knowledge about the past. These families and clans are recorded in patrilineal descent groups consisting of both biological relations and fictive kin that are the essential structures of Palestinian social organization and family life.[29] Among Palestinians, the village books reflect how kinship is constructed in groupings such as family (dar or 'a'ila), clan ('ashira or hamula), and tribe (qabila), whose existence (or lack thereof) varies according to the origin of the kinship group, location, and lifestyle (whether urban or rural; settled or nomadic; highland, coastal, or desert).[30]

Despite the clear-cut lists of descendants and the organized family trees that appear in the village books, these categories of identification are not (and never have been) as stable as they appear in these written records. The meanings of these constructions of family relations that connect individuals and families in webs of relations vary over time and from place to place.[31] Rhoda Kanaaneh argues in her study of Palestinians in the Galilee that "clans are constantly fracturing into new ones, new families are incorporated or expunged, and boundaries are disputed. Not only is it not a biologically determined clear-cut category, but the importance of clan and its role in shaping individual lives has fluctuated as well."[32] Despite the indeterminancy of these genealogies, Palestinian village book authors give them prominence because they represent culturally and socially significant accounts of origins and connections to communally recognized groups.

The village book authors present family histories and locate family origins in a variety of ways. When family stories of origin are included in the books, they reveal connections with the villages and cities of Syria, the Bedouin tribes of the Arabian peninsula, the farming communities and nomadic groups across the Jordan river, and travelers and soldiers from Lebanon, Syria, Egypt, Cyprus, and Iraq who settled in historic Palestine. Genealogical renderings of family history occasionally trace ancestors back to the purported forefathers of all Arabs, with links to pre-Islamic tribes and significant persons. "The tribe of Abu Sa'ad (also called Banu Sa'ad) came to our village and is from the tribe of Jadham of the Yamanite Qahtan. The Jadham came to Palestine and Egypt before and after the advent of Islam, and the Jadham's of Palestine are from the people of [the prophet] Shu'ayb, peace be upon him."[33] Others trace lineages to origins in a particular place. Thus family history begins with stories of the time the family's forefather arrived in the village. "The Dakwar family came to Kafr Bir'im in the seventeenth century from the village of Rmaysh al-Jabal in southern Lebanon. The family was founded by their ancestor Louis."[34] Origin thus forms the starting point of the genealogy, and the account focuses on when the forefather arrived at the village, which marks the beginning of the family history. What he did prior to arriving is, in most cases, not worthy of mention, or if it is mentioned, it is described as part of the reason for resettling in the village or as part of the journey of getting to the village. These stories of family origin are embedded in how we "do family," according to oral historians Kristin Langellier and Eric Peterson:

> The family-as-lived, replete with its multiple and contradictory meanings, is organized and maintained daily and over generations through a variety of discursive practices by which we "do family." Doing family embraces practices that present the family as legitimate and interpretable. One important strategy for doing family is storytelling—both stories to tell and secrets to keep.[35]

Social pressures and values constrain people's revelations about their families, wherever they live; in the case of the village books, the authors most often present a publicly acceptable origin story for families.

The information passed on orally about family genealogies and origins forms what people *believe* to be their histories. Often they preface their stories with "it was told to me" or "the old people used to say. . . ." For the most part, only people from the family know a specific family's lineage; thus authority is invested in those who memorize and record this part of the past.[36] According to one village book author, "a characteristic of the Arabs was, and still is, a special pride in himself, his lineage, his origin and branches, his fathers and grandfathers, and the tribe to which he belongs, a pride ['itizaz] that reaches the point of partiality ['asabiya]."[37] As Andrew Shryock explores in his ethnography of two Jordanian tribes, the 'Adwan and 'Abbad history is genealogy intertwined with events recounted in poetic form.[38] Because oral tales about family were heroic tales of battles won, other tribes defeated, and land taken over, they tended to focus on or at least come to some resolution that shows the glory and strength of a particular family.

Such accounts that seek to tell the origin story of a village, family, or tribe are not merely unquestioned renditions of genealogical facts. Shryock shows that transforming this information from story form into factual tradition requires citing proper sources and receiving the transmission from a chain of ancestors.[39] The desire for an origin and a past confounds some village book authors, who are aware of what is at stake in claiming a noble family history. One of the authors questions whether these genealogical traditions are real and possible:

> Only someone naive [sadhij] would believe that all of the residents in Najd, Hijaz, Yemen, the Arabian Peninsula, and the Gulf, generation after generation of children and grandchildren from the pre-Islamic period unto this time which we live in, have preserved the correct and uncontaminated lineages that connect them to 'Adnan or Qahtan, Qays or Yaman, or any tribe. Recording the lineages and planting [family] trees among the [individual] leaves are a habitual practice [sunna] followed by particular classes [tabaqat] of Arabs at certain times in order to be called honorable and chiefs, and to cover themselves with a semblance of superiority and aristocracy. Thus they take privileges that protect their establishments and interests at the expense of others of their same skin. All of the time they fabricate information and weave strands into these lineages, if they are overcome by mixing or forgetfulness or loss.[40]

Likewise, village book authors who are trying to make sense of all the origin stories told to them by the elders of the village often find themselves unable to come up with one narrative history, and thereby find the idea of one historical narrative for the village to be fractured. The authors of the book on the village of Kafr Saba explain that the residents of the village came from some fifteen different families and tribes, but the villagers could not agree on who was first:

> [The villagers] believe that the majority of the families came from southern Palestine. There are those who think that the first tribe to arrive in the town was the al-Walwail tribe, who make up about half the population of the village. Others believe that the Jabr family was the first. And another group believes that four tribes—al-Walwail, Jabr, Badeir, and al-Najjar—came and established the village, and the other tribes, like 'Allan, Farraj, Suwaylim, Abu Thabit, 'Arbas, Yassin, Taha, al-Balasma and al-Khatib, came later.[41]

These origin accounts of the village residents also reflect the prestige and power that are at stake in claiming to be the first families in the village, or the ones with the most significant origin. After the 1948 *nakba*, in the Palestinian diaspora, claims of family prominence have become more symbolic than before, and previously significant social and class structures have been rendered less relevant by the general poverty of refugee life, more opportunities for primary education for all, and the increasing irrelevance of *mukhtars* in local governance. Thus, although people still rely on family origin in their claims to be significant in village history, they have less to gain (land, roles as village leaders, and so on) than they might have had sixty years ago. In fact, the majority of the families, and the accounts of their origins in the village books, acknowledge that they are of humble origins—that they are people who came as footsoldiers with a passing army, who came because of a drought elsewhere, or who can trace their family to an ancestor who came to the village only six generations earlier.[42]

What is often not told in the stories of ancestors who moved from Iraq or Egypt or other villages is why they left those locations for Palestine. Undoubtedly many may have been forced to leave due to hard times, punishment, or fear. One man from the village of 'Ayn Karim recounted that his family's presence in Palestine was due to his grandfather's poor comportment toward his familial duty. In Lebanon, the grandfather had fallen in love with and secretly married a woman from outside his family. His family would not accept this act and drove him out; he *rahala* (traveled) to Palestine—hence his new "family" name, Rahil (traveler).[43]

In one of several versions of the origin story of the Palestinian village of Abu Kishk, the forefather is a stranger, Abu Kishk, who came from Egypt and worked as a guard for the local *amir*, or Bedouin tribal head, Ya'qub al-Harithi. The story relates how Abu Kishk ended up "saving" the tribe from an attack by outsiders, but could not become part of it until he brought his own family from Egypt to prove his own honorable origins.[44] This story reveals the concern that everyone had for the reputation of the stranger who is now going to become part of the tribe and live on the land. As the ancestor of this village, Abu Kishk's honorable conduct figures prominently in the story, and his respectable origin needs to be proven.

The absence of details about certain families is undoubtedly related to the geography of the diaspora—dependent on where people fled to and where the book is composed. Some of the smaller families only get diagrammed; others have little history and few names to fill in the family tree. The village book for Kafr Bir'im consists of interviews with the families who remained in Israel, and the authors and people interviewed note that it is impossible to know the details of the histories of village families who fled to Lebanon.[45] Because no one from these families was near enough to tell their lineages to the authors of the village book, their family histories could not be noted and were thus unintentionally expunged from the record. Whether included or not, these lists of families and the stories of their origin can create the greatest amount of controversy for the authors of village books.

READING FAMILY GENEALOGIES AS HISTORY

In my years of conducting research on the village books, this selective accounting of family prominence was the most common reason that people I talked to did not value a particular village book. Readers sometimes felt that a book promoted certain families and ignored others, or that an author was careless and did not include all of the village's families in the book.[46] If one family is featured too prominently, with pages of information about it and details of a noble origin, while the other families are reduced to a paragraph, the villagers object by going directly to the author, boycotting the book, and even asking for changes.[47] People I talked with about the village books critiqued some of them as being merely vehicles for a certain family to promote themselves; alternatively, those whose families are not included in their village's book often discounted any value in those particular village books.

During my research in the West Bank in 1999, I gave two of the Salama village books to a friend's father, a well-educated professional who had grown up as a refugee in the West Bank, been exiled by the Israelis, and then returned to the West Bank with the PLO in 1995. I asked him what he thought of the books. He dismissed them, saying that his family was not mentioned in them. He did not comment more on the content or on the project of documenting village life for other generations. I tried to figure out why his family would be left out. Salama was a huge village (some seven thousand people) and his family may have been small and maybe even a migrant family. Whatever its past may have been, clearly the family is significant today. In this case, and perhaps others, the village book reflects the family statuses that were significant in the 1940s, before the upheaval of 1948. They reflect the social structures that existed in the past, which everyone knows have changed in the present. Authors and readers have different ideas of how to record families in the books. Changing family status and people's reasonable desire for the representation of village families to be as inclusive and accurate as possible clearly affects how people read and respond to the village books today.

In fact, in my interviews with writers and readers of the village books, and in my ethnographic work in Syria, I discovered that the most controversial material in the village books according to the villagers is the genealogies and the reckoning of family origins and membership. Lists of family names would seem to be factual, straightforward, and unambiguous, but interviews with the authors of the books revealed that recording families and family names was the most fraught endeavor of their history-recording work. "It is the biggest disaster for the book," said one author, "that I wrote about the families; it would have been much better if I didn't write about them."[48] When I asked the author of the book about 'Innaba how he had chosen how to structure his material, he responded, "I started the book—organizationally, I started with the houses, the order of the houses (*tartib al-buyut*) and where they were built and how they were built in order not to upset the people. Because if I had started with the different families, they would say, why did you start with this family?"[49] He listed the thirty or so village families in alphabetical order, he told me, "to avoid conflict over who came first and who was last."

The letters received by the CRDPS about the village books they published also contain disagreements over the portrayal of family information. A two-page letter in minuscule handwriting from an older gentleman took the author and director to task:

> The question is [. . .] was what was written done in the spirit of truth or was it blind selfishness? It is as if the author wanted to say in arrogant boasting that there was no one in the village except his family that had any stature. [. . .] Was it for material gain or out of a sense of nationalism? If it was for national sentiments, then why cheat history and change the truth? Are there no literati or thinkers apart from that deluded author to record the history of 'Imwas and the region for future generations? I don't want to even discuss the Battle of Latrun that he described, most of which was naked untruth. However, what he mentioned about the families was as if only his family lived in 'Imwas. And only men, since he did not mention any women. He mentioned only a tiny bit about the other four families that made up the village. I want to ask him why he didn't mention the Hasan family [and from here the letter-writer fills a page and a half with the names of the villagers left out of the book].[50]

Although in his critique the writer references the larger issue of writing an accurate and truthful history, he dedicates his detailed letter primarily to correcting the geneaological material, clearly prioritizing this information over everything else about the portrayal of the village.

Such sentiments about the portrayal of the family were shared by the Shalabi family in Jenin and the surrounding refugee camps, who took out a quarter-page advertisement in a Palestinian newspaper on January 31, 1995.[51] Titled "Revealing the Truth," it contained a similar upbraiding of those responsible for the Zir'in book.[52] After quoting a verse from the Qur'an about ascertaining the truth,[53] the ad said that the family would like to clarify facts about eight points, almost all of them related to their family and the village *mukhtar*, Hajj 'Abdallah Salih al-Shalabi.[54] They concluded with, "We verify this information as the truth for the sake of history and place the responsibility on Birzeit University's CRDPS for the mistakes in the book. We ask that the CRDPS document the information mentioned above in a new printing of the book, and we reserve the right for ourselves to settle accounts, legally and in accordance with tribal law, with whomsoever provided this wrong information." Despite the veiled threats with which they ended the piece, they did not name the author, almost as if to protect him. The missing or incorrect information they objected to was no more egregious or grevious than other complaints I heard or read. In fact, it is likely less. That they mustered the family council to take a position and that they paid for the advertisement shows a collective sense of need to have their family history rendered correctly both in the book and for the historical record.

The issue of family heritage and history not only arises in the books but also resonates throughout all representations of the past that involve names and claims on the past. The problem of representing the histories of families in the village books is mirrored in the debates that take place among people and on Web sites about family prominence and historical material. An example appears in a debate that took place on PalestineRemembered.com. Photographer Maqbula Nassar posted a photograph of a beautifully preserved stone house in the village of Ijzim. Identified as "the home of the *mukhtar* Mas'ud al-Madi," a sign on the house labels it "the Castel."[55] The following posts appear underneath the photograph:

Post #48527: "My name is Muhammad al-Madi and my father and grandfather and his brothers and most of the Madi family were uprooted from Ijzim to Iraq. Now, sixty years later, we have fled a second time to the Syrian border because of the Iraqi sectarian militas. It pains me to see the house of our ancestor Mas'ud al-Madi, the *mukhtar* of the village. Most of the people of the village were of the Madi family; in other words, we belong to a good lineage, and have land, and houses . . . and now we are in camps, after sixty years of continual uprooting."[56]

Post #57641: "I am 'Abd al-Rahman al-Hasan from Ijzim and my father is Lutfi Amin Ahmad al-Shaykh Hasan. We are originally from the al-Bahhouri clan (note the double h). I'd like to clarify for brother Muhammad al-Madi that we were a large family like the other families in Ijzim, such as the al-Nabhani, al-As'ad, al-Jiyab, and so on, and my grandfather was al-Shaykh Hasan, who had a great deal of agricultural land and houses. According to my information, al-Shaykh Mas'ud al-Madi was not the *mukhtar* of Ijzim but it was someone else whose name I don't know. . . ."[57]

Post #57656, by Maqbula Nassar, the photographer: "Brother 'Abd al-Rahman, I'm sorry that these photos of your village engender feelings of clannishness and partisanship and the desire for a leadership (*makhtara*) rather than combined struggle and unity. This concern [for positions] is empty and overblown. . . . we are all refugees now."[58]

In fact, 'Abd al-Rahman is correct, and this and his subsequent posts strive not only for accurate historical information but also to recognize the other families in the village beyond the dominant al-Madi family. Later posts point out (and the Ijzim village book details) that indeed Mas'ud was never the *mukhtar*, but he was a *shaykh* (village and/or clan head), as 'Abd al-Rahman refers to him. The Ijzim book describes Shaykh Mas'ud as a prominent leader of the area who had a role in various historical events in the first half of the nineteenth century, including that Mas'ud and his son led the ranks of the revolt in their area against the Egyptian occupation (1831–1840). Ibrahim Pasha, the Egyptian ruler at that time, executed Mas'ud and his son and then captured his other sons.[59] In fact, the *mukhtar* position was instituted in 1860 by Ottomans long after Shaykh Mas'ud was gone.

'Abd al-Rahman responded six months later that he was shocked by the responses; his intention in mentioning the other families in Ijzim, he wrote, was so that they would not be ignored. He also acknowledged that "of course the al-Madi family has a long history in the region." He concludes by stating that "as regards the struggle for Palestine, I was and continue to hold my homeland dear and participate in demonstrations here in Washington."[60] His final words indicate that he understood the attack on his statement as questioning not just his knowledge but also his patriotism.

The many examples of readers' reactions to the village books and to other material produced about families reveal the importance placed on the inclusive representation of all of the families from a village. The context in which this information is published—in written form (the village book) or on the Internet—raises problems within the community, especially when the author writes about families other than his or her own while constructing a written document for the historical record. Village book authors tread this path carefully, and many of them include caveats on the inside of the front or back cover, along with their contact information, and ask readers to send in additional or missing information. This concern for registering information correctly indicates the power of individuals and families to affect authors' lives, but even more so it indicates how important the representation of the past is to people, particularly their inclusion in it, when recording village history in written forms that will endure. It was difficult in my research to extract from authors how they responded to these things beyond feeling outright frustration that their efforts were not appreciated and that people focused only on the missing information rather than on the wealth of material that had been published. This reaction to the books—that people see them as misrepresenting the village and the villagers—indicates that people take these publications of history seriously. Although they may not be moved to write a response or another village book, they do, however, acknowledge that these books have or will have influence in the community as a codified and accepted history.

GENDER IN THE FAMILY TREE

Because Arab society assigns family name and origin through patriarchal lineage, the vast majority of the genealogies discussed here have included only male ancestors and descendants and excluded women entirely from a written genealogical presence.[61] Thus the origin stories of these male ancestors tie them to when they arrived in Palestine. Other stories mark religious conversion as the point of origin, as in the example of the Habib family from the village of al-Kawfakha. According to Abu Ramadan, his family "was originally Christian, and our ancestor became a Muslim. The father of my grandfather, 'Ali Khalaf Hassan [from Gaza], he is the one who came to al-Kawfakha."[62] Undoubtedly men who migrated or fled from elsewhere married women from among the local villagers. Thus, female ancestors may provide families with a longer history in Palestine (and the village) than male ancestors reveal; ironically, however, women's origins are not recorded in traditional family genealogies.

Although the village books' authors emphasize patrilineal descent, and with it family knowledge, some authors do include information about women that falls outside of formal genealogies. Everybody knows, for example, the names of their mothers, grandmothers, and great grandmothers, these women's family names, and their places of origin. The information is known and communicated within the family, even if it is not written down. With the passing of generations, it is subsequently lost in the transition to formalized recordings of lineages. However, because of Palestinians' interest in recording their "lost" past, I would argue, contemporary Palestinian ways of recording and writing history are providing new opportunities for women to be included in this genealogical record.

For example, in writing his book on the village of Qalunya, the author utilized his personal knowledge of women's names and origins to craft his work. In a section entitled "Our Roots: The Residents of Our Village, from Ancient Times Until the Diaspora of 1948," he describes the different tribes and clans (hama'il wa 'asha'ir) in the village. He follows this standard, formal description of family origins with a fifty-three-page section on the residents of the village for the hundred–year period prior to 1948. One small section reads as follows:

Families [fasa'il] dar Salama:

- Salama Sha'ban Salama, married to Siriya 'Atiya (who is the mother of Hussein Salama Sha'ban Salama), in exchange for his sister Fatima Sha'ban, who married from the 'Atiya's of the Makhluf hamula.
- Hussein Salama Sha'ban Salama. He married three wives:
  'Othmana Othman Samur "Imm Salama"
  Subha Muhammad 'Abidrabbo from the village of al-Ram "Imm Muhammad"
  'Izziya Muhammad 'Ali Salama "Imm Ahmad." This was her second marriage after her first husband, Hamdan Barakat, died in the Ottoman army.
- Salama Hussein Salama Sha'ban Salama was married to Fatima Muhammad 'Ali Salama Sha'ban Salama 'Askar "Imm Sha'ban".
- Muhammad Hussein Salama Sha'ban Salama married two wives: the first was Ni'ma al-'Abid 'Othman Salah from the Makhluf family "Imm Hussein," and after her death, the second was 'Aziza Muhammad 'Atwa from the Makhluf family "Imm Khalil."[63]

The information recorded in this village book is exceptional, for a number of reasons. This work gives us information not recorded in formal oral genealogies, written family trees, or other historical documents. Instead, the Qalunya register gives us personal family knowledge, such as mothers' and sisters' names. The list also provides interesting information on how many men married more than one wife, either simultaneously or after the death of a previous wife, as well as how many women remarried. The author gives information about the family or clan the bride is from, or whether she is from another village entirely. Such documentation provides a rare opportunity to see, over a number of generations, women's presence in family histories, the relationships among neighboring villages indicated by marriages, and possibilities for understanding the social history of the village (numbers of multiple marriages, deaths, and marriages within or outside of the family, tribe, and clan).

In the preceding selection alone, which covers only three generations (the book continues on for three more generations) we find a variety of information that often is asserted to be either "characteristic of" or "unusual for" Arab societies and village relations, but rarely do we have actual data with which to work. In his outline of these six generations of the Salama Sha'ban Salama family, the author lists nineteen marriages. Among those there is one case of "exchange weddings," in which a groom from one family takes a bride from another family and in exchange a sister from the groom's family becomes a bride for someone in the other family (presumably to lower the wedding costs, because per agreement the husbands would provide less money and fewer goods to the wife and her family). In the Salama Sha'ban Salama family we find seven wives who come from other villages entirely, five wives who are cousins from the same family, three wives who come from other families within the same tribe (*hamula*), and three wives who are from other tribes (although within the same clan (*'ashira*)).[64] The author provides us with the data and summaries to understand the social relations of the time for this village—the marriage statistics, the nature of the marriages, and the women's origins and families.[65] He concludes his chapter on marriage and love with two tables from his one-hundred-year survey of marriages. Among all of the village *hamulas*, the percentage of men marrying outside the *hamula* averaged 32.3 percent, ranging between 22.5 percent and 39.2 percent (the outlier was 15 percent).[66] This marriage of relatives occurred in 144 of 445 marriages. However, the vast majority of these marriages, 133, were to other *hamulas* in Qalunya. The author enriches the readers' understanding of the village marriage patterns in these statistics by also listing each woman and including specific personal familial information (the women's names and family and village origins) that is often maintained for only a few generations within the family and which is rarely, if ever, included in larger, collective Palestinian written and oral genealogical histories. In this village book, specialized family knowledge known only to a small group of people is recorded in a larger collective history of the village. Thus village books, while often conforming to social norms and textual traditions, also reveal that there is neither one set of information that can be told, nor is there one way of telling it.

Another memorial book, for the village of Kafr Bir'am, includes women in its reckoning of family history. One family attributes its origin and family name, al-Susaan, to "our first ancestor, Susaan [*ummuhum al-ula Susaan*]." Another family (with five lineages) includes women in their genealogy, this time within the actual tree. No other information about this family is listed in the text, which is the Yusuf lineage of the Zaknun branch of the Daoud al-Risha family. Why this particular family includes all of the women is not clear to me. It could be that the information was taken from either family records (such as a Bible) or church records, both of which would have recorded all births. Alternatively, this information may have been recounted by a person, man or woman, who had taken an interest in family history and remembered (or recorded) such things.[67]

This concern with male lineages propels some village book authors to conflate their family origin and lineage (residing in male offspring and ancestors) with who can carry on the village history and stories. Thus, for some authors the loss of the village is recorded and remembered only in male frames of reference. This male-centered language persists despite the fact that Palestinian women, as Julie Peteet and Rhoda Kanaaneh argue, are envisioned as the carriers of Palestinian culture and expected to raise Palestinian children.[68] "It is striking how this focus on patriarchal continuity is deeply dependent on *female* reproductivity," writes Kanaaneh in her study of reproduction among Palestinians living inside Israel. It is a subject that "is not mentioned but simply assumed."[69] The language used in some of the village books reflects the notion that knowledge of village history, land, and origin rests in the male domain because it is the male's role to pass it on, whereas women are seen as passing on customs and traditions, such as songs, handicrafts, and knowledge of clothing and food. The footnotes in most of the village books (there are a number of exceptions, particularly among the CRDPS books) evince this bifurcated conception of knowledge about the village; women's names (one or two) appear as sources for information about songs and cultural information, but women are almost never cited in the other sections. Women's knowledge is thus categorized as relevant only to certain subjects and is not included as part of their overall experience of being members of village society.

This conception that men are the source of knowledge for the village slips, in a few cases, into the village book by addressing only the male reader in the introduction. The author of the book on Bayt Mahsir writes that it is the right of the generation that was born outside the village "to ask those who lived there and know its features, its ways of life, to put the truth between their hands." In addressing this new generation, he uses the masculine singular *akhi wa-ibn qaryati al-shabb* (my brother and young son of my village) throughout his introduction, finally declaring that "it is for you, my brother, that I write this humble research attempt [. . .] to introduce you to the village that you never saw. . . ."[70] One could argue, of course, that this specification of gender is due to the Arabic language. However, in their introductions most authors use the plural (which can be gender inclusive) to address readers. A number of authors do what Jimzu village book author 'Atiya al-Najjar did, which is to address both male and female villagers and readers:

> Jimzawi man and woman [*ayuha al-jimzawi wa ayatuha al-jimzawiyya*], to you my words are addressed. I speak about my village and yours, my homeland and yours, the land of all of our ancestors . . . with the scratch of a pen they erased the name of the village and with a bunch of explosives they blew it up, leveling its houses, erasing its landmarks, and with bulldozers they wiped out what remained so that it seemed to be completely destroyed. Despite all that happened to our beloved village, it remains alive in each of our hearts.[71]

During an interview I conducted in Jordan with the author of this book, he described to me his life's work as a teacher of Arabic and Islam in girls' schools operated by the United Nations Relief and Works Administration. Clearly he believed not only in the importance of teaching girls school subjects, but also in educating them about their village. Unlike the author of the book on Bayt Mahsir, al-Najjar explicitly addressed both genders, thus emphasizing that both should know the village's past and make it part of their heritage.

In contrast, the author's dedication to the 'Ayn Karim village book considers only male descendants and ancestors in his desire to hand on information about the village:

> To my son, who did not know that he has a homeland except through the memories of his father and grandfather, and from what he hears and reads, and from what he feels and his pain. I say to you, my son, you have a homeland, one that is dear and beautiful. [. . .]
>
> Your homeland, my son, is the truest essence, the most beautiful dream. It is the land that God blessed and made for the struggle (*jihad*) from the past until the day of judgment. . . . This "'Ayn Karim" is the birthplace of your father, your grandfather, and all of the ancestors before you. To it we shall return, and your children, and your children's children, and the children of all of your descendants, God willing.[72]

Later, in the introduction, the author talks about the butcher (who used to give him bones for his cat) and how the butcher's sons became the author's son's maternal uncles (*akhwal*) because the author married the butcher's daughter. So in fact the son's mother and her family are also from 'Ayn Karim. But neither the author's wife nor her parents nor his own grandmother—the maternal line of his son's lineage as well as his own—is part of this dedication that projects onto the male lineage exclusively the role of maintaining the stories of the homeland.[73]

Although public and accepted genealogical representations of family have historically precluded the inclusion of women as recordable members of a lineage, not all local and personal conceptions of family and village history subscribe to this vision. But perhaps because of the destruction of the villages and the threat to personal Palestinian identity in the contemporary political environment, this social norm is undergoing a transformation of sorts. Authors of village books are both reflecting past traditions of representation as well as creating new ways to include women's lives and experiences in the written record of pre-1948 Palestine, and recognizing them as contributors to and carriers of familial, village-based, and national identifications and sentiments.

. . .

Every Palestinian knows what village or city they are from via their family stories. The family knowledge that most people acquire is from their parents, aunts, uncles, and grandparents. This knowledge is passed down as stories about individuals' experiences in the village, the family's exodus in 1948, their genealogy, and stories of important, humorous, heroic, or otherwise significant events in the village. The village books, as this chapter explores, are positioned by their authors as collective repositories of village knowledge that build on and draw from both family stories and well-known published historical texts on Palestine. Citing al-Dabbagh's (and others') work provides authors with the opportunity to connect their work to the dominant texts and the most esteemed historians of modern Palestinian history, thereby gaining a measure of respect, and highlighting their own erudition by doing so. The village books also communicate, in both the collective narratives of the village and the stories of individuals, the value of what it means to be a villager, a Palestinian, and an Arab. In these assertions about village families and village values, people express their strong attachments to the village and to representing the past in ways that unify people.

What readers can take from these books is the collective ethos of what it meant to be a villager before 1948 and what it means to be a Palestinian and an Arab. This ethos valued living a life characterized by acts of generosity, shared concerns, and shared welfare. Although the idealization of village life in the village books obscures some of the conflict, it also actualizes the village values in seeking to focus on the greater concern of village unity. The focus on recording family names shows both the commonly used way of representing family— through the male lineage—as well as other ways that authors devise to represent genealogical information. These new ways reflect the desire to preserve all of the village knowledge in the face of the destruction of historic Palestine in general and of the village specifically. One element of this documentary impulse is the inclusion of women and their origins and backgrounds in these books.

Unlike the political metanarratives of Palestinian history, the village books focus on the details of village life, and thus open themselves up to disagreements over representation and unfair partisanship if they leave out or emphasize certain information. What these accusations and struggles reveal, among other things, is the importance of the past to people. If people did not care about the past or did not read the books or the Web sites, there would be no debate. The lively and contentious discussions that have resulted from the publication of the village books and the online debates are a clear indicator of how important this history is to people today.

4 WRITING A HISTORY, DEFINING A PAST

Amman, Jordan: 2004

In response to my question about what stirred him to write the book on his village of 'Innaba, 'Abdallah al-Sufi noted that he was inspired by an earlier book on the village that he considered ill-informed and harmful, because it was written by researchers not from the village.[1] One story in the earlier book propelled al-Sufi to write. In that story, the mayor was riding his donkey, hit his head on a tree branch, and was knocked unconscious. The story was told because the donkey, rather amazingly, brought the mayor back to the village coffee shop, unconscious and still on the donkey's back. Al-Sufi admonished, "History must have useful information, not information that is distasteful. Informative information with a point. What kind of information is this [in the story about the mayor and the donkey]? A ridiculous story (*maskhara*). Nothing, nothing else."[2]

Al-Sufi, a former librarian, maintained that his book was not a response but rather a correction (*tas-hih*). He added that writing history is not just re-cording information but also evaluating it:

> Some historians do not choose the material they include. Instead they write down everything, including the kitchen sink (*kull ma habba wa dab*). Yes, I meet with someone and get information from him. But shouldn't I choose the appropriate information to use? I want to write history. I am writing for others, not for me. So that others who have forgotten can benefit from the information. It is not to make fun of so and so or so and so. We need something people can benefit from, not silly stories and insults.

Thus, in his view, history should have a purpose, a goal. When I asked him what he thought "history" is, he said, "Everything that happened—that is history—*and* what people need for the future. The writer or collector should make sure that the history they are telling has a positive influence or reveals something negative to be avoided in the future." His view of history contrasts with that of professional historians who write about change over time, perhaps with an eye on the present and future but without explicit reference to it.

Al-Sufi said he sees a more active role for history among his readership, the young people not born in the village: "What good does it do for the new generation to know this meaningless information? [. . .] But informative information stays in your brain. When it has real meaning, it stays with you." I asked him what he meant by "real" [*haqiqiyya*], because events such as the donkey story are real in that they happened. "Yes," he said, "it did happen but it doesn't need to be made into a historical event [*la yu'arrakh*]. If something like that is written down, then it is just folly on the part of the person who tells it or writes it." Al-Sufi believes that historians should task themselves with choosing which events to relate and what they mean. As author of the 'Innaba village book, al-Sufi presents a clear vision of the history he wants to tell. His ideas about what constitutes history—information that is beneficial and honorable, and that does not show others in a bad light—are connected to the goals that the authors of the village books desire them to play in contemporary Palestinian life; they want them to serve as sources of knowledge and inspiration about origins, identity, and sentiment. Although silly or pointless stories, such as the one about the mayor and the donkey, do exist, al-Sufi believes that such material should not be part of written history or the values that one passes down formally to others; that is, not everything is history.

Then how do village book authors make choices about what information to put in their books? As documentary projects that aim to inform people about the village and record the past, the writing of the village books also shapes, in part, which subjects constitute history. The books' authors may believe that they are simply documenting knowledge about and sentiment for the village by focusing on certain topics and considering certain sources (and likely omitting others). The village books as a whole, and their authors individually, delineate what is to be known about the village, the framework within which that knowledge is to be written, and who or what can be the source of that knowledge. In fact, the authors take part in the process of composing a certain type of history focused on a particular village within a larger historical narrative about Palestine and Palestinians. Elizabeth Tonkin maintains that because humans are both individuals and members of communities, "individuals may therefore be supported or threatened by public representations of pastness that seem either to guarantee their identity or to deny its significance."[3] The interactions between the author of a book and the subject matter, between cultural values and dominant stories, between political goals and national causes, and between self and collective culture are all part of the representations of the past that create the narratives of village life.

This chapter examines how the choices that authors make in terms of selecting subjects to emphasize and others to ignore, as well as in choosing sources for information, affect the content and composition of history in the village books. In some cases, such choices reflect existing social and gender relationships in the village, patriarchal social structures, and economic class divisions. In other cases, authors choose ways to portray material that reflect the social and religious norms at the time of their writing. Still others openly write the books from the perspectives that they believe best document their history. Ultimately, however, they are defining a history of the village, in dialogue both with other authors and with their readers, one that is affirmed and contested as the books are published, read, revised, and countered. Moreover, this chapter explores how village book authors engage with the complex and complicated issues surrounding the representation of women, men, gender relations, religion, and land records, and the images of village life that result from their choices. For Palestinians, history in these village books is about Palestinians asserting what they want to tell others about themselves, which is subject to, among other things, strong internal forces within Palestinian society that dominate their memories as well as their ways of remembering and reckoning the past.[4]

WRITING VILLAGE HISTORY

The village books are written as local history, drawing on the methods used in historical research, oral history, cultural anthropology, and autobiographical writing. However, these books do not fit into the divisions of amateur history versus expert history that scholars have used to distinguish works of historical writing.[5] Because of the varying methods used to craft the texts, as well as their variations in narrative style, the village books are better seen as part of the written Arabic tradition of local histories. Also, the authors of the village books assume a variety of pro forma styles that suggest authoritative forms of history, which I explore here.

The village book authors use autobiographical, oral historical, and primary and secondary research methods to find the content for and construct their texts. All of the 112 village books in my collection include some sort of attribution to the sources used—either direct quotes from individuals, footnotes, or a bibliography of works cited or consulted. But the styles in which the books are written vary. Some authors rely on their own experiences and memories whereas other authors act as oral historians and quote individuals in colloquial Arabic. Other authors seek knowledge in historical sources such as Ottoman and British archives or secondary books on Palestinian history. Each of these styles of writing provides different perspectives on what history is, how information is collected and crafted, what can be used as sources for history, and how these sources can be read and understood.

Authors who were adults at the time of their exile in 1948 tend to rely on themselves and their knowledge of the village as the main source for their writing. The village book about Ishwa' by Deeb Ahmad Kan'aan, who was born in 1927, contains no footnotes or attributions of any sort other than a short list of references in the back that also mentions "individual testimonies of the people of the village" but without listing any names. When I interviewed Kan'aan, he relayed that he too remembered the village and its people, but he also consulted other elders like himself to make sure that what he was presenting was correct.[6] Similarly, Ribhi Mustafa 'Alayan, who published his book on Yalu in 1988, wrote, "I lived a good portion of my life in the village and know a great deal about it through my observations and personal experiences." He notes that he also conducted interviews with older people from the village.[7] These two men represent those who turn to their own experiences and knowledge to craft and inform their presentation of village history. They also talked to others and read certain books to remind them of events, to gather specifics or the names of people involved, and to prepare genealogies, but ultimately they saw themselves as the source, and their experience as providing them with their knowledge of the village's history. All of the village books rely on the authority of older men and women as those who knew the village and are able to recall and remember it today with the purpose of recording a history.

The vast majority of the authors, however, do not remember the village, or they were young children in 1948; they therefore turn to older individuals and written texts as sources. More than half of the village books have lists of the people the author or authors interviewed for their research (although authors who did not include a list of interviewees also told me they talked to elders). Writing about Kuwaykat village, al-Hajj 'Abd al-Majid al-'Ali recalled his experience in 1948 and how he managed to collect information about the village for writing the book: "We were forced to leave Palestine when I was 12 years old, so I remember my village, our village's land. But I also gathered information from the elders of the village and collected the information they told me."[8] Fadi Sulayma was twenty-six when his first book on his family's village of al-Shajara was published in 2003. In this book he creates an image of the village he never knew on the basis of his research with published accounts as well as from the stories he collected from older villagers. He retells stories of times long past, some of which he qualifies with "this rests on the conscience of the tellers; God is most knowledgeable" (*wa dhalak 'ala dhimat al-rawah wa allahu 'alam*),[9] thus placing the responsibility for the accuracy of the information on the teller. As a researcher and author, Sulayma was somewhat at the mercy of those who told him stories. As a young man trying to adhere to societal norms, he most likely felt he had to be respectful and trust his elders, but also wanted to include this qualifier with the stories. Book authors who never lived in the village they are writing about must constantly deliberate over what is told to them and who is telling it—over what and whom to believe and include—especially because they cannot turn to their own experience in the village.

Many village book authors engage in debates—both in the text of their books and in the process of collecting the information for writing them—about what constitutes village history. The village book authors respond to communal pressures about what should be presented in (or eliminated from) the books, and about what people believe to be correct information. It is on one level a debate about methodology. For some authors, the ability to write a village history requires access to the right information. For example, 'Atiya al-Najjar, from Jimzu village, writes in his village book about correcting information about the village:

> Others not from Jimzu have written about the village and, without intending to, they wrote wrong and distorted information. Thus many people from the village did not know the truth about the village sites and borders, the school, the classes, the number of teachers, the social behavior, and other things. This was upsetting and caused some villagers a great deal of pain and distress[....]
> I have done part of my duty by transferring, recording, and perhaps correcting

this situation [fixing an incorrect publication that upset people] as well as I was able, just as we lived it, and knew it. As the saying goes, the people of Mecca know its residents [*ahl Makka adra bi-sh'aabiha*].[10]

Al-Najjar justifies his own qualifications to write by showing he is from the village and therefore knows it:

I lived in the village and was aware of what was going on in the beginning of the 1940s. I knew its neighborhoods, streets, and alleyways, and I still remember the distinctive public spaces. I am unable to forget the threshing floor, the village association, the mosque, the *madafa* [guesthouse], the *zawiya* [clan meeting place or Sufi religious lodge], the cemetery, and the olive press; it is as if I can see them before my eyes. I still remember many of the traditions and customs of weddings and funerals, food and drink, festivities and celebrations. These events are indelibly engraved in my mind for the rest of my life. They say that the young are aware and remember all that happens around them. So I am passing along and recording these events that I witnessed with my own eyes and without exaggeration.[11]

Al-Najjar does not condemn those who wrote mistaken information about the village (he says they did it unintentionally), but his underlying message is that because of his knowledge and efforts he is writing the correct history. Whether his discussion of the village is correct or not is not my point (nor the subject of my work). His 450-page volume offers an extensive and fair treatment of the subject (and here I acknowledge my own limitations to judge the accuracy of his portrayal of the details of village life). My point is that his concern about history is both about making sure the information is correct and engaging the other members of his community who "know" the village. The writing of village histories is not an egalitarian venture in which everyone can add their voice. Such writing is tense with internal discussions about the veracity of the narrative and the representation of the village, and about who can speak and write about it. The community's responses to the books encompass evaluations of and declamations against those whom readers think have presented incorrect information or stories not worthy of being reprinted as village history.

WOMEN AS SOURCES OF HISTORY

As authors construct village histories in textual form, they document their sources in different ways. The use of women as a source of information for the writing of the village books depends on two issues: one, the subjects addressed, and two, the authors' individual perspectives on what constitutes history. Certain subjects, such as folklore, songs, and clothing, are seen as in women's purview and thus authors turn to women for information on these subjects, whether they cite them in their source list or not. The particular kinds of history that are emphasized in the village books means that women are largely absent as sources for the majority of the content. The authors I interviewed drew instead on the role of men, both as the public face of the village and as more knowledgeable about subjects of interest to the cause of "history." These ideas about knowledge and public roles are embedded within the patriarchal social system that gives prominence to elder male knowledge. In addition, drawing on cultural conservatisms about avoiding the appearance of women's names in public forums, the authors also mentioned to me that some women did not want their names mentioned.[12]

Women appear as oral sources in less than half of the village books.[13] Approximately forty of the eighty village books that included lists of people interviewed listed women as a source. I remarked to Kuwaykat village book author al-'Ali that he, unlike some of the other authors, interviewed and listed as sources both men and women. He responded, "I asked the women to tell me how they left Palestine. But I didn't take information from women about the village, because the men know more." I asked him to explain why and he said the men "were the ones who planted, cultivated, and harvested the land; they know their land and how it was divided." He clearly prioritized their experience as something to draw on. He cited a phrase from the Qur'an about why men are more reliable as sources: "Women," he said, "have to remind each other."[14] Yet for him, women's lack of experience did not hinder their lack of knowledge. His explanation would strike anyone, perhaps even himself, as contradictory, because he could rely on women to narrate about the events surrounding the exodus from the village in 1948, but not about the village lands. His comments indicate a general unease with using women as authoritative sources on subjects that men are supposed to be the most knowledgeable about in relation to the village.

When I asked authors about women serving as sources for writing their village histories, many said that they had talked to women but did not think to include them in their citation lists or chose to respect the fact that women did not want their names included. One author responded with retrospection when asked why he had not included his wife's mother or his own mother, both of whom were from the village, among those had passed on village knowledge and sentiment. He said that mine was a good observation and quite accurate, and that he should have considered it at the time of writing. He noted that he had not meant to imply that the young folks did not benefit from the stories of mothers and grandmothers, but that the father is always the *sayyid*, the master, in all realms, including the transmission of knowledge. Women would tell bedtime stories and riddles and sing songs, he said, but this is very different from the stories of what happened to the villagers, of how they were driven out of the village and forced into exile. Women provided him with songs and perceived trivial and folkloric information for writing his book.[15]

Certain subjects and sources of information cause considerable tension in how authors define and construct what constitutes history for them. As we have seen, many authors handle the gendered conception of knowledge by turning to men for information about land, space, genealogies, and agriculture, and to women for information about cultural customs, traditions, songs, and clothing. The one subject on which authors consulted both men and women seems to be the accounts of fleeing the village in 1948. This gendered division of sources of information results in specific ways of portraying history. Particularly evident is the authors' reliance on men for the majority of what they write about the village, which results in stories and portrayals of the village that are inflected by male perspectives and the socially dominant expectations of men. Thus the portrayal of certain subjects in these local histories often reflects the idealized image of the village that privileges men's roles. A collective reading of the books provides an understanding of the gendered tropes that the books follow, as well as the many instances in which authors provide other perspectives. In the rest of this chapter I explore how authors limit themselves to certain idealized notions of village life in some cases, while in others they provide broader, more reflective, and therefore richer perspectives on the local history of the village.

RELIGION AND GENDER IN THE VILLAGE: THE PRESENT IN THE PAST

Close examination of the treatment of religion and women in the village books provides an interesting contrast to the authors' portrayals of village values. Village book authors often idealize village values as tied to a time when social and family relations defined people's lives in small communities. Thus the village values are presented in the book as what was meaningful to the villagers at a particular point in history, even if the stories are about people who transgressed those values. Authors tend, however, to deal with religion and women in the exact opposite way; rather than idealize how they were in the past, they address both religion and women through the lens of modern sensibilities and impose on history today's modern conventions about religious expression, acceptable ways of worship, and contemporary ideals of men's and women's roles in society. The books thus not only evidence the pressures of maintaining particular images of the village, but also in some cases reflect the modern understandings of social and religious values that are imposed on the historic village. Exploring what subjects are left out and why gives us insight into the issues that were hidden from public discussions in the past (such as overlooking a particular family's poverty), but also reveals the modern sensibilities that push people to rethink how they lived in the past. Although many Palestinian villages consisted of both Muslims and Christians, few of the books go into the details of Christian religious practices, and thus my focus is on Islam.[16]

Religious practice among Muslims has changed dramatically over the last one hundred years. Both the scholarly work on pre-1948 life as well as Palestinian villagers who remember life in the 1940s give evidence of the types of religious worship and beliefs that were practiced in the first part of the twentieth century.[17] To be certain, the village *shaykh* encouraged the Muslim villagers to worship at the mosque, taught the children to recite the Qur'an, and led the ceremonies at religious celebrations. But village religious practices also encompassed a wide range of folk practices. Taufik Canaan, a Palestinian physician and ethnographer during the Mandate, described such subjects as Muslim saints and shrines, and "cups of fear," among many others in his thirty-five articles on Palestinian folklore.[18] Very little of this type of religious practice is mentioned in the village books, and if it *is* mentioned, it is denigrated as superstition. These practices were well-documented, however, by both Palestinians and foreigners in the early twentieth century.[19]

The 1970s witnessed another push in the preservation of this cultural heritage as important to identity in the changing global economic and agricultural system, and folklorists such as 'Abd al-'Aziz Abu Hadba at In'ash al-Usra Society in al-Bira, 'Abd al-Latif al-Barghuti, and Sharif Kanaana produced numerous monographs and journal articles documenting the changing customs and traditions. Many of the subjects of the articles in the *Heritage and Society* journal published by the In'ash al-Usra Society in the late 1970s mirror the subjects and organization of material that later appeared in the village books—for example, songs to send off and receive the Hajj (pilgrimage to Mecca) caravan, children's games and social change in the Palestinian village, the "evil eye" in Palestinian society, and the dower and wedding costs in peasant society.

Concurrent with this interest in preserving folklife and folklore in the 1970s, the practice of Islam among Muslims in the Arab world has increasingly been pushed toward orthodox beliefs proffered by movements both within established Muslim teachings and outside of them.[20] Even in 1927, Canaan noted that "the primitive features of Palestine are disappearing so quickly that before long most of them will be forgotten."[21] These new ways of defining Muslim belief and worship have normalized the power of a central religious authority to determine how to be Muslim. In effect, they have critiqued folk religion and previous practices as unorthodox and therefore unacceptable: activities such as sacrificing animals and bringing offerings to the shrines of holy men and women (*walis*), the very existence of the shrines and the holy men and women themselves, celebrations of special days for prophets,[22] and rituals around certain supernatural beliefs (*nidhr*, vows or prayers for divine intervention, for example).

Village book authors who are educated in government schools and in countries that regulate religion and who embrace this contemporary way of understanding Muslim practice find it difficult to condone or even chronicle the practices of Muslim villagers pre-1948. For example, Fadi Sulayma wrote that the villagers of al-Shajara were accused of being *Wahhabis*[23] because "they did not believe in the *mazarat* [shrines of the holy men and women] even though they were in the village, and they did not celebrate *mawlid al-nabi* [the birth of the Prophet Muhammad] or the *khitma fil-maatim* because they thought it all to be *bida'* [innovation] and without any basis in religion."[24] However, none of the other material on al-Shajara by older authors such as Mahmoud 'Issa or Mustafa Murad al-Dabbagh or at PalestineRemembered.com mentions this subject.[25] Furthermore, other Palestinian villages had local shrines that were frequented by villagers, and people made pilgrimages to the shrines of the various prophets in Palestine. What is perhaps the case instead is that the villagers from al-Shajara who Sulayma interviewed were uneasy with their memories of these rituals and beliefs that are not acceptable today, preferring instead to adhere to the modern and normative orthodox interpretation of Islam, which casts these folk beliefs as heteropraxy or errant Islamic practice.[26] Such a reinterpretation of the past is not an idealization based on nostalgia but rather an imposition of a modern understanding of proper behavior and belief onto people's practices in an earlier period.

More true to the documentary mission of the village book, the author of the book on Jimzu village deals with these Muslim folk religious practices in a different way. In describing the villagers' visits to the shrine of Shaykh 'Abd al-Qadir Ahmad al-Haj, a local Sufi from the village, al-Najjar explains that the shrine was a place for the making and fulfilling of vows or for prayers for divine intervention (*nidhr*) that necessitated the slaughter of an animal near the shrine and the undertaking of other rituals by the vow taker, or by the child upon whom the vow was made, which included stepping over the animal a number of times.[27] He comments, "it goes without saying that such practices are complete ignorance, and a crude violation of the conventions of Islamic law."[28] He similarly comments on the unorthodox burial of the *shaykh* in the mosque.[29] In these cases, al-Najjar evaluates (and critiques) the villagers' behaviors (in which he undoubtedly participated as a child), but as a documenter and chronicler of life in his village he chooses to include them in his description of the villagers' beliefs and practiced rituals. As a former teacher of religion in a girls' school, he knows the orthodox and proper forms of Muslim belief and practice, but as a documenter of village life, he does not eliminate from the historical record what he believes to be wrong behaviors or even things that might make the villagers look ignorant. His solution instead is to describe these beliefs and practices and then contextualize them from his present position. Al-Najjar's use of the past to record history and his use of the present to evaluate that history illustrates the value of memory as a source. We know of these practices at the shrines of holy men and women from accounts of village life written in the 1920s and 1930s,[30] and we know that they are condemned by today's religious *shaykhs* and by orthopraxy. But al-Najjar's account of people having once practiced these rituals that he now condemns shows the reader how transformations of practice and belief occur, the time frames in which such changes can take place, and the process by which authority can arise such that in one person's lifetime a ritual can go from being an accepted practice to being something that must be disavowed.

Similar to the role of contemporary religious belief, present norms about female behavior, male roles, and social conservatism also influence some people's recollections or the vision of certain authors as they construct the narratives of their village. Earlier in the chapter I discussed the concerns that some male authors had about using women as *sources* of history. Some authors also had difficulty including women's lives as *subjects* of history. The response of women readers to the books provided a few indications as to their reactions to these portrayals. One village book author, Ghalib Sumrayn, told me that he had gone on a picnic with about 150 members of his extended family. "A relative of mine said to me that a woman called Fatima Hamdan is upset with you about the book you published ten years ago, in 1993. After her husband's death she raised her children on her own and refused to remarry. And yet you didn't write her name in the book. So I said to him to salute her hard work and efforts and hopefully in the next edition I'll mention her name." This situation illustrates women pushing back against the patriarchal norms that restrict their presence as subjects in the village books.

In some of the books, women are even removed from the activities in which we know they participated. In the book on al-Shajara, Fadi Sulayma mentions that the village women did not take their goods, such as eggs and milk, to the cities to sell as did women from all of the other villages.[31] Sulyama's comment makes up the last part of a section on trade in the village where he describes the small shops in the village and says that prior to the 1936 Palestinian revolt the Jews in the nearby settlement of Sejara would buy from the al-Shajara villagers, most of whom saved their excess production for guests and the poor.[32] We know from many accounts, both oral and written, that village women regularly went to the cities to sell their agricultural and animal products (as they still did in the West Bank and Gaza until the most recent closures). Sulayma maintains that al-Shajara women did not sell their products outside the village (but he does not say why) and he acknowledges that this was different than in the other villages. Sulayma himself was not yet born at that time, so he relies on the memories of others. Given that individuals from every village marketed their products (whether grain, fruits and vegetables, or dairy products) in the surrounding towns and cities,[33] the removal of women from stories about marketing the products of labor seems to go against the custom of the time and suggests a more conservative revision of the role of women in village life. In contrast, for example, Sahira Dirbas mentions that

> [the villagers of al-Birwa] used to sell most of their products in the market in the city of Acre ('Akka). The women of al-Birwa (al-Birwaniyat) were accustomed to leaving early, walking and carrying on their head their cheeses and milk. They went along the plain, then took the Mujawaba path to al-Suwana and to Tel al-'Ayadya, and from there on the path parallel to the empty land next to the orchard of Na'im al-Salim on the edge of Acre and then down to the market.[34]

Women in villages all over Palestine made these treks to nearby cities and larger towns on market days or on specific occasions to sell what they had harvested or made, yet there is a contemporary reluctance, either by the women themselves or by men, to tell these stories. When I asked one of the authors of the village book on al-Walaja, Mahmoud Sulayman, about this issue he said,

> Unfortunately in our village and in nearby villages the man stayed at home more than the woman at that time. Let me give you an example. My mother, may God have mercy on her soul, in the morning before dawn would take the basket of agricultural products to Jerusalem to sell, then she would come home, do the laundry and cook, go to the fields and work harvesting, then go home, make bread, cook again, clean, get water from the stream, and sew and embroider clothes. . . . But I'm not going to publish this information: that the woman would carry all of this on her head and wake up at 3 A.M. to get to the market. . . . The smart reader understands between the lines that she was working hard. When we wrote in the book that "her hand combines with the man's hand"—what does this mean? She was the one who was working.[35]

Sulayman's comments illustrate the gendered role of male authors composing history and their concern for social norms. Given that the vast majority of village book authors and their sources are men, the stories of women that appear in the books reflect more the ways that men think gender roles should be portrayed rather than actual experiences. Although these authors see women as fundamentally part of the village, they clearly define a space for women that adheres to their contemporary ideas of female and male respectability and male responsibility.

Mahmoud Sulayman admitted that women did a huge amount of the work in the village and for the family, but he also suggested that featuring that information prominently in the book makes the men look bad. Instead, he and the other authors of the al-Walaja village book wrote that women were the equals of men:

> If historians praised women for some position or event that happened, their role was a natural one. The women of al-Walaja enjoyed quality [of life] that exceeded the description of the historians. We feel that we must put between the readers' hands, both men and women, what we have heard from the women of the village and some of the roles that women took on in al-Walaja and practiced over the generations in building the houses, raising children, and making ends meet [*kasb al-'aysh*].[36]

The authors of the book on Walaja then listed the different fields in which women played an important role: being lady of the house (*sayyida fi baytiha*), helping her husband in the fields and orchards, helping him sell the agricultural products, making household goods through knitting and embroidery, encouraging boys to go to school, teaching girls household skills, and helping her husband defend the land.[37] Another author described that in the village of Suba "we find that the women worked with and shared with the men in their happy times, sad times, and daily work."[38] In these visions of the past, the women *helped* the men with economic and political and nationalist issues while they took care of the household and the children.

The village history that is written in the books makes clear the gendered dimensions of family responsibilities (women take care of home and children while men are in charge of economics and politics) that reflect contemporary, urban ideals and lifestyles. One woman from a village in the Galilee who was married to a much older wealthy village landowner told me that she had been spoiled by her husband and knew nothing of working in the fields. As these examples illustrate, the idea of men providing for women so that they do not have to work is connected both to upwardly mobile class norms that were more urban[39] and to increased wealth that provided for the absence of women's labor. Both of these influences were likely ideals that few other than the elite in the village could even imagine. Today, however, among Palestinian villagers living in camps and lower-class neighborhoods in Jordan, the West Bank, and Lebanon, few women work outside the home due to issues around child care, education levels, and male control, and for other reasons.[40] Thus the retrospective refashioning of women's roles in the village reflects the changing gender divisions of responsibility and labor of the later part of the twentieth century (and now early twenty-first century). The elision of so much of pre-1948 women's work and responsibility suggests that the village book authors are interpreting the role of women in the village through their contemporary values that take pride in men's ability to take care of women and make life easy for them, and in women's total devotion to family and home.

The elimination of stories about the hard work that women undertook reflects on men's perception of themselves as providers for the family and on their unease with exposing how hard women in the village labored to take care of their families. Of course not all of the village authors write in this way. Mahmoud Sa'id's forty-page book on Tirat Haifa mentions "the fundamental role women had in agricultural work. The Tirawiya woman was used to going with her husband to the fields; in fact, during the olive-harvesting season, the whole family would go."[41] Likewise, in his book on Qalunya village, author

Ghalib Sumrayn included many descriptions of the work his mother did as a village healer, and of women's work in the fields and around the house.

Another notable exception is the book on the village of Mallaha by Yusif 'Ali 'Abd al-'Aal. Women appear in this book with regularity. 'Abd al-'Aal mentions the midwife in the village, Fatima al-Shamrukh, as well as a seamstress, Nazira, the wife of Rashid al-Imam. In all of the post-1970s photographs, including the professionally produced mosaic photos of various individuals around the family tree or a map of Palestine, women are pictured. The photos in other books show women from a distance or doing or wearing "folklore," but in this book they are pictured just as the men are. The author also includes a thirty-page section in which he writes about the various generations in the village from 1859 to the present, with paragraphs about notable ancestors. One of them, whose picture is also included, is Fatima Musa 'Abd al-'Aal, born in 1937. After describing her life, marriage, children, and difficulties, the author writes, "She was and will remain an exemplar of generosity and morals."[42] Why does the author of this village book include women in the narrative in ways that almost no other authors do? My conjecture on an answer involves a little-researched subject in modern Palestinian history and society: the Ghawarneh. This "group" of Palestinians is made up of "peasants originally 'imported' from the southern frontiers of the Ottoman empire, who consequently had weak clan structures and were subject to semi-feudal conditions in the *jiftliks* (government lands) of the Hula Valley of northern Palestine and of the Jordan Valley to the south. . . ."[43] This particular group has largely been forgotten, historically, and in modern times its members still receive some of the discrimination that accompanies their less-than-noble origins. They tend to be in the poorer, less well-developed camps in Syria and Lebanon. One researcher in Lebanon described to me how they are seen to "not be afraid for the honor of their women" and thus women take more prominent roles in society, including working and being pictured in books.[44]

Most of these books, however, portray women's participation in village life within a male-centric reality in that men provide the facts and interpretation of village life and are in charge of the things they consider important.[45] Men, as the primary tellers of history, are tapped to represent and tell women's experiences of village life. And when men tell these stories about women, as illustrated in some of the cases presented here, what occurs is a re-centering of authority onto men. Even the women authors, although they interview many more women than the men authors, echo the same authority structures in their books.

WRITING ABOUT POVERTY, DISEASE, AND SOCIOECONOMIC CLASS

In a manner similar to how women and Muslim religious practice in the village are treated in the village books, some potentially embarrassing or negative subjects related to village life are sometimes glossed over, left out altogether, or reevaluated through modern lenses. Poverty, disease, and economic and social class divisions tend to be totally ignored, both out of the collective desire to hold up the village as an ideal place and out of the descendants' desire to see it as such. In part the desire to present this vision of the village ties into the nostalgic view that many people have when they look back on the past in general.[46] But this elision by Palestinian authors also ties to their concern with portraying themselves as anything but hearty, hale, and supportive of one another. Palestinians have been keenly aware to deny British and Zionist discourses of governance and statehood that have tied modernity and development to *deserving* to live on the land. Such arguments have presented the case that Arabs and Palestinians do not deserve to be considered as having rights to the land because they were seen as impoverished, sickly, and unproductive.[47]

Historians and others with background knowledge about village life in the 1930s and 1940s and who read the village books might be surprised by the general absence of any discussion relating to taxation, poverty, and disease (in both people and animals). Contemporaneous reports published by the British Mandate (such as four commissions appointed between 1929 and 1930 to report on the conditions in the Arab rural economy) as well as contemporary scholarship present an image of impoverished Palestinian rural residents.[48] The discourse on these issues was one of outsiders looking in, but it was also perpetuated by Palestinian nationalists as points of needed action and the Mandate authority's negligence. One contemporary scholar writes,

> The mass of the Arab population were *fellahin*, peasant cultivators of the soil. They constituted a depressed class. Their lot was harsh. Their poverty and chronic indebtedness were legendary. Small, usually fragmented, landholdings; insecurity of tenure; poor soil, especially in the hill country where most of them lived; insufficient water; and lack of both education and capital, so necessary if they were to improve their farming methods, largely explain their poverty. The exactions of landlords and tax collectors, together with droughts and poor harvests, further reduced their capacity to significantly improve their position.[49]

In contrast, the village books describe traditional and changing farming techniques, noncapitalist market ventures, barter, and subsistence agriculture.

They portray how people lived their lives rather than judge the conditions under which they lived. In addition, in spite of their crushing poverty, Palestinians continued to thrive and more than doubled their population from 562,002 in the first British census in 1922 to an estimated 1,237,334 in 1946.[50] However, this trope of poverty and despair continues to be used by outsiders to describe Palestinian village life under the Mandate. This is not to say that Palestinian peasants were not poor, but to portray them only as such is to portray them as devoid of any agency, and even of any activity or emotion. I would argue that we need to read these sources together—village books, Mandate sources, nationalist tropes, and academic scholarship—in order to obtain a full picture of village lives in both their richness and their poverty, from the perspectives of the systems of administration and of those who negotiated living in those systems.

Interestingly, the village books contain almost no discussion of taxes or of British Mandate interventions in people's lives at the time, despite the fact that records exist for such subjects and they are therefore described in scholarly works.[51] The British Mandate shifted taxation of the rural sector from an Ottoman system of tithing to a property tax, and ultimately it seems that the tax burden on the individual decreased.[52] In the 1940s one of the tropes of British reform policy was that the crippling burden these taxes placed on the rural sector resulted in labor migration to the cities or people selling their land. Despite all of the matters that the Mandate government underfunded or ignored such as roads, water, education, labor, and agricultural development, it did spend time and resources on land taxation, health, and hygiene.[53] The village books rarely if at all address the government role in taxing villagers, vaccinating their herds, or eradicating diseases such as malaria.

A number of village books do, however, provide evidence of the government's role in these efforts by reproducing the taxation and vaccination documents given to them as part of the government's regulation of their herds. Sections on indigenous medicinal practices address the local ways developed to deal with broken bones, snakebites, stiff bodies, and enchantments. Most of the books also talk about death, funeral practices, and cemeteries, and describe the rituals surrounding these social customs, but very few of them describe actual causes of death and illness. A few mention the larger, more cataclysmic health disasters. For example, the Jimzu village book describes earthquakes and epidemics that struck the village, including peoples' memories of the 1902 cholera epidemic that killed many in the village.[54]

Because the central focus of the books is on what was meaningful to the villagers—their land, their families, and the communal spirit of unity and helpfulness—and although cooperation among villagers is undoubtedly an accurate picture of the *values* the villagers held, the economic differences among villagers and the importance of noble family origins resulted in poverty and social stratification. Although it is not explicitly addressed in the books, villagers knew the blight of class differences, of being poor, and of being from an unknown family. They also knew the prestige of having wealth and a powerful lineage. One author I interviewed told me about his extensive research doing interviews with people who were born in the village and of working closely with people to write the family genealogies. His efforts took two years and absorbed four hundred pages. Thus it was with some bitterness that he related to me how people from the most prominent family said to him, "Who are you to be writing this book? *Your* father was only an orange seller."[55] This incident, not the only one of its kind that I heard, clearly holds leftover social and economic hierarchies from the pre-1948 village. And although the rhetoric in the village books often talks about the cooperative nature of the village and how the villagers were all willing to help one another, this incident about who and from which family among the villagers is qualified to be an author elides this collective ethos of the village and reveals the unwritten class differences that existed then and obviously still do in some form.

My concern in raising this subject is not to point out that there were different economic and social statuses in the village—Palestinians today know that. Instead, my point is that these differences are not recorded as such nor emphasized in the books. Thus, in order to perceive these differences and understand the subtexts and meanings in these texts, one has to read them with the knowledge of a villager from that particular village, and one has to have heard the stories from relatives about who was rich and who was poor. Those who are reading these texts today certainly bring this knowledge to their reading (unlike me in my situation as a reader, for example). I would suggest, however, that as time passes and as educational and economic situations change in the diaspora, coming generations will have different background knowledge and be curious about different subjects. Also, because the books do not record such class differences, they do not therefore register (and preserve) for history the unfortunate circumstances of a certain family or the tragedies of disease, accidents, and poverty. Therefore, because people's fortunes have changed since 1948 and they likely have become enmeshed in their current class issues, the texts may end up substantiating the picture the authors seek to create of a more classless, unified society. Interestingly, this history creates a picture of a middle ground; it does not elevate everyone to the elite, nor does it make them all impoverished (as Zionist and British accounts are more likely to do). Instead, it removes both the elite and the poor and lumps them together with the people who had enough to survive and thrive. The resulting written history thus does indeed reflect the values that Palestinians held about village life before 1948 (if not the hard reality), and narrows the social and economic differences that separated the villagers.

The readers of these histories, particularly the new generations who hear stories from their parents and grandparents as well, also want histories of village life that correspond to an idyllic version and not one that is replete with the simple hardships of living in a village without electricity and running water. In part that is because they want their history of their homeland not to mirror their lives in the diaspora, where many of them face daily economic struggles and have always lived with their outsider status as Palestinians. The elision of class differences, poverty, disease, and the difficulties of village life from history influences how young people understand the village. Hussein al-Lubani from Damun village commented:

> This new generation thinks that we were all kings back then. They don't know that all the people were essentially shepherds, and there weren't any bathrooms or bedrooms. But they don't want to hear this—they want me to paint an image of our poor modest village to be that of something recent and modern. They don't want to accept the fact that we were riding donkeys and walking around barefoot.[56]

It is not necessarily only the nostalgia of those who remember the past that encourages authors to write about positive values and ignore those less-than-appealing aspects of an era or society. In addition, pressures by others—by descendants, parents, neighbors, and local leaders—to tell stories that fit into the dominant stereotypes or knowledge of village life also influence authors' choices of subjects. One person whose father was from Jaffa, known for its orange groves, recounted the following story that took place in the 1970s:

> I was fourteen when my uncle, who lived in Greece, visited us. For a certain reason that I knew later, my mother, who was a non-Jaffite, was quarreling silently with my father one day. When she said something about the many

orange orchards that the family had lost in Jaffa, my uncle, who did not know how much family history my father had told my mother, intervened and said to me, "Your grandfather did not have any orchards in Jaffa; he was a merchant in the wholesale market, not the owner of an orchard." My mother lived for twenty years of her marriage recalling stories about the family's glory and its orchards in Jaffa. As for my father, he never had the courage to tell her the truth.[57]

This story illustrates that people may have wanted to adopt a certain narrative about the past—a sort of channeled and misplaced nostalgia—and in the process have formed a certain idea of that past and that place and cling tightly to it. These ways we have of complicating history, of leaving out negative stories, of claiming what we do not have, and of reformulating the ways in which we see the past are all part of how we narrate history, of the role of our memories, and of how we incorporate history into our lives.

DOCUMENTS OF HISTORY: LAND RECORDS AND WHAT THEY REVEAL

Village book authors address land ownership in the villages from the perspective of the villagers, those who farmed on, grazed their herds on, and survived off of the land. Thus the authors include in the books detailed descriptions of the land, tables of land ownership, and reproductions of land deeds and records in order to present evidence of Palestinian rights to the land taken from them by Israel in the 1948 War (and after), as well as to reflect the economic structures within the village. Only occasionally do authors discuss the larger systems of administration, regulation, and taxation to which the villagers were subjected and in which they functioned, and the historical context of land ownership more generally: the changing land laws and ownership, inheritance practices, and the shift from systems of collectively and communally held agricultural land to private plots, started under the Ottomans and continued under the British Mandate.[58] In large part this is because the issue of land ownership in Palestine is an extremely complex historical skein to unravel and understand, and one that varies widely from area to area.[59]

The reproduction of village land ownership records raises the issue of how to understand both why authors reproduce them and how we as readers are to read them. The al-Birwa village book, for example, contains a reproduction of the entire collection of the listing of Claims to Land (Settlement of Title) documents, which makes up two-thirds of the total pages of the village book. These documents, part of the official recording of the land holdings by the

British government in Palestine, were created as the government made legislative changes with regard to land ownership, in this case requiring villages to transfer collectively owned land into private ownership.[60] The 115 pages of records include information on the number, parcel, category of land,[61] names of claimants (owners), shares, boundaries, and nature of the claim, as well as information about the productivity or use of the land—such as old olive grove, new olive trees, land without trees (*sleekh*), household garden (*hakura*), grapes, fruit trees, and *waqf* (endowment) of the Orthodox Church for the Christian cemetery.[62] These pages contain at least twenty-five claims per page and thus detail nearly three thousand plots owned and registered among a population of about fifteen hundred people in 1948 (with the entire land registered to the village being a total of 13,542 dunums).[63]

A close historical reading of these records would provide a major addition to the social history of the village by allowing for a better understanding of the distribution of village land among individuals and families, of the types of communal property and the ways shares were owned, and finally, of the ways in which people dealt with proportional shares of land.[64] For example, a historian analyzing the land registration records (*shahadat tasjil* or *kushan*) reproduced in Dirbas's book on Salama would find them to be an informative source for social history.[65] Not only do they reveal sales, transfers, inheritances, and divisions of land, but they also list, among other things, the type of property owned, the area, the owner (or seller) and the buyer (if it is a purchase deed), the date, the plot number, and the section of the village where the recorded land was located.[66] But the village books are not histories in the professional sense, neither are their authors trained historians, nor are the interests of the authors and the reading community shared with academics. Instead, Dirbas includes the records, as do other village book authors, as talismanic proof that the village's name appeared in official documents and that Palestinians owned land in the village. Although ideally I or other readers would have looked closely at this listing of claims and analyzed its contents, the rough reproduction in the books makes the handwriting very difficult to read. This is perhaps the most tantalizing, and frustrating, element of these reproductions: the copies of very old documents are often so unclear that they are hard to decipher, and in many cases they are only a small personal collection of the thousands of documents the villagers would have possessed. Both situations make it difficult for a scholar or professional historian to work with them. They remain, for both villagers and scholars, a suggestion of what existed, and they illustrate the incomplete and fragmentary nature of the written documentation of village life in Palestinian hands.

WRITING PEOPLE IN AND OUT OF HISTORY

These land documents, as official documents, also present the readers of the village books with a vexing dilemma in terms of understanding history.[67] Specialists in subaltern studies, oral historians, social historians, and historians of women, among others, have argued successfully and correctly that alternative sources such as personal accounts, oral histories, letters, and diaries can provide scholars and historians with more extensive and inclusive knowledge of women's histories, the lives of politically or economically marginal populations, and nonstandard historical contexts—topics often excluded from official histories. The village books, however, which are largely based on the very sources (memory and oral history) that are touted as providing more knowledge of the lives of disenfranchised people and women, do not discuss in any detail the indigenous systems of communal land rotation that would have ensured access to land for everyone in a family, or the inheritance laws by which women inherited property, or the resistances to landlords or government regulation. Thus the village books rarely address many of the inequalities in the villagers' lives that existed via the established systems or through the particular efforts of individuals.

The book on Mallaha by 'Abd al-'Aal, discussed earlier in this chapter, provides an example of some of the ways that changing land laws were potentially exploited by those who were more knowledgeable in the village, and it illustrates the patronage system that existed in many villages.

> [Our *mukhtar*] knew all of the other *mukhtars* in the area and most of the government offices in Safad and their employees. He did his utmost to prevent Arab land traders and thieves who worked on behalf of the Jews from breaking up the land of al-Mallaha. He was the owner and purchaser [of all of the village land], distributing land and supervising the sale of every inch of it. Even among the villagers themselves, anyone who wanted to sell their land sold it to the *mukhtar* out of fear that there would be problems. He would give the person what they needed. A few small-minded people accused him of being greedy and selfish, but he did it honestly and for the good of the village.[68]

The author here presents the *mukhtar* as nationalistic and working in villagers' interests while at the same time acknowledging that he gathered all of the village land in his name and the criticisms of his actions. The threat of outside danger in the form of selling land to Jewish settlers provides an explanataory framework for how the *mukhtar* served as master and protector, which may or may not have come with a great deal of power over the other villagers.

With neither stories or official records available, some of the smaller families, individuals, and the Bedouin in the area have fallen into historical lacunae. They have disappeared because of the destroyed documents, changing land laws in both the Ottoman and Mandate periods, and the scattering of villagers in 1948. Thus many individuals or small families who immigrated or were killed or died in 1948 and did not constitute a presence in the diaspora communities have likely been forgotten. Without someone to speak for them, they have no presence in the village books, and there is no assurance that their memory will be perpetuated in village history. Those communities that previously had been dispossessed during the late Ottoman and Mandate-era property-recording efforts that had privileged the more powerful village families have also been largely removed from memory. It is difficult to unearth these stories from the accumulated narratives that have been attached to the more powerful families and dominant origin stories. The village of Kawfakha, for example, came into existence in the late nineteenth century, a product of migration from Gaza. According to Walid Khalidi's *All That Remains* and al-Dabbagh's *Our Country Palestine*, as well as some accounts in the Kawfakha village book, Gaza city residents came to farm the surrounding land and founded the village.[69] Hajj Sha'ban al-Hilu, these histories note, established a pact with the Ottoman authorities promising that the villagers would serve in the army, in return for acquiring the land. However, an oral account quoted in the village book mentions how Hajj Sha'ban obtained the land that was being used by others.

> As we have heard and were told by the old people, Kawfakha was government land [*jiftlik*] during the time of Sultan 'Abd al-Hamid, and the 'Arab al-Qatatwa [Bedouin tribe of al-Qatatwa] lived on it. A man named al-Hajj Sha'ban al-Hilu came, he is the one who established the village. Hajj Sha'ban competed with the Arab al-Qatatwa and he said to them, "By God I have to get you off of this land." The Hajj went to the government and met the man responsible for government lands and told him, "I am willing to build up the ruins of Kawfakha, and we will serve in the army." The official gave him papers with everything written on them; they were written by a guy named Hafiz al-'Alami from Gaza. So the government

official told the Arab al-Qatatwa that there were people who wanted to inhabit [*ta'mar*] that land. The 'Arab al-Qatatwa said that we were here before the others. So the official said to them, if you are willing to serve the government and join the army, and let us take people from you [*wa yakhdu minkum anfar*], then you can stay here. They said, "We are ready." Then our men, Shaykh Sha'ban and his people, said, "Our ploy didn't work, so we better go to Shaykh al-Huzayl." So al-Huzayl was a shaykh of the Arabs, well-known and strong. They told him the story, and he sent word to the 'Arab [al-Qatatwa] and said, "You are going to accommodate Hajj Sha'aban's folks [*bidku tiftahu fi bayt al-sha'ba taghra*], by God, or I will finish you off [*ghayr aqta' diyarkum al-bu'ada*]." So they left; not one remained.[70]

In contrast to the "known" history of the village, this orally recorded account makes clear that Kawfakha was not settled on empty land and instead required the disenfranchisement of the local Bedouin who grazed herds there on the basis of, at the least, customary rights and land laws that allowed them access to state-owned land. In present-day memory and written accounts of the village's history, however, the local Bedouin are almost entirely absent, and they exist only as a presence against which the village came into existence.

In the case of women property owners, the official documents rather than the village books reveal women's roles in land transactions, sales, and purchases. The inclusion of land records in the village books depicts aspects of the historical record that, in the case of women owning land, the oral history and subaltern perspectives do not elucidate. In Dirbas's book on Salama, the sixty-six British Mandate land records show at least twenty-one transactions that involve nine different women as the sole property owner.[71] Of the twenty-one transactions, nine involve women selling land, three record women buying land, two are records of ownership [*tasjil*], and seven are records of property exchange [*tabdil*].[72] An additional two transactions involved men and women together as property sellers. Dirbas's inclusion of the original historical documents in the book allows readers to develop an understanding of a much more prominent role for women as landowners and as actors with economic and social power than the roles presented by the authors of village books.

Historically speaking, this high proportion of women involved in property transactions contrasts with recent scholarly accounts about women as landowners in the present. Annalies Moors provides cogent anthropological interpretation of land ownership among women in the Nablus area between

1920 and 1990. On the basis of in-depth fieldwork with a number of women and their families, she discusses women's involvement in land ownership through dowry gains, purchases, sales, and inheritance. She finds in the rural areas a *decline* in women's access to property as some women give up property rights to gain other rights in familial and marital relationships.[73] However, this decline might also be specific to the West Bank and highland region and not to the coastal areas or the Galilee. Work by Iris Agmon reveals that in earlier centuries, women (or at least urban women) were active holders, buyers, and sellers of land and property.[74]

The use of oral sources and memory provides a voice for Palestinians to assert ownership of land in the face of their physical dispossession by Zionist forces, but they also privilege a male and patriarchal vision of the village. Because women were seen as falling under the protection of their male family members, the presentation of land ownership in the village books absorbs women property owners into "the family," which is represented by the senior male in the family unit and under whose name the property is remembered and recorded in the books. For example, in the book on al-Shaykh Daoud, the seventy-seven houses of the village are enumerated and listed by head of family and architectural elements: seventy-one are listed under the name of a male family member, and six are listed by the names of the widows or unmarried women who lived in them.[75] In this reckoning of recorded houses, the ownership of the house is extended to the head of the household by asserting that this is his (or her) house. Thus, only the women who did not live with a man are seen as having a house, in terms of both physical ownership and household lineage status (which will end with their death). Women who owned (partially or fully, by buying or inheriting the house they lived in) were not included on this list if they lived there with their husbands, brothers, or sons. Thus the patrilocal, patrilineal, and patriarchal system of reckoning kin and residence subtly segues into registering the "ownership" of that space in a way that is meaningful to the villagers in social terms but presents an inaccurate and ahistorical image of women's role in property ownership.[76]

In contrast, the government land records show that village women owned property of all types—farmland, orchard land, and land with buildings—both whole parcels and partial shares. Despite the presence of official records in the village books, neither the records nor the books give us any sense of the actual actions of women and men in the village in this regard, and we therefore do not know if the women had any sort of decision-making role in buying, selling, or trading these lands. Based on what we know from current practice as well as from historical accounts, women's husbands, fathers, and brothers were often the public face on a woman's property, buying and selling in her name and running her business ventures.[77] Thus the fact that she owned property should not be read as anything more than that, but it does extend the possibility that women were, or could be, economically, socially, and politically influential. The more recent decline, or perceived decline, in women's property holdings may, as Moors suggests, stem from the fact that authors writing at the end of the twentieth century really may not have known that women were such major property holders as the documents bear out in certain villages in the first half of the century. Furthermore, one might argue that by omitting women as property holders from the village histories, the more conservative social values of the late twentieth century have overtaken the social customs and the implementation of Islamic laws that may have been practiced before 1948. (According to Islamic law, women retain their property and wealth in their own name upon marriage and inherit upon the death of their parents, husband, or children.)[78] Yet even those authors who are quick to point out that the village practice of worshiping at saints' shrines contradicts "true" Islamic practice neglect to point out this particular disregard of Islamic inheritance and ownership practice.

Thus land records as traditional historical documentary sources provide a more comprehensive and accurate picture of women's roles in village life, which are largely elided from oral histories. This elision contradicts, in some ways, what many scholars have argued about writing women's history.[79] In the discipline of history, these village books would be seen as subaltern or alternative historical sources that allow us more complete access to historical contexts and realities and more accurately represent women's lives. However, the official government sources provide us with material, such as land records, that allows us to understand other dimensions of women's lives in the village, whereas villagers' memories and oral histories eliminate that subject almost entirely, conforming instead to certain norms about village life that the community holds.

Ironically, Palestinians have turned to alternative and subaltern sources to write their own histories and challenge dominant portrayals of their lives, at the same time relying on socially dominant norms about village social structures, family dynamics, and gender roles. The evidence reflected in the documents and individual stories that are reproduced in the books suggests that the omissions in the books contribute to particular understandings of what constitutes "history." The history told in the village books does not question patriarchal forces, nor does it provide an understanding of women's economic power as property holders, or of the importance of land ownership within the older, communal rights system of pre-Tanzimat Ottoman Empire, or of those settled social groups that could assert power and privilege within the governmental system against the marginalized Bedouin or Ghawarneh. Current migration patterns, the errors of memory, and the influences of contemporary power result in the erasure from history of smaller families and marginalized populations while ensuring the representation of the most powerful social norms and the largest and strongest families in the village. The village books thus do not detail individual property rights or records, nor represent, as they may claim, an egalitarian vision of the village. Rather, they represent the powers, whether real or assumed over time, that have come to dominate how people remember the past and negotiate writing about it in the present.

. . .

As the village book authors write about the past, they also document more than just the events of pre-1948 village life. In this chapter I have explicated how their choices of subjects and sources result in a communally circumscribed vision of the past that in many cases represents social forces that promote some subjects and silence others. Of course individual authors, both intentionally and unintentionally, break with social and narrative convention and introduce historical subjects and methods of writing history that rupture the dominant portrayal of village life.

The ways in which Palestinians are writing and reading history in the village books provides examples of the replication of pre-1948 social structures, patriarchal forces, and social and economic hierarchies as well as contemporary ones. Most prominently, the inclusion and exclusion of women in the books reflects these forces. By failing to note the fact that women were property owners, authors reinforce patriarchal norms as well as communicate ideas about the village that may (or may not) reflect their own conceptions of women as property owners, today as well as historically. Given that today most refugees from a village, whether male or female, living in Syria, Jordan, Lebanon, Gaza, or the West Bank, own no property at all or at most a house in the refugee camp or a flat in the city, the issue of ownership is probably not one they deal with regularly. However, in writing the books and desiring to portray the village in a way that is communally accepted, the authors concern themselves with patriarchal authority that gives precedence to men's social and protective roles. They thus ignore women's roles as property owners and the pre-1948 villagers' adherence to Islamic law and women's rights of inheritance and property in marriage. It is the documents that are often included in the village books that reveal that women did own property, and bought and sold it, and that give names and numbers to those facts. The books do not say explicitly that women did not own property; rather, it is the absence of descriptions of women as property owners that contrasts with the documents. Likewise, the transmission of knowledge through patriarchal sources perpetuates the rendering of family histories and genealogies that largely exclude women. The village books that *do* include women's names and origins create a much richer history of Palestinian village life, although a history that reflects personal knowledge and not history as Palestinians have typically recorded it historically, in both oral and written form.

5 THE AUTHORITY OF MEMORY

Jerusalem, Palestine: 1923

In 1923, Khalil al-Sakakini, the prominent Jerusalem educator and man of letters, was astounded at an article he read in the Egyptian newspaper *al-Siyasa* (Politics). Written by Rosita Forbes and translated into Arabic, it claimed that "the [Arab] inhabitants all know that the only way to increase their wealth is by depending on Jewish capital holders and making use of their projects. . . . It seemed [to the author] that there was no disagreement in Palestine that cannot be solved between the Zionists and the Arab inhabitants."[1] Forbes, an English traveler and writer, had spent four days visiting Palestine and on her return to England wrote this account that so confounded al-Sakakini. The same newspaper then published his response, in which he sought to show that Forbes was wrong:

> Palestine is neither the North Pole nor the planet Mars. Popular opinion is not disguised or hidden. The national newspapers, the reports of the conferences, the associations, and the political clubs which represent the people, the delegations which travel east and west to announce public opinion—all of them have rejected the Mandate over Palestine, refused to accept the Balfour declaration, resisted Zionism and boycotted their projects. . . . If all of these things represent public opinion, then we do not know how Miss Rosita Forbes, who passed [so quickly] through Palestine [that she was] like a phantasm in front of our eyes, was able to discern [what she claims to be] popular opinion. . . . What Rosita Forbes is calling for has not been said by anyone. This government and the Zionists are carrying Diogenes' lantern, searching

the country for someone to say those things, and like Diogenes, they haven't found anyone.[2]

Both al-Sakakini's protest and the article by Forbes are now part of history and sources for understanding the past that can be read and analyzed. They show that even as early as five years into the British colonization of Palestine, Palestinians were well aware that they were fighting over who had the right to represent reality and the authority to narrate and represent their lives, opinions, views, and histories.

Global political forces, from the Balfour Declaration in 1917 to the present, have shaped Palestinian histories and lives, and thus also pushed Palestinians to see and represent their personal histories within the sway of these larger forces. Political movements have failed to bring them statehood or to rally global political will to their cause. Meanwhile, they have lived through the catastrophe of 1948, life in the diaspora or under Israeli military rule, civil wars in Jordan and Lebanon, the continued occupation of the West Bank and Gaza (which began in 1967), the aging and death of those members of the population who remember the *nakba*, and the struggle for Palestinian statehood. In this existence of dispossession, dispersion, and statelessness, collections of personal stories and memories are what Palestinians have in comparative abundance.[3]

These factors have all pushed forward those who might not have otherwise been able or willing to present their stories to the public. Since the 1980s, when Palestinian village books began to appear (and autobiographies as well), Palestinians have been making public their individual histories and collective experiences as a legacy that needs to be preserved and recorded. Elizabeth Tonkin believes that the timing of when people take an interest in recalling and preserving the past, as well as the nature of what they record, is critical: "A changing interest in the past is part of a present consciousness, and changes in social conditions appear to alter that consciousness."[4] This chapter explores how Palestinians see themselves, their lives, and their experiences: as material with which to promote the righteousness of their cause and as evidence of their existence.

For the authors of the village books, these individual, personal, and local stories enhance and enrich the broader historical narrative of the Palestinian past and define how they write and the information they choose to include. The idea of Palestinian historians using their own personal stories and memories to create a "history" presents a number of difficulties: first, turning memories that are told orally into accurate and acceptable written texts; second, dealing with the complex author attribution issues that come with rendering personal stories in written texts; third, using culturally and linguistically meaningfully forms to convey these narratives convincingly; and fourth, ensuring that these narratives are published and read and become part of the historical record. Not only are these books about Palestinians claiming the right to tell their own stories and thus exert control over their own history, but they are also about claiming the power invested in knowledge.

WRITING HISTORY DESPITE AND TO SPITE SILENCES AND SILENCING

For Palestinians, telling stories about life both before and after the creation of the state of Israel has been and continues to be a difficult task.[5] Because they have neither a state that represents them nor an official narrative of critical historical moments, Palestinians lack the narrative power of a unified founding myth that justifies their existence as a collective.[6] However, given the political situation of the Palestinians over the last sixty-plus years, the absence of a totalizing hegemonic power that advocates an all-encompassing historical narrative has allowed for the rise of many local and individual accounts of history.[7] From their diverse experiences have emerged the village books, as Palestinians have searched to find ways to legitimize their existence as Palestinians within a national discourse and self-understanding.

Further changes in Palestinian society following the 1967 War and the Israeli occupation of the West Bank and Gaza (the remainder of historic Palestine) forced a new reckoning with the Palestinian past.[8] Refugees from these areas were finally able to cross the border that separated them from their former homes and villages. The shock at what they found—whole villages completely destroyed, mosques and churches turned into stables and restaurants, Israelis living in and adding on to Palestinian houses—showed the Palestinians most forcefully that the past they recalled no longer existed. Hala Sakakini writes that on Tuesday, July 4, 1967, one month after the June 1967 War,

> my sister and I visited our house in Katamon, Jerusalem, for the first time in nineteen years. It was a sad encounter, like meeting a dear person whom you had last seen young, healthy, and well groomed and finding that he had become old, sick, and shabby. Even worse, it was like coming across a friend whose personality had undergone a drastic change and he was no more the same person.[9]

Sakakini describes their emotional reaction (in response to their physical encounter with the place) and personifies the homecoming as if meeting a person rather than a house. The profound alterations in the material landscape, and people's reactions to these visits, are rendered in visceral reactions and deeply emotive metaphors. Recorded in many different types of texts and both written and visual media, stories of the "return" visit to the home or village figure prominently in autobiographies, oral history collections, village books, fiction, and more recently, videos.[10]

Still, the pain of 1948 silences some Palestinians despite the encouragement to make their stories public. Two of my friends in Damascus (a brother and sister) told me the story of their pregnant aunt who had fled their village on foot during the fighting in 1948. She had her small daughter by the hand and they were separated from the rest of the family in the chaos. They told me the story with all of its details. The aunt and her daughter continued walking north, away from the gunfire and explosions, and the little girl tired along the way, so the mother had to strap her onto her back with her dress.[11] During this journey she went into labor and delivered the baby, alone and without help. The infant was stillborn, and she buried her where she had halted, in a location she did not know and cannot recall.[12]

More than fifty years later, the sister who told me this story heard her aunt tell it once, and the brother heard it from others in the family. He wanted to record it as part of their family history. After much prompting, they got their aunt to tell her story, but when they started to record her on their cell phone, she stopped and refused to continue. They assured her they would not record it, but she persisted in her refusal. She communicated to them that her life and suffering were not a story to be recorded, made permanent, and potentially passed on to others outside of her own family. This example illustrates the complicated role of individual experience as a source of history: some people choose not to offer their lives up to the collective historical experience.[13] I retell this woman's story here because it was told to me by my friends as an example of their struggles as the younger generation to extract these stories from their older relatives. And although I acknowledge their and my violation of her wish for her story not to be retold, I retell it here, suitably obscured, to illustrate exactly what this desire to make the personal a part of the public record evinces: a silencing process of the intimate, so that even something as universal as a tragic death cannot be told because of reluctance to bare one's personal pain and shame to the public.[14] This separation of the person from her story, and her descendants' conviction that her account not be lost, led to their willingness to use her account as part of Palestinian history, thus subsuming the individual, her sentiments, desires, and being, to the historical narrative that is deemed more important than the individual.

MEMORY AS A SOURCE OF HISTORY

Even in the twentieth and twenty-first centuries, which have been characterized by colonial rule, the growth of nation-states, and complex bureaucracies of administration that create pages of records, statistics, reports, and other documents, memory remains the primary way that experiences—both individual and shared—are maintained in both personal and community life. Huge swaths of contemporary human existence covering a variety of subjects are missing written and visual records and a documented archive to mine for understanding a given place or people or event. As we have tried to understand human experience, we have come to acknowledge that how humans record, recall, and remember their pasts is an integral part of understanding that experience themselves. Thus, when we examine memories of the past, we are able to envisage how they are enmeshed with the information and narratives that make up history, and to recognize the filters that make us see and understand things in certain ways that change over time.[15]

Memory's tight hold on the past, on what it means, and the need to transfer it to forms that will not fade recalls Salman Rushdie's comments on the use of his own memories when writing *Midnight's Children*, his novel about the partition of India in 1947. Trying to recall his Bombay childhood, he felt that "the shards of memory acquired greater status, greater resonance, because they were *remains*; fragmentation made trivial things seem like symbols, and the mundane acquired numinous qualities." Trying to understand these fragments of his past, Rushdie struggles with the emotions that give meaning to the "shards of memory":

> Meaning is a shaky edifice we build out of scraps, dogmas, childhood injuries, newspaper articles, chance remarks, old films, small victories, people hated, people loved; perhaps it is because our sense of what is the case is constructed from such inadequate materials that we defend it so fiercely, even to the death.[16]

Understanding how people hold onto and create meaning from memories when the places of that past no longer exist is part of understanding the history of people whose lives are framed by wars, displacement, and upheaval.

As those memories are expressed, written down, and shared with others, they portray certain meanings that have individual and collective roles in forming people's identifications and their senses of the past, the present, and the future. This shared nature of memories underlies Maurice Halbwachs's *On Collective Memory*: "If we examine a little more closely how we recollect things, we will surely realize that the greatest number of memories come back to us when our parents, our friends, or other persons recall them to us. . . . It is in society that people normally acquire their memories. It is also in society that they recall, recognize, and localize their memories."[17]

As so many scholars observe, memories are not stored as information in isolation from the rest of human life. Rather, they are subject to reinterpretation and reconsideration on the basis of new information, beliefs, experiences, and the unpredictable whims of our minds. Alessandro Portelli describes how the Rome-based oral history and folklore collective Circolo Gianni Bosio envisioned memory: "We never thought of memory as an archive, as a freezer that preserves data and meanings, but rather as a processor that transforms and elaborates them in osmotic fashion and yields ever new data and meanings that include the old ones—if only to deny or get rid of them."[18] In this sense, Susan Slyomovics notes that the village books that rely on memory as their primary source forge a new relationship between the former residents and their descendants, and between the former residents' memories and the books that in textual and visual form now enter the public domain. Slyomovics maintains that "the processes of collecting materials for, writing, and editing memorial books reflect the concerns of a shared authorship and a communal readership of survivors."[19] These concerns reflect the role of the present and other factors in how memories of the past are remembered and portrayed.[20]

Some people are loathe to see memory as a reliable source for understanding the past, for these (and other) reasons. Yet what scholars and others are saying is not necessarily that people misremember events or actions (which of course they do), but that over time their interpretation of those events changes or they give different meaning to particular actions. Our subconscious makes sure, however, that our memories generally make sense to us, and despite whatever else happens, our memories remain an essential part of a web of meaning-making by which we understand and interpret events and emotions. The result is an ever-changing, amorphous understanding of the events of the past, rooted in the present in which the memory is recalled and mediated by the audience and the purpose of the recollection, among numerous other forces. The interpretation and recording of memories is steeped in the varying influences of local dynamics, political forces, individual emotions, material circumstances, family relations, gender, class, education, and personality, among other factors. A noted oral historian believes that "people tend with the passage of time to be more rather than less candid. Near the end of a life, there is a need to look at things as honestly as possible to make sense of experiences over a lifetime. . . ."[21] Events and periods in people's lives that are somehow seen as defining the individual—such as marriage, birth of children, especially happy or traumatic events, including death, or as for the Palestinian refugees, the loss of home and community—occupy prominent places in people's memories.[22]

Of course people misremember, just as documents misrecord. However, despite what we know about the limitations of and influences on how and what we remember, we should not discount memory as a historical source, as many traditional historians are wont to do. Benny Morris's seminal 1987 book *The Birth of the Palestinian Refugee Problem* broke new ground in analyzing the 1948 War by using declassified Israeli archival sources. He did not, however, reference or rely on any oral sources in his research, which he justified by turning to the tradition of history as a discipline. He maintained that

> after careful and long thought, I decided to refrain almost completely from using interviews, with Jews or Arabs, as sources of information. I was brought up believing in the value of documents. While contemporary documents may misinform, distort, omit or lie, they do so, in my experience, far more rarely than interviewees recalling highly controversial events some 40 years ago. [. . .] I have found interviews of use in obtaining "colour" and a picture of the prevailing conditions. Only very, very rarely have I relied on oral history to establish facts.[23]

Morris's relegation of oral history to only providing "colour" to "real" history suggests more than just a historian's distrust of oral histories. His condemnation of memory as notoriously faulty overlooks two major forces: one, the power of those with the documents to create hegemonic historical narratives in environments where texts dominate; and two, the challenges to the historical record by those people without documents. They often force us to reconsider the primacy we place on texts as the only source of history, and compel us instead to consider their narratives of experience.[24] Regarding the 1948 War, no one doubts that crucial information about what happened will remain missing if we rely solely on written sources. Further, we underestimate the skills of scholars across diverse disciplines if we think they cannot work beyond written documents and interpret from oral sources. Just as historians learn to decode and read beyond the content of documents (which do, in Morris's words, "misinform, distort, omit or lie" in their own way), so too do scholars using oral sources and memory learn to decode and *hear* beyond the content of the material told to them.[25] In fact, Morris's own research proved what had long been asserted by Palestinians from their own experiences, which they told in oral histories and personal accounts about the events of the 1948 War but which had been denied by historians and others, until they had access to the written Israeli sources that were declassified in the 1980s.[26]

Other researchers investigating the events of 1948 have found that the Palestinian oral accounts of events often coincide with the records made by Zionist-Israeli forces. In Efrat Ben-Ze'ev's work examining the sources that discuss the events in the Palestinian village of Ijzim during the 1948 War, she concludes that "the villagers' oral accounts and the army documents often complement each other and sometimes converge."[27] The oral accounts focus on people, heroic actions, emotions, motivations, and the development of an internal logic to the turn of events. These subjects differ from the contents of an army intelligence report but nevertheless provide a perspective from the people who experienced the actions and activities described in the army report. Perhaps even more important than the information added by the perspectives provided in oral accounts is that people imbue their stories with the *meaning* attributed to those events by those who experienced them. Writing history requires understanding not just what happened, but also what it meant and means to the people who experienced it.

People who work extensively with oral histories appreciate the nonconformity of individual accounts to the dominant narratives. Alessandro Portelli's work collecting oral histories of the Italian resistance to Fascism and the Nazi occupation has convinced him that people telling their stories are "more articulate and credible historians than those professional writers and administrators of history. . . ."[28] People remembered the violence of the Resistance, and the class and civil war that occurred along with the patriotic war. Their individual stories and experiences fit into the larger picture, making it possible for Portelli to write a more nuanced and complete account, and thus a more accurate and correct depiction of the period. Although individual memories may fit into a larger historical structure of events, they do not necessarily submit to the dominant or hegemonic narrative of those events. Swedenburg researched collective and individual memories of the Palestinian revolt in 1936–1939, not to construct an "alternative history" of the revolt based on oral sources, but rather to understand how the revolt has figured into individual, popular, and nationalist memory in the present. His book *Memories of Revolt* examines the effect of the intervening years and events, the emergence and use of national signifiers, and individual versus official memories of the rebellion. He found that individual memories of the revolt were not overwritten by the larger political context and national narrative but competed with them in the rewriting of history to include internal social and political struggles, class issues, and strongly held values.[29]

Anthropologists have long worked to present people's perspectives on and expressions of how they understand the past and the role that history plays in their lives. Most anthropologists present readers with an understanding of a particular group or community by reconstructing how those people see the world. Some, however, like John Neihardt, Andrew Shryock, Keith Basso, and Penelope Papailias, have worked closely with local historians to understand how history is composed, transmitted, and received in the respective communities under study.[30] Basso, for example, shows how "Apache standards for interpreting the past are not the same as our own, and that working Apache historians [. . .] go about their business with different aims and procedures."[31] Recent scholarship by both anthropologists and historians engages local history-writing projects and local historians in order to expand our notions of the possibilities for using nontraditional historical material, methods, and narratives, and explores the reception of the history-writing projects within local and larger communities.[32]

In the context of understanding how local histories are composed, we must take into account how we as Western scholars assume that our conceptions of what constitutes history are universal. In examining Bedouin orally transmitted historical narratives, Shryock considers the impossibility of successfully rendering them within the predominately Western notion of historical scholarship. The models of history that we use to understand the past "become powerful tools for the conceptual subordination of other histories to hegemonically Western ones."[33] He mentions, among others, the chronological template to which history must conform in scholarly work. Basso reports that Apache historians find Western ways of writing history "obsessed with dating historical events," in addition to appearing "to be in search of final historical truths."[34]

Our own historical certitude and insistence on anchoring events within chronological frames does not allow for easily understanding how people experience a particular moment, both as it happens and later. James Olney writes that "it is in the interplay of past and present, of present memory reflecting over past experience on its way to becoming present being, that events are lifted out of time to be re-situated not in mere chronological sequence but in patterned significance."[35] The meaningfulness of a particular event may not become evident to participants or observers until after the event has passed. In the oral histories I collected about Palestinian life in Jerusalem before 1948, I asked each person I interviewed when they left their house in Jerusalem for the last time. Almost none of the people gave me a date, although some provided me with a month. Some of them I explicitly asked, "Do you remember the date?" Most replied no, they didn't remember. Answers ranged from the reconstructable ("Palm Sunday") to an event-related occurrence ("after our gardener was shot dead in the yard by a sniper" or "after the Dayr Yasin massacre") to the general ("in the spring"). What this line of questioning divulges, first of all, is my own interest and thinking in terms of chronological understanding and consistency. It also reveals that the people I talked to did not think only in chronological terms. When they left their homes in Jerusalem and elsewhere, they did not think at the time that it was the momentous event that it turned out to be. Not one of them thought they would *never* return, and thus the exact date and time they left were unremarkable to them *at the time*. Instead, it was the event that caused them to leave that remained embedded in their memory. This calendar-based chronological ambiguity poses a problem for the existence of Palestinian historical accounts within Western academic textual history. They do not conform to the academic historical standards developed in universities in the West, which would set them within a measured, date-oriented history. This calendrical chronology, much like the gold standard, provides us with a measuring stick by which to compare accounts. Those who already use that dating measure—states, armies, academics, bureaucrats—have set the terms for what constitutes reliable history, leaving those who do not to conform or be excluded.

In a sense, Benny Morris may be right: memories are inflected by various forces, ideologies, pressures, and physical factors that are part of how we as humans remember. But his argument assumes, first, that "we" (westerners, academics) write history in an entirely unbiased and universal manner (and that our chronological and big-picture ways of seeing history are not inflected by ideologies, pressures, and forces); and second, that history consists of only chronicling events. Instead, what memories of the past can provide us with is how people make sense of those events. Other communities and cultures in different historical moments also rely on using nontraditional historical material that does not just take the material as fact but also investigates the context in which it is embedded. The seminal work *The Slave's Narrative* brings together scholarship on autobiographical works of the eighteenth to twentieth centuries by slaves in the United States in order to "explicate the structure of the world these narratives represent."[36] Through understanding the structures with which we build our histories, we can better interpret the content of the material.

Oral historians and anthropologists also know that narratives, as versions of reality, consist of "one or more points of view rather than objective, omniscient accounts."[37] Raphael Samuel and Paul Thompson advocate for serious efforts to be made to include nonhegemonic narratives in history-writing because:

> the collective memories of minorities need continual active expression if they are to survive being absorbed or smothered by the historical traditions of the majority. Nor is this dominance a mere matter of numbers. The powerful have a breathtaking ability to stamp their own meanings on the past. Our tales of Empire are of the bravery and benign administration of a "master race," rather than of superior military technology or back-breaking slavery in plantation or pit."[38]

Perhaps in similar ways but for different reasons, textual and oral sources are faulty—the former for omitting so many voices and emphasizing the perspectives of the powerful and hegemonic over everything and everyone else, and the latter for intermittent reliability. Palestinians, by using their own stories and experiences, are pushing for their voices to be included in the historical record of the Arab-Israeli conflict. Their voices allow us to understand not only what happened and who was involved, but also what the past means to different people, including those outside of the dominant and hegemonic meaning-generating centers.[39]

THE AUTHORITY OF MEMORY

Palestinians writing about their villages find that few written records and history books bear the imprint of the villagers themselves. British Mandate sources are about governance: local councils, education, health and hygiene, taxes, and laws, among other topics. Ylana Miller employs these sources to interesting purposes in explaining the impact of the British Mandate government on village life in terms of administration, regulation, and education.[40] Her work reveals Palestinians' perspectives on government regulation at the time, but little of what was meaningful to them outside of this context.

The village book authors wish to tell the history of the village from the perspectives of those who lived there, with the sentiments of what it means to be from the village, with the idea of passing that information down to their descendants. As histories, the books express little engagement with or interest in the British Mandate sources on the village—the documents and materials that explicate official perspectives on Palestinians' lives. Thus the memories of those who lived village life are the primary source available to Palestinian village book authors for knowing about that past.

It is not just the village book authors who turn to those who remember as their primary source. When I talked to young and middle-aged Palestinians in Syria and Lebanon about where they get their knowledge of their village, most of them responded by citing their older relatives rather than written sources such as books or the Internet.[41] While living in Yarmouk camp in Damascus in 2008, I asked the people I met where they learned about the history of their village. I broached the subject with two first cousins while sharing with them pizza and a water pipe in a café in the camp. I asked them what sources they turn to in order to learn about their village history. Both are educated, politically aware and active women in their late twenties who I know have copies of a village book on their village. But they did not mention written sources or well-known histories; instead, they told me they get stories about their village from their grandmother. They insisted we go talk to her, which required a long walk through the camp (broken up by frequent pauses to comment on the dresses stylishly arrayed in the storefronts). When we got to the house, we joined Grandma and her sister, who were eating peaches and drinking coffee. Having a stranger shoved into her midst to hear her talk about her growing-up years did not make Grandma very comfortable, but she obliged with some stories of what she remembered. That these two educated and politically active young women thought their grandmother was the best source for learning about their village, despite the presence of a village book on the subject and a long entry about the village on PalestineRemembered.com, signifies the continuing relevance and power of firsthand sources to how individuals relate to their local history.

THE AUTHORITY OF EXPERIENCE

The village books compete with individuals to be a source of knowledge for others to turn to in order to learn about the past. My ten years of working on this subject and living in Palestinian communities revealed to me that lived knowledge of the past is the primary authority and source for Palestinians in knowing and understanding their histories. With the passage of time, however, the textual sources are taking over as the most complete record of village life as peoples' relatives who remember the village pass on. But until then, most people value and turn to the authority of experience for what they believe to be the most accurate and real source of Palestinian history.

Not only are people who have this kind of personal knowledge and experience sought out by others who want to learn from them, but their knowledge and information are sometimes set against other types of information about the villages, both in the village books and in people's discussions. For example, the British Mandate government's quantification and knowledge of the village is sometimes challenged. Dirbas opens her book on Salama village with the following statement: "Salama was one of the large Palestinian villages from Jaffa district that was destroyed. The number of inhabitants before their dispersal in 1948 reached 6,730 people (although it is thought that the number was almost 10,000 if the unregistered residents were also counted). The people of Salama were scattered during the *nakba*, and most of the village's buildings were destroyed by 1950."[42] Ahmad al-Bash, author of one of the five books on the village of Tirat Haifa, maintains that according to the official British Mandate statistics of 1945, the population of Tirat Haifa was 5,270. But according to the statistics and estimates of the villagers, the population in 1948 was between 8,000 and 12,000, and during World War II the Government Directorate of Food Control estimated that there were 10,000 people in the village.[43] And Dirbas's other book, on al-Birwa, includes a chart that lists the population of the village throughout the twentieth century and the 1948 population is listed as 2,000 people, which "includes the unregistered inhabitants, according to the accounts of the villagers."[44] In al-Bash's and Dirbas's books, the "unregistered inhabitants" of Salama, Tirat Haifa, and al-Birwa, who increase the population numbers, are set against the official British Mandate statistics for these villages. Both authors' texts thus defy the status quo of the time (the British Mandate government), its ability to properly count and monitor the people, and the historical legacy it has left behind in these numbers.

These authors instead give primacy to the personal experiences of the villagers, who they presume knew more about the situation in the villages. By using the population numbers in such a way, these authors make the population count of Palestine an issue closely related to the efforts of Palestinians to control their own history and to "know better" than others about their own lives, villages, and country. Dirbas, al-Bash, and others who have written village books and other texts on Palestinian history often privilege memory and what I will term "experiential" authority—the authority of eyewitness and firsthand experience—over the documentary authority commonly used in the writing of history.[45]

If we explore indigenous perceptions of the past by examining the social, historical, and cultural contexts in which they are generated, we can address the embedded nature of these memories and their function in the present. Renato Rosaldo's study of the Ilongot in the Philippines, for example, shows that the Ilongot believe in events that they have personally experienced or that were experienced by those they trust. In this context, an event is validated only through a direct connection to experience.[46] The ways in which knowledge is communicated expresses the differences between lived experience and outsider, technocratic knowledge.[47] For example, British Mandate reports on agriculture, wells, and such subjects are expressed in counting and measurement numbers, as exemplified in the two-volume *A Survey of Palestine*, prepared in 1945 and 1946.[48] This is not to say that there are right and wrong ways of knowing information, but rather that the way in which one knows, records, and uses information is contextual and tied to regimes of authority and power. An account by the author of the village book on Bashsheet illustrates the importance of this contextualization of knowledge.

> In the process of collecting stories, it became clear how rich the village was in water resources, as the *mukhtar* Hajj Yusif Abu Fuda describes: "There were more than twenty artesian wells. We had pumps on two of them, one for the trees, that was a Michelin, while the other was a Rustam, that was for vegetables. There were other pumps: with the Sbayh family, another with the Khadrawis, the 'Asqula family had one, so did Barhum, Hassan Hilal, Sa'd Hilal, the Hajj, the Sharqawis, the Salih family, the Hilal family, and so forth."[49]

The differences between the various ways of collecting and communicating knowledge depend on the purpose of the information. The British wanted statistics on mechanization and technology for agricultural development.

Although such development was important to the villagers, the wells exist within social worlds in which people and their relations with one another also matter, particularly when describing who had control over various resources in the village.

Palestinians use the authority of their own experience to challenge other forms of knowledge about themselves and about Palestine, a challenge that I personally experienced as well. In the winter of 1998, I gave a lecture in Arabic to the Jerusalem Forum in Amman, Jordan, a group consisting of Jerusalemites and others interested in the history of the city and its current political status. My talk focused on the modern history of Jerusalem and on the ways in which the history of the city has been written. The audience consisted of many older persons who had memories of living in the city, as either children or adults, before 1948. As part of my talk, I provided the British Mandate statistics for the population of the city, as estimated in 1946, which put the Jewish population at 99,320 and the Arab (Muslim and Christian)[50] population at 65,010.[51] The Jewish population was clearly in the majority, which my audience neither believed nor found accordant with their memories.

The animated discussion following my talk focused almost entirely on population statistics from British census sources that I had (innocently, I thought) quoted. The discussion began with statements by some that the numbers were just plain wrong; either the British had fabricated them or I had misunderstood them or I had (intentionally) used the wrong numbers. A few people suggested that statistics need to be taken seriously and could not be dismissed out of hand. The audience then began to discuss plausible reasons for the unreliability of the British statistics: the undercount of Arab women for social reasons, stemming from the inappropriateness of a male researcher knowing their names or seeing them; the undercount of young men because of leftover fears of Ottoman conscription; and the fact that the population statistics from 1945 are estimates from the census of 1931.[52] What became clear to me then and what is most relevant to retelling this discussion here is that these Palestinians did not treat these statistics as part of their history as I did and as other scholars do. Instead they saw these numbers as gathered by "others" about them, and thus they could be dismissed as a malleable tool that the British Mandate (and others) used to discredit Palestinian claims to Jerusalem and to divest Palestinians of their land.

The forceful response that my demographic remarks elicited from the Palestinian audience revealed to me the very real reactions that people have to the information that so many scholars, policymakers, government officials, social workers, UN and nongovernmental organization employees, and so on use as building blocks in our work. As an American academic trained in anthropological, historical, and theoretical methods, I had access to and saw as useful certain sources that my audience, at least in large part, did not have access to or perhaps did not respect. The statistics I quoted were at odds with their memories of an Arab Jerusalem, and their political sensibilities would not allow them to become aware of any perspective other than the "Arab Jerusalem" vision that had prevailed since 1948. The audience's reaction also spurred me to try and understand why they would not remember such an overwhelming number of Jewish residents in Jerusalem. In addition, the map of the Mandate municipal borders of the city shows that the population count included distant Jewish neighborhoods that Jewish residents had petitioned for and thus were included within the municipal boundaries, but did not include the closer Arab villages that wanted their own autonomy outside of the municipality's governance.[53] Therefore the audience's reaction to and Dirbas's and al-Bash's questioning of the British Mandate statistics argue for the Palestinian right to write their own history, and declare to know better about themselves than the foreign, colonial authorities.

Some of the village book authors, like the audience at the Jerusalem Forum, engage with the statistics collected about their villages. Ahmad al-Bash investigates why the actual census numbers for Tirat Haifa might be lower than other sources claim. He notes that the last actual census of Palestine was conducted in 1931 and then discusses that the number of people living in Tirat Haifa rose dramatically after this occurred because the village was so close to Haifa and it was cheaper for Palestinians working in the port and in the British military camps to live there rather than in the city. This increase, he says, "indicates the generosity of the villagers; their simple, trusting natures; and their lack of discrimination against outsiders." Other additions to the village population were men who came from elsewhere and married village women and then ended up joining her family or clan. This became evident to Al-Bash, he maintains, only when he examined the family histories of the village. Finally, he also says that the census did not count the people living in Khirbat al-Damun, an area east of the village, nor all of the Tirat Haifa villagers who were living in Haifa for work.[54] By citing all of these additions to the Tirat Haifa population, al-Bash asserts two elements of how census numbers are conceived: one indicates residency, the second indicates sentiment. It is standard practice for census numbers to be about residency, but al-Bash gets at an important issue related to how these numbers are used by Palestinians. Often people who want to know how many Tirawis (villagers from Tirat Haifa) there are today use the British Mandate statistics to show how many villagers there were at that time and then extrapolate how many Tirawis there are now. Thus, al-Bash includes in his assessment of the Tirawis those who were from the village but living in Haifa—because they remain Tirawis. He also includes those who lived in the village and may or may not have been on their way to becoming Tirawis. But this quantifying process of charting population by residency was abruptly ended with the displacement of villagers in 1948, freezing in time a particular number of and notion about the population, which the villagers build on by adding those who identify as being from Tirat Haifa but living elsewhere.

The writing of history and the recording of the past center not just on facts and events but also on the ability to know and generate knowledge. The British Mandate authority produced hundreds of thousands of documents about the general situation in Palestine.[55] According to Ann Stoler, the knowledge underlying claims of truth is mediated "by disqualifying some knowledges and valorizing others, by normalizing the communication between them, by establishing a hierarchy of knowledges."[56] As explored previously, Palestinians' historical perspectives in the world arena have been much lower in this hierarchy of knowledge because they were not the victors in the 1948 War, nor do they rely on written sources for the most part. Dirbas's and al-Bash's assertions about the village populations spurn the British Mandate's documentary history and turn to the experiential authority emerging from the villagers themselves—a knowledge that exists not in estimates of population growth based on a fifteen-year-old census, but in a lived, day-to-day knowledge and in a consideration of sentiment and who belongs to that village.

But what Dirbas, al-Bash, and Khalil al-Sakakini, whose writings in 1923 opened this chapter, do specifically, and what other Palestinian authors of village books do more generally, is invert the hierarchy of knowledges. Thus, within their own communities, directly and publicly, they assert that they know that part of the past better because they are using sources who lived that history. I am not advocating in favor of one or another of these sources; instead, my point here is to understand how Palestinians are engaging with and responding to the knowledge produced about them. Not only do the village books by and about Palestinians claim the right for Palestinians to tell their own stories and thus exert control over their own history, but they also claim the power they have invested in knowledge and knowledge production.

NARRATING MEMORIES

Memories also have meaning within the context of their forms of narration and communication. As people convey their memories to others through storytelling or writing, the narrative structure of how people communicate defines how the memory can be understood. "Memory needs a place, a context. Its place, if it finds one that lives beyond a single generation, is to be found in the stories we tell."[57] Elizabeth Tonkin's extensive work on how people talk about their pasts confirms that they

> are social beings who *must* bring previous understandings to their lived experience in order to interpret it. And, when they try to proffer this experience in words, they will turn to known formulations, modes and genres to do so. This may mean that deeply felt experiences appear cliché-ridden, but even the most "original" experience has to be represented through accepted rules of language and of narrative production.[58]

The process of expressing an experience from the past in language (oral or written) requires putting it in a structure and style that the audience can comprehend. In this vein, we know that as people communicate, they do so with a notion of their action: "human beings, including 'native informants,' never speak without attempting to form an idea, a theory, of what they are speaking about, to whom, and why."[59] Michael Kenny's work among the First Nations peoples in Canada explores how people put their memories into known frameworks, which inevitably alters the memory and its associations that were once inside people's minds: "They are dependent on an acceptable narrative frame for their telling—a place for memory, and a merging of individual and collective history."[60]

Furthermore, the form and content of memories are closely linked to the historical moment when memories take on a public role and presence. Kenny's work in Canada in the 1990s shows that it is not enough for people to express their memories; there also has to be a time and place for it to be heard. He found that "native people who endured the [residential] schools have a story to tell, but only lately has a space been opened up for the story to be not only told but heard, and not only heard but perpetuated in the collective memory."[61]

Once individual memories are told or become part of accepted public knowledge, they take on a role in forming a collective understanding of the past.[62]

In addition to the political environment and the social and cultural context that encourages (or discourages) people to tell their personal stories, the chosen modes of narration are bound by similar forces of social acceptability, cultural mores, and artistic expression. Alessandro Portelli proposes three different history-telling modes that provide "ways of organizing historical narrative in terms of point of view, social, and spatial referents." The first mode is the *institutional* mode, which is spatially located in relation to the nation or state in reference to politics and governments. In this mode, the telling of the story often switches to the third person impersonal. The second mode is the *communal* mode, which refers to the community in a local space and uses the first person plural. The third mode is that of the *personal*, which references the individual and his or her home space using the first person singular.[63] According to Portelli, narrators constantly shift in and out of these different modes, and "history-telling is precisely the art of combining the modes into meaningful patterns."

The meaningful patterns of history-telling, via the different referential modes that Portelli proposes, help those of us who listen to people's stories make sense of them.[64] What I find so compelling about Portelli's delineation of narrative modes is that they map onto my experience of listening to and reading Palestinian narratives about the past. In both textual and oral accounts, individual Palestinian narrators shift among institutional subjects (colonial government actions, political treaties, and state policies, and so on), local events (such as harvest seasons, weddings, economic strikes, and military resistance), and personal accounts (for example, their friends on the school playground, how the British broke into the house and arrested their father, and how they fled the village). When I was conducting oral histories, I construed these shifts in subject to my presence as a foreigner, and thus assumed that they wanted to make sure I understood the larger framework of political events in order to put their life stories into perspective. And although that was undoubtedly true, I have also come to see that even when Palestinians tell their stories to one another, they choose to create narratives that make sense of history with multiple referents—such as larger institutional forces, local community actions, and their own thoughts and deeds.

Ultimately, as people communicate their memories of the past, how they chose to form and cast their stories influences the ways in which others can understand and contextualize them, as both individual and communal explanations of historical circumstances. People who narrate their memories choose specific genres and methods of narration that are also part of a cultural memory, or perhaps a memory of culture.[65] The following section discusses the cultural and narrative specificity of the types of narration chosen by the village book authors within the context of the Arab historiographical tradition.

NARRATING MEMORIES IN THE VILLAGE BOOKS:
ARAB HISTORY AND THE ACADEMIC PRESENT

Arabic has been a written language for a millennium and a half, and texts of a historical nature have appeared in a variety of forms since the ninth century CE.[66] Arab historiography consists of written historical traditions imbricated with Arab oral and narrative styles.[67] As was usual throughout much of the world, literacy was low prior to the mid-twentieth century. The huge advances in literacy across economic classes and gender in the Arab world in the last fifty years has begun to change people's relationship to oral narratives and performances.[68] As illustrated earlier, Palestinians still turn to their older family members for these individuals' recollections of the past. At the same time, they are educated in Arab and Muslim history and read both old and modern history texts. Built thus from both oral and written traditions, Palestinians' contemporary understanding of history is made up of a bricolage of sources, styles and subjects.

Palestinian village book authors, as educated, literate Arabs, draw on both the tradition of written history that they learn in schools and the environment of oral transmission via the stories they have heard from their elders. They all incorporate memories, communicated to them in oral form, into their texts. This transfer to the written book form entails the authors choosing from among narrative styles and engaging with the historical influences surrounding the use of oral accounts in historical texts.

The village book authors rely on two different styles and languages. Some of the authors, particularly those who wrote the first books in Birzeit University's CRDPS village book series under the supervision of Sharif Kanaana, create texts that rely almost entirely on the oral histories they collected for the project. Many of these authors quote the interviewees verbatim in colloquial Arabic. This style follows the conventions in folklore and heritage studies and an academic style used in anthropology.[69] A few other village books not in this series also adopt this story-telling colloquial mode of writing history. The vast majority of authors, however, use a different narrative style: they collected stories and memories of the past and then rewrote the text in their own words in modern standard Arabic.[70]

These two styles of composing texts based on oral accounts harken back to early Arabic composition styles that continued into the twentieth century. Stephen Humphreys describes how early Islamic history was written down in the ninth century but retained attributes of the oral-based transmission system of the previous centuries. In these early written histories, the authors of the texts have different roles. In one style, the author's role is organizational: he divides the history into subjects and then quotes stories from known narrators related to that subject. Humphreys refers to this as the *compilation* style. In the other style of history-writing, the one that is more common today both in Arabic and in modern academic history, the author relies on the stories and narration of others and then retells history in his or her own words.[71]

These early examples of how oral material became texts illustrate Mikhail Bakhtin's belief that the interaction between spoken and written genres fundamentally affects the written text; speech genres, as reflected in "certain types of oral dialogue," penetrate written language and fundamentally change literary styles.[72] In the Arab world, oral and written forms have interacted for centuries. This is illustrated in Arabic literature and history, where oral compositions were recorded later as written texts, influencing generations of scholars and poets, who also memorized them as part of their corpus of knowledge and could cite and recite them from memory.[73]

The compilation style retains the authority of the quoted person, who as narrator remains responsible for the information that he or she recounts, to tell the story. This style of compiling quotes has largely faded in the twentieth century but can be seen in parts of al-Dabbagh's monumental work *Our Country Palestine*, which all of the village book authors reference.[74] The second style, the reauthored and rewritten version, subsumes authority for the proffered information under the name of the author. It is this style that the majority of the village books are written in, for reasons that will be elaborated on shortly. In a sense, these two styles of writing pit oral history techniques—which grow out of an egalitarian sense of allowing everyone to participate in the recording of history—against collective forces that want to control representation and the author's authority to include and exclude.

As history-narrating styles shape some of the authors' choices of voice and attribution, other communal and political forces also fashion how stories are put into written form and published. Palestinians fear the power of the state or military authorities to inflict punishments on the basis of what is written and attributed to them. In the introduction to the first volume of the *Destroyed Palestinian Villages* series, project supervisor and coauthor Sharif Kanaana explains some of the issues that the CRDPS dealt with when collecting oral histories of people from 'Ayn Hawd village:

> Among the difficulties we faced was the reluctance of those we met to grant us information. They either feared offending others from the village or, as was the case most of the time, they feared punishment by the Israeli authorities. For these reasons, and out of respect for the feelings and desires of the villagers, we will not ascribe the quotations or detailed information to specific people. Instead we will mention all of the names of those who helped us with information, and reference the information in this book to all of the villagers as a group.[75]

The aura of communal disapproval and retributive fear constrains and restricts how authors attribute stories to individuals. 'Abdallah al-Sufi, author of the 'Innaba village book, and I discussed how to collect information from a variety of former village residents, and the type of picture that such a method would create of the village. His hesitation in talking to everyone and including what they said was that he wanted both to get accurate information and to ensure the collective approval of his representation of the village in his book.

> We have a village association here in Amman. I left 'Innaba when I was thirteen. But the people in the association left when they were in their thirties or forties, so they knew the information that I wrote about, or at the very least knew it better than I do. And I wanted to make sure the information was correct and acceptable. To that end, I took the handwritten draft of the book to them with everything in it, and we sat a number of times with men in their seventies and eighties and we went through it line by line. And they agreed that the information in my book gives an accurate picture of the village to the coming generation, their children and their children's children.[76]

The authors, especially those who are from the village they are writing about, often want (or are pushed) to include certain subjects, ignore others, and create a collective representation of the village that people will accept.

One author structured his process of mapping the village with this collective pressure to remember (and forget) in mind. Nabil al-Sahli from Balad al-Shaykh, a village on the outskirts of Haifa, said that one of the ways he as an author negotiated potential problems both with individuals' memories and with getting collective approval was to get his informants to correct one an-other. He gathered old people from the village together and then they "walked" through the village, talking about each house on the right and left of the path and who owned it. The old men altogether, he said, could remind and correct each other so that no one claimed more than their fair share of land and no one was forgotten.[77] These accounts illustrate the role of the individual's story and how it functions in a text compared to an individual story or individual memory of an event that is then exposed to a collective process that negotiates its truth value, its representativeness, and its value to village history.[78]

READING VILLAGE BOOKS

The questions that arise around the advantages and disadvantages of the different forms of writing history and the attribution made by authors also allow us to explore how people read and understand the stories within the narrative choices that authors make. The different styles of narration are also concerned with issues of authority and responsibility for the informa-tion rendered. The compilation style (the first style) of history-writing, which puts individual stories side by side, makes the storyteller responsible for his or her own story and decreases the authority of the author. At the same time, it makes known the source of the information and, if presented in colloquial Arabic, also jars the readers into awareness of social and class differences by writing in the village dialect. (The Palestinian village dialect is almost never written, because if someone knows how to write, they can write in stan-dard Arabic or modified colloquial Arabic.) The reauthored style (the second style) of history-writing, in which the author uses sources without attribu-tion and retells events in an omniscient voice, devolves the authority for the information onto the author himself or herself. As it usurps an unnamed individual's knowledge, it also protects the identity of the original oral narra-tor, and standardizes the presentation into a textual form that is authoritative in the modern period and acceptable among the educated classes.

Two examples from stories about education in the two different narrative styles allow me to elaborate on how each style might be read and under-stood. The following story illustrates the collective representation of the re-authored style:

> Al-Walaja, like the neighboring villages, had the *kuttab* system of education at the end of the Ottoman period and the beginning of the British Mandate.

[In the *kuttab*] the students studied Islam, the Qur'an, the Arabic language, and arithmetic. Students stayed in the *kuttab* until they had finished reading the Qur'an. A celebration would be held for this occasion and the *shaykh* and students of the *kuttab* would go to the house of the student who had completed the reading to have lunch. Students who finished a part of the Qur'an would also distribute sweets to their fellow students. This situation lasted until 1938. The boys of al-Walaja would study in the home of the teacher for a minimal fee.[79]

This narrative style removes personal impressions and experiences and offers the information as a factual component of the village history. It is also a story that every villager can tell and that can be adopted by all, even if they or their parents or grandparents did not go to school; there *was* a school in the village and this is what happened in that school. Such a presentation of the material collectivizes an experience that was not collective. Studying in the *kuttab* is a unique memory in al-Walaja, privileged to only one sector of the population (boys) and further constrained to only those whose families could afford not only the trifling fees but, more important, the absence of their sons' labor. However, in this narrative, the story is told as if it were a shared event to which no one person is attached. Historical events are made timeless and agentless in this way. The school simply exists in the home of the village teacher, an individual whose name is never specified.

I interviewed one of the four authors of the Walaja village book about their methods of collecting information and composing the text. He said that they each met with a number of old men and wrote down their stories. Then the four authors met and pulled out the things that at least two of the old men agreed on and put them into the first draft of the book.[80] As did many authors I interviewed, they thought this method would provide them with the most accurate material, which may be the case. However, in addition, it also ensured the most agreed-upon representation. They then composed the stories in their own words and language, using the reauthored style of history writing. They chose collective methods to write history that turned individual stories and memories into unobjectionable (and anonymous) stories vetted and accepted by people who use them to represent the history of the village. Thus, by presenting collective portrayals of village life, the authors of the village books ensure that they are telling about the village in a general, factual manner.

Contrast the preceding account of education with the following description from Birzeit University's CRDPS village book about Miska. The inclusion of this person's story in his own words closely follows the compilation style of history-telling, in which an individual's story is told, followed by another person's story. This narrative style portrays a complex and multivocal image of the past. I include one story here to provide an idea of the content and storytelling element of this narrative style.

> The room for the *kuttab* was in the center of town, very close to the mosque. It was in the guesthouse of Dar al-Dahmasi, then they moved it to the east, maybe to Dar Jabr. Shaykh 'Abd al-Hafiz al-Zuhd taught in it, and he had studied in Nablus with Shaykh 'Abdallah Sufan. Then the *kuttab* was in the *matban* (storeroom) of Sulayman Abu Tahun in Bab al-Zawiya, which belonged to Salim al-Dahmas. Shaykh 'Abd al-Rahman 'Abd al-'Aziz taught the children there. He used to teach in Kafr Saba and would also come teach in Miska. Nabiha, the daughter of Yusif al-Shina'a, snuck in among the students when she was little, and she learned [how to read and write] and could read the Qur'an really well. After Shaykh al-Zuhd, we had a man come from Tulkarm named 'Arif al-'Awwad, and he was truly educated and had studied a lot and wrote poetry. He taught the children of Miska during the British Mandate period. [. . .] After the Second World War, Ahmad Samih al-Khalidi, the education inspector, came to our village while touring the country to chose students for fellowships. He asked me the first question, "Son, do you know—slowly and quietly because I can hear an ant walking on the ground—the genealogy of the blessed one [Muhammad]?" I told him yes, so he said, "Tell me, so I can see." So I said, "He is Muhammad bin 'Abdallah bin 'Abd al-Mutalab bin Hashim bin 'Abd al-Munaf bin Qusai bin Kulayb bin Malik bin al-Nidhr bin Kinana bin al-Ghazina bin Mudrika bin Mughiz bin 'Adnan." He told me, good job, and asked me, "Fine, clever boy, do you know how to divide? If someone gave you ten pounds and told you to divide them among four, how much would each one get?" I told him, two and a half pounds. He said, that's enough. He wrote down that this student must be given a scholarship to go to Jerusalem. I was about ten or twelve at the time. My relatives got upset and didn't want to send me, and my mother said, Oh my God, my son go to Jerusalem?! I was the only child of my mother and she didn't want me to go away from her. She went and begged Inspector al-Khalidi that he not take me.[81]

I include this full story with all of the names and details, despite its length, to illustrate the qualities of this individual account that explicates not only the personal but also the collective history of education.

The authors of the village book have allowed this man to tell stories of education from his perspective that are richer and more detailed than the other account. But such individual stories are also communal: "It shows that far from dealing only with ourselves when we tell about the past, we incorporate the experience of a multitude of others along with our own; they appear in what we say through our marvellous capacity to express other perspectives."[82] Thus we also learn about the village in general from this individual story—that certain villagers had extra space that they could provide or rent out for a school. The teachers were not local; they instead came from other towns and villages and also taught elsewhere. This man's story allows for the gendered basis of education at that time to come to light. The fact that a girl wanted to go to school with the boys (there seems to have been no school for girls in Miska at this time) and was ultimately allowed to stay and learn the Qur'an implicitly informs us that *kuttab* education was almost exclusively for boys and she had to sneak in, but ultimately neither the shaykh nor her parents objected to her attendance. These personal remembrances are rich with names and places, and here the storyteller also tells of his own success in school. He relates his opportunity to go to Jerusalem and complete his studies.[83] This story can be read and understood in the larger context in which the events took place, and as illustrative of other things uncontextualized and hinted at in documents and photographs. For example, the Balad al-Shaykh village book reproduces the Palestine matriculation certificate of Yunis 'Abd al-Hafiz al-Sahli, who, like the narrator in the Miska account, was likely recruited because of his high marks to attend the Rashidiya secondary school in Jerusalem, from which he graduated in 1943. But the Balad al-Shaykh book does not tell the story of how a villager from near Haifa left his home and went to Jerusalem to attend one of the best high schools in the country at the time. No story accompanies al-Sahli's certificate, and his tale is untold.[84]

The Miska villager's nuanced and detailed account of his educational experiences would be flattened by a generalized paragraph on education before 1948. This personal story, and all those that are rendered in this style, is told here as an experience that happened to someone and that sheds light on the society and education system of the time. But they can also just be retold as a meaningful story. This type of narrating and history-writing brings these voices (complete with their village pronunciations and idioms) into written forms and public spaces where they can be read, recited, refuted, enjoyed, acknowledged, and recognized by others.[85] Most important, by maintaining the narrative words and style of the storyteller, individual experiences become part of, rather than stand in for, collective experiences.

.   .   .

As Palestinians explore writing about their past, in the absence of other historical sources they find that their own memories are what remain and are available to them to tell their history. Without Palestinian accounts told on their own terms, we would have little material with which to reconstruct their experiences and lives. Palestinians, as individuals telling their stories and as village book authors, take oral testimony and recounted memories and turn them into narrative structures that rarely conform to Western historical forms. The subjects and narrative styles used to write these culturally situated memories are specific to the Arab historical and cultural past.

The authors of the Palestinian village books have set out to make a written record—where none existed—of the places of their past and to create a new body of written knowledge documenting that past. Their primary sources, by their own design and by virtue of what exists, are the memories of people who lived in the villages. As Margaret Somers theorizes, narratives are crucial to the creation, propagation, and persistence of social life, social practices, and social analyses.[86] In some cases, these memories are almost all that is left of villages destroyed more than sixty years ago whose populations are displaced in two, three, or more countries. But memory takes precedence over what limited written documentary evidence exists, not only because memory is Palestinians' own source, but also because the written sources were made about them by others (largely the British Mandate authorities).[87] For Palestinians, writing histories of villages long-ago destroyed on the basis of the stories and memories of their inhabitants constitutes a public declaration of their memories as a valid source for presenting their perspectives and experiences. This assertion of their past exists within strong institutional opposition to the use of Palestinian memory as a historical source, precisely because giving it validity means taking seriously what is expressed.

Personal memories serve to validate what existed and to give testimony to a Palestine once registered as a tangible entity on maps. People have felt compelled to tell and record their stories as part of a larger trend to counteract the effacing nature of Israeli-centered history. The texts and oral accounts that come from people's memories assert the physical, emotional, and moral attachments of the Palestinians to their homeland. In a difficult atmosphere in which Palestinian assertions of historical rights and the applicability of international laws are contested and the documents of the past are regularly deconstructed and reinterpreted, Palestinians have turned to themselves and their memories as historical sources. Take, for example, the conversation between Salman Rushdie and Edward Said, published in Rushdie's *Imaginary Homelands*. Rushdie asked Said, as a Palestinian, "Doesn't this need to go back again and again over the same story become tiring?" Said replied,

> It does, but you do it anyway. It is like trying to find the magical moment when everything starts. . . . But it is very hard to do that because you have to work out everything and get past a lot of questions in the daily press about why Palestinians don't just stay where they are and stop causing trouble. That immediately launches you into a tremendous harangue, as you explain to people, "My mother was born in Nazareth, my father was born in Jerusalem. . . ." The interesting thing is that there seems to be nothing in the world which sustains the story: unless you go on telling it, it will just drop and disappear.[88]

In telling the story of Palestinian history, of when that history started, even noted literary scholar Edward Said turns to the personal to illustrate the past. With increasing frequency, Palestinians tell history through their personal stories and family chronicles, or by writing histories of a particular time that incorporate personal accounts as part of the narrative.[89] Personal experience counters historical renditions of events by becoming a source that can be negated only by proving that it did not happen, a difficult task in the majority of cases.[90] By focusing on how Palestinian village book authors base their work in the authority of memory, this chapter has analyzed how those authors claim an authority of experience both to prove their existence and to counteract their discursive displacement from history, a dispossession that tries to mirror their physical displacement from Palestine. We move next to discussing how Palestinians map the village cartographically as well as in stories and poems, in ways that reflect this authority of experience.

6 MAPPING THE PAST: THE VILLAGE LANDSCAPE

London, England: 1950s

"Are you the Canaans of Nablus or the Canaans of Jerusalem?" my mother would ask. My father, who prided himself on knowing every inch of Palestine, often joined in. But sometimes he was stumped when someone cited the name of a small village. He would worry at it until he found it. "Ah," he would suddenly say, "it's in the district of Jaffa! Why didn't you say so at first?"

For years, I thought this obsession with places and family names and who was related to whom was just a quirk of my parents. My sister and I used to imitate them in our bedroom after a particularly grueling interrogation with some hapless Palestinian visitor and laugh and shake our heads. It took me years to realize that after 1948, establishing a person's origin became for Palestinians a kind of mapping, a surrogate repopulation of Palestine in negation of the *nakba*. It was their way of recreating the lost homeland, as if the families and the villages and the relations they had once known were all still there, waiting to be reclaimed.[1]

Ghada Karmi, in this recollection of her family's life in London, recognizes her parents' interrogation of other Palestinians as part of maintaining Palestine in the diaspora—as she says, of "recreating the lost homeland." In the face of the 1948 War, its upheaval, and the destruction of communal and family ties, Palestinians have maintained these mental maps that assign Palestinians to geographical locations and origins, even if those places no longer exist on the ground. The pre-1948 physical places and all that attended them have become conceptual and memorial spaces maintained and shared through many forms and forums.

In this chapter, I present the different methods of mapping the past that are employed in the village books: cartographic maps, lists, poems, journeys, and maps of return. The different forms used to map the places of the past suggest a variety of ways in which these spaces are shaped and claimed as places, post-1948, through the authority of knowledge and experience. These maps that people create are not only about mapping what is gone, but also about mapping certain places that remain as markers of what was once there. Because Palestinian maps of the pre-1948 landscape consist not only of place names, as is common in cartographic representations, but also of experiences, values, and idealizations, understanding how Palestinians represent pre-1948 spaces and places in visual and verbal forms relates directly to the identities that Palestinians are actively creating in the present.

HISTORIES OF PLACE

In form and content, the Palestinian village books share similarities with many other books and manuscripts while also clearly evoking an indigenous tradition of Arab-Islamic writings about places. In terms of content, the village books are part of a genre of a certain kind of writing about destroyed places, a genre neither entirely original nor solely devoted to the destroyed Palestinian villages. As discussed previously, the village books share many similarities with the Jewish memorial books about the communities destroyed in Europe during the Holocaust, as well as with the Armenian and Bosnian books. In terms of both form and content, the village books, however, have grown out of a hybrid Arab historical-geographical writing tradition that produces place histories. The Encyclopedia of Islam's entry on history describes the local histories of urban cities that were first produced in the eleventh century CE and continue up to the present. These local histories

> used a systematic catalogue of a city's important sites and monuments as the framework for the presentation of a wide variety of historical and biographical materials. Typically, an urban topography would proceed site by site, describing the circumstances under which a particular edifice was erected, then appending biographical sketches of the key persons associated with that monument. In this way the physical fabric of the city is linked to the men and women who created and sustained it, and embodies their purposes, values and acts.[2]

This tradition of writing about places encompasses more than just physical spaces; it also connects those spaces to people, events, actions, social relations, and cultural production.

Contemporary Arab authors continue to write local histories in this form about extant villages and cities in Syria, Lebanon, Jordan, and Palestine, among other countries.[3] I have collected more than one hundred such books in Arabic. The authors of these local histories, particularly those about rural areas, concern themselves with documenting the past, especially in terms of folklore, heritage, and cultural traditions.[4] Like the books about the destroyed villages, they include descriptions of agricultural practices, genealogies, and material objects such as coffee roasters, dresses, and house decorations, among other subjects, and they contain pictures of the village then and now ("now" being a built-up, modern lived-in space as opposed to the forests, fields, and piles of rocks that are pictured in the books about the destroyed villages). Similarly, they chronicle the changing village landscape and culture, and rely largely on memory and on mentions of the place in traditional history texts to compose these narratives. Unlike the books about the destroyed Palestinian villages, however, the local histories document a geography that is still inhabited and that connects the villagers' lives to these places. Theirs is a geography of possession—a geography that may describe longing for long-gone ways of life while still being present in the place. This fundamental difference between the local histories of still-extant villages and the books about the destroyed villages marks how the authors denote, remember, and write about these places and spaces. The authors' own displacement engenders a desire to document in ways that recreate that absent physical space, and this chapter explores the visual, verbal, and experiential mappings of the destroyed villages that are included in the village books.

MAPPING THE PAST

For the Palestinian villagers who became refugees in 1948 and were separated completely from their places and lands, their memorializations of the village later on in book form can be understood as an attempt both to recreate and present the village as it existed prior to 1948, and to emphasize their historical claims not only to the past but also to the present and future.

Creating maps hinges on several issues, and what is seen and what is to be represented are central aspects of what the final map will look like. The Palestinian village books convey maps not of a time forgotten but of places that no longer exist. Creating maps of those places relies on the author's specific memories, as well as on the memories of those he solicits. We all know that people look at a landscape and see completely different things, depending on their age, education, gender, historical knowledge, and national identity, among many other factors. The act of seeing, then, is completely tied up in the historical processes that humans create and in which they participate. The act of transferring what is seen and internalized into a representation for others pushes us to consider form, language, politics, ideology, and history—all of which are part of my analysis.

Not all was destroyed in the villages. Certain landmarks remain: the minaret of the mosque of al-'Abbasiyya, now an Israeli 1948 War commemorative site; the *mukhtar's* house in Ijzim, turned into a bed and breakfast inn; the roofless and windowless school in Kafr Saba; the locked churches in Ma'loul and Kafr Bir'im; the mosques in 'Ayn Hawd (refashioned as a restaurant), Salama (once a club but now closed), and al-Ghabisiyya (disintegrating behind rolls of razor wire), among others. Contemporary photographs of pre-1948 places that still exist are presented as evidence of the village's past and continued presence; visual documentation of ruins supplement the stories and documents presented in the books. These visual and verbal representations record places whose functions have changed and that stand as markers for all of the rest of the Palestinian village now absent, for the most part, from that physical space. The fact that the villages no longer exist, either in space or in social worlds, does not lessen their representative power. And just as the physical recording of these memories in books is inscribed by the past, the act of maintaining this information as knowledge reinscribes the history of what existed and what Palestinians experienced.

To the villagers in the present, places function differently from the other subjects recorded in the memorial books. For example, villagers may still sing the wedding songs, or at the very least revive, perform, or record them; likewise, family lineages are part of a continual process that the villagers modify as they have children and their children have children—affected by the diaspora of 1948, but not erased. Even material practices such as embroidery and basket making are revived in forms of modern dress and home decoration. These cultural practices and material objects are tied to a notion of "tradition" that draws on a "past" but is also incorporated into the body of the "present," linked through cultural continuity, continuing social traditions, and modified material practices. The village places, however, are physically unavailable, either because people are separated by war and borders from their villages or the actual places have been plowed under, forested over, or allowed to fall into ruin.

In the face of this physical removal and distance, the village memorial books focus on retaining place names in order to record and memorialize places that no longer exist, that cannot be revisited, photographed, or even re-created. Pierre Nora proposes a useful way to think about how humans conceive of places in the past: as *lieux de mémoire*, realms or sites of memory, which are concrete places, objects, and gestures that symbolize a break with the past. As Nora explains, "The moment of *lieux de mémoire* occurs at the same time that an immense and intimate fund of memory disappears, surviving only as a reconstituted object beneath the gaze of critical history. This period sees, on the one hand, the decisive deepening of historical study and, on the other hand, a heritage consolidated."[5] Palestinians position the village and its physical spaces as carriers of all that was pre-1948 history, creating maps in a variety of forms to recall and record village places in order to recreate and connect them to the social worlds and natural landscapes of pre-1948 Palestine.

MAPPING THE PHYSICAL LANDSCAPE

The maps that Palestinians make of destroyed villages are not just about the physical places they record, but also about the complex world expressed in social, natural, labor, economic, and kin relations in the village. As Denis Wood explains, "the very point of the map [is] to present us not with the world we can *see*, but to point *toward* a world we might *know*."[6] Visually striking for their detail, the cartographic maps in the village books illustrate the physical landscape of the village, its buildings and lands. The variety of maps that authors include in the village books situate the village within historic Palestine and the villages around it, as well as providing details about the village layout and landscape. In fact, 60 of the 112 books in my collection contain some sort of drawn map of the village; some are very general, others are filled with incredible detail. Drawn after 1948, the maps mark what the mapmaker or author deems to be the essential components of the village, neighborhood, or town: wells, caves, valleys, hills, paths, plots of farmland, buildings, mosques, churches, trees, cafes, and stores. The Dayr Aban village book, for example, includes six maps that mark, respectively, the locations of the houses in the three neighborhoods of the village, the roads and agricultural areas, the springs and valleys, the hills and mountains, the landmarks and borders, and the religious and archaeological sites.[7] These maps, like all maps, express different ways of seeing the world, marking what is important at a particular time or place or to a particular population.[8] Here they map physically visible spaces—roads, houses, wells, orchards—that were used by the villagers, thus creating a geography of everyday life in two-dimensional form. The maps and lists of these elements define a particular village and the intertwining relationship between geography and human habitation. Any reading of these maps suggests the close relationship of the villagers to the land.

The geography, however, has been significantly changed. The maps cannot now be used, because the intervening years have brought new places, new buildings, new people, new farming techniques, and forests and shopping malls onto the village lands.[9] Are they then just maps of the past or maps of memory? Given the Palestinian-Israeli struggle over land, the very act of creating the map of the past claims an authority to know—by listing names of places, people show their knowledge of that place—and to imprint their presence on the land through this authority of knowledge. This authority serves to maintain Palestinians' ties to pre-1948 Palestinian land; by showing their intimate and familiar relationship to as well as their former dependence on the land, the maps help individuals continue to define themselves as Palestinians and as belonging to a particular village. While Palestinians create a visual representation of what was once physically there, at the same time they also assert an origin for who they are today in the social world of Palestinians in the diaspora. And they chronicle what existed and still exists in the natural world (hills, springs, trees) of then and now.

This assertion of the authority of experience, expressed through the cartographic representation of what once was, exists in contrast to the Zionist and Israeli discursive, then actual, uprooting of Palestinians from the land. The Zionist discourse of the late nineteenth and twentieth centuries propagated the idea of Palestinians as aliens to the land, invaders, and not deserving to live there because of their lifestyles and sentiments.[10] The idea of an uprooted people, according to Liisa Malkki, is one of a people living on the margins, a people that has been stripped of the specificity of their experience, having no recognizable cultural topography.[11] When someone (or something) is without roots to a place or a space, it becomes easy for others to move, assign to another place, or give it another ascriptive belonging.

These beliefs preceded the physical removal of Palestinians that occurred during the fighting of the 1948 War.[12] Although the Jewish state that was designated in the Palestine partition plan of 1947 was to have a population of 500,000 Jews and 416,000 Arabs,[13] the Israeli census (population registry) in

1948 recorded a total population of 806,000, of whom 145,080 were Arabs.[14] The low number of Arabs, despite the fact that the new Israeli state included territories beyond its UN-designated borders, was a result of the evictions of Palestinians and their exodus during the 1948 War. In the years that immediately followed, Israel received huge numbers of immigrants from the Arab countries and Europe[15] while the Palestinians in the north of the country and the Triangle continued to be transferred outside of the borders.[16] These population removals have continued to the present, particularly since the 1967 War, in Israeli government policies and support for the settler movement in the West Bank and Gaza Strip, and in extraditions, targeted killings, denial of residency and family reunification permits, and a multitude of bureaucratic policies and military actions that prevent Palestinians from living in Israel, the West Bank, and Gaza.[17] Despite the displacement of more than half of the Palestinian population in the 1948 and 1967 Wars, Palestinians have maintained a sense of themselves as members of a Palestinian nation through practices such as remaining connected to their natal villages, towns, and cities.

MAPS OF PLACE

In the village books, Palestinian authors create other ways beyond the cartographic maps of mapping the physical landscape—in descriptions of places and in lists of natural features and names. For example, the Dayr Aban village map includes the names of such places as Jabal Haqrus, 'Ayn Umm 'Abbus, Hariqat Aslan, Shi'b Bir al-Nahal, Shi'b al-Husayniyyat, Wad Qarayqa', and al-Marj.[18] These place names evoke mountains, springs, land with a creek running through it, valleys, a long-ago fire, and flatlands. By learning these names, the village descendants can also learn about the topography of the landscape. Furthermore, lists of natural and man-made landmarks reveal the names and locations of what Palestinian villagers conceive of as the important places in the village. They reveal that the relationship of the peasants to the landscape is derived from knowing and harnessing its productivity for work and life in a particular landscape. Like cartography, mapping places through lists retains the knowledge of names and places, even if they have been divested of social meaning, significance, and context. Divorced from their everyday use and their history, these places are made meaningful through the list form, which quantifies them as knowledge, signifying Palestinians' relationship to the land through knowledge of it.

Other narrative styles that provide village place names are more descriptive but serve similarly to show the authority of experience. Mahmud Sa'id's book on Tirat Haifa describes the crops and the places they were grown in a way that only someone with knowledge of the land could comprehend.

> We were lucky in Tirat Haifa because hills are the best place to grow grapes, and we had them at *Khirbat Yunis* [Jonah's Ruins] and *al-Masliyya*. The people of Tirat Haifa also grew figs and almonds next to grapes on the hills. There was a big grape vineyard near the pool of the spring, and in a place called *Farash al-Halaqa*, which belonged to the Abu 'Issa family, and they had grapes and many trees. Another place was at the end of *Wadi Fallah* [Peasant's Valley], which was the one that began at the end of the area called *Imsakkar Babu* [Closed Its Door], which stretched east about 1,000 meters from the bridge on the main road between Haifa and Jaffa, east of the 'Atleet police station. This was a fertile area for bananas and pomegranates, and at the higher reaches of the valley to the east there was a waterfall, which made an attractive place with the many fruit and pine trees.[19]

This description of the land in Tirat Haifa for growing grapes and other fruit is evidence that the narrator (or his source) is someone who knew the land and worked it. His story is like a cartographic map that indicates only vineyards and orchards, with the narrative map jumping from marked place to marked place, and described in relation to other landmarks known to the villagers (the hills, the pool, the valley). The narrative style takes knowledge of the land into account, and for a reader who has never been to the place or heard detailed stories, it is difficult to envision or understand the spaces and how they connect to each other and to the village without that knowledge. But their connection to the villagers themselves is clear.

For many village book authors, preserving the names of significant places is more than just an act of geographic nostalgia or an element of authoritative claims to knowledge. According to anthropologist Kathleen Stewart, recalling and remembering places allows us to create "a narrative space opened against the naturalized flow of the everyday." She believes that "*places* on the side of the road stand as icons of things that happen and the people they happen to."[20] In this sense, recalling certain places also references events associated with them, and the significant moments in individual memories and the villagers' collective lives. In the case of the village of Qalunya, maps and descriptions provide the locations of all of the springs in the village, but the author's account of the different wells not only lists and locates them but also describes who owned each and what role the wells played in the villagers' lives.

> Among the other notable wells in the village were the well of the Mosque of Shaykh Hamad; the well of Muhammad 'Ali Salama 'Askar; the well of Dar Khalil in al-Matayin, east of al-Jifir; the well of Dar 'Isa Hamdan; and the well of al-Msawwis on the lands of al-Safha, the one that a village woman fell into when she accompanied her husband to work on the land there.
>
> The people of the village dug a collective well on their land in the area of Dayr Nahla, near the village of al-Qubab, that everyone benefited from during the harvest and threshing. I remember perfectly the well of Mustafa Ramadan, in the area of Bayt Mazza. It was the only well that had water in it year round, among the seven wells found there, that belonged to the clan of 'Askar in Bayt Mazza, the northernmost part of our village of Qalunya. Those wells were known as "rain-fed wells" and were known from Roman times. The winter rains would collect in them; the wells depended only on the rains and surface runoff [collected through small channels], and had no underground water source. Unfortunately, I have seen how neglect has affected these wells; they are now dry all year long.[21]

As the stories associated with this list of wells suggest, the wells played a key role in villagers' lives. The villagers' knowledge of the natural resources and how best to use them—in this case, how to store rainwater, as passed down from Roman times—are also used to mark the author's knowledge of the village and to enhance the readers' familiarity and intimacy with the land. These accounts tie people, incidents, and groups to particular geographic features, creating ties between physical locations and the shared history of the village.

The author of the Mallaha village book, Yusif 'Abd al-'Aal, narrates through his father's stories not only the physical area of the village but also the characteristics associated with each place his father remembers:

> My father told me in his many recollections of al-Mallaha about the cooperation and affection between the families and villages in Palestine. He talked about the village of Baysamoun and its residents, Jahula and its people and our alliances with them, 'Almaniyya and its clean air and orchards, al-Khalisa and its generosity, and the al-Nabi Yashu' with its evening parties, *dabka* dancing, and endless amounts of meat. . . . He told us about the weddings and festivals, about the fish [. . .], the wheat and the corn and the oranges. [In detailing all of these things,] he told a story of going with his friends to a wedding in al-Khalisa

village, and when they arrived, seeing the black goat-hair tents set up for the guests, each almost fifty meters long. He also remembered that there was so much food and so many guests that the trays of *mansaf* (meat cooked in yogurt and served with rice) had to be distributed with help.[22] He said that he had never seen in his life such generosity.[23]

Through this recollection, the immediate environment around the village is re-created, if only in broad brushstrokes. Although 'Abd al-'Aal acknowledged in our interview that his book is really more the history and stories of his own family, within a narrative place structure, in the book he presents the village as part of a larger whole, which he also deems should be known. "We must teach our children everything about our homeland, our village, our history, and our identity, through knowledge and information, not just emotion. We must do that through studying books and maps and history. This way they will know Palestine . . . and Safad and Haifa and al-Ja'una and Mallaha and al-Khalisa and Jahula . . . and all of Palestine."[24] He places the importance of being Palestinian within the frame of places—from the larger homeland to the big cities to the small villages.

Mapping the homeland is made possible, the authors of the village book believe, through making connections between places and experiences. Deeb Kan'aan writes in his book on Ishwa':

> The homeland is not just land; it is more than that: fields of infancy, playgrounds of childhood, caprice of youth, the councils of elders [*majalis al-uns*]. It is the collection of life's memories filled with the cares and feelings of hope and pain. The stone in a place has a meaning, as does the tree; the homeland is the relationship between a person and their environment and all that it contains of people, animals, birds, plants, stones, and earth. If you visit the ruins with a guide, you'll find the stones and trees will tell stories, and you'll enter a world where the dead live and the place throbs with life, surrounded by relatives and friends.[25]

Kan'aan's description of the places in the homeland links individuals in a village farming culture that was dependent on the land and on people's knowledge of it to survive. But he asserts that the homeland is also made up of all the human relationships and the emotional ties that people build between each other and to spaces. This connection, he says, can be found even if the place is in ruins; someone can provide the stories that tie people to the physical landscape.

Some of the village books take on the task of educating readers about the village terms for the landscape. The book on Dayr Aban contains a list that explains the terms used to describe land:

al-shaqa: about ten dunums [10,000 square meters]

al-shi'b: land that has a shallow creek running through it

al-maris: long strip of level agricultural land

al-marah: high, flat land that slants slightly

al-jisr: smooth agricultural land that stretches between two higher places

al-jura: agricultural land that goes up on all sides, a basin

al-marj: flatland, plain

al-diba: raised agricultural land that drops down on all sides, the opposite of *al-jura*

al-ta'mira: land planted with fruit trees that is also rocky

al-misha: flat agricultural land with moist soil and wild bushes surrounding it. . . . [26]

This key would allow someone not from the village to read the place names and understand that, for example, *shi'b al-husayniyat* is the "land with the shallow creek of the foxes." Not many people aside from the peasants who farm the land have much knowledge of or even use for this vocabulary, as I found out when trying to decipher these place names. Because they are un-voweled in these books,[27] I had to ask people how to pronounce some of them so I could transliterate them into the Latin alphabet. I found that it was only people who had heard their parents speak these names and agricultural terms, or those who were old enough to remember village life, who could answer my questions. If young people do not know how to say them, then these words become names *to be read* in stories or on maps, and are no longer spoken in everyday life. So, although the village books seek to transfer this knowledge to the coming generations, that transfer is taking place in written form—not for use in navigating the village landscape or knowing where crops are to be planted, but for creating a record of the past.[28]

STORIES AS MAPS

The stories in the village books map a lived space that has depth and meaning beyond its physical, cartographic presence. The social context for the names we put on maps comes from stories, which Michel de Certeau believes define how we see places. Stories endow places with specifically selected contextual meanings. Every story, he argues, is a journey through space because it projects experience onto places through the actions of historical subjects.[29] Without a social context, the names in the lists of places and on the maps of locations of the natural and human-built environment remain just names, teetering on the edge of becoming, as the well-known Palestinian folklorist Sharif Kana'ana fears, "only names on old maps."[30] They serve as a record of history, but history that is removed from the experience of those who read the books but do not know the land. For the many who lived in and remember the village, however, these place names conjure up stories and experiences. "The symbiotic relationship between the landscape and the oral tradition is crucial," maintains Deborah Tall, because "without the land the stories will fade; without the stories, land becomes less meaningful."[31] This concept is illustrated clearly in the village book for Majdal 'Asqalan, which includes a picture of a tree in the middle of a field. The photograph itself reveals nothing other than the tree. The caption, however, reads as follows: "Majdal 'Asqalan: Seventeen martyrs of the 1936 revolt, who are known as the 'Imran Shushar group, rest under this tree."[32] It is only through the story told about the tree, about this place, that we are able to know the significance of the tree and its history in the lives of the villagers. It is the picture with the story that gives meaning, though only one of many possible stories and meanings, to this place.

Through these accounts, the places and names take on meanings beyond their role as just location markers; instead they become signifiers and ideographs of a specific past that is embodied in the names and embedded in their social construction and transmission. Working within the Western Apache naming system allowed linguistic anthropologist Keith Basso to understand how "commemorative place names, accompanied by their stories, continue to accumulate, each one marking the site of some sad or tragic event from which valuable lessons can be readily drawn and taken fast to heart."[33] In the Palestinian context, although the villages are destroyed and the people have been removed from the land, the stories still exist, and in some cases they continue to build on each other. Another of Palestinian photographer Maqbula Nassar's photographs of the village of Ijzim on PalestineRemembered.com shows a stone house with a red-tile roof. In the comments section under the photo, Hussein 'Omar Khadr 'Ali Balalta from the West Bank posted the following on March 8, 2008:

> This house with the red tile roof is the house that my grandfather Khadr 'Ali Hussein Balalta built. It is just northeast of the Ijzim mosque. It was completed in 1947 and they did not really get to enjoy it except for a few months because

[shortly thereafter] they fled to Jenin [in the West Bank], first to the Janzur refugee camp and then to the Nur al-Shams camp. In 1967, a few months after the Israeli occupation of the West Bank, when people were allowed to visit the 1948 areas, a relative of ours who lived in al-Furaydis [a village inside Israel] came to visit us in Jenin. I was about seven years old at the time. He took us—my grandfather, father, mother, and me—to visit Ijzim. We got out of the car in front of the house and an old Jewish man asked us what we wanted. My relative told him in Hebrew that these people own this house and they just want to come in and look at it. He refused and a heated argument ensued in Hebrew between him and my relative, for about ten minutes, and he threatened to call the police. Ultimately he agreed to let us enter for two minutes, without "the old guy" (saying *zaken* in Hebrew), in other words, my grandfather. I have not and will not forget the image of my grandfather going to the mosque and climbing up to the roof, where he squatted with his cane in hand and looked to the north over the village and wept. We returned to Nur al-Shams refugee camp and my grandfather became ill and died six days later. From that day, every time we've been able to, we have visited the house, although we've not been able to get too close because a major military or police officer lives there and has a guard. But these visits ensure that all of the grandchildren of Khadr ʿAli Hussein Balalta, and their children too, know the house very well, with the promise to my grandfather that we will make sure our children know it, generation after generation.[34]

This family's history remains intertwined, permanently, with this physical place (the house) because of the significance of its loss. In this man's account, he suggests that the house accumulates stories with each visit and revisit. Not only is the story of the grandfather building the house told to all who are present on the visit, but the stories of what happened on each subsequent visit are recounted as well. Without this story, visitors to this Web site would see only a renovated Palestinian home in the village of Ijzim, now taken over and renamed Kerem Maharal. But this Web site uniquely allows Palestinians to bridge the diasporic geography of their lives in order to connect the past to the present, photographs to stories, and family histories to Palestinian histories.

In the Palestinian village books, most of the stories tell of a collective history, not individual experiences. Susan Slyomovics described this context in her book *The Object of Memory: Arab and Jew Narrate the Palestinian Village*:

> The Palestinian Arab past, as it is imagined, recounted, written, and drawn from memory, involves images and descriptions of specific places and actual

settings. Projects commemorating places of memory not only are imaginatively constructed and reconstructed but, according to the French historian Maurice Halbwachs, are also collectively espoused: only communally do we remember. Individual memory, he argues, depends for its articulation on the social groups to which the memorist belongs.[35]

Thus the village book authors tell stories of the village using the collective *we* or *they* and rarely the first person *I* to talk about the village places, just as Palestinian accounts of the *nakba* often do.[36] I have written elsewhere that we should see the village books as "collective autobiographies," as the experiences of individuals and their rememberings conflated into a past that everyone in the village shares.[37]

Palestinians story the places of their past as a "shared past" that in these books takes over the representation of the village in narrative and visual forms of verse, personal recollections, collective histories, maps, and artwork. Representations of people's activities transform the physical place—buildings of a neighborhood, the village square, or a tree—into meaningful spaces of village and communal life. In the village memorial books, the stories associated with places usually center around communal places that were important at certain times and for events that were shared by all of the villagers. As sites of daily activities, these communal spaces take on a particular symbolic role for the village. Even when these stories are told by an individual in his or her own words, as are the stories in the village book for Bashsheet, they illustrate collective experiences. Here Ahmad Muhammad al-Duwairi tells of the area around the tomb of the prophet Sheet,[38] which had a large sycamore tree next to it:

> During Turkish times, they put a metal box in the tree, and the rich put in any extra coins they had, and the poor could take out what they needed. That tree stayed there until we were evicted from the village, and then it was removed by the Israelis. Weddings were held there because the land was collective, and it was a chance for people to visit the tomb, and it provided a space to cook.[39]

As this story illustrates, villages were divided into a variety of areas where communal activities took place, such as the village center; the empty land next to the mosque or church; the fields, wells, and springs; or the threshing floor of the village. In the village book about Qalunya, the author writes:

> Many memories link us emotionally to the threshing floor [of the village] that was so dear to us. The threshing floor was the ground of our youth and childhood

games. On that floor many celebrations took place. During wedding parties, women danced and girls sang, men danced the *dabka*, and old men danced the *sahja*. On this floor the mats were spread, rugs laid out, and *mansaf* [meat cooked in yogurt] and big bowls of *jarisha* [wheat cooked with yogurt] were offered for both men and women. On this floor we took pride in showing the harvest of grains and fruits, represented in the threshing and winnowing days of each year.[40]

The threshing floor of a village is a carefully cleaned and hardened space that is out in the open and serves as the functional space where people thresh and winnow grain. In this description of the space, however, it is invested not *only* with the memory of its useful function but also with other seminal parts of the collective village life that occurred there: celebrations, hosting and feeding guests, and childhood games. By presenting the account in this fashion, the author allows everyone from the village—men, women, children, old people—to have a memory of it. The hard work of harvesting, threshing, and winnowing the grain, as well as cooking the *jarisha* and *mansaf*, is absent from this account, which focuses instead on the villagers' good times together.

The mention of places also inspires people to recall certain values or characteristics. Keith Basso describes the moral behavior that accrues to each place in the Western Apache context and how the stories of those places regulate and instruct people's behavior by their everyday visibility in the landscape.[41] For Palestinians, places are connected to collective values, such as the generosity offered during weddings mentioned earlier, which are recalled when places are mentioned. In addition to highlighting the meaningful social practices and communal values evoked by certain locations, some authors also use place names to summon a location's known character, thus tying the place to the natural features of the landscape—the olive groves, the wildflowers, the hills of *za'tar* (thyme). Poetic verse, as in the following poem, illustrates how specific names of village sites are called on to invoke memories of life in the past:

Trip in the Ruins of al-Walaja [*Rihla fi atlal al-Walaja*]
   by Mustafa Khalil al-Sayfi

I'm thirsty. . . . Where are the springs and wells?
   Nothing, only wasteland and desert,
Nothing but murky wilderness
   The earth of the fields covered in stones.
Where is "al-Dhuhur" of almond buds
   And the "Hadayif" surrounded by wildflowers

Where are the fields and birds of "al-Khalayil"
  And "Wadi Ahmad," the grounds of the partridges
Where is "al-Hina" and its flowing water
  Its shade sheltering resting travelers
Where are the guests who suddenly appear
  And in the quffeh the coals are lit [to cook for them]
So that in every house the men clash
  Like a huge wave, opening the way for a tornado
As a result of their love for the guests
  They compete, young and old
And they threaten to divorce their wives if their offerings aren't touched
  They are all butchers when it comes to hospitality
[. . .]
On the "Jurun" were playgrounds
  On the "Habayil" was a house
Is there still enough in the coffeepots
  For people to stay up late and drink?[42]

This poem recalls various places in the village, reflecting on what they were known for and linking many of them closely to the generosity of the villagers toward their guests. The vestiges of the villagers' forefathers that are called on in this poem suggest a shared ethos of hospitality embodied in the traditions of offering coffee and slaughtering an animal for a meal (rather than in specific examples of visitors and the generosity shown to them).

In the village books, the poems about places, like the story maps, differ from the lists and the physical maps of location markers in that lists and physical maps concentrate on remembering what was in the village in order to perpetuate them for future generations whereas the poems and stories create a direct emotional relationship between memory and the places of the past. In the poem just presented, the author invokes the *atlal* (the ruins), a poetic form from pre-Islamic and classical Arabic poetry, to lament the places of memory. In the *atlal* form, the poet visits the abandoned places of his past and bemoans his lost beloved.[43] This poem about the village of al-Walaja, for example, laments the lost village and merges the abandoned places and the beloved into one. The poetic journey through the spaces of the village recalls the "traditional" *atlal* poet describing the physical characteristics of his beloved, such as her eyes and hair, which is paralleled in the al-Walaja poem by the poet as he describes the physical spaces of the village by place name and enumerates their virtues and the characteristics associated with each place, for example, al-Dhuhur of almond buds, the Hina with its flowing waters. This use of a classical Arabic poetic form and the content of lamenting loss and celebrating generosity inserts this memorialization of the village into a larger Arab social and cultural context, thus idealizing and contextualizing the sentiments of attachment and longing into a known emotional expression and form.[44] The stories and poems associated with the places of the village tell of the events, memories, emotions, and values that are communicated in the books as things shared by all of the villagers and as elements of village pride, thus creating a memory and a past for the village that can be collectively presented as authentic.

JOURNEY MAPS

The village book authors also reconstruct the village landscape in journeys, real or imagined, through the village, in both the past and the present. Journey maps allow the author to reconstruct a voyeuristic visit to the village. The trip through the natural and manmade landscape is a convention also found in school geography books for children, such as Jordanian school textbooks of the 1950 and 1960s.[45] Narrating the directions to and locations of the village, the author takes the reader on a journey that places the names that appear on the maps within a human relational framework embodied in the physical return to the village space. These journey maps provide the reader with the ability to virtually traverse the village as it existed before 1948 and experience it through the eyes of its inhabitants, as this example from Dayr Aban suggests:

> This is a trip through the lands of the village by which we will get to know the major landmarks and the location of these places in the basic structure of the village. We'll make this trip on a day in the month of June 1946, and we'll begin in Jerusalem, where we will take a car from the city, heading west for twenty-three kilometers, where we will reach Bab al-Wad at the western edge of the Jerusalem hills. Then we'll change our direction and head south; the lands of the villages of Bayt Mahsir and 'Artuf are on the left, and the lands of 'Isalin, Ishwa', and Sar'a are on the right. After nine kilometers we'll reach the police station on the eastern side of the main road. . . . The private mill of Ibrahim Shuraym, and the droning of the motor as it grinds the Dayr Abani wheat, is the first landmark of the village that we pass by, located to the north after we pass the bridge over the valley of Abu Khashaba. . . . If we face to the north, we will be pleased to see two important landmarks: Hawwuz al-Mayya [the water pool],

which lies 150 meters off of the main road, and the village girls are standing in front of it—they have come to fill their containers with the water from the spring of Marjalin; and the elementary school of the village, with its large garden ringing with the voices of the students in their classes and the sound of the tools working in the beautiful garden of the school.[46]

This account of the village begins from a landmark that everyone knows (Jerusalem) and takes the reader from the approach to the village into the different areas, noting their landmarks and people. Such a process could be traced on a map, and all of the significant locations are commonly represented on the village book maps, including the book about Dayr Aban. But this journey account also describes more than what can be represented on a map or in statistics; it fills in for readers the author's historical memory of the constant hum of the mill motor, the vision of women filling water containers at the spring, and the sounds of schoolchildren and work. This journey map endows these spaces with a sensory element that pushes readers to imagine observing or participating in village life, as if they were standing there hearing the children at play or the grinding of the wheat.

Other journey maps, such as the one in the memorial book on the village of 'Imwas,[47] describe the setting of the village and the actions of its inhabitants as if in a folkloric tableau:

Among the famous landmarks of the village is the tomb of Shaykh 'Ubayd (Abu 'Ubayda 'Amr bin al-Jarrah) and the tomb of Shaykh Mu'ala (Mu'adh bin Jabal), and next to Shaykh 'Ubayd was a big *sidr* tree [*Zizyphus spini-christi*], as old as 'Imwas. Under its shade the village elders would sit chatting in the evenings [*yatasamarun*] and playing *seeja* [*mancala*, a board game]. When the tree's fruit ripened (*al-dom*) you would see the village children in large numbers racing to pick it. The tree was surrounded by the central cemetery of the village, and between the cemetery and the buildings of the village was a large empty square, which became the bus stop. [. . .] The street continued onto a high bridge that crossed over the Shalala valley, which collected the rainwater and the water of the spring ('Ayn Nini). The young men would go to the bridge in the evenings to chat with each other and stroll along the empty main street until reaching Dayr al-Latrun [the Latrun Monastery] or the school. While they walked, they passed by the wide gate and large walls surrounding an old church. . . . After school the boys and young men liked to go to the sports field on the *awqaf* [religious trust] lands around the tomb of Shaykh Mu'ala.[48]

In these journey maps, readers can relive an idealized memory of village life in which the social system is orderly and people are in their places doing their expected tasks: young women fill their containers at the well, old men sit in the village center playing a board game, the children are in school or roaming freely in a large mass, and the young men claim the streets in the evening whereas during the day they have their own space on the outskirts of the village, away from the houses. Those doing much of the work—both women and men—are absent from the public village space because their work keeps them either out in the fields, inside the homes, or working outside of the village. The image conveyed is one of well-ordered, stable tradition.

The journey maps provide for a unique conflation of personal and communal memories. They allow the author, as the journey maker, to choose the historical time for the trip, along with the elements that will be revealed to the visitor, thereby deciding what is important to map and narrate. As such, the journey map is not only embedded in the collectively held representation of meaningful parts of the village, but it also presents the village as an object of a tour, with the author as guide. The journey map presents an individual's understanding of the landmarks, sights, sounds, and flavors of a place in a selected image of daily life, disconnected from seasons, conflicts, weather, health, and the myriad other unappealing or unmemorable aspects of daily life. Because these journey maps are created by individuals, they differ depending on the author. However, they are written in a similar style and conform to a similar vision of the village as a site for the folkloric and the traditional, a place where life was pleasant, satisfying, and idyllic, and marked and circumscribed by the natural world around it.

Some village book authors construct journey maps on the basis of an actual return trip to the village. These maps do not present the "traditional" folkloric view of what the village looked like, but rather describe the two worlds the author is in—the world of the place itself and the world of his memory of the place. 'Abd al-Majid al-'Ali from Burj al-Barajneh camp in Lebanon describes in his village book a trip he made in 1977, twenty-nine years after being displaced from the village in 1948:

> My cousin from Kafr Yassif went with me to Kuwaykat, our village. Even though we could have gone by car, I wanted to walk over the path between the two villages that I had taken for five years, back and forth to my school in Kafr Yassif from 1943 to 1948. We passed by the Maymas spring, near the hilltop of Khirbat Maymas. We

crossed over the bridge of Wadi al-'Assafiya and reached the edge of the village lands, where I stopped, bent, and kissed the ground. I saw that it was planted with vegetables, and marked with numbers, from the edge of the Rummana hills in the east to the Baharat hills in the west. My cousin told me that the Israelis spray pesticides from helicopters and the numbers are indicators for the pilots about the progression of their work. We went into the cemetery through a fence that continued north up to the Jubayl[. . . .] We walked among the rubble remains of the houses in the middle of a pine forest planted by the Israelis after they destroyed the village. We reached the place of the house I was born in, and I stopped, recalling all of the houses that had been there, especially the neighbors' houses, and the shop of Ibrahim al-Jishi, and next to it the shop of 'Ali Hussein—the two places where we used to buy our goods. All of this had become ruins, and I bent to pick up a pebble to take to my children and grandchildren, so that they will not forget that they have a house in Palestine. . . . [49]

As this story illustrates, the imagined journeys described in the village books about Dayr Aban and 'Imwas differ from the return journey of al-'Ali to his village. Although some of the natural landscape still exists, the markers of Israeli presence and use of the land are also evident; the story thus records history in the form of showing change over time. Despite the destruction, al-'Ali chronicles how he finds some evidence of his house that he can take back to his family as a symbol of their heritage and inheritance (past and future). These journey maps, whether they describe the imagined past or a more contemporaneous return, present the village and the landscape as the author experienced it or as he wants us as readers to experience it. We, however, are limited to the verbal descriptions of places that for him were lived in, seen, and heard.

MAPS OF RETURN, MAPS OF WHAT REMAINS

The village books and Palestinians today tell stories of the continuing existence of certain elements of the pre-1948 landscape that have not been destroyed. As the return journey of al-'Ali illustrates, stories of return show that someone knowledgeable can find the remains of the destroyed villages. A dwindling number of houses, mosques, churches, cemeteries, and schools still exist. The formerly Palestinian cities of Jaffa, Haifa, Acre, Tiberius, Safad, and Beersheba present their former residents with a different kind of experience on their return visits, because the majority of their houses are still standing. Many urban refugees have chronicled their own or others' return visits to their homes, and their encounters with the current residents.[50] Returning to and reading these landscapes invokes another way of seeing and understanding, as Carol Bardenstein describes in her article "Threads of Memory and Discourses of Rootedness: Of Trees, Oranges and the Prickly-Pear Cactus in Israel-Palestine."[51] Bardenstein as well as Meron Benvenisti, Jonathan Boyarin, Sharif Kanaana, and numerous other scholars explore this returning-to-remains in academic texts, and countless Palestinians search out, visit, and document these remnants of the past.[52] Village books, return-journey videos, Web sites, oral history collections, autobiographies, and movies all contain accounts of returning to village spaces and searching out the remains and what is recognizable. What is seen and how it is interpreted are parts of the maps of remains and the maps of return that people create.

What is missing from the landscape on the return visits occupies 'Abd al-'Aziz Abu Hadba, author of the village book on Dayr Aban. He notes that the trees the villagers planted had been neglected, so most of them had died and another section of them had been burned. He adds, however, that "the cactus remains as the landmark of the village, impossible to destroy. It says, 'Here was an Arab village, and here Arabs lived.'"[53] As someone who took refuge in the West Bank, he and his family were able to visit the village frequently after 1967 (until the Israeli closure policy that began in 1991 instituted checkpoints and travel permits). The book is full of pictures of him and his family at the village sites. He describes what the visitor would find:

> Starting from the east at the cemetery, we notice that a number of the graves have been destroyed and the bulldozers have buried others. The main cemetery of the village is easier to find, but none of the graves can be identified. Heading west, we are at the shrine of al-Shaykh Muslim, but we find that nothing remains other than a fig tree that has sprouted again in the depression behind the shrine. [...] Walking quickly, we reach the clear remains of the al-'Omari mosque, and the two graves in its courtyard are damaged, revealing the bones of those buried there. The school and courtyard are completely destroyed and even someone who lived in the village would have a difficult time locating them except by using Wadi Qarayqa' as a reference. Toward the north was the shrine of Abu Hassan Najd and the nearby graves associated with the Wa'ara family (descendants of Abu Hassan), which were destroyed in 1973. Similarly, the mill, the first landmark upon entering the village, is gone. Nothing remains of it today, although remnants were there until 1970.[54]

Abu Hadba's description of what he knew, what remained, and what was destroyed in the intervening years reveals his intimate knowledge of the history of this place. His knowledge of the past allowed him to chronicle the changes, and to indicate how the physical landscape had been transformed.

There is little visible, distinctive evidence that many of the villages were once there. In the late 1980s and early 1990s, the researchers of the encyclopedic *All That Remains* visited each of the 418 villages, which they then catalogued, describing 292 (70 percent) of them as totally destroyed, and 90 villages (22 percent) as largely destroyed.[55] Scholar Carol Bardenstein maintains that, confronted with such physical destruction, one therefore "has to rely on landscape readings, because little else remains."[56] She tells of going, at first alone, to the Palestinian village of al-Ghabisiyya in the Galilee, where she never could see more than the pine forest planted over the village by the Jewish National Fund. On another visit, this time with former villagers, they showed her how to discover more: rubble from buildings, the round stone of the olive press, and "two towering palm trees that used to flank the entrance to the [*mukhtar*'s] home, the only two such trees in the village," which marked the location of the missing house. "Their former function of demarcating status and authority seems mocked by the fact that they now rather ridiculously 'flank' an empty space, announcing only a lack or an absence."[57] Benvenisti describes the trips to destroyed Palestinian villages as "botanical" because "the silhouette of the village was preserved by cactus hedges, fruit trees growing wild, certain varieties of grasses and brambles that thrive in the ruins of inhabited sites . . . [and] cultivated or wild plants that served as signposts in a landscape from which the human element has disappeared."[58] Majdal 'Asqalan was a small town on the Mediterranean coast north of Gaza. Heavily invested in the textile industry, it also contained multistory buildings, including a number of religious buildings and shrines, schools, a bank, and government buildings. Much of it has been destroyed or modified, and the main mosque has been turned into a museum. The cemetery and many of the other religious shrines have been erased; these include the *zawiya* (tomb or hospice) of Abu Shusha, the *zawiya* of al-Shaykh Shakir ("erased, only indicated by the fig tree"), the tomb of al-Shaykh Asa'ad ("erased, only indicated by the pomegranate tree"), and the tomb of al-Shaykh Muhammad al-Ansari.[59] The absence of the actual markers of these significant sites of village memory invests the surrounding trees with the power to represent what is gone.

The transformations in the landscape make it bewilderingly difficult for those who are able to return after long periods to orient themselves. Ghalib Sumrayn, author of the village book on Qalunya, described to me his return visit to the village when I asked him about the map he made of the village while living in Kuwait. The map is reproduced in the village book as well as printed as a large color poster.

> It is very important to put the map in the book to focus on the things that you want to talk about and to communicate that information to others. In 1970 I visited my village. I'm sorry to say that I had to ask some of the Israeli Jews how to locate it [because everything had changed so much]. I took my seven kids, my wife, and her parents. We came through the West Bank. We found a busdriver from Hebron to take all of us to Qalunya. My father-in-law knows every inch of the village land, but we couldn't find our way in it, because the village had changed; the old houses were destroyed and the streets were paved. The hill in the village was called the Shfair and my father and my uncle owned land there, but this hill had been leveled and a new Jewish settlement was built there called Mevaseret Zion. I stood there in our village with my father-in-law, and I started to tell my kids, here was your grandfather's house, and this land used to belong to us in the past. . . . The driver of the bus noticed that I was going to faint, so he called my father-in-law to take me back to the bus before anything bad happened to me. [. . .] When I went to Palestine I wanted to stay for a month, but I stayed for only nine days because I could not bear it. This is why the map is important—so that people can see their destroyed village.[60]

This return trip not only showed Sumrayn how much of his village was destroyed, but also proved to him the value of recording this information and creating for others a map, which he would make in the years following his visit. He proposed that the map could serve as a reference to everything that cannot be seen with the eyes.

For many people who return to visit their villages and homes, an important part of the visit is to gather herbs and grape leaves and eat the fruits of the remaining trees. These acts, occuring daily, yearly, or once in a lifetime, are embodied performances of what it means to be from the village—not only doing what one (or one's ancestors) used to do, but also ingesting the place by consuming the land's produce. For Palestinians, the embodying element of this—making what was once yours, yours again by eating it—is never questioned. Instead, it is repeatedly requested and performed as a right and a ritual. When the authors of the *Hikayat Qarya* (Story of a village) oral history collection returned to the village of Bayt Thul with one of the villagers named Umm ʿAli, she began to collect herbs and plants. "She continued picking the leaves until what she had clutched to her chest sprouted from her like a large bush. That was Umm ʿAli, or maybe that's what we remember: A tree of wild herbs and greens moving with amazing grace over the stones of the destroyed villages, assuring, comforting, and reminding us of our descendants who are awaiting us."[61] Umm ʿAli's behavior of gathering the products of the land reinforces the physical connection to the past. A photo from the Dayr Aban book shows the author and his family eating figs in the village. It is not just that the visit is undertaken, but that it is also recorded, published, and shared. These acts of consuming the natural world of the village assert Palestinian connections to and embodiment of the land and the soil, a leitmotif of Palestinian exile.[62]

As physicals marker of Palestinian villages, the trees, cacti, and other botanical species also serve as symbolic mediums for expressing sentiment and identity in activism, art, and literature. The 1987 film *Does the Cactus Have a Soul?* chronicles people returning to visit their villages.[63] The title plays with the fact that cacti are sometimes the only surviving evidence of the existence of the village; the film asks if they have also been invested with the spirit of that past. These products of the earth—orange and olive trees and cacti—are an essential visual vocabulary in the iconography of Palestinian art, in particular in literature and political poster art.[64] Palestinian artist Rana Bishara has used dried and living cactus as material for her sculptures and installations. In an interview, she describes cactus as "a symbol" of the *nakba*

> because it has tenacious roots and grows wherever you throw it; and that is what Palestinians do out of necessity. In Arabic, cactus is called *saber*, which is also the word for "patience," and because Palestinians use patience a lot as a weapon of hope for the future. Cactus has become a symbol of resistance. It is also a symbol of the heroism and tenacity of villagers who were violently evicted from Palestine by Israelis in 1948. Since traditionally cactus is a protective fence, when in 1948 Israelis demolished and bulldozed our villages, the cactus would grow again and etch out the boundaries of family homes and plots, revealing Israeli crime in graphic outline.[65]

Some remaining elements of the Palestinian built landscape are easy for Palestinians to locate because they have been transformed for other purposes.

Meron Benvenisti, Sharif Kanaana, Walid Khalidi, the PalestineRemembered .com Website, and many others chart the transformations that have taken place in the remaining buildings, particularly mosques and shrines.[66] For the most part, the Palestinians who remained inside Israel have been cut off from tending to these buildings—even the churches and mosques.[67] According to Benvenisti's field research, only forty village mosques remain.[68] After the end of the military administration of the Palestinians inside Israel in 1966, they could travel without permits and more easily access their former villages. Groups of villagers and nongovernmental organizations organized clean-up campaigns to take care of cemeteries and places of worship.[69] In addition, political movements—first the leftists, then the Islamist movements—have adopted some of these sites and have raised money to renovate them. Benvenisti writes about the struggle of the villagers from the destroyed village of al-Ghabisiyya, all of whom are Israeli citizens. In the early 1970s they set up a committee "whose principal activity was to try to renovate the village mosque and cemetery, which were left standing after all the houses were blown up in 1955."[70] Despite letters to the authorities and promises in return, the Israel Lands Administration has actively dismantled any changes the villagers made to the mosque, confiscated their belongings, and sealed it and erected a fence around it.[71] In other villages, such as Kafr Bir'im, Saffuriyya, and Suba, the built landscape was removed and archaeological sites were excavated.

As Benvenisti chronicles in *Sacred Landscape: The Buried History of the Holy Land Since 1948*, destruction, both intentional and through neglect, plagues the old buildings. The village shrines for the Judeo-Christian-Muslim prophets and holy men and women have been "newly discovered" as the shrines of exclusively Jewish prophets and holy men, ancient and medieval.[72] Today these shrines are the sites of organized pilgrimages and referred to on signs as Jewish shrines, and Jews go to them for spiritual healing and interventions, much like Jews, Christians, and Muslims used to do before 1948. Israeli museums and art galleries built in Palestinian mosques and houses host displays of Israel's archaeological heritage and engage with global modern art movements.[73]

The Palestinians in the diaspora who write about their villages often know little of what has become of these places, especially if they have been appropriated and incorporated into Israelis' lives. Even if they do know that a mosque has been turned into a museum or restaurant, or a religious shrine has been made into an exclusively Jewish shrine, they rarely acknowledge the extent to which that place has become part of the everyday life of Israelis. Their lack of knowledge is the result of a combination of forces: their inability to access these places, their lack of knowledge of Hebrew, and perhaps most strongly of all, their desire not to know or acknowledge how Israelis have transformed the landscape in the last sixty years.

Some parts of the remaining Palestinian landscape that have remained have been imbued by Palestinians with a power to resist destruction, a power that carries over from pre-1948 cultural traditions.[74] One late night in 1995 I set out from Ramallah in a taxi with the driver, Abu Omar, and some other passengers headed for the airport in al-Lyd/Tel-Aviv. The headlights illuminated fleeting spots on the road winding west down the plateau toward the sea—including, surprisingly, a very small domed tomb in the median between the eastbound and westbound roads. When the Palestinian man in the front seat asked about it, Abu Omar said that when the Israelis were expanding this road, they tried to knock down the tomb. Each time the bulldozer driver approached the tomb, the engine would sputter to a stop. Over and over this happened until finally they decided just to leave it and build the road around it. This story is not unique. Later I read in the village book for the coastal village of Salama about the "tomb of Shaykh Hasan: It is a holy shrine (*maqam*) for the people of the village; the women made a sacrifice to it and visit it to place candles. This *maqam* fills people with amazement because the Zionist occupation has tried to destroy it a number of times. Their bulldozers break down by some miracle and cannot destroy it. So instead they put a fence around it and left it."[75]

The supernatural power of these religious buildings is a carryover from earlier times. As mentioned earlier in the chapter, the book about the village of Bashsheet describes "the tomb of the prophet Sheet," which was a site of blessings (*baraka*) and of vows or prayers for divine intervention (*nidhr*). A story by Yusif Abu Fuda, retold in the book, relates that before 1948

> some people from Dar Abu al-'Aysh (who were part of Dar Abu Hilal) bought the land adjacent to the tomb, and one of them said to the worker, go knock down that tomb because the people that come here mess up this land, so go get rid of it, we no longer have any need for the prophet Sheet. So, I'm telling you, the worker went and whacked it two or three times with his pickaxe, which then broke. The next day the man who told the worker to get rid of the tomb went to Jaffa, where his son went swimming and drowned. And after five days the worker died in his sleep.[76]

These stories told across the different eras are about the power of the shrine and are not just limited to those that focus on Palestinian defiance of Israel. They help Palestinians to explain how certain things have remained. The tombs have supernatural force, the fruit-bearing trees that Palestinians planted before 1948 keep reseeding themselves and have natural powers to keep growing, and cacti cannot be killed.

I include these accounts of the power of the tombs and plants not, of course, to verify that these events happened, but rather to show how Palestinians, in continuity with previous eras, invest both built places and elements of the natural environment with the power to resist. They both resist their own destruction and symbolically mark for Palestinians the (failed) attempts of others to erase their presence and history from the land. All of these accounts about tombs reveal, in a way, one of the ways in which Palestinians see Israelis—as another passing power occupying the land and infringing on their space.

People create maps of what remains in stories and accounts of return that describe the physical landscape as they see it at the time of their visit; they also conjure up the landscape and village as it had been. Missing buildings are reimagined and detailed, and people recognize trees that mark the locations of once-important village sites. They find places that resist the destruction, places that they can anchor stories to—stories from both the past and the present. Through these descriptions they express either their own or their ancestors' relationships to these places; and through their return visits they keep alive memories of the places of the past. All of these things and more are what these places of pre-1948 village life mean to Palestinians today.

MAPPING THE PAST AND MEMORIES OF PLACE

Balad al-Shaykh, Israel: 1993

One hot summer day in 1993 I set out with my camera and a friend to visit Balad al-Shaykh, a destroyed Palestinian village just east of Haifa and most well-known for its cemetery, where 'Izz al-Din al-Qassam was buried. A Syrian exile and militant fighting against European colonialism in the region, al-Qassam fled to Palestine in the 1920s and worked as a preacher and activist among poor and working-class Palestinians in Haifa and the Galilee. He was killed by the British Mandate (Palestine) police in November of 1935. His funeral rallied thousands of Palestinians and served to mobilize nationalist activism, including the 1936–1939 Arab revolt against the Mandate rule.[77] When I visited Balad al-Shaykh in 1993, the giant Israeli Nesher cement plant loomed nearby and the cemetery was surrounded by a wall with a dramatic carved-stone gate at the entrance, just meters off the road. Several small workshops had been built along the eastern wall, facing out toward the road, with their backs to the cemetery. After photographing the cemetery, including a recently replaced modern headstone for al-Qassam and the beautifully carved white marble marker of Sami Taha, general-secretary of the Palestinian Arab Workers Society who was assassinated in 1947, we panted over to the shade of one of the workshops. The carpenter working there, a Palestinian living in Nazareth, kindly offered us cold water. I commented on the ruinous state of the cemetery, the exposed bones, the broken headstones, and all of the marble that had been removed from the tombs over time. The carpenter, accustomed to the transformation that had been taking place to Palestinian sites over the previous fifty-five years, to the destruction of the villages, and to the neglect of what remained, looked up from his work and said to me flatly, "They stole the entire country and you're getting worked up about a few pieces of marble?"

I tell this story here to show the range in which Palestinians assess the destruction and dispossession they have endured. Those who survived it and live in it today, like the carpenter, see more than just the narrow lens of a neglected cemetery and pilfered headstones. They live in vibrant communities among the ruins, still sing the village songs (as well as make new ones), know their extended families, plant tomatoes, go to universities, and speak Arabic and Hebrew seamlessly. They live not obsessed by these dead people. Nor do they see cemeteries necessarily as national symbols for which they should be responsible, because the ones in their own communities are taken care of by the familes of those buried there and by the churches and Islamic *waqf* administrations. In this sense, as localism pushes people to represent their communal histories, it also cedes responsibility to the community. With all of the Balad al-Shaykh villagers in the diaspora, its cemetery has largely been abandoned.[78]

Palestinian village books present themselves as entrusted with documenting and passing on the history of the villages—what remains and what was destroyed—from the perspectives of those who lived in them. Thus they have produced (and continue to produce) various ways of mapping the space of the village past, whether in the form of physical maps or as lists of place names, stories about a particular place, poetry about the village, or re-created journeys. These geographic maps of the village take physical spaces and turn them into lived places by telling stories of human lives and experiences that are inextricably tied to those very places. These maps of the past endure, to a great extent, through forms of writing and imagery that are removed from the land as it now exists. At the same time, they map spaces that can be shared by all of the villagers—wells, springs, sentiments, and journeys—in one way or another.

As evidenced in this chapter, the past that is mapped consists of memories and idealizations. The village books seek to re-create and reclaim the physical village by taking the villagers' experience and rendering it verbally as well as visually and in print. Through maps and lists of village lands and landmarks, Palestinians claim the village through knowing it; through poems about the village places they show sentiment and emotional attachment; and through journeys that take readers on tours of a repopulated village they re-create an idyllic peasant life and show their connections to those places. Although each village book portrays the unique places of the village's past, the sentiments, emotions, activities, and associations affiliated with those places are made to correspond to a greater narrative of what it means to be Palestinian at this historical juncture. Ultimately, geographic nostalgia for the village places and the peasant lifestyle is rooted both in local memories and experiences and in Palestinians' current status as landless and dispossessed refugees.

7 IDENTITIES AND HISTORY

Al-Yahudiyya, Palestine: 1930s

Around 1932, the inhabitants of al-Yahudiyya, a village of some six thousand residents located on the plains thirteen kilometers east of the city of Jaffa, changed the village's name to al-'Abbasiyya.[1] For reasons that seem apparent today, the Palestinian Arab villagers were no longer comfortable living in a village whose name in modern Arabic meant "Jewish." The village name al-Yahudiyya had lasted through centuries of changing rulers and empires; it was mentioned in Joshua 19:45 of the Hebrew Scriptures (Old Testament), as Yehud or Jehud, a Caananite town given to the sons of Dan following the Israelite conquest of Canaan.[2] It continued through the Byzantine Empire, early Islamic rule, Umayyads, Abbasids, Mamlukes, Crusaders, Ayyubids, four hundred years of the Ottoman Empire, and into the British Mandate over Palestine. At some point in its history, the village's name was also associated with the name of the Biblical prophet Judah, the son of Jacob (in Arabic, *al-Nabi Huda bin Ya'coub*), whose tomb was in the village and the site of local Muslim venerations.[3] Shortly after the village was captured and emptied of its inhabitants in 1948, Jewish rabbis consecrated it for Jews as the burial place of the same Judah (*Yehuda Ben Ya'akov* in Hebrew), and it has since become "a place of pilgrimage, prayer, and for miracles and healing of the sick."[4]

That the villagers had not changed the village's name prior to the 1930s speaks to the centuries of acceptance of the name al-Yahudiyya. The predominantly Muslim villagers who had lived there for a thousand years or so (with what we know were some Jews and Christians in the twentieth century) did not find anything objectionable about the name. One could conclude, then, that references to Jews and things Jewish were part of the known and accepted landscape of Palestine throughout the ages, regardless of the rulers' religion or policies. What precipitated the willingness to change the name were modern political developments: the dramatic changes brought about by the late-nineteenth-century rise of the Zionist movement, and the British colonization of Palestine that began in 1917. These changes in demographics and the political demands being made by Jews both inside and outside the country for a Jewish homeland in Palestine that would deny the Palestinians national rights to the land made it difficult for Palestinian Arabs to continue to call their village al-Yahudiyya. Their choice of al-'Abbasiyya as the new name for the village evidences other ways the villagers had of identifying themselves, in both local and broader religious and ethnic terms. According to Hussein al-Lubani, the name was changed to al-'Abbasiyya, "on the basis of al-Shaykh 'Abbas, who was buried there and thought to be al-Fadl bin 'Abbas, the paternal cousin of the prophet Muhammad, while others say the village was named after the Arab Abbasid empire as a good omen."[5] As this explanation shows, the new name references other dimensions of Palestinian identity—a local identification with a village shrine and a broader identification with the Arab and Muslim past. Despite the name change, however, in formal correspondence with the Mandate government authorities, villagers continued to refer to the village as al-Yahudiyya.[6]

As this story of how the village name was changed and used illustrates, Palestinian villagers in the first half of the twentieth century lived through intersecting political forces that affected both how they defined themselves and how others defined them. Adding to their own growing sense of Palestinian nationalism, they were both claimed and excluded by others: in the colonization of Palestine by the British Mandate, through the increasing power of the Zionist movement, and under the influences of a strong Arab nationalism and a rising Muslim-oriented political movement. In these periods, they formed and reformed how they thought of themselves as Palestinians and Arabs, which influenced and was influenced by how others thought of them. With these political forces in mind, this chapter addresses the particularities of Palestinian identity in the twentieth century, primarily as expressed in the village books.

The theoretical underpinning of this chapter is grounded primarily in practice-based theories about identity that embrace the complex and multivalent nature of identity expressed individually and collectively in national, religious, ethnic, and other identifications. In rethinking how we analyze and conceptualize identity, the village books provide us with the opportunity to understand both how identity is expressed and how scholars explicate it. The village books, written starting in the 1980s, illuminate how Palestinians in the present look back on pre-1948 relations with the Jewish communities in Palestine, as well as on their own sense of being Palestinian, Arab, Muslim, Christian, and other expressions of self-identification within a contemporary nationalist existence. The final part of the chapter explores how the village books express a Palestinian village identity that is land-based—not just a connection to Palestine as a geographical and political entity, but also a connection to the history of their village through the ages. In claiming the entire village history as their own, Palestinians assert a connection to that space over time, branching out beyond other common identification markers such as ethnicity, religion, and nationalism. Palestinians share this sense of a land-based identity with many indigenous peoples. Such expressions of affiliation are often heard, read, and studied only by outsiders when those peoples are threatened—a legacy of displacement and colonial policies wherever and whenever it has taken place.

PALESTINIAN NATIONAL AND REGIONAL IDENTIFICATIONS

Scholarly focus since the 1980s on the constructed nature of nationalism provides us with a considerable sheaf of theoretical material with which to explore the political, historical, and cultural forces that form nationalist sentiment and bodies.[7] In historic Palestine, the widespread formation of Palestinian national sentiment in the late nineteenth and, particularly, the early twentieth centuries has been examined by Rashid Khalidi in his *Palestinian Identity: The Construction of a Modern National Consciousness*. Combining examinations of elite family papers and newspapers from the World War I and British Mandate eras, he shows how the economic and political changes in the World War I period and immediately afterward resulted in "so profound a transformation of the sense of self of the Arab population of Palestine [. . . that it] resulted in the emergence of a Palestinian national identity where a few decades before no such thing had existed."[8] A crucial element of Palestinian and other nationalisms in the Arab world, as noted by Khalidi and others, is that these nation-state nationalisms were not exclusive and that local loyalties, religious ties, and sentiments to Arabism existed concurrently.

Palestinian expressions of Palestinian nationalism, in the form of sentiment and action, have engendered more debate (and discrediting) than coeval national movements in the area, such as in Jordan, Syria, Lebanon, and Egypt. This is because unlike these other national movements, Palestinian nationalism was competing with the Zionist movement for the national claim to and political sovereignty over the same land.[9] None of these countries, with the exception of Algeria, faced the arrival of large numbers of organized foreigners who sought to settle the land with the aid of colonial authorities. With the development of nationalist movements in the area, Palestinians began to think of themselves as a nation, and since 1948 they have faced two issues (among others) that have prevented them from forming a nation-state: the denial of territory and the absence of a viable (and representative) government to govern the territory and people. Thus Palestinians lack the state power that other nation-states have to educate and mold its citizenry and create hegemonic narratives about the state or nation. Palestinians today do not live in a single geographic area, nor do they have control over the more common institutions of a state that provides citizens with a history and identification practices, such as money, an army, museums, schools (with the exception of the West Bank and Gaza), and archives, to name a few. Despite this lack, Palestinians express national feelings about being Palestinian—sentiments that unite them across borders and time.[10] Also, despite international expectations (or perhaps because of them) that after 1948 they would soon assimilate into the other Arab countries, Palestinians have continued to self-identify as Palestinians with shared understandings, agreed-upon labels, and definitions of what certain sentiments and practices mean.[11] Conversely, perhaps the absence of a nation-state fuels the continued desire by Palestinians to assert and keep alive collective narratives of national commonalties.

In addition to the primacy of national identity for Palestinians, they also embrace regional, local, and family histories as both separate from and part of national identification practices. Palestinian village history, as told from the perspective of its residents, reflects the memories of local, family, ethnic, national, and religious identifications, and provides a framework for narrating history, as well as for claiming the authority to tell these stories as a viable and legitimate history.[12] Acting in concert with and in counterpoint to larger national collective understandings of history, smaller and more local accounts of village, city, and family history connect directly to the national struggle for recognition through people's claims to a distinct and documentable past in Palestine. At the same time, they highlight their own lives, experiences, and identifications.

Given the historical role of nationalist struggle in twentieth century Palestine-Israel, and the exclusionary nature of Zionism, the national struggle influenced Palestinians' lives both before and after 1948, and still affects how they remember the past in the present. The conflict is thus often framed as between Jews and Arabs or Jews and Palestinians. However, Palestinian textual and oral histories eschew this interpretation of an inherent groupness to Arabs and Jews, or of an inherent antagonism between them. Instead, recollections of the past by Palestinians often include memories of Jewish neighbors, merchants, and classmates that challenge the contemporary nationalist and exclusivist visions of the past that reflect the configuration of the post-1948 conflict.[13]

In this vein, Victor Kattan, in his new study of the origins of the Arab-Israeli conflict entitled *From Coexistence to Conquest*, proposes that "it was European anti-Semitism and British colonialism which caused the conflict in Palestine."[14] He shows how the British alarm over Jewish immigration to Great Britain found a solution in the Balfour Declaration, which granted a homeland to Jews in Palestine. "Before then," Kattan states, "Palestine's Jews intermingled with Muslims and Christians, with whom they communicated in Arabic and Turkish. It was only with later waves of Jewish immigration caused by European anti-Semitism that conflict ensued."[15] Kattan's work communicates a scholarly ethos that most would agree with: as we look back at historical periods, we must use sources and material to understand those periods through the lens of what was happening at the time, and discern the influence of what happened subsequently on how those periods came to have meaning. These efforts allow us to refocus our understanding of the past and create history in ways that more accurately reflect contemporaneous understandings and the power of the events that followed to shape our present rendering of that past.

Although religion is often seen by many commentators as the crux of the Palestinian-Israeli conflict, the majority of Palestinian recollections of life before 1948 subsume confessional identity—be it Jewish, Muslim, or Christian—within discussions of moral values such as generosity and friendship, within political affiliation and sentiment, within communal ideas of shared language and culture, and within other commonalties such as residence and business. In the context of living together, Palestinians express the importance of relational identities such as kinship, friendship, and political sentiment as much as categorical identities such as ethnicity, religion, and nationality.

These relational identities are threatened when people violate the shared understandings that have bound them together as neighbors, kin, and political groups, and are strengthened when people honor or build on them. Examples of each of these relational identities, in addition to chauvinistic groupness based on religion and political beliefs are detailed in this chapter.

RETHINKING IDENTITY

Most theories of identity and nationalism attribute only certain meanings to Palestinianness, imposed by the constraints inherent in the word *identity*. Rogers Brubaker and Frederick Cooper, in their article "Beyond 'Identity,'" take issue with the use of the word *identity* as an *analytical* category because, they argue, it has two major problems related to strong and weak understandings of the term. In the strong sense, they believe, we think of identity as a defining characteristic that all people have, and we therefore see their actions and behaviors only as products of something inherent in all people. Such a concept of identity implies strong notions of group boundedness and homogeneity. There is no room for change, development, flexibility, or strategic deployment of identity. However, when we try to soften that strongly deterministic way of thinking of identity "by stipulating that identities are constructed, fluid, and multiple," we end up with another problem. This current, more popular solution of thinking of identity as constructed and shifting "leaves us without a rationale for talking about 'identities' at all and ill-equipped to examine the 'hard' dynamics and essentialist claims of contemporary identity politics."[16]

The authors argue instead for dividing the ideas that are subsumed under the word *identity* into three categories in order to analyze the multitude of concepts that are referred to when people write or talk about identity. "The language of 'identity' [. . .] blurs what needs to be kept distinct: external categorization and self-understanding, objective commonality and subjective groupness."[17] They propose instead the analytical use of the term *identification*, which, as a noun derived from a verb, can be seen as a "processual, active term." If we describe a person or a group's identification (as opposed to identity), we are implicitly thinking of them undertaking an action or professing a belief or feeling, rather than just describing their state of being. Also, because identification is a process, "it does not presuppose that such identifying (even by powerful agents such as the state) will necessarily result in the internal sameness, the distinctiveness, the bounded groupness that political entrepreneurs may seek to achieve."[18] *Identification* can be defined or expressed by the self or by others, making the concept less ambiguous than *identity* because "it invites us to specify the agents that do the identifying."[19] In this sense, identification captures the experiences and practices of people in order to express how we think about ourselves and others, and does not just rely on ideologies or stated beliefs. "Identification—of oneself and of others—is intrinsic to social life; 'identity' in the strong sense is not."[20] In this vein, "'identification' calls attention to complex (and often ambivalent) *processes*, while the term 'identity,' designating a *condition* rather than a *process*, implies too easy a fit between the individual and the social."[21]

Brubaker and Cooper suggest using the term *self-understanding* to "designates *one's own* understanding of who one is,"[22] because it preserves the concept of agentive and individualistic nature of self that forms post-Enlightenment rational thought and understanding of how people think. Acknowledging the power of "coercive external categorizations" to define how an individual understands himself or herself, they propose that analyzing self-understanding through examining individually expressed sentiments allows us to comprehend the power of political, social, and cultural hegemonic forces.

Complementing, contrasting, and influencing this self-understanding is the concept of a collective identity, which Brubaker and Cooper argue connotes "the emotionally laden sense of belonging to a distinctive, bounded group."[23] This concept, they assert, is more effectively expressed through the terms *commonality*, *connectedness*, and *groupness*, rather than *collective identity*. "This will enable us to distinguish instances of strongly binding, vehemently felt groupness from more loosely structured, weakly constraining forms of affinity and affiliation."[24] It also allows us to understand the forces that make for strong groupness at different times and in different places, and for weak affiliations at others, rather than, as most analyses of identity do, attribute the mere fact of belonging to a group as invoking an inherent chauvinism.

Furthermore, by providing more details about the type of identifying, we can then describe "*relational* and *categorical* modes of identification."[25] Relational identification suggests "position in a relational web" (kinship, friendship, or patronage, for example) whereas categorical identification implies "membership in a class of persons sharing some categorical attribute (such as race, ethnicity, language, nationality, citizenship, gender, sexual orientation, etc.)."[26] Within categorical identification, however, external categorization "developed by powerful, authoritative institutions," in particular the modern state, has played an important role in both practiced and analytical conceptions of identification and categorization.[27] These terms also allow for both modes of identification to exist simultaneously, as they do in reality.

Brubaker and Cooper advocate the use of these more nuanced and accurate linguistic descriptions that map onto a much more sophisticated analytical understanding of how identity exists, functions, and is manipulated in the world. They encourage us to stop using identity as a catchall term to express how individuals see themselves, how people define themselves, how we see others, how people align with and act on the basis of how they think of themselves and others and form rigid groups that exclude others. The terms they use instead—such as *self-identification, groupness,* and *identification practice*—capture more accurately the ways we think analytically about how identity functions in people's lives and in the world. These ways of thinking about identity allow us to understand identity as both lived by individuals and subject to the forces that push or pull people to group themselves in certain categories of national, religious, or ethnic affinity. Most important, as I discuss shortly, these conceptualizations of the various types of identification allow us to see how affiliations with these groups wax and wane over time. Because this book is a study of the writing of history and of people declaring their affiliations and self-identities, I base the discussion of Palestinian identity in this chapter largely on this practice-based conception of identity.

The fluctuating strength and weakness of affiliations and groupness, considered in the ways that Brubaker and Cooper encourage us to examine identity, is revealed particularly when analyzed over time. Thus, looking back historically to see how people thought of themselves and others reveals not only a different basis of groupness than exists today, but also the total demise of once salient, meaningful, and powerful groups. In the Palestinian case, we know of the disappearance of the once-strong identities of Qays and Yaman. In the nineteenth and extending into the early twentieth century, the genealogical division of central highland Palestinian families—from Nablus down to Hebron—centered on whether they belonged to the Qays or the Yaman. Also popular in Syria and Lebanon, Qays and Yaman were "expressed as clan alignments" that attributed the origin of the family to an ancestor from the pre-Islamic period in the Arabian Peninsula.[28] Political alliances were brokered, blood was shed, fields were harvested, and marriages were made or refused on the basis of this identity. According to Salim Tamari, Qays and Yaman were not actual biological lineages but "putative genealogies" of an ancient origin that people could shift in and out of—flexible categories that allowed alignment and realignment with feudal lords, regardless of other identifications, such as religion. Ramallah, for example, an entirely Christian village before 1948, was 90 percent Qays and 10 percent Yaman, and the two Christian Yamani families would align with the nearby Yamani villages of al-Bira and Baytunya (almost entirely Muslim) against Qaysi Ramallah. They favored this allegiance of origin over religious identification. Moreover, the categories of Qays and Yaman ensured not only protection and patronage but also people to help during harvest times. The villagers of Dura were Qays and would come to Ramallah to aid in the olive and fig harvests.[29] Despite the gravity and importance of these identities in the nineteenth and early twentieth centuries, people do not think in these ways today. No one thinks of themselves in these terms, and no group sentiments exist on the basis of these divisions. Many of the village books mention these affiliations, but they are groups without power, action, or even meaning. And although some people may know if they are from Qays or Yaman, no one from the Yaman refuses to let their daughter marry someone from the Qays, as they might have one hundred years ago, and no one travels tens of miles to help with a harvest in order to join their Qaysi brethren.[30]

MEMORIES OF TOGETHERNESS AND MEMORIES OF DIFFERENCE: JEWS AND ARABS IN PALESTINE

The historical reconstructions of village life expressed in contemporary village books address the issues of communal relations—among the villagers (as Muslims and Christians), and between the indigenous and immigrant Jewish communities. This section discusses how Palestinian villagers interacted with and what they thought of the Jewish communities around them, as well as how Palestinians today remember and record that part of their past. In many cases, the largely diasporic audience of the village books has had little to no contact with Israelis and Jews over the last sixty years, with the exception of wars and resistance fighting, and the occasional meeting in a third location. Of course some of the books were written and published by authors living in Israel, the West Bank, and Gaza who have had daily contact with Israelis since 1948 and 1967. But two-thirds of the books—some 80 of the 112 books in my collection—were published in Jordan, Lebanon, Syria or elsewhere.[31] The current paradigm of relationships in Palestine-Israel, which categorizes people as "Jews" and "Arabs" (or "Palestinians"), provides an opportunity to understand the effect of the present on the memories of the past. Fueled by modern national movements, these categories have come to be understood as mutually exclusive in the present era.[32] Most important is that although these groups are currently bounded and separated by national sentiment and geographic borders, these designations have changed dramatically over time.

Historically, the Ottoman *millet* system allowed local groups to govern their own communities in terms of family and social laws; it also created groups to which people had to belong in order to be part of society. With the bureaucratization of governmental administration at that time, religious, ethnic, and national categorizations were developed as means to enumerate and record group belonging for legal reasons and on identity cards and passports. These acts reified categories as necessarily groups that people belonged to on the basis of religious belief—Jews, Muslims, Christians—and loyalty to empire—Ottoman or foreigner.[33] With the rise of Zionism as a national movement, Arab Jews were pulled into a different group affiliation—from Jewish and Arab to Jewish and Zionist—while non-Arab Jews were categorized as "foreigners."

Technically, *Arab* designates a group of language speakers and, more recently, sentiment toward a larger community, whereas the term *Jew* implies religious belief and a sense, currently, of a people. Neither term excludes the other, however. People identified themselves as (and were identified as) Jewish Arabs or Arab Jews. As Ella Shohat and Joseph Massad explore, however, in the current environment most Jews who speak Arabic and were raised in Arab countries do not claim an Arab identity.[34] What constitutes Arabness and Jewishness are not innate but rather are defined by the dominant powers at any particular time—and in recent times in the Middle East, both of these labels have developed chauvinistic national elements that often exclude the other. This is not to say that they are equally chauvinistic; through the power of its state and military, Israel has violently and through the creation of an apartheid legal system been able to drive out, refuse to let in, or otherwise remove Palestinians from Israel, the West Bank, and Gaza. Palestinians have never had such power; their struggle, using both violent and nonviolent means, has been early on to eliminate the state of Israel, but since the 1970s it has been to have their own rights recognized. After 1948, many of the Arab states enacted oppressive laws that singled out their Jewish citizens, forcing many of them to leave, which combined with covert and overt Israeli activities to encourage Arab Jews to immigrate to Israel. This Israeli national and religious chauvinism has meant that Jews from Arab countries and the Arab people with whom they used to live have been suppressed under the hegemonic Ashkenazi (European) character of the Israeli state. According to Gidon Giladi, immigrant Ashkenazi Zionists believed in their own "qualitative and cultural superiority to the Palestinian Arab people and the Arab Islamic community, including those Jews who came from Arab countries."[35] The elimination of a sense of Arabness among Arab Jews has been as much related to political ideologies as to colonial ideas of culture. Shohat believes that "erasure of the Arab dimension of Sephardim is crucial from a Zionist perspective, since Israel has ended up in a paradoxical situation in which its 'Orientals' had closer cultural and historical links to the presumed enemy—the 'Arab'—than to the Ashkenazi Jews with whom they were forcibly merged into nationhood."[36] As Israelis have redefined (and degraded) what it means to be Arab, Jews from Arab countries have been divorced from (and have divorced themselves from) those with whom they shared language, culture, and history for centuries.[37]

At the same time, since the advent of the Zionist movement at the end of the nineteenth century, Arab communities in Palestine have had problems, both semantically and actually, with including the Jews in their midst. Palestinians have viewed (and continue to view) the influx of foreign Jews from Europe and Russia or the Soviet Union and their desire to found a Jewish national home in Palestine as a colonial project and something to fight against. Palestinian attacks on the Arab Jewish communities of Safad and Hebron in 1929, for example, in response to British concessions to the Zionist movement, reveal that some Palestinians grouped together all Jews and blurred the line between Arab Jews and the Ashkenazi Zionist immigrants. At the same time, many of these Jews were rescued from the angry and violent Palestinian mobs by Palestinian families.[38] The attacks on Arab Jews during this time and the identification of Arab Jews with the Zionist movement that disenfranchised and drove out the Palestinian Arab population make it difficult to delineate clearly the sentiments of the Palestinian population—Jews, Christians, and Muslims—toward one another. Shohat posits that with the growth of Zionist institutions and power in Palestine, Palestinians began to see "all Jews as at least potential Zionists,"[39] a fear that destroyed shared cultures and friendly relations but worked to the advantage of the Zionist movement to separate Jews from Arabs in the minds of Palestinians.

This ambiguity existed in both personal and community relationships, however, which were at times close and neighborly and at other times rife with suspicion. It shows the quickly altering ideas about what it meant to be Jewish,

Arab, Palestinian, and Zionist within this continually changing mix of political affiliations, self-understandings, cultural practices, and social relations. One example of the transformation in relationships and the difference between culturally similar Jews and foreign Jews appears in the village book on al-Shajara. On the one hand, the book mentions Kurdish Jews from Mosul arriving in the area during World War I. They came escaping the famine that had also hit their lands, they settled in the village "among the Arab families, and they shared our customs and traditions." The author lists the names of some of the families and their children; his narrators clearly wanted to show that they knew and remembered them by name. They later moved to the nearby Jewish settlement of Sejara, a result, he says, of the insecurity during the 1936–1939 Palestinian revolt and the association of all Jews with Zionism, as mentioned earlier.[40] After a page and a half of their customs and wedding songs, the author writes that "from this study of our village we can conclude that the Kurdish Jews were much more part of the Arab environment than what you might call the Israeli environment."[41] At the same time, the author mentions the land disputes that the villagers had with the nearby Jewish settlement, including a court case, and the land confiscated from the village by the British Mandate government for Jews in Palestine.[42] The dichotomy between how the Palestinians remember and write about the Jewish residents of Palestine whom they accepted and remembered warmly (even though they left the village to live in the settlement) and how they remember and write about the Jewish foreign settlers is based on a shared culture and values, and not solely on religion.

In Palestinian communities, the sixty years of wars, invasions, militant movements, refugee status, military administrative rule, military occupation, borders, and separation walls since the 1948 War affect how they remember their past relationships with Jews. On the basis of her work among Palestinians living in the Galilee inside Israel, Rhoda Kanaaneh expresses the fear that the present dichotomy between Jew and Arab has gone so far as even to erase "any *memories* of hybridity."[43] But these years of conflict do not necessarily wipe out all memories of shared spaces and interactions; instead, it is perhaps because of the conflict, and out of nostalgia for remembering times of less conflict, that Palestinians tell stories and highlight their memories of interactions with Jews. These stories also reflect the cultural identification that Palestinian Arabs felt with Jewish Arabs (or non-Arab Middle Eastern Mizrahi Jews), born of a feeling of groupness based on shared values and cultural similarities. In interviews I conducted, people expressed to me a nostalgia for the time when they had good relations with their Jewish neighbors, a nostalgia for what might have been, they said, without the creation of an exclusive Jewish state that took their land. At the same time, they also expressed memories of Jews framed by a nationalist fight for land, resources, and control.

Despite the political ideologies that separated Jews and Palestinians in the twentieth century, the village books express how Palestinians recall shared spaces, religious occasions, and mercantile relations with Arab Jews, whom they regarded as part of the indigenous population. Between the village of Lifta, which was right on the outskirts of Jerusalem, and Jerusalem was an area that the villagers called Shaykh Badr and that the Jews called Romeima. The oral histories collected in one of the village books mentions that living in Shaykh Badr were mostly "Eastern Jews" (*yahud sharqiyyin*), whose "ways of life were close to Arab ways."[44] One woman recalled, "We used to buy things from them and they would buy building stones from us. A normal relation like neighbors, no rivalry. We were all one. . . ."[45] Another person reported, "We used to live in Romeima, and we were totally mixed among the Jews. There were friendships and other relations, and they would visit us on the *eid* [feast day] and eat with us. The relations were good between us and them."[46] The stories in this book describe how people used to sell their products at the market of Mahne Yahuda and go to Jewish doctors in Romeima or Mahne Yahuda before the first Liftawi graduated from medical school and became the local doctor. These memories even free these Jews of responsibility for the events of 1948. One Arab resident of Shaykh Badr/Romeima recalls that the Jews of Romeima were not the ones fighting. To this day, they say, the Liftawis retain relations with the Jews of Romeima: "It was the Zionists who began the hostilities. The old Jews' characteristics and behavior were eastern, closer to Arabs."[47]

Individuals' stories also reveal incidents of religious intermarriage, which in general was rare. One man I interviewed from 'Ayn Karim told me that his mother was from an Orthodox Jewish family from the Mea Shea'rim neighborhood in Jerusalem. Upon receiving news of the marriage, her Jewish family behaved as if she had died. She lived in 'Ayn Karim, converted to Christianity (the religion of her husband), and became a refugee with the rest of the family in 1948.[48] Muslim men married Jewish women as well: the Lifta book tells of Fahmi Ibrahim Abu Sa'ad of Lifta, who married a Jewish woman; and a similar story about Muhammad Sadiq al-Madi is told in the book about Tantura.[49] Notably, the only recorded incidents of intermarriage I found were of Jewish women marrying Arab men.

The books also publish some evidence of the daily interactions and relationships between Jews and Palestinians during the Mandate period. The book on Bashsheet tells the story of one man who says, "If we got sick, for example, if someone's eyes hurt him, he would go to Yibna to a Jewish woman doctor whom we called Imm Yusif."[50] Another example appears in two of the village books about Salama village, which reproduce a number of petitions that were submitted to the assistant district commissioner of al-Lyd and al-Ramla by the *mukhtars* and populations of the surrounding villages requesting that the Salama Bus Company be allowed to take its vehicles all the way into the city of Lyd.[51] Reproduced in these books are two other Arabic petitions, one English petition, and one Hebrew petition explaining the situation. Because the majority of village book readers do not know Hebrew well enough to read the document, it seems as if the documents are present there in the three languages in order to provide an example of cooperative efforts that transcended competing national interests in order to provide transportation for all of the residents of the area, and specifically by an Arab transportation company. That the village book authors chose to reprint these documents also indicates the willingness of contemporary Palestinian authors to represent this aspect of the past.

However, the content of the three petitions reveals fundamentally different interpretations of responsibility. The Arabic and English petitions submitted by the Palestinian villagers say that the government's unwillingness to allow the buses to enter the city makes it difficult for many people who have to walk the rest of the way into the city, particularly women and children and those who need to go to government departments, courts, and the police.[52] The petition in Hebrew has a much different request from the *mukhtars*[53] and citizens of HaTikva: "We would like very much to ask that the government give instructions to the Salama Bus Company to continue the service so that the S12 will continue on to the city of Lod [Lydda or al-Lyd]." So, although Palestinian villagers know that it is the government that has restricted them from entering al-Lyd (and there are other documents that prove this), the people from HaTikva have framed it as something that the (Arab) bus company refuses to let them do. In some ways, this lack of communication and the politics of blaming ensured the separation of the communities that was taking place.

So why do Palestinians hold on to these documents and reproduce stories of coexistence and cooperation when the present circumstances clearly pressure them toward narratives of conflict and division? It would have been very easy for authors not to include these stories of living together and cooperation, and for narrators not to tell them. On some level, including these documents reveals the authors' concern with documenting the past as they experienced it or heard about it or found material about it, and these relations were an element of that past. However, it also reflects that Palestinians felt an affiliation with those with whom they could work and with whom they shared their values and who respected them. So, rather than Jewishness being at issue for the Palestinians recalling their relationships prior to 1948, they express their connections and affinities with the people with whom they shared values and a sense of citizenship. It is, as I mentioned earlier, a nostalgia for what might have been.

However, Palestinians do tell critical stories about some Jews and Brits. In particular, the people—both Jewish and British—who were behind the colonial project that resulted in the stunting of Palestinian political and national ambitions and the creation of the refugees in 1948 come under verbal attacks and were the subjects of negative stories in the village books. In the climate of contemporary Arab-Israeli relations, the stories about antagonisms between Palestinians and Jews are not surprising. The conflict-driven accounts in the village books reflect the struggles between Zionists and Palestinians. In these stories, Jews are often included when discussing the nationalist activities of the villagers and their resistance in concrete ways to the Zionist movement, in particular as regards land sales and during the 1936–1939 revolt, which was a negative turning point in Jewish-Arab relations. These larger national issues are portrayed as being at the heart of village life during this period, and as reflecting the larger concerns of all Palestinians. As part of their history, villagers from Kawfakha narrate how they refused to sell any of their village land to a nearby Jewish settlement that had been established in 1941. According to one narrator, a village man got in a fight with his brother. In order to spite him, the brother decided to sell their three hundred dunums of land to the head of the Jewish settlement (*kabaniya*) of Dorot:

> The head of the settlement and his guards came to our town riding on horses and they had eggplant, tomatoes, and potatoes with them as a present. They went to the house of the man who wanted to sell the land. Our *mukhtar* asked what they were doing and why they had come here. They told him what had happened and that the men were coming to buy so-and-so's land. The *mukhtar* (may God have mercy on his soul) approached them and said, "Wait, *ya khawaja* [Mister], wait. Don't ever enter this village again. We don't have anyone here who wants to sell

land. If you ever come back again or buy one inch of land from it, you know what will happen." I swear to God, the kids threw rocks at them, and they ran off and never returned. The important point of the story is that there was no cooperation between us [the villagers and the nearby Jewish settlers].[54]

In this account, the *mukhtar* protects the villagers from the settlers who wish to take advantage of the feuding within the village. The pettiness of the brother who would have sold land to the Jewish settlers is given a central role as the *raison d'être* of the land sale, which by this time was well known to be an antinationalistic act. The *mukhtar* appears as nationalistic and also as aware that such a sale would have brought into question the reputation of the entire village; thus he is portrayed as defending the village and the nationalist cause against the actions of the one villager. This is not to say that villagers did not cooperate with the Jewish settlers or sell land to them, although evidence shows that the majority of those who sold land were absentee landowners or land-owning urban notables.[55]

In the village book about Abu Kishk, one of the villagers tells a story to illustrate relations between the villagers and Jews after the 1936–1939 revolt:

My father came across some people from al-Qar'an with twelve head of cattle. He asked them, "Where are you taking those cows?" "We're going to sell them to the Jews," they replied. My father had his pistol at his side and he grabbed it and— bang, bang—killed all twelve cows so that they couldn't sell them to the Jews.[56]

At this time, two of the strategies of the six-month strike at the outset of the 1936–1939 revolt were the boycott of Jewish (and British) businesses, and to not pay taxes to the British Mandate authority. Amos Nadan shows that in the two years before the revolt it is estimated that "the Arabs supplied about 61 percent of Jewish consumption from local vegetable produce," whereas that number dropped to 26 percent during the revolt.[57] It would seem that both the desire and the pressure to participate in the strike were significant.

Furthermore, the exclusivity of the Zionist movement contradicted the neighborly relations and shared values that had characterized how Palestinians saw Arab Jews. The Zionist movement during this period was intent on building a Jewish state at the expense of Arab society in Palestine. Two slogans of the Zionist movement were to support *'Avoda 'Ivrit* (Jewish labor) and buy *Tozat 'Ivrit* (Jewish products).[58] The Jewish National Fund (JNF) was established in 1901 at the Fifth Zionist Congress to "purchase land in Palestine as an inviolate possession of the Jewish people."[59] Both JNF land and land purchased by the Jewish Agency were not to be leased or sold to non-Jews. In the leases to Jews, fines were prescribed for leasees who employed non-Jewish labor, with provisions for their eviction from the land.[60] In this milieu of colonial and exclusionary attitudes and policies, many Palestinians (although not all), felt it was a Palestinian nationalist duty to avoid cooperating with Jews because of their exclusivist activities and their visions of a Jewish state that excluded Palestinians. Hence the story of a Palestinian who would punish another Palestinian and shoot his cows for cooperating with Jews.

In the large sections about the events of the 1948 War in the Palestinian village books, the authors often include stories about attempts by both the villagers and the nearby Jewish settlements to dissuade military attacks. The al-Shajara village book mentions that the leader of the Kurdish Jews tried to broker an agreement with the al-Shajara villagers before May 15, 1948, that neither group would fight, but the al-Shajara villagers (given that by this date some 200 to 300 thousand Palestinians had already been displaced from their villages and cities) wanted to fight and defend their land.[61] In Wadi al-Hawarith, just preceding the war of 1948, the leader of the Bedouin tribe called for peace with the local Jewish regional council, but the "Haganah attacked the tribe's remnants, 'advised' them to leave, and then *assisted by the local Jewish settlements*, systematically destroyed the houses and huts at . . . Wadi al-Hawarith . . . making a return all but impossible."[62] In the Israeli attack on the coastal village of Tantura, population 1,500, on May 22–23 of 1948, a large number of the village men were put in prison, others were killed, and the rest of the villagers were expelled first to the village of al-Furaydis and then beyond the Israeli borders.[63] The village book tells the details of these events, including a story of two unarmed Palestinian men that the Israeli Haganah forces found on the eastern edge of the village. They told the men to stand facing one of the tall rock formations in the village and lifted their guns. But "one of the Jews from Zichron Ya'akov accompanying the Haganah forces knew one of the men—Yahya bin Muhammad Khadr al-Madi—who lived in the village. The Jewish man felt bad and lauded al-Madi's character and behaviors, so they pardoned him. But they executed the other man, Mustafa Abu Jamous, right there."[64]

Although the intertwined histories of the residents of Palestine prior to 1948 are mentioned in these local histories of village life, they are not called on to represent the collective experiences of Palestinians and Jews under the Mandate and during Ottoman times. Instead, Palestinians who currently live in the diaspora and have no contact with Israelis (or even non-Israeli Jews) find it hard to accept the stories of personal contact and friendships between what have now become quite rigid categories of Israeli Jews and Arabs. Because the Israeli state now categorizes Jews as one collective, and because contemporary Palestinians have been faced with violence and disenfranchisement at the hands of members of that state, the idea of Jews and Arabs being neighbors, colleagues, and friends may indeed be only a fading memory. Yet many Palestinian urban and rural residents told stories from pre-1948 of collegial work relations, mercantile ties, and neighborly relations with Jews in Palestine. Palestinian collective narratives, particularly public ones espoused in statements and books, largely ignore these pre-war interactions of commonality and read into history a continual bitter line of conflict and being attacked. Israeli Jews have invested in a European Ashkenazi Jewish experience that defines them and a history of the Yishuv (the Zionist Jewish community in Palestine prior to 1948) that glosses over the experiences of living with Arabs and shared neighborhoods and in some cases even positions itself in opposition to them.[65] This dominant Israeli memory has come to represent the identity politics of the present, especially for Israelis. Despite the varied individual memories of the past, the antagonistic history of the present situation has hegemonized the national and collective understanding of those periods, largely effacing Palestinian and Israeli collective narratives of shared commonalities and experiences while emphasizing the national conflict. In the context of living apart, the identities that separate people, such as political ideologies and religion, become more salient, especially as people use them to mark and inform difference, possibility, and privilege.

ARAB, PALESTINIAN, MUSLIM: SENSES OF GROUPNESS, CHANGE, AND CONTINUITY

One group sentiment that has bound Palestinians together from the nineteenth and twentieth centuries and into the present is a sense of being Arab. What it means to be Arab has changed over time, as has who is included in the group, to reflect the various sentiments, affiliations, and interests around which people create connections. For many centuries, prior to the *nahda* and the Arab renaissance of the nineteenth century, the appellation of the plural *'Arab* in Arabic connotated the nomadic Bedouin, and settled people in cities and villages would not have used it as a label of self-identity. However, as Arabic speakers, they would have contrasted themselves with non-Arabic speakers, and in contrast to other non-Arabs, might have portrayed themselves as Arabs. But one of the difficulties in understanding identity in the past is that, there are very few (or no) sources to access for popular and everyday understandings of how people thought of themselves at that time.

In the nineteenth and early twentieth centuries, the people living in historic Palestine created new ways of thinking of themselves as a collective, and this period witnessed the rise of the *Nahda* (Renaissance), in which Arabness and the Arabic language were seen as a heritage to be reclaimed and revived, a heritage that grew out of the Arab Muslim ages of intellectual creativity, scientific discovery, and strength of empire. The *Nahda* movement emerged during the fading of the military power of the Ottoman Empire, the strong Turkification of that Empire, rising nationalist sentiments elsewhere, and the European economic, political, and cultural penetration of North Africa and the Middle East. During this time, Arabness was about pride in the past, about a shared history, and about emphasizing Arabic as a mother tongue. This sense of being Arab crossed religious lines while celebrating the fact that Arabs and Arabic had spread throughout the Middle East under Muslim rule. During the *Nahda* and well into the twentieth century, Christians, Muslims, and Jews participated in creating a literate society that used the Arabic language in periodicals, fiction, poetry, essays, theater, and history texts. [66]

During the political liberation movements of the 1930s to 1960s, Arabness developed new political meanings, and people endowed it with a way of thinking—a political belief in a unity built around this ethnolinguistic identification. This Arabness built on the previous sense of shared bonds of language, an origin in Arabia, and shared Arab ancestors—all of which still had little to do with religion, except the acknowledgement of the connection between Arabs and Arabic via the Muslim conquest.[67] The concept of being *Arab* became a nationalist way of thinking of the self and others, and Arab nationalism was the political movement espoused by Palestinian leaders and movements in the 1950s and 1960s throughout the Arab World. I narrate Palestinians' Arabness in this way in order to draw on Brubaker and Cooper's understanding of identity: Arabness is a sense of groupness that fluctuates over time, and the historical pasts with which it is associated sometimes creates weak affinities of lifestyle and heritage, and sometimes strongly binds people together in political movements.[68]

Although linguists and archaeologists have discovered ancient references to Arabs as nomads living on the fringes of state powers,[69] what ties contemporary

Arabic speakers to the people of the ancient past is an identity constructed around a continuity they have established with that past. Palestinians' sense of Arabness is closely associated with the Islamic conquest and the settlement and migration of Arab tribes from the south. Throughout the more than thirteen hundred years of Muslim rule, Palestine (and all of the other areas under that rule) existed not as a separate nation-state but as part of a larger territory in which people moved and traveled among the various areas. This sense of shared history and language provides Palestinians with a connection to greater Muslim and Arab identifications in which they understand their local and family origins and claim a history and an identity.

Detailing the distinct history of a village or city or family within the context of the larger history of Palestine, the Levant, and Arab tribes provides people with access to a past that ties them to a more powerful historical narrative of Arab migrations, the Islamic conquest, and local resistance to the Crusades. The authors and narrators of the village books describe places and their inhabitants in terms that emphasize pre-nation-state identities, ways of conceiving of themselves and the past within a cultural system of identification that continues to have meaning. Mikhail Bakhtin speaks to the relation between collective knowledge passed on through families and larger narratives of the past: "The national ideal is represented by ancestors."[70] Placing family, tribal, and village origins within a Muslim identity gives Palestinians a history in the land that stretches back many hundreds of years. Because the history of Palestine is part of the Arab and Islamic past, Palestinians can claim to be Palestinian, Muslim, and Arab, sharing "natural" historical, linguistic, cultural, and social ties to larger groups.

Slyomovics found in her study of the Palestinian village of 'Ayn Hawd that the five family lineages (*dar*) of that village trace their descent back to one of Saladin's generals who was given land in the Haifa hills for his role in the Battle of Hittin against the Crusaders.

> The historical and genealogical connection to a medieval past and the awards from their heroic leader, Saladin [Salah al-Din], illustrate the ways in which contemporary Palestinian narrative is not separable from the Palestinian people's existence in Palestine and their subsequent displacement from their homeland. The Palestinian national narrative cannot be reduced to a response to Zionism; in the case of the history of the Abu al-Hayja's in Ein Houd, the story stems from Saladin's twelfth-century conquests.[71]

Such ties to the past exist in memory as much as in written documentable history. Abu al-Hayja ("the Daring") was the nickname of the governor of Irbil District in Iraq. He served as commander of the garrison at Acre during the Crusader siege of the city that lasted from 1189 to 1192. Although he returned to Iraq and died there, "several members of his family remained in the country under orders from the sultan and settled on spacious tracts of land that they had been granted in the Carmel region, in the Lower, Eastern, and Western Galilee, and in the Hebron Highlands."[72] In the village books, the origin of 'Ayn Hawd is told through a collective memory that ties the village to a specific event and person, one that has credibility within the narrative of Palestinian, Arab, and Islamic history.

The village books also posit a much less direct family or historical connection to Arabness through citing the pre-Islamic Arab past. Most scholarly and popular conceptions of Arabness are tied to Islam, but Palestinians also cite an Arab history that pre-dates the Islamic conquest. The Bayt Nabala book describes the Ghassanids, an Arab Christian group that lived in southern Syria, Jordan, and Palestine in the third century CE prior to the coming of Islam to the region.[73] The village books also adopt pre-Islamic historical information about Arabs, and the educated conjectures of scholars, archaeologists, and philologists who posit that the Canaanites migrated out of the Arabian Penninsula and spoke a semitic, proto-Arabic language.[74] The author of one of the village books on 'Ayn Karim, for example, traces the history of Palestine and its people back to the Canaanite migration from the Arabian Peninsula around 3,500 BCE into the Holy Land.[75] In this way, by connecting themselves to the Canaanites, Palestinians not only tie themselves to a sense of Arabness, both ancient and modern, but also claim a pre-Israelite past on the land that continues to inform how people think about themselves in the present.

Palestinians cite the many civilizations that pre-dated the modern period as proof that through these histories they themselves have had a long existence on this land. In the same ways that the modern Zionist movement claims an ancient historical and ethnic connection to the land of Israel for the Jewish people, Palestinians claim an ancient historical and ethnolinguistic connection to the same land as the Arab Canaanites and Philistines, as mentioned in the Hebrew Scriptures. Thus Palestinians are claiming not just a physical connection to the land and space, but also an ethnolinguistic connection to Arabness, to origin, and to language. The village memorial books demonstrate this sense of family and ethnoliguistic history as essential to national claims to the land.

One book declares that in discussing the tribes and families of the village, "our subject is not the study of the lineages, as much as it is remembering and confirming [dhikr wa-tathbit] the names of the families and tribes of al-Walaja to demonstrate their presence and roots there since olden times to the present."[76]

Some Palestinians, from both villages and cities, are not of Arab origin but are Circassian or Albanian or from other ethnic origins.[77] These identities are acknowledged and recognized as a heritage and origin, and in most cases they are then situated within a Palestinian national identity, which until recently has been an inclusive, territory and sentiment-based political identity that includes all those who lived in historic Palestine and express a political belief in their belonging to a Palestinian nation. The villagers of Umm al-Faraj, from the Acre district, attribute their origins to Circassian Mamlukes removed from Egypt under the reign of Muhammad Ali.[78] Their knowledge of their own past provides them with other frameworks in which to understand their family and village history. However, as one of these villagers, a refugee in Lebanon, attests, "Palestine will stay in my heart forever and ever, whether I am from Turkic background or not."[79] This author's sentiments and identity as Palestinian in no way contradicts or takes away from his ethnic origin (which he calls his background), thus allowing him to assert a Palestinian identity. "For me," he says, "I am proud to be from Turkic origins, but I am more proud to be a Palestinian, as is my father."[80] Not only does he express his sentiments about being Palestinian, but he also attributes the same to his father, and thus his national identity is also part of the family patrimony. His ethnic background as a Circassian Turk is another layer of his family and his village's history and identity, which have been subsumed within a Palestinian national identity. In this case, and in many others, village and city origins and inhabitants are situated within Islamic and Arab history, which allows the village book authors to emphasize both the national and the ethnocultural identity of their family or village.

VISIONS OF THE PAST: A LAND-BASED IDENTIFICATION

In 1998, fifty years after the founding of the Israeli state, Palestinian poet Mahmud Darwish penned "The Palestinian People's Appeal on the 50th Anniversary of the Nakba. He invoked Palestinians' history in the following terms:

> Not emerging from the darkness of myth or legend, we were born in the
> pristine daylight of history on this land which gave birth to the most ancient

of civilizations. On this land humanity found its way to building its first home, to planting its first wheat grain, to creating its first alphabet. From the hills of Jerusalem, the first prayers of gratitude rose to the Creator. Our land, modest in size, hosted vast cultures and civilizations, both in conflict and in harmony, our own culture emerging from the fullness of this diverse and rich heritage. Our human history began with the history of humanity. Our Arab history began with the history of the Arabs. The consciousness of our national history began with our resistance to conquest and greed, which beset our land.[81]

In his description, Darwish summons up multiple pasts and identities—an ancient history tied to the Fertile Crescent and the advent of human history, a religious connection to the first monotheists, an Arab history, and a national history under siege. This conception of the Palestinian past—as a continuous movement of time that shaped Palestinians into the diverse group they have become—imagines the Palestinian homeland as a *place* the history of which has shaped who Palestinians are today. In this view, Palestinian understandings of their history as a people not only are tied to the creation of a modern nation-state, but also invoke an inheritance of all that has happened on the land for everyone who has been there.

This way of thinking, in terms of a land-based identification category, is in opposition to the ethnic and religious identification that defines Israeli identity as a Jewish state for a group of people identified as Jews (although it does give citizenship to non-Jews.)[82] Palestinians have rooted their sense of nationalism in a discourse that emphasizes the connection between people and the land, a territory-based sense of identification. A national connection to a territory and the history of that territory is of course a common element of nationalism. Although Palestinians also connect to other identifications—political beliefs, religion, ethnicity, clan, family—and connect them to their sense of being Palestinian, the ways in which they think about their villages and the land of Palestine suggest that in the twentieth and twenty-first centuries, Palestinians anchor themselves within a web of history, knowledge, and connection to the *land* of Palestine.

Palestinian national identification is framed by geographic origin and sentiment toward Palestine, which is why they call themselves Palestinian.[83] The village books frame each community within Palestinian national terms and delineate the village's geographical relation to the nation. Dirbas, for example, tells us that "al-Birwa is one of the Arab Palestinian villages from the Acre District that was destroyed in the 1948 War. . . ."[84] In these village book narratives, the authors represent each village as similar to all other Palestinian villages, in particular because of their shared national fate. Another book relates that "Suba represents one village among the hundreds of Palestinian villages that were erased from the Palestinian map in 1948."[85] Geographical descriptions also situate the villages within the national context: "Al-Faluja is an Arab Palestinian village that lies in southern Palestine."[86] And the authors of one of the books on the village of 'Innaba write, "'Innaba (with a fatha on the b) was one village in the district of al-Ramla."[87] The authors place the villages and the experiences of the inhabitants as representative of and part of a national identity that is defined by geographic borders in relationship to other villages and cities in historic Palestine.

In the village books, the authors place the villages not only within the land of historic Palestine, but also within the historic chronology that took place in Palestine. The village books tell the stories of the villages as not only a history of a people, but also as the history of that place. They connect the destroyed Palestinian village to the pre-modern and pre-national history of the village, claiming as part of their own histories the entire record of human habitation on that land. In particular, the ancient pre-history, Canaanite, Philistine, Jebusite, Israelite, Greek, Roman, Byzantine, Islamic, and Ottoman pasts are described as part of the heritage and history of the inhabitants of those same places on that same land.[88]

These connections of the village to the ancient past are evidenced in origin stories, in the meaning of village names, and in the archaeological evidence that the authors include as part of the historical record. Regardless of what exists in the historical record, what interests me here is how Palestinians retell the history of the villages to include all of the historical record. "The relations of people to place," according to Liisa Malkki, "tend to be naturalized in discursive and other practices."[89] By recalling and reworking stories of the past that connect people to places, they "impart familiar repeating shapes to discursive historical memory. . . ."[90] Take, for example, the summary about the village of Abu Shusha from the CDRPS Web site:

> Abu Shusha was situated on the south slope of Tall Jazar where the coastal plain meets the Jerusalem foothills [. . .], and was linked by a secondary road to the Jaffa-Jerusalem highway to the northeast. Tall Jazar has been identified with

the Old Testament city of Gezer, but settlement may date back as early as the fourth millennium BC. Excavations conducted in Abu Shusha in the early 1900s turned up artifacts that date back to the third millennium BC (the early Bronze Age). Prior to Roman times, it was documented that the city was controlled by the Canaanites (who built a wall around it), Egypt (it was mentioned as one of the cities Thutmose III conquered, circa 1469 BC), and the first Jewish kingdom (Solomon is believed to have turned it into a major stronghold).[91]

In this reckoning, the successive ancient civilizations are rendered as part of the history of the village. Village book authors tell these stories so that villagers can know this history and thus connect themselves to it and claim it as part of their village's patrimony.

CANAAN AND THE HISTORY OF THE LAND

Contemporary scholars have made the case that colonialism, biblical studies, and the Zionist movement narratives have gone hand in hand in accentuating Israelite history and disregarding other histories in the same geographical location.[92] Politically this religious championing of the ancient Israelite past, based on ancient Jewish claims to the land given to them by God as evidenced in their religious scriptures, has been and still is used to justify the creation of a modern Israeli state. Although it is based in these religious beliefs, the Zionist movement grew out of national movements in Europe in the nineteenth century. Biblical scholars and Zionists were delighted to find in the nineteenth and twentieth centuries that the Palestinians living in the Holy Land were, as the Europeans and Americans patronizingly described them, living as they did in "biblical times."[93]

Textual scholarship and archaelogical excavations anchored the biblical scriptures and stories to actual physical places in the Holy Land from the late nineteenth century to the present, and archaelogy has focused largely on periods related to the Old Testament (Hebrew Scriptures). Nadia Abu El-Haj shows in her *Facts on the Ground: Archaeological Practice and territorial Self-Fashioning in Israeli Society* that "archaeological practice generated a historical knowledge and epistemology that became almost second nature in representations of and arguments about nation, homeland, sovereignty, national rights, history, and heritage for decades to come."[94] This search for a biblical past and its use as the basis for a modern-day nation state has resulted in ignoring pre-Israelite history and the centuries that followed the Israelite presence, all of which were fundamental to the development of the land, history, trade, and languages of historic Palestine and the peoples who lived there.[95]

The village book authors both draw on and contrast themselves to this particular historical record generated by archaeologists and biblical scholars intent on finding a history that "supports European intellectual and spiritual claims of continuity with the Bible and its past."[96] The village book authors and Palestinians in general have sought their own origins outside of and parallel to this "biblicalization" of their existence. They ascribe their origins to Canaanite civilizations in geographic Palestine that pre-date the Israelite kingdoms and who spoke West Semitic languages and lived along the Mediterranean coast from present day Lebanon south to Gaza and to the Jordan river in the east.[97] The authors of the al-Walaja village book declare, for example, that "Palestine was known in the past as the land of Canaan, and al-Walaja village was a part of it."[98] But because, as I explore shortly, Palestinians want to be Arabs, they do not claim the Canaanite past as an ethnic origin necessarily; rather, it is a land-based origin with ethnic undertones. Most archeological theories on the subject suggest that around 2500 BCE, migrants from the Arabian peninsula settled along the Eastern Mediterranean and became some of the early semitic groups in the area, such as the Canaanites and Amorites. Meron Benvenisti finds that by claiming this ancient past as Canaanite, Palestinians "stand the Israeli claim to 'the *fallahin*'s [peasants] being living proof of the ways of life of our ancient (Jewish) forebears' on its head; living proof they are, but of the life of those who predated the Israelite tribe, that is, the Canaanite-Arabs."[99]

Benvenisti describes the process that took place between 1948 and 1951 in which the JNF's naming committee "assigned 200 new names" to the formerly Palestinian villages and lands that were now emptied and part of the Israeli state.[100] He asserts that "choosing a name for one of the Jewish settlements that were springing up in or beside abandoned Arab villages was generally quite uncomplicated: the committee simply restored the ancient Hebrew name that had been preserved, almost unchanged, in the Arabic one."[101] Although he notes that the intervening centuries of Palestinian Arab Muslim presence were ignored, he does not acknowledge that the ancient Hebrew names may have been adopted from Canaanite place names. The normalization of the biblical as the origin of these place names relies on the Judeo-Christian-Islamic scriptural tradition rather than on a studied and informed exploration of the historical record.

Among the examples of the "name-restoring" work, Benvenisti cites the Palestinian village of Yibna, renamed Yavneh. The name appears in the Hebrew Scriptures as Yavneh (or Jabneh). However, the scriptural reference to Yavneh is to a Canaanite town (not an Israelite town) that is mentioned twice in Joshua to describe the division of land after the Israelite conquest of parts of Canaan.[102] In addition, in 2 Chronicles 26:6–7, it is mentioned that Uzziah, King of Judah, "took the field against the Philistines and broke down the walls of Gath, Jabneh, and Ashdod; and he built cities in the territory of Ashdod and among the Philistines. God aided him against them, against the Arabs who lived in Gur baal, and against the Meunites."[103] But the history that the Israelis drew on in renaming the village in 1949 is not the biblical accounts, which show that Canaanite Yavneh pre-dated the Israelite presence. Rather, Benvenisti cites Yavneh's importance as a Jewish site much later: following the destruction of Jerusalem in 70 CE, it hosted a reconstituted Sanhedrin for twenty years, until centers of Jewish learning and religious leadership were established in the Galilee.[104] While Zionist discourse cites biblical scriptures to claim Jewish rights to the land, in this case, the scriptures indicate the presence of others prior to the Israelite presence, something not consonant with the Zionist version of pre-modern history. The careful selection of historical moments chosen to build national narratives (an action not unique to Israelis or Palestinians), elides ill-fitting information and validates that which bolsters the chosen story. But the continuity of village names over the millennia suggests a more rooted connection between names and places that changing populations maintain, in spite of modern exclusionary nationalist readings of history.

As Palestinians claim an ancient past as their own, they challenge the dominance of the religious scholars and political ideologues who have positioned Israelite history on the land as the only one of relevance in the Holy Land. Palestinians do this in part by tracing the etymologies of their village names back to the Canaanite period, to names that they still use in some form today. 'Abdallah Abu Sbayh, in his book on the village of al-'Abbasiyya, mentions the Canaanite history of al-Yahudiyya village along with the history of other villages in the surrounding area: Jaffa (whose Canaanite name was Yafo), the village of Yalu (formerly called Ilon), Sayidna 'Ali (called Arsuf), and Hadid (called Haditha).[105] Village and city names are traced in encyclopedic form in books like Hussein al-Lubani's *Mu'jam asma' al-mudun wal-qura al-filastini-yya wa tafseer ma'aniha* (Lexicon of Palestinian city and village names and explanations of their meanings), which describes the Palestinian village of Jimzu, located on the rolling plains east of al-Ramla: Gamzu, which means "many sycamores," was the name of a Canaanite city on this spot. It was then called Gamza in Roman times.[106] The variations in names and how they are carried through the ages illustrate the deeply rooted connections of the places to many histories.

This connection to the ancient past appears not only in the continuing use and knowledge of village names, but also in the village places that were part of people's lives. Palestinians not only claim a pre-Israelite connection to the land, but they also connect themselves to the two thousand plus years of history from the Greek conquest to the present. This type of history is evidenced most often in archaeological remains and in references in Greek and Arabic sources; thus it cites different authorities than those who tell the history of the Holy Land only from biblical sources. These types of village history seek other historically significant empires and nodes of time to which to anchor themselves: "The Greek and Roman oil presses still remain, carved into the rock of our village Bayt Mahsir, long after those Empires faded and were defeated by the Arab Muslims. Likewise the monumental olive trees from that era stand until today."[107]

These places in the village are not just remnants of a past claimed by the villagers, but they are also spaces that the villagers used and that were part of their lives. The list of significant places in the village book about al-Walaja refers to "al-Charcha, a hill above the village to the northwest. They say this hill is called this because of the remnants of an old church in the village."[108] Al-Charcha acquired a different meaning for the villagers, as related in this story from PalestinianRemembered.com:

> *Ala al-charcha ya walagia ala al-charcha* [To the Charcha, Walaji, to the Charcha]: When we were young children, my beloved Father (*rahemaho Allah*) used to tell us stories about al-Walaja and the special hillside, called the Karka (*charcha* in al-Walaja dialogue [sic]). When the people of al-Walaja of any Hamoulah used to get into a fight with another, they used to call each other by saying "Ala al-charcha ya walagia ala al-charcha." This hillside was very rocky and steep, therefore, whoever gets up to the top first wins the fight. And the winning was by throwing rocks and stones at the people down below.[109]

The church, from the Byzantine period most likely, was part of the villagers' everyday lives—not only a site that the Muslim villagers call by its former name, but one that functions differently for them today.

The village books illustrate how ancient-, classical-, Byzantine-, and Islamic-era ruins are incorporated into the lives of the villagers in a multitude of ways. A few kilometers from the village of Dayr Aban lie the ruins of Bir al-Limon (the Well of Lemons), from which villagers used to water their herds until 1948. It derived its name, stories tell, from long-ago lemon trees. The people of the village believed that the well water had healing properties because the sun never touched it.[110] Carved in relief on one of the walls above the well was a cross in a circle surrounded with leaf designs. Villagers told two stories associated with the well: one about two separated lovers who were reunited at the well, only to die there also;[111] the other about an old unmarried man from the Dyarba family who went to Bir al-Limon to water his sheep but found someone blocking the entrance to the well. After asking him repeatedly to move but to no avail, the Dyarba man shot him with his rifle. "The man did not fight back but said, "Go, and may God eliminate your offspring." And that's what happened. There aren't very many of the Dyarba to this day."[112] These ancient places in the village, like Bir al-Limon, are not just remnants of past peoples and civilizations; they are also places of meaning for the villagers that connect the past to the present. Bir al-Limon existed for them without a lemon tree in sight—although villagers said that on some days you could catch the scent of the blossoms from long ago.[113] This well and the story associated with it also explain a social issue for the villagers: why there are so few people of the Dyarba lineage.

By incorporating these ruins and structures from previous civilizations into their own, the village descendents integrate the land itself into the identifications they are making with being from this village. In these books, the relationships of the villagers to these places are lived, not generated by a state power or national myths.[114] History here is not only unearthed and used to legitimate the present and subsumed into a national narrative; it is also expressed as part of the lived environment of the villagers.

· · ·

The vast majority of studies of contemporary Palestinian identity focus on how Palestinian identity is formed and transferred in the absence of the nation-state. For both the Palestinians who remained and the diaspora populations, national identity has been retained, built and cultivated through nonstate efforts, such as political movements; family stories; cultural movements in poetry, music, and art; community events; and student activism, among other influences—including, most recently, the village books and other texts.[115]

Palestinian identification practices and feelings of groupness *as Palestinians* provide them with a strong categorical identity as members of a nation, and at the same time allow them to express long-standing relational modes of constructing their identification practices vested by religion, ethnic origin, kinship, and family. Thus, as is evident in narratives of modern Palestinian life and history, Palestinians understand and frame their accounts with overlapping senses of a greater Palestinian national identity that binds them together and not only allows for but at times encourages the expression of ethnic, religious, and other relational and categorical identification practices that make up the diversity of Palestinian national identifications.

8 CONCLUSION:
CONNECTING GEOGRAPHIES OF DISPOSSESSION

Palestine: 1948
Al-Rama, Israel: 1960s
Jerusalem, West Bank, and al-Rama, Israel: 1984
Nazareth, Israel: 1990s
Damascus, Syria: 2000s
Beirut, Lebanon: 2003

In the 1960s, Palestinian poet Samih al-Qasim, who has lived in Israel since 1948, composed a poem entitled "I Will Tell the World" (*Ahki lil-'alam*). In this poem, he expresses what it was like to remain living among the destroyed Palestinian villages, seeing arrested lives, frozen in time:

> I will tell the world, I will tell . . .
> About a house whose lantern was broken,
> About a hoe that cut down an iris
> And a fire that destroyed a braid of hair.
> I will tell stories about a goat that was not milked,
> About a morning cup of coffee never drunk
> About a mother's bread that was not baked,
> About a mud roof sprouting grass.
> I will tell the world, I will tell. . . .
> Forgotten daughter of my neighbor,
> I still have your doll, in my care.
> The doll is with me, so please return,
> On the back of the eastern winds.
> Hanna, I don't remember your features,
> But I long to remember. . . .
> In my heart, I can hear your footsteps.
> [. . .]
> I will tell the world, I will tell. . . .[1]

For those remaining inside Israel, the silent yet expressive scenes of the emptied villages, untended orchards, and destroyed homes described in the poem confronted them every day on their trips to work and to their remaining fields.

Poetry became a potent medium of expression for many Palestinians who remained inside Israel: al-Qasim, Mahmud Darwish, and Tawfiq Zayyad, among others. Their poems have now crossed borders in spoken, written, and musical form as musicians across the Arab world have created a repertoire of songs that are revolutionary, in both content and musical form.[2] "I Will Tell the World" has been put to music, hauntingly and passionately, by at least four musical groups. In 1984, the avant-guarde musical group Sabreen, made up of Palestinian musicians from Israel and the West Bank, created a fast-beat chanting song on their album *Smoke of the Volcanoes* (*Dukhkhan al-barakin*).[3] Another Palestinian musician, Rim Banna, who lives and works in Nazareth, Israel, and performs in many parts of the Arab world, composed a lyrical lament of the poem with her husband, Ukrainian musician Leonid Alexeienko.[4] Dima Orsho, a Syrian singer and composer, produced a song of the poem that showcases her operatic soprano.[5] And Ziad El Ahmadie, a musician in Lebanon, composed music for a chorus to the words of the poem in 2003.[6]

Many Palestinian poems have been adopted by singers and musicians as the lyrics for their songs, which has meant that the poems are heard by more than would read them on paper or the computer screen. When people hear this particular poem, they know it refers to Palestinians' experience of dispossession, despite the fact that it does not mention 1948 or the *nakba*, or make any other reference to date or place. It does, however, express the haunting emptiness of a once-vibrant life stilled, a depopulated landscape, and the desire to make those memories come back to life and to see people from that past. This poem and the images it creates, both when it is sung and when it is listened to, is part of an act of testimony of remembering, like so many other actions undertaken by Palestinians.

Al-Qasim's poem proclaims that he will "tell the world" about these stories, and this act of putting one's own experiences forward as evidence preoccupies Palestinians in their search for justice. Latin America has witnessed the emergence of textual accounts (*testimonios*) that describe the personal experience of people who recall their lives on the peripheries and margins of political, economic, and social centers of power.[7] In Latin America, *testimonios* subvert the authority of colonial bodies or local elites to write history. But Palestinian accounts do not necessarily emerge from the margins of Palestinian society (although some do). Instead, Palestinian narratives of life before 1948 are figured as collective testimonies of those who were marginalized within the global state-system and in the struggle over Palestine.

Palestinian village books and other material about Palestinian history challenge the politically dominant forces, both within and external to Palestinian society, and assert representational power. As part of exploring how Palestinians think of themselves and write their histories, I have charted the geographies of displacement that resulted from their dispossession in 1948. In my efforts to chronicle their processes of recording that history, I have also witnessed Palestinians reconnecting across that geography to their families, to their heritage, to their history, to other Palestinians, and to the social and spatial structures that were familiar to them. This chapter examines some of the many ways that Palestinians relate to their villages and their histories, and it examines how Palestinians reconnect across the geographies of dispossession that characterize their lives.

LIVES AS REFUGEES

Charting what happened to Palestinians during the fighting that occurred in 1947–1949 and how they rebuilt their lives as displaced persons illustrates the various ways that people made use of the connections within and to their villages. The fighting displaced more than 750,000 Palestinians from their villages and cities, along with at least 20,000 Jews who were also made refugees, most of them from Jerusalem and Hebron. The village refugees fled in stages, many of them first finding shelter near their villages in caves, forests, and other villages. In addition to continued military attacks that frightened people into fleeing further, Israeli trucks were brought in to move them to war-time borders.[8] Benny Morris chronicles the phases of refugee movement throughout this period. The first wave occurred between November 1947 and April 1948 and was from the urban centers; middle class and well-to-do families moved to safer areas inside and outside of Palestine, along with the villagers who lived along the coast.[9] The second wave of refugees occurred in April and May of 1948, bringing the total number of people already displaced at the time of the founding of the Israeli state to some 200 to 300,000 Palestinians, emptying Haifa, Jaffa, Tiberius, Safad, Baysan, and Acre, along with the surrounding towns and villages, of their Arab inhabitants.[10] The third and fourth waves occurred after Israel had come into existence and the Arab armies had attacked. Far fewer people fled of their own accord during this period, and most were forced out through direct military attacks, aerial assaults, and the targeted removal of villagers. Many tried repeatedly to return.

The displaced found refuge in all of the surrounding countries, within Israel, and in the parts of historic Palestine that were annexed to Jordan (the West Bank) or governed by the Egyptians (the Gaza Strip). In the Galilee, most people fled to Lebanon and Syria. From the central and southern parts of the country, people went to the West Bank, the Gaza Strip, and Jordan. When the United Nations Relief and Works Administration (UNRWA) for Palestinian Refugees came into being in 1950 and registered the refugees, Jordan (including the West Bank) had absorbed more than 500,000, while the Gaza Strip held almost 200,000, Lebanon hosted 127,000, and Syria provided for 82,000.[11] In the 1967 War, an estimated 300,000 to 400,000 Palestinians were displaced again, many for the second time, mostly from the West Bank.[12]

Refugees' lives and status have varied over time according to the governments, policies, and politics of the countries in which they reside.[13] In Jordan they were granted citizenship. In Syria they have neither citizenship nor the right to vote, but otherwise they have the same rights to education, health care, and employment as Syrians. In Lebanon they are excluded from Lebanese citizenship, schools, numerous jobs, and state services.[14] In Gaza and the West Bank, since 1967 up to the present the Israeli military administration circumscribes their lives.

Registered refugees have access to UNRWA services for primary education and primary health care.[15] As of June 30, 2009, UNRWA's records show 4,718,899 *registered* Palestinian refugees. Of this total, 1,385,316, some 29.3 percent of the total registered, live in refugee camps. The percentage has varied somewhat over the years: in 1953, 34.6 percent of the refugees lived in camps, in 1965 it was 39.1 percent, and in 1980, the percentage was 32.9%.[16] Although the number of refugees living in camps has decreased slightly over time, it would seem that the camps have become the permanent homes for generations of Palestinians.

This displacement from their natal villages and the refugees' reliance on the local and international community to rebuild their lives has resulted in new residential patterns and social and family relations. From 1948 to the present they have negotiated among local, class, and familial bonds, with a strong national sense of connectedness, and more recently with religious categorizations, and they have given new meanings to local and national symbols of village life.[17]

Throughout this period as well, many people, including Palestinians, have asked why they have not been better treated by the governments of their host countries, and why they have not been integrated or given citizenship. The answers to these questions are multifarious and complex. In short, however, it is worth noting that host countries were open and generous in the early years, and then rigidified regimes of administration and exclusion with the passing of time. De facto integration has taken place in some countries, most notably Jordan. But it is commonly cited that neither the Palestinian leadership nor the Arab countries wanted to integrate the refugees, fearing that the population would lose a desire for justice and for return. These arguments are not terribly convincing, in large part because historically Palestinians have remained tied to the idea of Palestine, despite, for example, the relatively low percentage of the population living in camps. The refugees remain today discriminated-against minorities, either by law or in practice, as evidenced most recently by the Palestinians who fled Iraq and were held at border camps for years in Syria and Jordan while Iraqis passed freely back and forth. Treated poorly by host governments over the last sixty years, and still seen as poor recipients of United Nations aid, they continue to evidence the power of the twentieth-century dispossessions in the twenty-first century.

RE-CREATING AND REORGANIZING THE VILLAGE IN THE DIAPOSRA

Up through the early 1950s, Palestinian refugees repeatedly relocated as they searched for places to live and work. Some found themselves able to rent accommodations in urban areas or towns. Others were moved or moved themselves to the areas that became the refugee camps, under the aegis of the international aid groups and then ultimately UNRWA. Two different residential and social patterns developed in the camps out of the efforts to provide the hundreds of thousands of displaced people with shelter and aid. The first pattern resulted from the refugees' shared displacement: people found themselves living with people they did not know, and thus remade social relations on the basis of the proximity of camp life. One wedding held in the first years of exile is described as

> commensurate in simplicity and sadness with the situation in which we all found ourselves. The sound of the reed flute [*mijwiz*] kept time to the stamping of the feet of those few people dancing the *dabka*; to the songs in the throats of the singers, thick with longing and sorrow; and to the women singing their wedding wishes amid tears. The chaos of the camp made for a social melting pot, because here a Bedouin family was next to a peasant family, which was

next to a family from the city. The hand of fate had dragged them from their previously disparate lives and varied social standings to meld them together in a single crucible.[18]

Thus the 1948 diaspora worked in some ways to mix social and economic classes that might not have lived together before, similar to what rural migration and urbanization had done in the 1930s and 1940s in Palestine.[19]

As this mixing of populations was taking place, however, people were also trying to remake their villages in the camps, both by settling in camps on the basis of village origin and by creating familiar spaces of village and home. Julie Peteet describes how refugees in Gaza and Lebanon settled ultimately in a "familiar and safe social landscape" by organizing the camps into areas on the basis of family ties or village of origin.[20] Rosemary Sayigh tells the story of Abed Bisher from Majd al-Krum who had been a resistance fighter against the British and ended up in Lebanon during the war. Abed's son described his father's role in establishing the Shatila camp:

> [My father] managed to procure twenty tents from UNRWA—it had started then—and he went to all the places where Majd al-Kroom [sic] people were scattered and brought them to Beirut. The twenty tents were taken, more people came, my father got more tents. He had to keep in continuous contact with UNRWA for things that Palestinians needed—distributions of milk and rations, tents and so on. Then the offer came from UNRWA to my father to become camp leader for a salary of LL 75 a month. At the time this was great. My father had no objection, we needed the money badly. So he was officially appointed on condition that he agreed to take in around twenty-five families from Yaffa [Jaffa] who were occupying the Kraytem Mosque.[21]

Although not noticeable to an outsider, and although modified significantly today because of population growth and decline, the camps for many years maintained the social familiarity of the village. One example of this is illustrated in women's choices of attire, explained in Julie Peteet's work on the large urban camps of Shatila and Burj al-Barajneh in Lebanon. She describes how women wore their formal visiting clothes when they left their village area within the camp, but they stayed in their informal house clothes when in their own village neighborhoods inside the camp—an indicator of the familiarity and intimacy of the "village space" in the camp that they would have shared in the village.[22]

Another form of shared physical space was created in the diaspora, largely outside the camps, that mirrored similar spaces that once existed in the villages: the *madafa* or *diwan* (guest house). Susan Slyomovics details how in the pre-1948 village the guesthouse served as a communal space: a place to solve disputes, for guests to be fed and spend the night, and for collective gatherings for happy and sad occasions.

> Historically, the *madafah* maintained by clans or subclans, have served not only as communal mechanisms for discharging the sacred duty of hospitality but also as arenas for activities designed to reinforce and perpetuate the kinship group as a social unit by casting into high relief the relation of kin among themselves on the one hand, and the relations of the group with the rest of the world on the other.[23]

In Jordan, largely due to the influence of similar Jordanian practices, the Palestinian refugees have set up either family *madafas* (listed for governmental registration purposes as *diwans*) or village charitable organizations.[24] For example, the al-Walaja Cooperative Society, established in 1968, has branches in Amman and al-Zarqa'; the 'Ayn Karim Charitable Society, established in 1964, is located in Amman near the Royal Sports Club); and the al-Muzayri'a Charitable Society, established in 1980, is located in the Ashrafiyya neighborhood of Amman. These groups' activities include the granting of loans to members, specific loans for education, the availability of the social hall for funeral receptions (*li-istiqbal al-mu'azzin*) and weddings, fixing problems that arise in or between families, and accepting donations for the needy among the members.

These societies thus replicate a shared community space and bind people together by gathering them on special occasions.[25] Because a number of the village books were published under the auspices of and distributed by these village societies, a crucial element of the local identities that the members of the societies espouse is the shared cultural memory of the local and national past that is reconstructed and recreated in the books.

In the chaos and upheaval of the 1948 War, as people rebuilt the spatial bonds that had connected them, they also turned to and modified social structures that had existed in the pre-1948 Palestinian village. For both villagers and those trying to manage the refugee population, these structures provided stability and security. One such social structure was a simplified system of local leadership. Villages in pre-1948 Palestine were headed by *mukhtars*, and in some cases also by a local council that usually consisted of the heads of local families. In small villages there would be one *mukhtar*, but in larger villages there were usual a number of them, each representing a signficiant family in the village.[26] The *mukhtar* position, established in 1861, was an Ottoman creation. The *mukhtar* was to be the representative of the village and chosen or elected by the villagers.[27] The *mukhtar*'s job changed over time, but in addition to registering births and deaths, and collecting and allocating taxes,[28] he served as liason to the central authority, and his duties included signing official documents such as land transfers, bills of sale, and so on.[29]

The role and job of the village *mukhtar* continued under the British, who saw these individuals as "sources of information and as instruments of control."[30] Moreover, the British tried to manipulate the office by taking over the power to appoint or reject individuals for the role. In her book on Mandate governmental regulations of Palestinian villages, Ylana Miller quotes a letter sent in 1924 by the Muslim Christian Society in Jerusalem complaining to the Executive Committee of the Palestine Arab Congress about the British Mandate authorities' takeover of the administration of these local offices:

> The election of *mukhtar*s has always been one of the rights of the people, since it is they who elect their *mukhtar*s and it is they also who demanded their resignation when the need arose and they approved of that. But now it appears that the matter of appointing and dismissing the *mukhtar*s is restricted to the governors alone. . . . It should be demanded of the government that they restore the election of *mukhtar*s to the people.[31]

Palestinians saw these positions as expressions of their own choices and internal power structures over representation and leadership. Their objection to the new British Mandate's intervention in their internal affairs mirrored Palestinians' negative reactions to British colonial rule of Palestine. Even on the village level, local interest in choosing local leaders clashed with the government authorities, who blocked certain individuals and put forward others. The *mukhtar* was also held up by villagers as a nationalist leader protecting their interests and land, or in other cases was removed by them for not taking on this role or for being corrupt.

Palestinians saw the *mukhtar*ship as a representative (not to be confused with democratic) process and they fought for their right to choose their own local leadership. This type of investment in a leadership system did not just disappear in 1948. Thus, during the 1948 War and its aftermath, these village leadership structures were relied on by the refugees themselves and were tapped into by the relief organizations providing aid to the refugees (first the Red Cross and the American Friends Service Committee, and then UNRWA). Peteet's work details how food aid was distributed under the aegis of the village *mukhtars*—because they had knowledge of the villagers, or at least of the family clans that they had represented, and could thus serve as the intermediary between the relief organizations and the people, to effectively get aid to them, to count the number of people, and to regulate and monitor the aid distribution in a way that the aid organization could not. Undoubtedly this process assisted in the distribution of aid, as well as continuing to empower the more powerful families.[32]

The governments of the host countries turned to these local leaders as well, often to move people to temporary residences. Whereas they sometimes brought in police to clear areas, they also tried other means. Peteet includes the story of the founding of Nabatieh camp in Lebanon as told by the son of a *mukhtar*:

> In 1955 the government [of Lebanon] decided that there were too many smugglers between Palestine and Lebanon and that it could affect the security situation—military operations could be undertaken. So they decided to gather all the Palestinians in the area. They coordinated with UNRWA to build this camp for these stray groups of people near the border area. They attracted them in a number of ways. My father was the *mukhtar* of our village. So they said to him, "We have places for you and your people—you are not obliged to pay rent and there will be a school." So there were certain motivations to accept the camp.[33]

In these various ways, both government and humanitarian assistance authorities fostered relations with the men who had been the village leaders. Thus the first years of the refugee displacement preserved in exile some of the internal social structures of the village, and the loci of power remained invested with certain families and individuals who had existed prior to 1948 in the village, thus providing ways for the *mukhtar*s to continue to play a leadership role in exile, as village representatives and in their brokering role with outside authority.

Because the *mukhtar* was chosen by the people, this form of leadership did not require the existence of the village to continue immediately following 1948. But as time passed, the person in the leadership role no longer had the ability to represent the village or even a certain family or clan in the village, because the villagers were dispersed in different camps and in different countries.

Representative elections for the *mukhtar* no longer reflected the composition of the village, or even family interests, but rather the composition of the camp.

RECONNECTING TO THE VILLAGE VIA RETURNS AND RESISTANCES

After 1948 and through the early 1950s, people found ways to go back to their villages. Not many attempted this, but some did, and the cost was high. Some succeeded in returning permanently to live inside Israel, but for most, their goals were to get the crops, provisions, and possessions they had left behind and to visit the family members who had remained. Many were killed on these cross-border infiltrations, which served to discourage all but the most daring, and these returns predated the military raids of the Palestinian resistance some years later.[34] Ilana Feldman's research on refugees in Gaza describes people's efforts post-1948 to remain connected to the homes and villages in which they no longer lived. She poignantly makes the point that maintaining a "refrain of home" allowed Palestinians to survive. It was acts of holding onto and retelling memories, of returning to their villages to retrieve their possessions, of stealing things from Israelis, or of engaging in militant actions that "helped to keep the tragic realities of Palestinian history from utterly destroying Palestinian community and political life."[35]

For others, these returns brought to the diaspora the reality of the transformed village landscape and Palestinians' political impotency. Returns were depressing more often than triumphant. Matar Abd al-Rahim tells his father's story of returning to visit his parents, who had remained in a village (Nohaf) that was now within Israel:

> Toward the end of 1951 my father decided to return to Occupied Palestine [Israel]. We spent our days anticipating his return to Syria, and in constant fear for him as he crossed without papers into Jordan and then into Palestine. All of the worst scenarios crossed our minds. Maybe he wouldn't make it. Even if he did make it, how would he return across those same borders? If he was caught by Israel, they would accuse him of spying for an Arab country. And if he was caught by an Arab country, they would accuse him of spying for Israel. Then, one evening there was a gentle knock on the door and our minds were put at ease. My father told us his story, or at least what he wanted us to know. Torn, dirty, exhausted, after secretly crossing the same paths he had known so intimately during the revolt, he had arrived at his family's house in Nahaf. He spent three days in the house with his mother, father, brother, and extended

family. At night he would walk around the village recalling his memories of his life there. By the time he returned to us, he was no longer the same man. Gone was the optimistic, strong man I had worshiped all my life. His hope for life disappeared with his homeland and home.[36]

This story illustrates some of the psychological effects of being a refugee. The clandestine returns sometimes drove home the meaning of the expulsion and the transformations of the land, causing debilitating distress and despair at the realization of the permanency of their displacement. Older people in particular came to realize that they would face the end of their life in exile. Hopes and dreams were easier to maintain without knowing how the villages had been transformed into Israeli towns, kibbutzes, and cooperative farms (*moshavs*); how they were being lived in by other people who now made these places their home.

Early on in the 1950s, in addition to playing a social and symbolic role, the village also served as an organizational point around which Palestinians formed their resistance to Israel in attempts to influence politics and regain their former homes. Because there was not yet widespread or organized resistance of the kind formed by Palestinians in the 1960s, Palestinians instead mounted individual attempts to return or to fight Israelis that were not coordinated with others. Ilana Feldman describes how armed infiltrators from the Gaza Strip chose to go to their former villages and the areas around them because they knew them, rather than go to unknown areas that were perhaps better "targets."[37]

Even with the rise of the organized Palestinian resistance in the late 1960s, the villages figured into individual fighters' lives as they mixed their individual desires with the goals and purposes of the guerrilla actions. The following story, told by someone about his "comrade" in the Palestinian resistance, illustrates the meshing of individual and nationalist actions:

Walid fled his village as a boy in 1948, and amid the chaos and fear, he found himself alone in Lebanon. He thought his family had preceded him there, but instead they had hidden in the mountains and returned to their village after the fighting stopped, and ultimately became citizens of the Israeli state. Walid eagerly joined in the first *fida'i* [guerrilla] work, with the goal of sneaking back to his village in Occupied Palestine and seeing his family, about whose fate he knew nothing. [. . .] He found the house in the darkness of the night and knocked quietly on the door. His brother Mahmoud, who was only three years old when he last saw him, opened the door. [. . .] [After entering the house,] Walid grabbed his father's hand, kissed it several times, hugged him tightly, and then kissed his chest where his heart was. His mother, he learned, had died three years earlier. He left on the seventh night, walking, crying, laughing back to his exile, carrying with him renewed faith and the conviction that he would continue to struggle for his people so that they would not dissolve into the darkness of history.[38]

In this story, the fighter goes off on his mission, only to find himself searching for his village and the family he left behind. After spending time with them, he leaves to return to his new family in the resistance and to the larger cause of fighting for the homeland. The moral of this story (which is retold in fiction as well, such as in Ghassan Kanafani's *Return to Haifa*) is that confronting loss through their return spurs people to increased nationalist dedication and willingness to fight for their homeland.

The Palestinian resistance movements, which together formed the Palestinian Liberation Organization (the PLO), channeled these energies and dedication and created cadres of trained fighters, in the sort of state-within-the-state movement that the PLO ran in Jordan until 1970 and in Lebanon from 1969 to 1982. Yezid Sayigh analyzes how the PLO's attempts "to achieve social control [were] continuously contested by rival state centers (especially Israel and Jordan)" and how "its own development as a statist actor was ultimately contingent on the existence of a counterpart: a society with a common 'sociological space.'"[39] The resistance movements that formed in the 1960s created compelling forms of popular political organizing and diminished the power of the village *mukhtar*s. Peteet shows how people found new leadership within the political factions and resistance movements that sprang up and ran the camps in Lebanon following the 1969 Cairo Accords.[40] Today the institution of the *mukhtar* still exists, although it is probably a more symbolic than administrative position in many instances, fulfilling some of the same roles as prior to 1948—solving problems, representing the village, and serving as intermediaries with local and governmental officials. In Syria, the body that *mukhtar*s represent has shifted; they now represent neighborhoods in the camp. They are elected or appointed by local councils, and to a certain extent the roles they take on depend on their interests, abilities, and standing in the community. Similarly, today the PLO political factions have also lost a great deal of their political power, both internally and with the governments of the countries in which they operate; they have been replaced in some cases by the rising militant Islamist movements.[41]

PALESTINIAN IDENTIFICATIONS WITH VILLAGE AND NATION

To be certain, the myriad ways in which Palestinians engage with and connect to their villages of origin, as described in this book, are embedded within the village as part of the Palestinian nation, homeland, and national identity. People do not see themselves only as Zaynatiyya (from the village of Imm al-Zaynat) or only as Khawalda (from Imm Khalid) or only as Shajarna (from al-Shajara village), but also as Palestinians from those villages. Their textual, scholarly, and cultural productions, in addition to their expressions of self and identity, exist within national discourses about being Palestinian, and place the village within larger narratives of what it means to be Palestinian. In the village books, the details of cultural expressions and social customs such as wedding songs, names, marriage patterns, allegiances, and even migrations reveal the significance of Palestinian villages and village life, and how the villages figure into larger national discourses and expressions of Palestinian national identity.

As discussed previously, Palestinian national identification is framed in terms of geographic origin and sentiment toward Palestine, and hence the name Palestinian. Palestinian nationalism has been and continues to be a land-based identity, rooted in a discourse about an integral relationship between people and the land, unlike other identification practices in which people think of themselves in categorical ways that bind them to other people, such as shared ethnicity, religious affiliations, common language, or national origin. This conception of nationalism is intimately tied to the Palestine that was designated by the British Mandate borders and by the *nakba* in 1948. Just as ethnic and religious identification defines Israel as a Jewish state, Palestinians also claim that being Arab is part of their Palestinian identity, which therefore includes both Muslim and Christian Arabs, as well as non-Arab minorities such as Armenians, Turkmen, Bosnians, and so on, as do other Arab states in the region. Although Palestinians connect with all of these identifications, the ways in which they think about the village and the land of Palestine suggest that in the twentieth and twenty-first centuries, Palestinians have particularly anchored themselves to the land. A refugee from the village of Yibna, now living in Gaza, describes himself within the complex layers of being Palestinian today:

> I am someone from Gaza. I and the Gazan are Palestinian. . . . Abroad—
> for example, in Amman—they don't say that I am from Yibna. They call me

Gazan—in Saudi Arabia, Gazan; in Egypt, Gazan. . . . I say I live in Gaza. If you ask me about my name, I will answer [Abu Ayub] from the people of Yibna. . . . I don't say I live in Yibna but I say [I am] "from the people of Yibna." . . . In the UNRWA file we are registered as being from Yibna. Everyone has his *balad* [village] registered. . . . A refugee remains a refugee, but the Gazan is Palestinian and I am Palestinian too.[42]

This complex explanation by Abu Ayub encompasses both his self-understanding and how others identify him—all of which he amalgamates into a whole that incorporates multiple identifiers. Every Palestinian at multiple times in his or her life goes through this recital of connections to place, home, citizenship, and ethnicity.[43]

The village books narrate these identifications by connecting the destroyed Palestinian village to the pre-modern and pre-national history of the village and claiming as part of the Palestinians' own histories the entire record of human habitation on that land. In the diaspora, this identification is no longer lived out by virtue of inhabiting the space. Instead, it is outwardly declared in the personal names that people adopt to connect themselves to their villages. The *nisba*, or name from place of origin, is a common way that people acquire Arabic names once they are no longer in that place. For example, al-Baghdadi is from Baghdad, and al-Maqdisi is from Jerusalem (called al-Quds or Bayt al-Maqdis in Arabic). One of the village books about Zanghariyya, for example, reflects how people adopted these names.[44] In the list of people imprisoned and killed in the struggle with the British and the Zionists before 1948, the men are listed—for example, Muhammad Salih, Faris al-Muqbil, and Khalid Hassan al-Faza'—by their given name, then their father's name, and perhaps a family name.[45] In the section on the history of resistance between 1948 and 2000, the last name of almost all of the thirty-five men (killed, imprisoned, fighters, and so on) is al-Zanghari, the *nisba* of al-Zanghariyya village.[46] What this says is that before 1948 the men did not need to be known by their village name because they lived in the village. The name of Hussein al-Lubani, who wrote the village book for al-Damun, indicates that someone in his ancestry came from the village of Lubya (al-Lubani), but on the cover and title page of his book he writes that he is also Hussein 'Ali al-Lubani "al-Damuni." Similarly, the author of one of the Bayt Mahsir books lists his name as 'Ali Muhammad Isleem al-Mahsiri, from the clan of Isleem (as described in the genealogies), plus indicating that he has added his village of origin to his family patronym. As refugees, Palestinians mark their connection to their natal villages through adding the village names into theirs, thus connecting their personal histories to the larger context of Palestine as a homeland and identification.[47]

THE VILLAGE RECONFIGURED: NEW TECHNOLOGIES, NEW CONNECTIONS

Not surprisingly, new technologies, particularly the Internet, have changed how people relate to and commemorate the Palestinian villages, and how they relate to each other as villagers. In the 1950s and 1960s, refugees sent letters to each other across borders via the Red Cross. Radio messages and greetings were read on the air at certain times, which served to reconnect families who did not know where their relatives were, and also to pass news across otherwise closed borders. People have found and continue to find ways, using new technologies, to make connections between geographically distant locations bounded by borders they cannot physically cross.

One example of how people connect is the exchange and republication of village books. Jamil 'Arafat is a prolific author who writes about the destroyed villages and lives in a Palestinian village on the outskirts of Nazareth in Israel. He organizes some of his books according to the British Mandate administrative district in which the villages were located. He has written books on the villages in the districts of Haifa, Baysan, and the Galilee, among others. His book on the villages and tribes of the Baysan subdistrict, for example, contains the details and stories of thirty-six villages and a number of Bedouin groups, with two to ten pages for each. Using a combination of oral history and Hebrew and Arabic sources, 'Arafat compiles encyclopedic entries on each village, including what is unique about it and how it fits into the larger regional and national context (both before and after 1948).[48]

Three hours away from Nazareth as a crow flies, a day and a half with an American passport, and impossible with 'Arafat's Israeli passport, is Yarmouk refugee camp in Damascus, Syria. When I asked for village books in the bookstores in the camp, I was repeatedly given 'Arafat's books, but because neither political nor diplomatic relations exist between Syria and Israel (and thus there is no mail, telephone, or other contact, not to mention trade or diplomatic relations), his books should not be easily found there. However, the Dar al-Shajara publishing house in the camp found a way to obtain 'Arafat's books and reprint them as part of their broad-ranging Keeping Alive Our Oral Histories Project. In addition, the editors provided to these readers living in Syria an introduction about the importance of these books in which they emphasized the necessity of connecting those who remained in "the homeland" to those outside in the diaspora. Because Palestinians can meet in third countries and route mail through others, such connections are possible. Furthermore, the advent of political relations between Israel and Egypt in 1979 and between Israel and Jordan in 1994 has made closer meetings easier in recent years.

Another example of how Palestinians maintain connections is through commemorative activities. The destroyed village of Saffuriyya in the Galilee shows how Palestinians from the village who are now living in Israel, Syria, and elsewhere retain connections to it.A few kilometers from the destroyed village, hundreds, perhaps thousands, of Safafra (people from Saffuriyya) still live in Israel, in a neighborhood in Nazareth called after themselves, Hayy al-Safafra. A number of books have been published about this village, which held the most land in the Nazareth District, some 55,378 dunums.[49] Yarmouk camp also contains a neighborhood called Saffuriyya, and many Safafra reside there. A prominent Saffuri, the late Hisham al-Maw'id, put great effort and many resources into creating the Palestinian Heritage House (*Bayt al-Turath*), which highlights Saffuriyya.

I asked people living in the Saffuriyya neighborhood of Yarmouk camp what they knew about this destroyed village. In addition to describing its geographical location, many of them knew that in May 2008 it hosted the March of Return that marked the anniversary of the Palestinian *nakba*. The March of Return is the work of a movement of Palestinians living inside Israel who seek recognition of the right of refugees to return to their homes. As part of their activities, each year they enact a march on the site of a different emptied village.[50] In 2008 approximately fifteen thousand people participated. On this occasion, right-wing Jewish Israeli counter-demonstrators attacked the group as the marchers were leaving the destroyed village; the Israeli police then turned on the Palestinian and Jewish Israeli marchers and subjected them to beatings, tear gas, threats of opening fire with live ammunition, and arrests of some Palestinian participants (all of whom were subsequently released without charge).[51] Multiple videos posted on YouTube (http://www.youtube. com) and other Web sites allowed Palestinians in Syria to learn of this incident and watch people chased and beaten by Israeli police, despite the fact that the March of Return took place across embargoed borders.

Technology also provokes unique publications that center on the village as an organizing principle. Phone books have been created that contain all of the names and contact numbers of people from a particular village, as well as the destroyed village's history. Published inside Israel, *Iqrit 2002*, for example, lists itself as a "guide to the families in the diaspora [*shatat*]" (with diaspora here meaning "outside of the village"). The village of Iqrit was emptied "temporarily" by the Israeli Defense Forces in November of 1948 and the villagers have never been allowed to return. They have settled instead in cities and villages inside Israel, such as Haifa, Nazareth, Abu Sinan, al-Rama, Tarsheeha, and Sakhneen, although some were also sent to Lebanon.[52] This book presents a short history of the village, and includes an alphabetical listing of the villagers' names, addresses, and phone numbers (and those of their spouses and children), and another list based on their current places of residence inside Israel. The villagers from Lifta living in Jordan produced *Lifta Guide 2004*, which contains some twenty-five pages of historical information on the village (interspersed with advertisements from sponsors), followed by thirty plus pages of male names and phone numbers, arranged according to family name. Although these books provide the major information about the village's history that they think the reader will need, they concentrate much more on the villagers who are living today (and on how to contact them).

Some of the village books share this focus on the present and on the names and locations of the villagers and their accomplishments. The populations of most of the villages have grown into the thousands and tens of thousands, so lists of names are not feasible. Instead, what a number of authors have done is include the names of college graduates and their field of specialization. Qasim al-Ramahi, himself a retired school headmaster, authored a second edition of the village book for al-Muzayri'a in 2004 and included a section entitled "Educational Renaissance 1948–2003." He provides both the numbers of graduates and their fields of study (medicine, dentistry, pharmacy, nursing, laboratory science), identifies those with doctorates, and lists their names and specializations. The section is divided into two subsections: one list and page of pictures for men, and one list and page of pictures for women.[53] Other village books have similar chapters that read almost like a who's who among contemporary villagers.

These new technologies and ways of cataloguing villagers also engender generational alliances and divides. In particular, contemporary life reveals the complex ways that refugees relate to and create knowledge about the village that spans generations and builds on their relationships across borders and boundaries. In a study of the communities from three destroyed

Palestinian villages near Haifa, anthropologist Efrat Ben-Ze'ev shows how knowledge of the past is maintained and reproduced among different Palestinian generations. For people still living in Israel and able to visit their village, as well as those who live in Jordan and the West Bank, the older people who remember the village "retain memories of specific places, events, smells, and colors."[54] Ben-Ze'ev contends that the younger, more literate generations find other ways to commemorate the village, though still with as much passion, by returning to the villages, collecting photos, and writing books about the villages. In my research, however, I found no such easy generational division. As many second- and third-generation refugees wrote village books as those who were raised in the village. Both young and old organize and participate in the celebrations held in diaspora communities that commemorate the village, such as "Saffuriyya day" in Yarmouk camp. In my experience, people's participation in these actions and activities centers on their own willingness to engage with these sentiments, whether individual, local, or national. I have also encountered people (and heard stories about others as well) who were unwilling to tell the stories of the past to their children or grandchildren, and unwilling even to look at pictures of the contemporary village or to visit it. Matar 'Abd al-Rahim, whose natal village still exists and has a population of some ten thousand Palestinians who are citizens of Israel, told me:

> My son works in an Internet shop so he showed me pictures of Nahaf from today. I didn't recognize it because of the tall apartment buildings. My village was simple. I lived in a small house surrounded by a yard. The people that we knew, the places we used to sit and talk . . . all these things have changed. I don't want the village to be like this; I want it as it was before. I used to think that if I returned, I would find everything still the same. I don't want anything to change. I want the people to be the same, but people die and are buried, and the village changes.[55]

'Abd al-Rahim balked at contemplating the transformations to the village and what it might mean for how he relates to his memory of the village.

In the 1990s and into the early 2000s, people figured out how to make return visits using visitor permits obtained by family members in Israel for their elderly relatives in Syria and Lebanon. Many recorded their visits with videocameras and now pass around the recordings (first as videos, now as DVDs). Not only are they circulated among family members, but they are also available at local music and video shops. They often begin with just footage of landscapes, crumbling stone walls overgrown with weeds, vistas of the village's setting. Disembodied narration describes village places, for example, "This was the nearest well," and "That was your aunt Haleema's house." Visitors who are seeing the village for the first time in fifty years sometimes appear on camera expressing confusion about this landscape that they think they should know but that does not reveal to them the village they once knew.

I came to understand that the majority of these videos are not about the village per se, or at least not about the physical village—in part because the village does not exist. Instead, they are full of the *villagers* who remained—no longer in the village, for the most part, but internally displaced within Israel. They are "present absentees" (as they are known in Israeli discourse) who exist in implicit reference to their visiting relatives from the diaspora, who are the "absent absentees."[56] The videos they make on these return journeys contain images of long tables covered with copious amounts of food made to honor the guests, and panning sweeps of the insides of houses showing pictures on the walls, sofas, and doorways with people standing in them. The cameras turn to capture kids playing, tractors, cars, horses, shy relatives, and long, steady scenes of people sitting quietly and uncomfortably for the camera in living rooms. The compact discs on which these images of the village are often stored are such an ordinary modern technology that people sometimes hang one from their car's rearview mirror as a decoration. Yet they also hold them dear because they contain precious stories of return and images of newly discovered relatives and of people's natal villages.

Return visits thus reveal for refugees that although the physical destruction of villages has made it impossible to revisit them as they once were, Palestinians can still reconnect to the villages via the villagers. They allow people to remember the villages by hearing and telling stories that reanimate the depopulated and destroyed landscape. Although these videos are purportedly about the village, they are really showcases of the people. A young woman dressed in jeans and with her short hair brushed off her face confidently and coyly perches on a rock in her destroyed village while she exhorts the camera to "say hello to Auntie Fatima and her husband, and tell her son congratulations on his new baby." She sends her regards to people she likely knows of but has never met, because the bonds of family relations are broken by the boundaries of nation-states; yet these new forms of technology are allowing new connections to be made and to exist in forms other than face-to-face contact. Other people travel to visit relatives with passports, but Palestinians live in a world in which governments, political antagonisms, and security arrangements make it possible for only a few to pass through the borders that separate people from one another.

Abu Sameeh was one of a few older Palestinians in Syria whom I met who managed to get a permit to return to his village for a visit in 2000. He was more than eighty years old when I interviewed him in 2008. His sponsor was his daughter, who had married a man from one of the villages in the Galilee and gone to live in Israel. Abu Sameeh showed me pictures of his destroyed village and of him pointing at the local well, standing in the cemetery, and praying on the ruins of the mosque. He also had pictures of himself taken in places that were relevant to his own personal history, and others taken in places that were of historical importance to Palestine—the cities of Safad and Acre, and near the site of the battle of Yarmouk between the Muslim and Byzantine armies in the seventh century CE. Abu Sameeh's grandson, who was not allowed on the visit because he was too young (in his thirties), sat with me as we looked at these photos. He later told me that he had made new connections as a result of his grandfather's visit. He talks regularly to his young cousins from inside Israel via an Internet chat program. The ways in which people make connections between the past and the present cannot be predicted. As Breckenridge and Appadurai explain, "Diasporas always leave a trail of collective memory about another place and time and create new maps of desire and attachment."[57] The memories and attachments that link families also create new landscapes, and for Palestinians, crossing borders reveals that the villages are more than just places of the past; they are also the villagers in the present.

GEOGRAPHIES OF DISPOSSESSION

As we have seen, since 1948, Palestinians have not lived in a single geographic area or in one political entity, and they do not control the common institutions vested by a state—institutions and powers that provide citizens with a shared history and with structures and sentiments by which they might identify themselves as a collective.[58] These institutions propagate (and impose) knowledge and feelings that inculcate citizens through such bodies as ministries of culture, information, and education, and through schools, media, militaries, archives, museums, money, and so on.[59] Palestinians thus lack the state power that educates and molds its citizenry and creates and propagates hegemonic narratives about the state and nation that have been so effective in creating and maintaining them. Despite the expectations (or perhaps because of the expectations) of the major world powers that Palestinians would assimilate into the other Arab countries soon after 1948, Palestinians have continued to self-identify as Palestinians with shared understandings, agreed-upon symbols, and broad definitions of what certain sentiments and practices mean. Whether granted or denied citizenship by their host countries; integrated into the population, as they have been to varying degrees in Jordan and Syria; or ostracized as they are in Lebanon, they self-identify and are identified as Palestinians. Even today, Palestinians who have never seen or been to the land of historic Palestine continue to express feelings about their family's village that tie them to national feelings about being Palestinian, and they maintain connections to people across borders that not only propagate family ties but also contribute to creating to what it means to be Palestinian today.[60] As they live in these places and make their homes there, they live in a present that they actively entwine with the past, a present unimaginable without the past, and they engage with people and places that enables them to cross borders of both time and space and maintain a sense of what it means to be Palestinian today.

The 1940s through the 1970s witnessed significant actors in Palestinian history composing historical and political narratives about Palestinian nationalism and politics—metanarratives that relied on historical events that they used as evidence of their dispossession and their claim to rights. When Palestinians from villages across Palestine, whether they still live in their villages or live as refugees or as internally displaced persons, turn to the most well-known and respected histories of Palestine, they find little information on their villages. In an effort to amend this situation, Palestinians began almost forty years after the *nakba* to turn to their own memories and to the recollections of their community elders to write books about the village. These books have allowed them to elaborate on their social history and on their lives despite the fact that few documents exist that provide such information, even as they face a continuing, systematic denial of the Palestinian presence in history. These efforts to create books about the villages have coincided with the efforts of local research institutions to collect oral histories and, years later, to produce fictional and nonfictional television programs on the Palestinian villages.[61]

Modern narratives of Palestinian history and expressions of Palestinians' relationships to the places of the past allow us to examine the manifestations and different forms of power relations in their lives—both global forces such as colonialism, state violence, and nationalism, and local social and political pressures, such as gendered discourses, class hierarchies, and struggles for control. Throughout this book I have traced some of the activities of Palestinians in the contemporary diaspora and the connection of those activities to the past, commenting on the influence of these forces as they have exerted pressure on both individuals and communities and as they have generated resistance and creative responses across the generations of Palestinians living today. It behooves us to understand not only how Palestinians express their relationships to their past and how the past informs how they think of themselves in the present, but also why they maintain and cultivate their national and local identities. Most important,, by clarifying "who the people involved take themselves to be" we can open ourselves to how they fit into the global world in which we live.[62]

Despite this focus on the villages and villagers as symbols, markers, and important elements in diaspora Palestinians' relationships to their origins and to Palestinian nationalism, strong feelings exist about how this knowledge should be situated and used within the Palestinian community. I asked Matar 'Abd al-Rahim, who has written three autobiographical volumes, what it was like to write about a place he hadn't seen in almost sixty years. He replied as follows:

> I want to write about loving the village and people and what that love means. What is life and why does it happen in the ways we know it? But I won't write about the stones of the village, nor record how many families there were or that sort of thing. There is someone here who wrote a 360-page book about Saffuriyya village. He wrote all the names of the villagers and about who got degrees and graduated from university, and who didn't. But this kind of writing is useless. What is useful about saying that I have had a cousin and he studied at the university, and also we used to have a tract of land and we used to plant this crop or that one? I don't want to write like this. Why keep crying over ruins? I must cry over our cause as Palestinians and the world. I would like to understand how this world works, about God, and about our feelings as humans. I don't want to write about stones, or about how we used to have a big house and whether we were rich or poor.[63]

'Abd al-Rahim clearly felt that such detailed knowledge of the village, both past and present, was extraneous to the more important task of having the proper sentiment toward the village, the larger Palestinian cause, and human rights.

A similar statement was given to me by Abu Ayham, from the village of Tirat Haifa, who wanted to talk to me when he heard that I was doing research on Palestinians' memories of village life:

> When we talk about return, people want to go back to their village, their house, rebuild on their land . . . but how can we do that—everything was destroyed and the Palestinian population has grown. And what if a university has been built on the land—are we going to destroy that? Why do people grab on to something specific—this rock is from al-Tira, for example—when it is bigger than all of that; it is a homeland that has been occupied (*watan muhtall*). The right of return is a human or humanitarian (*insaani*) right and not a Palestinian right. The history of the world is a history of occupations and revolutions, and we are part of that.[64]

As I have shown, historic Palestine—its villages and cities, homes and orchards, schools, herds, stones, weddings, mosques, churches, mills, shops, and crops—remains important to who Palestinians are today. Chronicling the stories of Palestinian farmers, teachers, fighters, poets, midwives, merchants, Bedouin, landowners, and shepherds provides Palestinians in the diaspora with communal stories to which to anchor themselves. As Palestinians document their histories of land and struggle, they reconfigure their contemporary expressions of Palestinian identity, of self-identification with the transformational events in the past, and of the forces pushing them toward particular forms of national identification in the future. Thus, while Palestinians maintain knowledge of their villages, recreate spaces and social structures that build on known aspects of village life, and write books documenting the past, they also think of themselves within national, global, and universal definitions of what it means to be Palestinian in the twenty-first century.

REFERENCE MATTER

NOTES

Preface

1. The 1948 Arab-Israeli War began in 1947 when the United Nations voted for the partition of Palestine into Arab and Jewish states on November 29, and ended in late 1949 when the final armistice treaty between Israel and Syria was signed. The 1948 War created the state of Israel in what had been the British Mandate of Palestine and is thus called by Israelis the War of Independence (*milhemet ha-atzma'ut*). It also resulted in the displacement of half of the Arab population of Palestine and is thus called the *nakba* (catastrophe). A number of Arab states joined the war after the British withdrew on May 15, 1948.

2. The 112 village books of which I have copies are listed in the first part of the Bibliography. I have heard of ten more but have not read them and thus they are not included in this list. In addition, village books continue to be published each year. The list in the Bibliography was compiled in late 2008 and thus does not include any that appeared after that.

3. Swedenburg 1990, p. 19.

4. al-Madi 1994, p. 236. I modified his quote slightly. He wrote, "the people of my village" rather than just "people," and "next edition" instead of "next work."

5. Kanaaneh 2002, p. 21.

Chapter 1: Geographies of Dispossession

1. The fighting began in late 1947, following the United Nations decision to partition Palestine into a Jewish state and an Arab state, and continued until Israel reached separate truce agreements with Egypt, Lebanon, Jordan, and Syria in Rhodes between February and July of 1949 (Shlaim 2000, pp. 41–47). Because the British formally withdrew on May 15, 1948, and Israel declared itself a state, the war is commonly referred to in English and Arabic as the 1948 War. The Israelis refer to it as the War of Independence.

2. 'Awadallah 1996, Rumman 2000.

3. Rumman 2000. This archaeological site is highlighted in Israeli tourism brochures (from which Rumman got the photographs). Rumman's book is the only book in my collection in which the author conducted historical research with the *sijil* court records from the Ottoman period.

4. Salih 1988, al-Mahsiri 2002.

5. Zerubavel 1995, Cohen 1993.

6. Jewish National Fund map of the Martyrs' Forest. http://www.shtetlinks.jewish gen.org/Mazeikiai/MapM.jpg. Accessed August 15, 2009.

7. Saffuriyya's population in 1944–1945 was 4,330, and the villagers owned 55,378 dunums of land (of which 13,630 were public lands). One dunum is one thousand square meters. W. Khalidi 1992, pp. 350–351.

8. Evans 2007.

9. Benvenisti 2000, Golan 1997, Kanaana 2000, Shai 2006.

10. W. Khalidi 1992, Benvenisti 2000.

11. Slyomovics 1998, pp. 201–203.

12. Everyday life has been strikingly written about in different forms by De Certeau 1984, Scott 1985, Scheper-Hughes 1992, among many others.

13. Dirks, Eley, and Ortner 1994, p. 17.

14. The British occupied Palestine and some of the surrounding areas in 1917 and imposed a military rule over Palestine. The Mandate was established in 1920 and finalized in 1922.

15. The Sykes-Picot agreement was an understanding reached by Britain and France in 1916, without consulting the inhabitants of the country, about the post-war division of the Ottoman Empire that ultimately led to the British Mandate in Iraq, Transjordan, and Palestine, and the French Mandate in Syria and Lebanon.

16. See McCarthy 1990 for detailed population statistics. Many works have been written on the Zionist movement and the growth of the Jewish communities in historic Palestine. See, among others, the Jewish Agency for Palestine 1947, Lockman 1996, Stillman 1991, Sufian 2007, Wasserstein 1991.

17. All UN documents related to the Palestine question are available at the United Nations Information System on Palestine (UNISPAL), http://domino.un.org/unispal. nsf. See Kattan 2009, pp. 151–166 for a discussion of the numbers.

18. For the most detailed combing-through of the United Nations Conciliation Commission for Palestine records of property lost, which were compiled in the years after 1948, see Abu Sitta 1998, 2004. See also Fischbach 2003 and 2008 on this subject.

19. These narratives of loss made swift entry into publication. In the summer of 1948, before the war had ended, Constantine Zurayk (Qustantin Zurayq) published *Ma'na al-nakba*, which describes "the meaning of the *nakba*" and outlines a plan for Arab unity. (It was later published in English in 1956.) In 1949, Musa 'al-Alami composed

his provocative *'Ibrat filastin* [The lesson of Palestine], which contains a sharp criticism of the lack of democratic ideals within Palestinian society, and a plan for rebuilding Palestine following the *nakba*. These texts and others like them saw the *nakba* as both a catastrophe and a catalyst for action. Their authors, shattered by the destruction of Palestinian society, the massive refugee movement, and what they saw as the success of a colonial project among them, used the platform to advocate for social and political change. Of a more descriptive nature is 'Arif al-'Arif's massive *Nakbat filastin wal-firdaws al-mafqud* (The catastrophe of Palestine and the lost paradise), a chronological narrative of events based on al-'Arif's and others' knowledge of the events that took place during the war. Al-'Arif's work is a six-volume series. Each book was originally published in a different year, beginning in 1956 (and the whole series was reprinted in 1980). One volume is dedicated to *sijil al-khulud* (record of immortality); it lists the names of martyrs who died in battles for Palestine between 1947 and 1952.

20. Abu Sitta 1998, 2004. The total number of depopulated villages, hamlets, settlements, and towns is estimated to be between 290 and 472. The most comprehensive study and the clearest on its methods for including and eliminating population settlements is the massive *All That Remains* (W. Khalidi 1992), which estimates the number of villages to be 418. According to this study, Israeli topographical maps chart 290 villages, Benny Morris's 1987 study lists 369, and the Palestinian encyclopedia published by Hay'at al-Mawsu'a al-Filastiniyya gives 391 (among other sources on the subject). Appendix IV of *All That Remains* (pp. 585–594) consists of a comparison of the sources and evaluates their methods and relative strengths and weaknesses.

21. The number of displaced Palestinians has been continually contested, particularly by people attempting to lessen or increase the number for political reasons. Most scholars generally agree with the UN number, which it was somewhere in the vicinity of 750,000 (J. Abu Lughod 1971). As regards the Bedouin, W. Khalidi (1992) estimates that 70,000 to 100,000 Bedouin should be added to those numbers. Abu Sitta's calculation for the Bedouin from Naqab/Negev is 90,000. Unlike Khalidi, however, he documents in detail each of the displaced Bedouin tribes by family name, locale, and population (1998, pp. 28–35, 56–57; 2004). According to Wakim and Beidas (2001, pp. 33–34), the Bedouin were expelled both during the fighting in 1947–1949 (when they either fled and were not allowed to return or were forcibly relocated) as well as after the armistice. Most of the urban centers in Palestine before 1948—Acre, Haifa, Safad, Jaffa, Jerusalem, Tiberius—had mixed populations of Palestinians and Jews, although some were almost entirely Palestinian—Nablus, Majdal 'Asqalan, Gaza City, Baysan, Beersheba, Nazareth, Shefa 'Amr—and one was almost entirely Jewish—Tel Aviv. The vast majority of the Palestinian inhabitants of the cities that were incorporated into the Israeli state in 1948—Acre, Haifa, Safad, Tiberius, Majdal 'Asqalan, Beersheba, Jaffa, and Baysan—including Greek, Armenian, and other non-Jewish residents, either fled or were expelled during the war and after. Most of the current Palestinian inhabitants

of those cities in Israel are internally displaced people who came from the surrounding villages.

22. These IDPs are labeled by Israeli governmental bodies as present-absentees, meaning they are subject to the Absentees' Property Law 5710 of 1950 (see Kretzmer 1990), despite the fact that they are present in the country (Wakim and Beidas 2001).

23. Jordanian Jerusalem (between 1948 and 1967) encompassed 2.5 square miles out of the total of 12.5 square miles that was municipal Jerusalem prior to 1948. Jones 1975, p. 223, quoting Mayor Ruhi al-Khatib. See also Katz 2005 for more on Jordanian Jerusalem. Approximately thirty thousand Palestinians remained in what became the Arab half of the city after 1948, and it also absorbed some of the 30,000 non-Jewish refugees from the part of the city that fell under Israeli control. More than five thousand Jewish refugees from the Old City were sent to the Israeli side.

24. Wakim and Beidas 2001. See also W. Khalidi 1992, which details that half of the refugee population (some 383,150 persons) came from these villages while the remainder came from the depopulation of the cities (241,016) and the Bedouin communities (70,000 to 100,000). According to W. Khalidi, the total number of refugees ranged between 714,150 and 744,150 (pp. 581–582).

25. The United Nations established the United Nations Relief for Palestine Refugees in November 1948 to assist Palestine refugees and coordinate relief efforts. For more details on the early provision of services, see Feldman 2007, al-Mawed 1999, Peteet 2005, Yahya 1999.

26. http://www.un.org/unrwa/publication/pdf/figures.pdf

27. al-Mawed 1999.

28. R. Sayigh 1994.

29. For more details, see Feldman 2008.

30. Feldman 2007, 2008; Jones 1975.

31. Benvenisti 2000, Kanaana 2000, Masalha 1992, Pappé 2006.

32. These statistics are according to the researchers Ghazi Falah, Sharif Kanaana, Kamal Abdulfattah, Albert Glock, and Sharif Elmusa, who visited all of the village sites in the late 1980s and early 1990s. Their work is the basis for the volume *All That Remains*, W. Khalidi 1992, pp. xviii–xix: "Of the 418 villages, 292 (70 percent) were totally destroyed; 90 villages (22 percent) were largely destroyed, which means that only a small percentage of the houses were left standing (20 villages in this category had only one surviving house). Eight villages (less than 2 percent) had only a small percentage of their houses destroyed, while 7 villages (less than 2 percent) survived but were taken over by Israeli settlers. [. . .] The level of destruction of 20 villages (5 percent) could not be determined. [. . .] In addition, another 69 villages and a number of towns remained with part or all of their population inside the borders of the new Israeli state."

33. Almost every village was photographed while documenting the villages for the *All That Remains* (W. Khalidi 1992) project, although not all of them appear in the book.

Those photographs and ones taken by Palestinians, Israelis, and others have been posted in each village entry on http://www.PalestineRemembered.com

34. Part and parcel of the colonial project was an obsession with the Holy Land, which was accorded special status in the nineteenth-century European consciousness, and which also took the form of religious projects and proselytizing among the population (Jewish, Christian, and Muslim). This "biblification," to quote Nassar 2006b, occurs in many photographs and postcards, and in other narrative forms. See Moors and Machlin 1987; Nassar 2006a, 2006b; van Oord 2008.

35. Gabbay 1959, p. 24. Ben-Ze'ev's work on the Palestinian village of Ijzim illustrates the multiple perspectives inherent both in representing the past and in the expressions of both the conquered and the conquering. A Jewish officer's description of the village after it was captured in July of 1948 encapsulates the ways in which Jews who became Israelis saw the Palestinians, and how Israelis did not understand Palestinians' connections to their villages. In his experience, "there were villages that we would walk into and the houses were barren and poor. Shacks. . . . But in this village there were stone houses, streets, two-story houses. You could tell the population here had a different standard of living. It also explained to us why they insisted on staying there. They were surrounded and should have left much earlier" (Ben-Ze'ev 2002, p. 23). Palestinians, of course, did not share these sentiments. They saw their existence in Palestine as connecting them to the land both historically and in the present. It was not just through fourteen hundred years of Arab and Islamic history that they could trace their presence, but also through centuries of living on the land itself.

36. Abi-Mershed 2010, Comaroff and Comaroff 1992, Fleischmann 2003, Sbaiti 2008.

37. Shohat 1997. The Mizrahim (which means "Eastern Jews," in Hebrew), or Arab Jews, are also called Jews from Muslim countries. One smaller group that is subsumed into them is the Sephardim (often confused in English as one and the same). The Sephardim, however, are Jews who were expelled from Spain (Sepharad in modern Hebrew) in the fifteenth century and absorbed into north Africa, Turkey, and Egypt.

38. Shohat 1988, 1997. Most European Jewish communities are called Ashkenazim and have a long history in Central and Eastern Europe. The communities of the Mediterranean, along with those in North Africa and Southwestern Asia, are the Mizrahim. As their Arab cultural norms and language were looked down on, one of the ways in which a few chose to prove themselves was through serving in Israeli intelligence as Arab specialists. Thus, while their culture and language were denigrated in wider Israel, at the same time those same skills were used by the state to protect that society. See Shenhav 2006, pp. 1–12, for his personal experiences.

39. Kalvarisky, an agronomist, was an immigrant to the country in 1895 and one of the founders of the Brit Shalom movement (which ceased to exist in 1933), which saw as necessary the coexistence of Jews and Arabs.

40. Atran 1989, p. 740. Conversation dated August 8, 1935.

41. See R. Khalidi 1997 for details on the rise of Palestinian nationalism in the late Ottoman and early Mandate periods.

42. Anderson 1991, Gellner 1983.

43. Anderson 1991.

44. Khalili 2007.

45. Brand 1988 deals with this subject most comprehensively for the period through the 1980s.

46. Hammer 2005.

47. Parmenter 1994, pp. 84–85.

48. Tonkin 1992, p. 2.

49. Dalen et al. 2009. Other words were used to describe specific types of historical writing, particularly before the mid third century AH (*anno hijra*, used to designate the Muslim calendar, which began in the year of Muhammad's *hijra*, that is, flight from Mecca to Medina), or ninth century CE, but also up to early modern times, and include *akhbar* (reports, narratives), *sira* (biography), *maghazi* (campaigns of the Prophet), and *futuh* (conquests). See Shryock (1997) for a modern discussion of how *akhbar* narratives fit into the historical and genealogical narratives and poems of contemporary Bedouin in Jordan.

50. Comaroff and Comaroff 1992, Dirks 1992, Lockman 2004, J. W. Scott 1991.

51. Geertz 1983.

52. Geertz 1973, 5.

53. Said 1979, pp. 272–273.

54. Kenny 1999, p. 437.

55. Clifford and Marcus 1986.

56. Abu-Lughod 1991, p. 148.

57. Abu-Lughod 1991, p. 158.

58. Dirks, Eley, and Ortner 1994, especially p. 39.

59. Sider 2005, p. 173.

60. White 1980.

61. Foucault 1978, 1980; cited in Dirks, Eley, and Ortner 1994.

62. Dirks, Eley, and Ortner 1994.

63. Dirks, Eley, and Ortner 1994, p. 8.

64. Portelli 1997, p. 143.

65. Papailias 2005.

66. Samuel 1994, p. 8.

67. Malkki 1992.

68. Peteet 1995, 2005; Feldman 2007. Extending Malkki's argument, many studies of Palestinians by non-Palestinians define the refugees as "the problem" that needs to be fixed, whereas the uprooter is seen and accepted as a member of the world community. This attitude is prévalent in studies by Artz 1997 and Gabbay 1959, among many others.

69. Abu El-Haj 2001, Silberman 1989, Zerubavel 1995.

70. Abu El-Haj 2001, Benvenisti 2000, Swedenburg 1990.

71. Benvenisti 2000, p. 4.

72. Other documentary projects that provide oral histories on this subject include the *nakba* archive created by Diana Allan and Mahmoud Zeidan, which has more than eleven hundred DVDs of interviews with 1948 refugees living in Lebanon [http://www .nakba-archive.org]; and the interviews posted at PalestineRemembered.com

73. Slyomovics 1998, 1994.

74. United States Holocaust Memorial Museum 1996; Bauer 2001.

75. The Mizrahi Jews (or Mizrahim) are those who once lived in Yemen, Iraq, Iran, Syria, Lebanon, and Central Asia, among other places.

76. The Mizrahi Jewish population formed half of the Jewish population in Israel until the immigration of more than 700,000 Jews from the former Soviet Union in the 1990s.

77. On numerous occasions, other citizens vented on the local Jewish population their anger at Israel and its treatment of Palestinians, which created a climate of fear and intimidation. See Stillman 1991.

78. Stillman 1991. Shenhav 2006 details and analyzes this history. He also describes the relationships created between Arab Jews and Palestinian refugees, and the various bodies that introduced plans for working out compensation and "exchange" of property.

79. Slyomovics 1994; 1998, pp. 1–7. For an extensive introduction to and excerpts from memorial books by the Jewish communities in Poland, see Kugelmass and Boyarin 1998. One of the commemorative sites in the Martyrs' Forest is for the Polish province of Turek. The certificate issued by the Jewish National Fund records that 2,500 trees were planted in their memory. See "We Remember Jewish Turek!" at http://www.zchor.org/ turek/turek.htm. Many of the memorial books are also available in innovative forms with pictures and texts on the Internet. For example, the Yurburg Lithuanian Jewish community's memorial book is available at http://www.jewishgen.org/yizkor/jurbarkas/ yurburg.html. The *yizkor* (memorial) books are described at this Web site as "memorials to Jewish communities destroyed in the Holocaust. They were usually put together by survivors from those communities and contain descriptions and histories of the *shtetl* [small Jewish town in Central or Eastern Europe], biographies of prominent people, lists of people who perished, etc. They are often embellished with photos, maps, and other memorabilia.

Yizkor books are valuable to genealogists, since the books may include biographies or photographs of relatives, or may include family members in a list of people who perished. *Yizkor* books also give important background information about the history and Jewish life in a particular shtetl. Yizkor books can be valuable, not only to genealogists, but to anyone wanting to learn about Jewish life and culture in the communities that vanished in the Holocaust." http://www.jewishgen.org/yizkor/faq.html#q1. Accessed August 15, 2009.

80. Kuglemass and Boyarin 1998, p. 1.

81. Slyomovics 1993, 1994, 1998.

82. I had many conversations with colleagues in the Arab world about how to characterize these books—including whether *memorial* (*tidhkari*) *book* is the correct term for them. I defended the use of *memorial book* at the time because it allowed these books to fit in with other books on destroyed villages around the world. Although that might make sense on some level, the fact is there are no links among the different geographical groups in the genre, and the Palestinians never use the word *memorial* in their titles or descriptions. Thus the grouping of these books into a genre is useful only for understanding comparatively how people remember and memorialize loss of homes and places. (Thanks to Marwan Khawaja and Sulayman al-Dabbagh, among others, for their insights on this subject.)

83. Hammer 2005, R. Khalidi 1997, al-Mawed 1999, al-Maw'id 1998, Nassar 2002, Parmenter 1994.

84. R. Khalidi 1997.

85. Milton-Edwards 1996, Robinson 1997, Lybarger 2007.

86. Interview with Hussein al-Lubani, Damun village, in Tripoli, Lebanon, June 6, 2005.

87. Abu Ahmed ('Issa Ahmed Musa Sulayman) in Kana'ana and al-Madani 1987a, p. 42.

88. Sayigh 1979.

89. During 1948 and even after the war, none of the banks, with the exception of the Arab Bank, gave people access to their bank accounts. To this contextual understanding of what the loss meant add the fact that the years of World War II were prosperous ones for Palestine (unlike for Europe), and thus most people had enjoyed a significant increase in their standard of living.

90. Diab and Fahoum 1990, p. 66. Words of Umm Jamal Qarafi'.

91. Boym 2001, p. 3.

92. Boym 2001, p. 3.

93. Boym 2001, p. 4. During the eighteenth and nineteenth centuries, nostalgia was also a soldier's disease. Although the condition among troops challenged military leaders fighting wars on distant soil and was punished by threats and violence, the sicknesses associated with nostalgia were seen as an expression of the powerful tie of the soldier to the homeland, even if he was not willing to fight or die for that country.

94. Written by Muhammad Khallad, a lawyer, who contrasts his memories of the past with how those who return to visit the village experience it. 'Atiya 1991, p. 46.

95. This meaning became popular in the twentieth century; compare "Transferred sense (the main modern one) of 'wistful yearning for the past' first recorded 1920" in *Online Etymology Dictionary*, Douglas Harper, Historian, http://dictionary.reference.com/browse/nostalgia. Accessed December 8, 2008.

96. Stewart 1988, p. 252.

Chapter 2: Village Books: Local Histories, National Struggles

1. Fendel 2007.

2. Rapoport 2007a.

3. Rapoport 2008.

4. Following the establishment of the State of Israel on May 15, 1948, regulations were established to deal with what were termed *absentee property* in December of 1948 (Emergency Regulations [Absentees' Property] Law 5709), and then eventually established the Absentees' Property Law 5710 of 1950. This law transferred the property of all those who were not in their place of residence on September 1, 1948 (or before) to the Custodian of Absentee Property. According to Sabri Jiryis (1973, pp. 88–89), "the Custodian was regarded as the legal holder of all property belonging to absentees, and was allowed to sell such properties to a Development Authority [. . .]." The Development Authority (Transfer of Property) Law of 1950 forbade the transfer of lands "it had obtained from the Custodian or others to any party but the state, the Keren Kayemet [JNF]; an organization engaged in settling the Arab 'refugees' who had stayed in Israel; or a local authority, on condition that the Keren Kayemet should have the prior right to buy such lands as the Development Authority might offer for sale" (). The law continues to be amended and interpreted.

5. Fendel 2007.

6. Rapoport 2007b.

7. Cohen 2007.

8. Dirbas 1993, p. 13.

9. One book was published in Cyprus and another two were published in the United States. Mahmoud Issa (1997) wrote an account of his village in English and published it on the Internet, but I did not include it here because it does not appear as a book.

10. Dirbas 1993, p. 8.

11. Kanaʿana and ʿAbd al-Hadi 1986, Saqr 1990.

12. Two of the villages represented in my collection—ʿImwas and Yalu—were emptied in the 1967 war.

13. The six villages are from the districts (*liwaʾ*) of Haifa (the village of ʿAyn Hawd), Jaffa (Salama village), Ramla (ʿInnaba village), Jerusalem (Dayr Yasin village), Hebron (al-Dawayima village), and Gaza (Majdal ʿAsqalan town). The first two books were about ʿAyn Hawd and Majdal ʿAsqalan.

14. Abu Fadda 1985, Hadeem 1985. A number of early studies, such as Ahmad Abu Khusa's *Biʾr al-Sabiʿ wa al-hayat al-badawiyya* (Beersheba and Bedouin life), (published in 1982, and Yusif Haddad's *ʿAdat al-khutba wal-zawaj fi qaryat al-bassa al-filastiniyya* (Customs of engagement and marriage in the Palestinian al-Bassa village), published in 1984, were prototypes of these local histories, although their focus is folklore and traditions. They both build on Arabic work by al-ʿArif (1933/2004) that is based in early anthropological descriptive and categorizing work. Research in English was also being published at the same time by Granqvist 1931–1935/1975, 1947 and Canaan 1927, 1933.

15. Kanaʻana and al-Madani 1987c, cover page.

16. There are no indications in the text that the authors from this first group in the Birzeit village book series were from any of the villages they researched. In addition to these books, the only other books written by people *not* from the village about which the authors are writing are the two books by Dirbas (on Salama and al-Birwa), and a book by Fadi Sulayma on Dayr Yasin. Muhammad Amin Nimr wrote about two villages—Kharbitha bani Harith (2005) and Shilta (2001)—but he was born in the first and raised in the second.

17. The villages written about in these books are Kafr Birʻim, Safad District; ʻAyn Hawd and Tirat Haifa, Haifa District; Lubya, Tiberius District; Zirʻin, Jenin District; Kafr Saba, Miska, and Qaqun, Tulkarm District; Dayr Yasin and Lifta, Jerusalem District; Salama and Abu Kishk, Jaffa District; ʻInnaba and Abu Shusha, al-Ramla District; Bayt Jibrin, Hebron District; and al-Faluja, al-Kawfakha, and Majdal ʻAsqalan, Gaza District. With the exception of the villages of the northern Galilee whose inhabitants ended up in Lebanon and Syria, the chosen villages represent most of the areas of Palestine that became Israel in 1948. These works do not cover, however, the large number of Bedouin communities that were displaced by the creation of Israel, in particular those from al-Naqab (the Negev) area, who ended up either displaced within Israel or as refugees in Jordan.

18. Kanaʻana and al-Madani 1987a, p. 14; Kanaʻana and al-Kaʻbi 1991b, p. 15.

19. Kanaʻana and ʻAbd al-Hadi 1986, p. 9.

20. The authors include Kanʻaan 1998 (on Ishwaʻ), Salih 1988 (on Bayt Mahsir), among numerous others. With many authors, it was difficult for me to tell whether they were born in the village because they did not indicate their birth year and thus I had no way of knowing how old they were in 1948. Although Saqr's book on Salama is not framed as an autobiography, its detailed explanations of places and events from the 1948 War are comparable to memoirs written by Palestinians who were also old enough to participate as fighters in the 1948 War, such as that by Bahjat Abu Gharbiyya 1993.

21. Kanaʻana and ʻAbd al-Hadi 1986, p. 7.

22. Kanaʻana and ʻAbd al-Hadi 1986, p. 7.

23. Correspondence dated September 11, 1995.

24. ʻAwadallah 1996, on Suba village; and al-Ramahi 2004, on Muzayriʻa village.

25. Copies of correspondence kindly shared with me by Saleh Abdel Jawad, 2008, al-Bira, West Bank.

26. Susan Slyomovics details the work of Sharif Kanaʻana as head of this project in *Object of Memory* (1998).

27. The books in the Birzeit series published under Saleh Abdel Jawad's leadership are fundamentally different from those in the first part of the series. They are significantly longer; the authors decided on the organization and content of the book, with the editorial input of Abdel Jawad; they use various kinds of documentation rather than

just oral histories obtained from a small group; and they have covers featuring a picture of the village.

28. I have not been able to travel to Gaza since the late 1990s, so I collected these four books in Jordan. There are perhaps many more. I also was not able to find out more on the National Center for Studies and Documentation (*al-markiz al-qawmi lil-dirasat wal-tawthiq*).

29. Slyomovics 1993, 1994, 1998; Baylouny 2006. Baylouny describes the growth of family charitable societies in Jordan.

30. Interview with 'Abd al-'Aziz Saqr, Amman, Jordan, June 1, 2005.

31. I insisted on buying books from them, which they of course refused, but we usually settled on them giving me a free copy that they inscribed to me, and then I would buy extra copies to take and donate to libraries in other countries.

32. The Birzeit book on Salama (Kana'ana and 'Abd al-Hadi 1986) reproduces documents and photos on 27 of its 84 pages. Dirbas's book (1993) is harder to calculate because the documents and photos are woven into the text, but they fill about 130 of its 241 pages.

33. According to Forman 2002, p. 61, "the Judicial Process of 'Settlement of Title,' or 'land settlement,' constituted the core of British land regime reform in Mandate Palestine. This process, which relied on topographical and cadastral survey, exact mapping and extensive judicial investigation of land rights aimed at identifying an owner for every parcel of land in the country. British reformers sought to transform the traditional usufruct rights of the indigenous, majority Arab population and the minority population of European Jewish settlers into rights of ownership."

34. Dirbas 1993. The articles from 1945 describe the installation of pumps and pipes to bring drinking water from the local well to the village (p. 72), and considerations taking place to join Salama to the Jaffa municipality (p. 85). The clippings from 1946 include a complaint by the Salama Cars Company against the British authorities who raided its office in Jaffa and allegedly stole goods and money, and reports about Jewish attacks on buses (pp. 94–96). Reprints from August 15, 1947, detail clashes between the Jews and Arabs on the edge of Jaffa–Tel Aviv, which included Salama residents (pp. 104–111).

35. It is not mentioned what the "mid-western sector" (*al-qita' al-gharbi lil-mintaqa al-wusta*) is, but it is likely a regional division of one of the political groups (such as al-Futuwwa or al-Najjada).

36. For more on the Salama Bus Company and its schedule between the Jewish settlements and Arab villages, see Chapter Seven.

37. Dirbas 1993, p. 59 (*Sharikat al-Fannaneen bil-Quds* [Artists Company in Jerusalem]); Kana'ana and 'Abd al-Hadi 1986, p. 76 (*al-Matba'a al-Tijariyya—Yafa* [Commercial Press—Jaffa]).

38. The Futuwwa [Youth] Group in Palestine was formed in 1935 by Emile al-Ghuri, gradually dissolved after the 1936–1939 Arab revolt, and then re-formed in 1946. Similar

groups existed in other Arab countries. They were modeled (organizationally, not ideologically) after the youth movements of the Nazi party in Germany. They built on the already prevalent Boy Scout movement, which was common in urban areas from the beginning of the century. The Palestine Arab Party (*al-Hizb al-'Arabi al-Filastini*) attempted to join together the Futuwwa and Najjada groups (the Najjada was founded in 1945 by Muhammad Nimr al-Hawari as a scout movement), which together numbered more than ten thousand members, in order to harness their skills (limited as they were) in defense of Palestine. The goal of both the Futuwwa and the Najjada groups was to train young men physically and morally, to teach them nationalist sentiments and how to fire a gun and carry out other military drills (Khalaf 1991, p. 143).

39. Dirbas 1993, pp. 133–151. The diary reproductions consist of seventeen pages from 1947 and six pages from April 17–28, 1948. Advertisements for *Al-Wihda* newspaper appear twice ("the mouthpiece of the loyal and honest leadership"), suggesting that perhaps it was the publisher of the daily agenda book. *Al-Wihda* was a daily newspaper started in 1945 by Ishaq 'Abd al-Salaam al-Husseini in Jerusalem.

40. Saqr's book does not include pictures or documents from before 1948.

41. Moors and Machlin 1987; Nassar 2006a, 2006b; van Oord 2008.

42. A *qumbaz* is a long, open shirt that extends well below the knees and is closed by wrapping it around the body and holding it in place with a belt (as with a robe). It is often made of a striped fabric. See Weir 1989 for more on this subject.

43. Kana'ana and 'Abd al-Hadi 1986, p. 52.

44. The word that Dirbas uses for "masked gypsy woman entertainer" is *jankiyat* (plural feminine), who are wedding entertainers, likely gypsies, in Egypt. Not surprisingly, given Salama's connections to Egypt, such traditions could be found in Salama as well as in Gaza. Conversation with Salim Tamari, February 2010.

45. Dirbas 1993, pp. 77–80. There are a number of other wedding songs (all of which follow a specific meter and rhyme in Arabic). The translations provided here are not literal and miss many of the subtleties of the colloquial references. I edited them heavily for the English reader.

46. Dirbas 1993, p. 173.

47. Tamari 2009, p. 7.

48. Dirbas 1993, p. 37.

49. Kana'ana and 'Abd al-Hadi 1986, p. 51.

50. Interview with 'Abd al-'Aziz Saqr, June 1, 2005. Amman, Jordan.

51. Dirbas 1993, pp. 44–45.

52. The Balfour Declaration was a letter from British Foreign Secretary Lord Balfour to a Jewish community leader, Baron Rothschild. It expressed the favorable disposition of the British Cabinet to "the establishment in Palestine of a national home for the Jewish people" as long as doing so did not "prejudice the civil and religious rights of existing non-Jewish communities in Palestine."

53. The fighting actually began in 1947 after the UN voted to partition Palestine on November 29, 1947, and ended officially with the Armistice Agreements signed by Israel with Egypt (February 24, 1949), Lebanon (March 23, 1949), Jordan (April 3, 1949), and Syria (July 20, 1949).

54. Saqr 1990, p. 93.

55. Khalili 2007, p. 214.

56. As the research of Julie Peteet, Rosemary Sayigh, and Ilana Feldman shows, soon after 1948, Palestinian narratives portrayed Palestinians as uprooted peasants, impoverished and dispossessed of all means of supporting themselves and reliant on aid. Pamphlets printed by the Palestine Arab Refugee Office aimed to move world opinion on the very real suffering of the refugees. Ilana Feldman discusses how "the category of 'refugee' proved to be important not only for managing relief, but also for the rearticulation of Palestinian political identity in the aftermath of dispossession" (Feldman 2007, p. 130).

57. T. Khalidi 1981, p. 68.

58. Y. Sayigh 1997, chapters one and two.

59. Y. Sayigh 1997, p. 71. The ANM was founded by Palestinians George Habash and Wadiʿ Haddad, along with Ahmad al-Khatib (a Kuwaiti) and Hani al-Hindi (a Syrian), and they found a pan-Arab hero in the rise of Egyptian President Gamal Abd al-Nasir in the 1950s. Sayigh states that "the overriding commitment to Nasir, his philosophy on political, social, and economic issues, and his regional agenda was to be the determining influence on the ideology and behavior of the ANM for over a decade" (p. 75).

60. Y. Sayigh 1997, p. 92.

61. Palestinians began what came to be known as the Resistance (al-Muqawima) to fight against the Israeli occupation of their homeland. The Resistance consisted of all of the Palestinian armed liberation movements of the time, which eventually joined together to form different factions of the PLO (and continually broke off from it). Rosemary Sayigh notes this process in the title of her first oral history: Palestinians: From Peasants to Revolutionaries (1979).

62. Khalili 2007, p. 61. The Palestine Research Center (Markaz al-Abhath al-Filastini) in Beirut was attached to the PLO and during this period produced many publications, including a series of books on Palestinian cities that were precursors to the village books. Yet these books focus only on cities or large towns and are textbook-like accounts of their location, geographical information, history, architecture, and significant monuments. This way of telling the stories of Palestinian places parallels what Khalili sees as the influence of the nationalist commemorative discourse: "much bottom-up history was suppressed in favor of heroic narratives which form the basis of all nationalist histories" (Khalili 2007, p. 62). The cities' histories are punctuated by the stories of great Arab and Muslim men and women from those places who were leaders, religious figures, literati, and patrons—strands in a glorifying Palestinian narrative.

63. See Rubenberg 1983 and Cobban 1984 for more on this subject. Khalili (2007, pp.

62–63) describes how even after the Research Center's archive was taken in 1982, a car bomb planted in Februrary 1983 "gutted" the six-story building, killed eighteen people, and destroyed the research work being done at the time—oral histories of survivors of the Sabra and Shatila massacre that took place in September 1982.

64. Tamari 2009, p. 1.

65. See Nazzal 1978, Peteet 1991, R. Sayigh 1979, and http://www.nakba-archive.org, among others.

66. See R. Sayigh 1979, Falah 1989, R. Shafir 1989, Gorkin and Othman 1996, and others.

67. See Edward Said's conversation with Salman Rushdie (Rushdie 1991, pp. 166–184) as an example of the role that telling memories plays in Palestinians' lives. This primacy of the personal past and memory is particularly the case when Palestinians interact with non-Palestinians (see Hassan Khader's story of pretending he was Yemeni to avoid the never-ending questions and conflict, in Khader 1997). Among Palestinians too, storied interactions of "who met whom when and where" are part of everyday interactions with one another.

68. 'Alyan 1988, p. 3.

69. Most of the memorial books address the reasons for undertaking such a project in their introduction.

70. Kan'aan 1998, p. 8.

71. Abu Khiyara, Fanush, Sulayman, and 'Ashur 1993, p. 10.

72. Interview with Ibrahim 'Awadallah, from Suba village. Interview conducted in Amman, Jordan, June 4, 2005.

73. Interview with Hussein al-Lubani, from Damun Village. Interview conducted in Tripoli, Lebanon, June 30, 2005.

74. Suhmata n.d, p. 160.

75. The Absentees' Property Law of 5710/1950 defines an absentee as follows: "a person who, at any time during the period between the 16th Kislev, 5708 (29th November, 1947) and the day on which a declaration is published, under section 9(d) of the Law and Administration Ordinance, 5708–1948 (1), that the state of emergency declared by the Provisional Council of State on the 10th Iyar, 5708 (19th May, 1948) (2) has ceased to exist, was a legal owner of any property situated in the area of Israel or enjoyed or held it, whether by himself or through another, and who, at any time during the said period—(i) was a national or citizen of the Lebanon, Egypt, Syria, Saudi Arabia, Trans-Jordan, Iraq or the Yemen, or (ii) was in one of these countries or in any part of Palestine outside the area of Israel, or (iii) was a Palestinian citizen and left his ordinary place of residence in Palestine (a) for a place outside Palestine before the 27th Av, 5708 (1st September, 1948); or (b) for a place in Palestine held at the time by forces which sought to prevent the establishment of the State of Israel or which fought against it after its establishment."

76. Wakim and Beidas 2001.

77. See Jiryis 1976, Robinson 2003, Zureik 1979.

78. I have accompanied Palestinians on some of these visits, and we collect grape leaves, figs, thyme, grapes, wild asparagus, and other plants that were once part of their orchards and gardens and are now growing wild. They bring them home and eat from their land (see Ben-Ze'ev 2004). When I went to Kafr Bir'im with a woman whose family was from there, we came across other Kafr Bir'im families coming from Haifa and elsewhere to picnic there. The guard at the archaeological site did not charge any of us the entrance fee.

79. Both of these organizations are located in Israel. The Association for the Defense of the Rights of the Internally Displaced Persons in Israel, at http://www.group194 .net/?page=commitees&Id=17, is a largely Palestinian organization formed to organize Palestinian IDPs. Zochrot, at http://www.zochrot.org/index.php?id=184, is a group of Israeli citizens working to raise awareness of the *nakba* in Israel. Accessed January 9, 2009.

80. Kan'aan 1998, p. 8.

81. Interview with Ghalib Sumrayn, Amman, Jordan, April 30, 2005.

82. Interview with Ghalib Sumrayn, Amman, Jordan, April 30, 2005.

83. Thank you to one of the anonymous reviewers of the manuscript for the clarifying comments.

Chapter 3: Village History and Village Values

1. W. Khalidi 1992.

2. In addition to al-Dabbagh's *Biladuna Filastin* (1965), the other encyclopedic source was W. Khalidi's *All That Remains* (1992). The availability of that book's information on PalestineRemembered.com allowed children without access to it in print form to read the book. With the passage of time, the website has become a virtual repository of information about the village. It is, as this book explores throughout, a popular alternative to printed village books.

3. Al-Dabbagh tells the story that he wrote this work not once but twice. He had to toss the six-thousand-page handwritten, unpublished manuscript over the side of the boat in which he and his family were fleeing the fighting in his neighborhood of al-Manshiyya in Jaffa in 1948 (al-Dabbagh 1965, Vol. 1, Part 1, pp. 7–8). He also mentions that in 1947 he had published a previous Volume 1, Part 1, but following the loss of Palestine in 1948 (and the rest of his work), he reconceived of the project and published a new Volume 1, Part 1.

4. Hay'at al-Mawsu'a al-Filastiniyah 1984.

5. W. Khalidi 1992. Khalidi is the editor, but the research for and writing of the text was done mainly by Sharif Elmusa and Muhammad Ali Khalidi, with on-the-ground site visits conducted by Sharif Kana'ana, Ghazi Falah, Kamal Abdulfattah, and Albert Glock, and the editorial work of William Young and Linda Butler.

6. In the West Bank, in Gaza, and inside Israel, the Arabic version of *All That Remains* was quickly pirated and reproduced in a copy so poor that the photographs were unrecognizable, even though the book was sold for the same price as the original IPS edition. The costs to IPS of getting the Arabic book from Beirut to Cyprus and then to

Jerusalem limited the numbers sent and sold by IPS, which made the pirated edition much easier to obtain for the majority of people in the West Bank. Personal communication, head of IPS in Cyprus.

7. Interview with Ibrahim ʿAwadallah, from Suba village. Interview in Amman Jordan, June 4, 2005.

8. Interview with Ghalib Sumrayn from Qalunya village. Interview in Amman, Jordan, April 30, 2005.

9. These texts focus on telling Palestinian history so as to show the consequences of the political actions and the behavior of political actors within the framework of the fall of Palestine in 1948. Written by authors who were both participants in and analysts of Palestinian history, these books are invaluable for understanding Palestine prior to 1948, the events of the *nakba*, and the effects of the war and displacement on the population. Many additional books on the Palestine tragedy are written in this same big-picture-history style and were published in Beirut, Cairo, Damascus, Baghdad, and elsewhere. They all focus on Palestinian losses in and rights to the occupied land. See Hasso 2000, and Stein 1991 for more on these subjects. ʿArif al-ʿArif's *al-Mufassal fi tarikh al-quds* (A detailed history of Jerusalem), with its encyclopedic description of life in that city in the chapter "Jerusalem as I Saw It at the Outset of 1947," is in some ways unique. Al-ʿArif relies largely on British statistics and his own memory to list and describe the Arab neighborhoods, religious sites, markets, libraries, schools, roads, gardens, museums, industry, businesses, workforce composition, standards of living, and characteristics of the population (1992, pp. 327–388).

10. Tamari 2009, p. 57.

11. Al-Dabbagh 1965, vol. 6, p. 110. He does not mention how Motza was destroyed or by whom.

12. Al-Dabbagh 1965, vol. 6, p. 110.

13. Keith Basso, in his work on Western Apache narratives of the past (1999), explicates the lesson-based moral codes embedded in stories that are told in connection to a certain place.

14. Abu Khiyara, Fanush, Sulayman, and ʿAshur 1993, p. 9.

15. In the village book about Jimzu, the villagers worked together for a larger national purpose during the 1936–1939 Arab revolt: "Often they would gather up the sheep and cows through the village at night to erase the footsteps of the resistance showing their movements. This made it difficult for the occupation forces to trace them and catch them" (al-Najjar 1996, p. 43). Here and elsewhere these values of unity are portrayed within the framework of Palestinian nationalist struggles as well as local concerns.

16. I have been unable to find Erza in any of the publications listing Israeli settlements in the area. I have therefore transcribed it according to how it could be read in Arabic, although the actual name of the settlement in Hebrew may be different.

17. Sumrayn 1993, p. 40.

18. Malkki 1995, p. 54.

19. Shryock 1997.

20. Kanaʻana and ʻAbd al-Hadi 1990, p. 20.

21. Sulayma 2003, p. 178.

22. This account contains many possible interpretations, particularly when read through the lenses of James Scott's analytical work on resistance to power in *Weapons of the Weak* (1985) and *Domination and the Arts of Resistance* (1992).

23. Al-Madi 1994, p. 78.

24. Ben-Ze'ev 2002, Miller 1985.

25. Interview with ʻAbd al-ʻAziz Saqr, Amman, Jordan, June 1, 2005.

26. Saqr 1990, pp. 82–84.

27. Interview with ʻAbd al-ʻAziz Saqr, Amman, Jordan, June 1, 2005.

28. Other examples include the village book on Dallata, in the Safad area in northern Galilee, which had an estimated 360 residents in 1945. This 117-page book devotes ten pages to the families of the village, listing the father and sons and where they are living today. Hummayd 2000, pp. 40–49. The village book on Qidditha, also in the Safad area, has 52 pages of spreadsheets listing the villagers in residence from 1875 to 1997, the names of wives and children for the five major *hamulas* in the village, the number of families in the *hamulas*, the head of each family in the village in 1948 and their descendants, where they live now, and the number of males and females, among other subjects (Dakwar 2001, pp. 35–87). The village book on Qaqun contains 23 pages of family trees, some extending back fourteen generations (al-Mudawwar 1994, pp. 52–75).

29. Barakat 1993, al-Haj 1988.

30. Anthropologists have described these kinship systems among villagers in both Palestine and Jordan. See Antoun 1972, Asad 1975, A. Cohen 1965, Lutfiyya 1966, Shryock 1997. The Bedouin of the Naqab/Negev render kinship in other terms—six *qaba'il* (tribes) are divided into seventy-seven *'asha'ir* (clans) (Falah 1989, pp. 57–58).

31. The website http://www.PalestineRemembered.com also features a place on each village's page for people from that village to list their name, their "Clan/Hamolah[sic]," and where they currently reside. By recording names in this way, the site provides another way for people to identify themselves with their village of origin, despite (or perhaps because of) their present distance from that village. Some people choose not to fill in the box that identifies their clan—for the village of Dallata, for example, 11 of 31 people did not name their clan; neither did 14 of 35 for Qalunya, nor did 25 of 112 for Tirat Haifa. Accessed January 11, 2009.

32. Kanaaneh 2002, p. 129.

33. Sumrayn 1993, p. 90. Shuʻayb is one of the prophets mentioned in the Qur'an. It is surmised that he is identified with the biblical Jethro (the father-in-law of Moses) or his uncle (Rippin 2009). According to the second edition of the *Encyclopedia of Islam*, Qahtan is, "according to the consensus of opinion among Muslim genealogists, historians, and

geographers, and in popular tradition, the ancestor of all the South-Arabian peoples [. . .], whence he is sometimes known as 'father of all Yaman,' the Yamanis themselves being called *banu qahtan, qaba'il qahtan,* or simply *qahtan.* He thus corresponds to 'Adnan . . . , the common ancestor of the northern Arabs[. . .]" (Fischer 2009). (Arabic spellings have been altered to fit the available fonts.)

34. Kana'ana and Ishtayya 1991, p. 10.

35. Langellier and Peterson 1993, pp. 55–56.

36. Reynolds 2001, Shryock 1997, Slyomovics 1998.

37. 'Atiya 1991, p. 21.

38. Shryock 1997. See chapters four and five in particular.

39. Shryock 1997, p. 107. These stories rely on the same validation mechanisms as the *hadith* (the sayings and traditions of the Prophet Muhammad). Verifying and judging the soundness of a *hadith* relies on the *isnad,* a Muslim historiographical tradition that evaluates the accuracy of the *hadith* by examining the chain of transmitters through which it was passed down, which thereby provides authority for the validity of the information.

40. Sumrayn 1993, p. 85.

41. Kana'ana and al-Ka'bi 1991a, p. 12.

42. There is a limit, however, to how humble they will portray themselves. No one professes to be of slave origin or a sharecropper or to have been exiled from another village (although undoubtedly some were).

43. Interview with Yusuf Rahil, Jerusalem, February 5, 1999. I always thought that the family name was related to *Rachel,* but he informed me that his grandfather was from the Khazin family and was given or adopted the name when he came to 'Ayn Karim.

44. The short version of the story: While on pilgrimage, the *amir* entrusted his lands and families to the *amir* of a neighboring tribe. The neighboring amir took a fancy to the daughter of the absent *amir* and decided to marry her immediately. Her male relatives, wishing neither to insult the neighboring amir nor to marry the girl off without her father's approval, were at a loss as to what to do. Abu Kishk, who was merely a guard, suddenly agreed to the marriage of the girl to the neighboring *amir,* much to the shock of the tribe. He explained his action to them as part of a plan to stall, thereby giving them five days to devise some way out. The neighboring amir detected their deception and attacked the tribe, and it was the stranger, Abu Kishk, who saved the daughter (from a fall into the river and kidnapping by the neighboring amir's men) and defended the tribe. The amir returned and offered his daughter's hand to the stranger, although the other tribesmen did not accept the liaison because it came from outside the family. The stranger, angered by the rebuff, set off to Egypt to bring his family from the village of al-Kishkiya to show that his father was well known and respected. He brought his father, uncles, and cousins and they took over part of the amir's land, "from Wadi al-Hawarith to al-Qibb" (Kana'ana and 'Abd al-Hadi 1990, pp. 5–7).

45. Kana'ana and Ishtayya 1991, p. 8.

46. Some of the books are explicit about this focus, for example, 'Abd al-'Aal 2005, and the two books on the Turkmen tribes of Marj ibn 'Amir (Khatib 1987, al-Shuqayrat 1999).

47. I do not mention names here in order to respect the wishes of those I interviewed, as well as to not unnecessarily incite others against particular books.

48. Anonymous interview.

49. Interview with 'Abdallah Isma'il al-Sufi from 'Innaba village. Amman, Jordan, June 8, 2005.

50. Correspondence dated April 29, no year.

51. The clipping I read did not include the name of the newspaper. It must have been either *al-Quds* or *al-Ayyam*, the two most popular newspapers at the time.

52. Mar'i 1994.

53. Qur'an 49:6—"O ye who believe! If a wicked person comes to you with any news, ascertain the truth, lest ye harm people unwittingly, and afterwards become full of repentance for what ye have done" (Asad 2003).

54. The issues they raised were, among other topics, that al-Shalabi was appointed *mukhtar* of the village during Ottoman times, not under the British Mandate as the book indicated; that al-Shalabi's *diwan* hosted fighters in the 1936–1939 Arab revolt and Zir'in was the headquarters of the Arab Liberation Army (*Jaysh al-Inqadh*) in the village during the 1948 War; that the names of people who owned shops were other than what was mentioned; that the al-Shalabi family was the largest landowning family in the village; and that a number of families were left out of the genealogies.

55. Picture #7876, http://www.palestineremembered.com/haifa/ijzim/picture7876 .html. Accessed December 23, 2008. "The Castel" is on the sign in the picture, but the Web site spells it "The Castle." It is currently (in 2009) both a private home and a bed and breakfast located in Kerem Maharal. http://www.web4u.co.il/code_english/main .asp?pID=551. Accessed August 18, 2009. The new residents of the house list it as from the eleventh century and as a crusader castle. The home page clearly indicates how the present residents understand history, characterize Arabs, and ignore the villagers who were uprooted:

"The Castle" is a crusader site going back to the 11th century, positioned on the highest place in Kerem Maharal, facing the Eastern slopes of the Carmel mountain range and Maharal Valley. "The Castle" was one of the sea fortresses on the king's path (HaBonim, Dor and Atlit). "The Castle" is located at the top of a historic barrow, tracing back to the days of 1st Temple and even to an earlier age. In the days of Islam, the site was called "Dir Al-Omar," after a hedonist Arabic prince, Amar Tzalah A-Din [sic Salah al-din], who with his men took control over whole areas, leading a strict and terrorizing regime over the entire region. Many tales are told of the valley called "Baha Valley" and of "The Castle," which was the ruler's residence. Up until the foundation of the country, "The Castle" was home to a very rich and influential Arabic family, the El-Mahadi [sic al-Madi] family, who dominated the whole area between Haifa and Hadera. The mosque residing at the foot of

"The Castle" was built by the El-Mahadi [sic al-Madi] family, in the 17th century. Kerem Maharal was built on the location of the large village Igazim [sic Ijzim], which was a prospering community throughout history. Many properties were destroyed by a government order after the war in 1967. "The Castle" was to be destroyed as well, until Tsilla came across it while traveling the area." http://www.web4u.co.il/code_english/main.asp?cat_id=2062&pID=551. Accessed August 18, 2009.

56. Translated from the Arabic. Posted August 8, 2008 at http://www.palestine remembered.com/Haifa/Ijzim/Picture7876.html

57. Posted November 20, 2008 at http://www.palestineremembered.com/Haifa/Ijzim /Picture7876.html

58. Posted November 20, 2008 at http://www.palestineremembered.com/Haifa/Ijzim /Picture7876.html

59. Al-Madi 1994, pp. 74–76.

60. Post #82345, posted July 7, 2009 at http://www.palestineremembered.com/Haifa/ Ijzim/Picture7876.html

61. Moors 1995, Peteet 1991, Rothenberg 1998–1999. Shryock 1997, p. xi, briefly mentions the hegemonic structures of history-making among the tribes in Jordan that parallel the patriarchal descent structure and are entirely androcentric.

62. Kana'ana and al-Madani n.d., p. 16.

63. Sumrayn 1993, pp. 93–95.

64. One wife was listed by her name and she didn't seem to fit into any of the families or *hama'il* listed in the book.

65. He does not specify in the book the sources of the names in this list of Qalunya families, but he told me in an interview that he obtained them from the various village elders, both male and female.

66. Sumrayn 1993, p. 229.

67. Kana'ana and Ishtayya 1991, p. 8. Two people quoted in other parts of the book are Father Yusuf al-Susaan and Nimr Zaknun. However, there are no footnotes to attribute any of the information in the book to a particular person, nor is there a list of those interviewed for the project. There is a fine example of the presence of women in genealogies and photographs in the Mallaha village book ('Abd al-'Aal 2005). This is likely due to the fact that the Mallaha villagers are from the Ghawarneh, a mixed people—nomads, former slaves, and so on—who have different norms about female roles than other Palestinians. Almost no research has been conducted on this subject, so much of what I have written here is based on casual conversations and observations.

68. Kanaaneh 2002, Peteet 1999.

69. Kanaaneh 2002, p. 128.

70. Al-Mahsiri 2002, pp. 12–13.

71. Al-Najjar 1996, p. 1.

72. 'Atiya 1991, p. 3.

73. Linguistically, and as author 'Atiya mentioned to me, the plural words in Arabic

for fathers and grandfathers (*aba'* and *ajdad*) can also be used to mean parents and ancestors; thus these references are less gender-specific than they imply in the singular. It is possible to use other words for parents (such as *walidan*) that include both sexes.

Chapter 4: Writing a History, Defining a Past

1. Kana'ana and Ishtayya 1987.

2. Interview with 'Abdallah Isma'il al-Sufi, June 8, 2005.

3. Tonkin 1992, p. 10.

4. According to the authors I interviewed and my examination of the bibliographies of the village books, some authors, but by no means many, read other Palestinian village books. In particular, they read other books about their village, but a few also cite books on other villages.

5. Papailias 2005.

6. Interview with Deeb Kan'aan, July 16, 2005.

7. 'Alayan 1988, p. 4.

8. Interview with al-Hajj 'Abd al-Majid al-'Ali, January 7, 2005.

9. Sulayma 2003, p. 45.

10. Al-Najjar 1996, p. 3. This common saying implies that people know best the people of their hometown.

11. Al-Najjar 1996, p. 2.

12. Of course there could also have been other reasons why women did not want their names mentioned: that they did not want to be seen as usurping the men as sources, or they were embarrassed by the request and did not see themselves as having a big role, or they truly were modest, among other reasons.

13. People conducting oral histories of Palestinians have made less of an issue of this subject and the oral history collections of Palestinians are rich with women's voices. This is because, first, women live longer so are sometimes the only people available who had lived in the village to talk with about it. Second, oral history can focus more on certain topics, such as women's experiences; see Fleischmann 1999, 2003; Gluck 1977; Gluck and Patai 1991; Peteet 1991; Sayigh 1994, 1998. Third, older women play a more prominent role in their families than they do in public, where the older men are dominant. So when people want to know information about their family, they often turn to their grandmothers or aunts.

14. Although technically in the Qur'an the phrase is in the context of contracting a debt, the principle of requiring two women as witnesses so that one can remind the other has been applied more broadly. Surat al-Baqara 2:282. "O you who believe! When you deal with each other in contracting a debt for a fixed time, then write it down; and let a scribe write it down between you with fairness; and the scribe should not refuse to write as Allah has taught him, so he should write; and let him who owes the debt dictate, and he should be careful of (his duty to) Allah, his Lord, and not diminish anything from

it; but if he who owes the debt is unsound in understanding, or weak, or (if) he is not able to dictate himself, let his guardian dictate with fairness; and call in to witness from among your men two witnesses; but if there are not two men, then one man and two women from among those whom you choose to be witnesses, so that if one of the two errs, the second of the two may remind the other[. . .]." The Holy Qur'an, translated by M. H. Shakir from Tahrike Tarsile Qur'an 1983. http://www.usc.edu/schools/college/crcc/engagement/resources/texts/muslim/quran/002.qmt.html. Accessed August 18, 2009.

15. I have made this interview anonymous.

16. Few of the village books cover the primarily Christian villages. This is in large part because the majority of the all-Christian villages were not attacked, nor were their populations exiled. Two books talk specifically about Christian faith in the villages: Kana'anah and Ishtayya 1991, about Kafr Bir'im; and Haddad 2002, about al-Bassa. Other books mention Christian villagers but do not cover their religious practices specifically.

17. Canaan 1927; Granqvist 1931, 1947.

18. Tamari (2009) describes the work of Canaan in a chapter titled "Lepers, Lunatics, and Saints: The Nativist Ethnography of Tawfiq Canaan and His Circle." The *ta'sat al-ra'b* (cups of fear) were inscribed with verses from the Qur'an, filled with water, and left out overnight under a full moon to be drunk by those afflicted with problems.

19. See, for example, Canaan's articles published in the journal of the Palestine Oriental Society, along with his mongraphs on the Palestinian village and Muslim shrines; the volumes of Hilma Granqvist (1947/1975, 1931–1935/1975), who wrote about the village of Artas; Rogers 1862 and Dalman 1928–1942.

20. Rippin 1993, Deeb 2006, Mahmood 2005.

21. Canaan 1927, p. v.

22. See Canaan 1927 and Granqvist 1931–1935/1975 and 1947/1975. See also Halabi 2006 on the celebrations around the Nabi Musa (the Prophet Moses); and Tamari 2009 on al-Nabi Rubeen.

23. *Wahhabism* is a conservative Muslim movement that began in the Arabian penninsula in the eighteenth century. It is the type of Islam practiced in Saudi Arabia today.

24. Sulayma 2003, p. 127. I was not able to figure out what the *khitma fil-maatim* refers to.

25. See, for example, Issa 1997 and al-Dabbagh 1965. Al-Dabbagh mentions al-Shajara village in vol. 6, part 2, pp. 426–429. al-Shajara village also has a page at http://www.palestineremembered.com/Tiberias/al-Shajara/index.html. See Canaan 1927 for his ethnographic work in the 1920s on the common practice of visiting Muslim saints and shrines.

26. Heteropraxy is practices or beliefs at variance with an official or orthodox position.

27. Next to the shrine, as with many shrines in Palestine and Jordan, was a large tree, this one a carob said to be five hundred years old.

28. Al-Najjar 1996, p. 92.

29. Al-Najjar 1996, p. 86. He relates that the story told by the villagers is that after they prayed over the dead body of the shaykh in the mosque, as is the custom, they were unable to move his body and therefore they buried him there.

30. Canaan 1927; Granqvist 1931–1935, 1947; Halabi 2006.

31. Sulayma 2003, p. 104.

32. Sulayma 2003, pp. 103–104.

33. See, for example, Doumani 1995 and H. Sakakini 1990, which contain accounts of village women marketing their products in nearby cities.

34. Dirbas 1992, p. 22.

35. Interview with Mahmoud Sulayman, Amman, Jordan, May 3, 2005.

36. Abu Khiyara, Fanush, Sulayman, and 'Ashur 1993, p. 99.

37. Abu Khiyara, Fanush, Sulayman, and 'Ashur 1993, pp. 99–100.

38. 'Awadallah 1996, p. 199.

39. Fleischmann 2003.

40. Peteet 1991, Rosenfeld 2004, R. Sayigh 1979.

41. Sa'id 1991, p. 19–20.

42. 'Abd al-'Aal 2005, pp. 138–139.

43. Y. Sayigh 1997, p 49.

44. I am grateful to Sylvain Perdigon, who shared with me his thoughts on this subject based on his research in southern Lebanon refugee camps in 2006.

45. Village book authors, for the most part, even when they talk about women in the village, do not turn to women villagers for their stories and perspectives. Dirbas's account (1992, p. 46), quoted earlier, of women walking to the market in Acre from al-Birwa, in all of its details, must have come from people who knew the overland route, yet she did not interview any women for the book.

46. See Boym 2001, Habib 2007, Kotre 1996, Rosaldo 1989, Stewart 1988, Tall 1993.

47. See Peteet 2005, chapter two; and van Oord 2008.

48. Nadan 2006, pp. xxv–xxvii and 9–11, discusses these commissions and the resulting Johnson and Crosbie report in detail and various authors who have written about it.

49. Tyler 2001, p. 160.

50. The last British census of the population of Palestine was in 1931, therefore all official population numbers after that are estimates based on birth, death, and immigration records. W. Khalidi 1971, pp. 842–843. See McCarthy 1990 for more on this subject.

51. See Asad 1976, Bunton 2007, Khalaf 1997, Miller 1985, Nadan 2006, and Sufian 2007, among others.

52. Nadan 2006, pp. 28–31.

53. Fleischmann 2003, Sufian 2007.

54. Al-Najjar 1996, pp. 58–60.

55. Because of the sensitive nature of his comments, I have chosen to make this interview anonymous.

56. Interview with Hussein al-Lubani, Tripoli, Lebanon, June 6, 2005.

57. "Samira Tells the Story of Her Family," http://www.yafa.org. Quoted in Tamari 2005b, pp. 176–177.

58. Dakwar 2001; Dirbas 1993; Kark and Gavish 1993; Saqr 1990, p. 79; Stein 1984.

59. See Firestone 1990; Nadan 2006, chap. 6, pp. 261–296; Stein 1984; Atran 1986; Tyler 2001; Moors 1995.

60. Dirbas 1992.

61. These include the *miri* (private), *matruka* (public), and *waqf* (endowment) categories.

62. Church *waqfs* are listed on pages 112 and 137 in Dirbas 1992.

63. W. Khalidi 1992, pp. 9–10. The land ownership numbers are 12,939 dunums registered to Arabs, 546 dunums to Jews, and 57 dunums of public lands. A dunum was approximately one thousand square meters (it varied slightly in different times and under different administrations).

64. With the caveat that this is merely the listing of those claimants whose land was not listed in the survey or was listed incorrectly. The size and quality of the reproduction of the records in the book makes them challenging to read, however.

65. Dirbas 1993 says that these records "represent 6 percent of the Salama village land," although it is not clear on what basis she makes this statement.

66. Many of the same names appear in the records, and at least half are for someone from the Abu Nijim family, not only because the Abu Nijim's owned a huge portion of the village land, but also because the Abu Nijim descendants were the major source, as discussed in Chapter Two of Dirbas' book (1993).

67. These documents of private land ownership exist within a larger framework of the evolution of property ownership, leading toward privatization in Palestine. The village books talk about *musha'* (collectively held land), *mulk* (privately owned land), and so on. However, in Palestine at that time, the reason for the existence of such records was that the British were enforcing the division of the land into private parcels, with the idea that the land would be developed and made more productive.

68. 'Abd al-'Aal 2005, p. 31.

69. W. Khalidi 1992, al-Dabbagh 1965.

70. Kana'ana and al-Madani n.d., p. 7; story told by Abu al-'Abid, born 1912.

71. Five of the sixty-six records are impossible to read from the photocopies and because of the poor qualities of the originals, but at least two may also contain women's names. Two sisters, Mary and Victoria, the daughters of Amin Nasif, sold two two-room buildings with a well to Sa'id Muhammad Salih and Mustafa 'Abd al-Qadir Abu Nijim in separate transactions. Two transactions were by Fatima 'Abd al-Raziq Abu Nijim and three were by her sister Safiyya 'Abd al-Raziq Abu Nijim; both sold their land to Mustafa 'Abd al-Qadir Abu Nijim (perhaps a cousin), who owned the bus company. He seems to have been a wealthy man and the pictures he took of events in the village are used

throughout both the Dirbas book and the CRDPS book on Salama. Mustafa Abu Nijim's dairy logs are also reproduced. Two other sales were by Safiyya 'Abd al-Raziq Abu Nijim to Mahmud Muhammad Yusif Abu Nijim.

72. The nine women sold four plots of farmland (*ard muftalah*) and five one- or two-room buildings with wells, all in separate transactions. They bought one plot of farmland, one piece of land for building on, and one *hakura* (household garden). The other transactions were all with farmland.

73. Moors 1994 and 1995. Doumani 1995 discusses a number of cases from the Nablus court records of village women approaching the court to adjudicate their usurped inheritance. Atran's 1986 work on *musha'* lands makes no mention of women as landowners, although there could be any number of reasons for this. First, in the villages he studied—Umm al-Fahm, 'Isfiya, and Dalat [sic] al-Karmel—women might not have gained land through inheritance. Second, and more likely, although women may have "owned" shares of *musha'* land, they would likely have handed over "representation" of those lands to their fathers, brothers, sons, or husbands. Third, Atran may simply have failed to address the issue.

74. Agmon 2006.

75. 'Abd al-'Aal 1999, pp. 46–49.

76. One might consider that the problem of recording ownership in the village books stems from cartographical limitations, which then manifest in interpretive difficulties. Imagine the problems of space and clarity in trying to put the name of every owner of every house or olive grove into a .5 x .5 centimeter square. A number of other books do map the village in this way, for example, as on the cover of the Qatra village book (al-Qatrawi 2000) (see Figure 1) and in the map in the book on Qalunya (Sumrayn 1993). As a result, the name tied to the land (as the property owner) is that of the senior male family member. In effect, the fact that women's roles in owning, buying, and selling property, of inheriting it from relatives, and of passing it down to their children are never mentioned in these books indicates a much greater historical omission than not putting names on a map.

77. Moors 1995.

78. An-Na'im 2002, 102–103. See also Ahmed 1992, Esposito 1998, Fluehr-Lobban 1993, and Moors 1995.

79. Peteet 1991, Sayigh 1979.

Chapter 5: The Authority of Memory

1. Al-Sakakini 1925, p. 47. Forbes is quoted from the editorial page of issue 158 of *al-Siyasa*, which was published under the editorship of Muhammad Husayn Haykal from 1922 to 1934 as the "mouthpiece of the Liberal Constitutionalist Party." For more information on the newspaper, see the Library of Congress at http://lcweb.loc.gov/rr/amed/nearest.html, an article on early press censorship at http://ahram.org.eg/weekly

/2000/512/chrncls.html, and a biography of Haykal at http://www.sis.gov.eg/VR/figures/
english/html/haykal.htm. Accessed September 2009.

2. Al-Sakakini 1925, p. 48. Diogenes carried a lantern during the daytime in Athens,
searching for an honest person, whom he claimed he never found.

3. According to the introduction of an autobiography published in the West Bank
by Birzeit University, "in the absence of an archive or national museum, the collection
of documents and personal experiences from oral history is an important part of our
work[. . .]to preserve personal experiences and the accompanying events in order to
rewrite history in new ways and by earnest Palestinian pens" (al-Mudawwar 1999, p. i).
This autobiography, one in a series, along with the series on the destroyed Palestinian
villages, was researched, collected, and published by the CRDPS, first under the direc-
tion of Sharif Kanaana and then under Saleh Abdel Jawad.

4. Tonkin 1992, p. 11.

5. al-Rimawi 1998.

6. Anderson 1991, Gellner 1983, Malkki 1995.

7. Swedenburg 1995/2003.

8. In this war, Israel occupied the Jordanian-controlled West Bank (which included
East Jerusalem), the Egyptian-controlled Gaza Strip, the Syrian Golan Heights, and the
Egyptian Sinai, which was returned to Egypt following the Camp David Accords in 1978.

9. Sakakini 1990, p. xi.

10. For autobiographical accounts see Lila Abu Lughod 2007, Edward Said 1999b,
Hisham Sharabi 1993, Salim Tamari and Rema Hammami 1998, among others. Ghassan
Kanafani's 'A'id ila Haifa (1987) and Elias Khoury's Bab al-Shams (1998) best represent
fiction works that deal with this subject. I deal with the subject of return videos in the
final chapter of this book.

11. This was likely a common way to carry children, with the skirt part of the dress
lifted and tied around the mother. (She was of course wearing either an underdress
or sirwal, that is, cotton trousers). My friends explained these details to me because in
this day and age strollers proliferate in the camp and no young people wear these long
embroidered dresses.

12. She then came across a Christian man in a village in Lebanon who took her
home and fed her and made her sleep in his house with his wife while he slept in the
guest room. She then found her way to Tyre in Lebanon and eventually found her family.
This story was told to me in summer 2008 in Damascus.

13. Brison 1999, Malkki 1995, Sturken 1999, Hirsch 2002.

14. The brother and sister allowed me to retell this story because I heard it from
them. I have obscured details and names so that their aunt is anonymous to everyone
but the three of us. Thus she as an individual and her story are now disconnected from
each other.

15. Fields 1994, Knapp 1989, Kotre 1996, P. Thompson 1994, Tonkin 1992.

16. Rushdie 1991, p. 12.

17. Halbwachs 1992, p. 38.

18. Portelli 1997, p. 44–45.

19. Slyomovics 1998, p. xiv.

20. Portelli 1991, 1997.

21. Yow 1994, p. 18.

22. Rubin et al. 1986.

23. Morris 1987, p. 2.

24. Scott 1985.

25. Portelli 1991, 1997.

26. See Esber 2008; Kana'ana and al-Ka'bi, 1987, 1991a, 1991b; Kana'ana and 'Abd al-Hadi 1986, 1990, 1991; Kana'ana and Ishtayya 1987 and 1991; Kana'ana and al-Madani n.d., 1987a, 1987b, 1987c; Masalha 1992; and Nazzal 1978. A number of other factors are undoubtedly involved: first, the difficulty for Israelis in soliciting oral accounts from Palestinians, particularly outside Israel-Palestine; second, the lack of Arabic skills among scholars of Israel in the academic establishment; and third, the political climate in the Israeli academy, in which revisionist history of Zionist historical narratives is not always accepted or appreciated.

27. Ben-Ze'ev 2002, p. 25.

28. Portelli 1997, p. 139.

29. Swedenburg 1995/2003.

30. Neihardt 1996, Shryock 1997, Basso 1999, and Papailias 2005.

31. Basso 1999, p. 31.

32. Sahlins 2004, Papailias 2005, Maddox 2006, Shryock 1997.

33. Shryock 1997, p. 28.

34. Basso 1999, pp. 33–34.

35. Olney 1985, p. 149.

36. Davis and Gates 1985, p. v.

37. Ochs and Capps 1996, p. 21.

38. Samuel and Thompson 1990, p. 18.

39. The point here is not that people don't misremember. Rather, it is that historical accounts written using only documents give us a certain kind of history, just as inflected and limited. In the western academic and popular historical traditions, we prioritize history written from documents. Keith Basso (1999, p. 32) shows how narratives are formed and performed by a particular people in a particular time and place in his research among Western Apache historians: "For people like Charles Henry and Morley Cromwell, the country of the past—and with it Apache history—is never more than a narrated place-world away."

40. Miller 1985.

41. Hammer 2005, al-Hardan 2008.

42. Dirbas 1993, p. 7.

43. Al-Bash 2001, p. 71.

44. Dirbas 1992, p. 38. The British Mandate's official statistics for al-Birwa were 1,460 people.

45. Dirbas is not alone in using memory and experience as sources to challenge the knowledge presented by others about the village—what others have portrayed as historical or statistical facts. In the village book about Kafr Bir'im, the population statistics from numerous sources are presented: "The number of residents of Kafr Bir'im was 554 in 1931 (276 men and 278 women) [footnote to *Survey of Palestine 1945*]. The population grew to become 710 in 1945 [again, footnote to *Survey of Palestine 1945*]. The population reached 1,010 in 1948 [footnote to 'an interview with Father Yusef Susaan,' the local priest]" (Kana'ana and Ishtayya 1991, p. 5) This book, as do those by Dirbas, gives voice to the experience of members of the community, and counters the authority of the Mandate source. It is entirely accordant that the priest would be a reliable source of local, detailed knowledge of the population, because he would be the one to record births, baptisms, and deaths.

46. Rosaldo 1980.

47. Mitchell takes on this subject masterfully in his *Rule of Experts: Egypt, Technopolitics, Modernity* (2002).

48. These volumes report that the government conducted a survey of some 2,550 wells and boreholes, chiefly on the coastal plains, in 1934 and 1935, and that "water levels were recorded in order that any future change might be easily detected" (p. 399). The Institute for Palestine Studies reprinted these survey results in 1991 and thus they are now widely available.

49. Shahin 2002, p. 13.

50. This population included Greeks and Armenians, who were not Arab but were Christian, as well as other small Christian communities.

51. McCarthy 1990, p. 69. At that time, 97,000 (96 percent) of the Jewish population lived outside the city walls in the area now know as West Jerusalem. The remaining 2,400 lived in the Old City. The Palestinian population was divided between 33,600 living within the Old City and 31,500 living outside the walls.

52. For more discussion of the issues around the 1931 census and the 1945 census estimates, see McCarthy 1990. My point is not that the Arabs were undercounted—it may even be that the numbers for the Jewish population should be higher. My point is that the numbers are not as certain as they may seem.

53. A number of distant Jewish neighborhoods to the west had been gerrymandered into the city borders—for example, Bayet vaGan, Beit ha Kerem, and Giv'at Shaul. These neighborhoods were further outside the city than a number of Arab villages, such as Lifta, Silwan, al-Tur, Bayt Safafa, and Sur Bahir, that were not included in the municipal population within the British Mandate boundaries. See Davis 1999a, 1999b; Dumper

1997; and Tamari 1999, p. 10 for further discussions on this issue. Although these neighborhoods would not have added a huge number of Jewish residents to the population, their distance from the heart of the city would suggest that they were not part of the city's residents. Also, the fact that the Palestinians were clustered inside the old city and in neighborhoods near the walls would make them seem more of a majority in those areas. The map made by Sami Hadawi that appears in *Jerusalem 1948*, edited by Salim Tamari (1999), provides some idea of the population distribution within the municipal boundaries.

54. Al-Bash 2001, p. 71.

55. See, for example, *A Survey of Palestine* (Palestine Government 1991), which has 1,139 pages (including the index) of tables, statistics, and summaries about Palestine. The chapters provide information on the following topics: immigration, land, agriculture, irrigation and drainage, forestry, fisheries, trade and industry, finance, law and order, social services, labor and wages, town planning, food and clothing, communications, the press, community and religious affairs, political parties, international agreements, concessions and mining, and war economic measures. It should also be noted that Jewish institutions and agencies kept detailed statistics on their own populations, and the British used these statistics in their reports. No parallel institutions did the same for the Arab population.

56. Stoler 1995, p. 77.

57. Kenny 1999, p. 421

58. Tonkin 1992, pp. 86–87.

59. Portelli 1997, p. 12.

60. Kenny 1999, p. 431.

61. Kenny 1999, p. 431.

62. Halbwachs 1992.

63. Portelli 1997, p. 27.

64. In similar fashion, Janet Hart describes two types of narratives that emerged from her work on women's memories of the Greek resistance during and after World War II that tie together the individual and collective natures of narrated memories: ontological (subjective) narratives and mobilizational (intersubjective) narratives. Whereas ontological narratives can be understood in terms of the narrator's portrayal of his or her actions, mind-set, and development, the mobilizational narratives place the narrator within the larger framework of collective sentiment and values. Both forms of narrative are interpretations of events rather than a mirror of the events themselves.   Hart 1996, pp. 52–53.

65. Kluitenberg 1999; Bal, Crewe, and Spitzer 1999.

66. According to the Encyclopedia of Islam entry for Ta'rikh a variety of terms were used in addition to Ta'rikh: "*akhbar* (reports, narratives) may be older and in any case was very widely used down to early modern times. Until the mid-3rd/9th century, in fact,

works of history were as likely to be identified by their subject matter—e.g. *sira* (biography), *maghazi* [*q.vv.*] (campaigns of the Prophet), *futuh* (conquests)—as by a word naming the literary genre or class of knowledge to which they belonged" (Dalen et al. 2009).

67. Humphreys 1991, Shryock 1997.

68. Shryock 1997, Ayalon 2004.

69. This is likely because of Kanaana's academic training and work as a folklorist. It is not clear why other books published elsewhere do this.

70. The one subject for which even these authors use individual stories, however, is the events of 1948.

71. Humphreys 1991.

72. Bakhtin 1981, pp. 65–66.

73. Makdisi 1990, Tibawi 1972.

74. Al-Dabbagh 1988, vol. 10, pp. 142–155. For example, the eleven-page section on Jerusalem before World War I comes from the description of the city in 1910 by Yusuf al-Hakim al-Ladhaqi, one of its judges. It discusses the following topics: Jerusalem and social life, culture, the Christian sects, the Russian institution, the conflict between the Greek Orthodox Patriarchate and its Arab members, the Aqsa Mosque and the tomb of Nabi Musa, the excavations in al-Haram al-Sharif (The Temple Mount), and Jews in Jerusalem. Al-Ladhaqi's description of the city is followed by the travel account of Lebanese-Egyptian author Jirji Zaydan, who visited the city in 1913 and wrote about his trip in his magazine *al-Hilal*.

75. Kana'ana and al-Ka'bi 1987, p. 5. 'Ayn Hawd was the subject of the first volume. The majority of the other volumes do not express these same difficulties, and the majority also cite the teller by name and birthdate within the text.

76. Interview with 'Abdallah Isma'il al-Sufi, June 8, 2005.

77. Al-Sahli 2001. At the same time, this book falls into another problem area that besets a number of books I discussed with people and read—that of the total dominance of one family in the subject matter and source material for the book.

78. It is in this sense that I refer elsewhere to these books, authored by those from the village, as collective autobiographies. The author of the village book, like the author of an autobiography, maintains control over the representation. In this case, it is not only the author of the book but also the community (or a section of it) that influences and enforces how the village is represented. Davis 2007b.

79. Abu Khiyara, Fanush, Sulayman, and 'Ashur 1993, p. 69.

80. Interview with Mahmoud Sulayman, Amman, Jordan, May 3, 2005.

81. Kana'ana and al-Ka'bi 1991b, pp. 51–52.

82. Schrager 1983, as quoted in Tonkin 1992, p. 41.

83. It seems that his family does prevent him from going to the school, although it is not explicitly stated as such in the text.

84. Al-Sahli 2001, p. 100.

85. As part of a paper I presented at a conference in Beirut, I read this story as it appeared in colloquial Arabic. The roomful of scholars, all educated Palestinians who spoke both urban dialects and Modern Standard Arabic, thus had to listen to me re-count this man's story in a village dialect and in his own words. I found it to be an interesting act of upsetting class barriers in that I was able to bring a voice into a group of people who likely never would have collectively sat and listened to the man's voice if he had delivered the words himself.

86. Somers 1994, as described in Brubaker and Cooper 2000, pp. 11–12.

87. Add to this fact the absence of any Palestinian archive, and the fact that the limited British Mandate archival sources are in English and located in London or Israel.

88. Rushdie 1991, p. 178.

89. English and Arabic sources.

90. See Davis 2002, Amr and Katz 2009, Qasmiyya 2007, and Tamari and Nassar 2007. The vast majority of Palestinian autobiographical works come from the hands of well-known politicians, military leaders, prominent men of letters, and elites who, with few exceptions, were on the forefront of Palestinian society and politics. As such, the struggle for Palestine through the writing of its history was still being promoted by the upper class that constituted the leadership of Palestine before 1948. However, the *nakba* forced profound changes in Palestinian society in terms of educational levels, class status, and opportunities for advancement, and these changes eventually created opportunities for new voices to be heard. Autobiographies by Palestinian women are al-most entirely by women from elite families. Two were published in the Birzeit University *Pages from Palestinian Memory* series—Hanun 1998 and Salah 1992—and three through personal initiative—al-Sakakini 1990, Shahid 2000, and Tuqan 1990. Men who have be-come successful reflect on their own self-made status and their lower- or middle-class origins, which they have transformed through education and effort. See, for example, works by Muhammad 'Izzat Darwaza (1993), a historian and intellectual; Yusif Haykal (1988, 1989), the former mayor of Jaffa; Hisham Sharabi (1993), a sociology professor at Georgetown University; Abdelhameed Shoman (1984), founder and director of the Arab Bank; and 'Izzat Tannous (1993), one of the chief negotiators and petitioners of the Mandate Government on behalf of Palestine. See Nabil Badran (1980) for statistics and a description of the education situation in the diaspora.

Chapter 6: Mapping the Past: The Village Landscape

1. Karmi 1999, 40.

2. Dalen et al 2009.

3. I am grateful to Beshara Doumani, who encouraged me to seek out the compari-sons between these local histories and the books about destroyed villages.

4. Books about the Palestinian cities that were emptied of their inhabitants have also been written, but they differ fundamentally from the village books in that they tend

to focus on places and their histories, on notable people, and on *events*. They are more like *Biladuna Filastin* (al-Dabbagh 1965), or the local history texts described by Dalen et al (2009) earlier, or they are autobiographies told within the context of the city's history.

5. Nora 1989, 12

6. Wood 1992, p. 12.

7. Abu Hadba 1990, pp. 180, 186, 188, 192, 195, and 300.

8. Adams, Hoelscher, and Till 2001; Agnew and Duncan 1989; Jackson 1989; Porteous 1990; Shurmer-Smith and Hannam 1994; Tuan 1996.

9. Bardenstein 1999, Kanaaneh 2002, Zerubavel 1995.

10. Boyarin 1996; W. Khalidi 1961; Masalha 1992; Nassar 2006a, 2006b; Obenzinger 1999; Peteet 2005, pp. 34–46; Peters 1984; Said 1979.

11. Malkki 1992; 1995, pp. 6–7.

12. Peteet 2005, pp. 34–46.

13. Report of the General Assembly 1947: "Jewish State: 500,000 Jews and 416,000 Arabs and Others. Arab State: 8,000 Jews and 715,000 Arabs and Others. Jerusalem: 100,000 Jews and 106,000 Arabs."

14. State of Israel, Central Bureau of Statistics 2009. According to this report, in 1948, 82 percent of the population, or 660,920 people, was Jewish. The 1948 Census "had the primary function of establishing the Population Registry (PR)." The next official census occurred in 1961. See also Kamen 2005, p. 2.

15. Israel absorbed between 750,000 to 900,000 Jews from Arab and Muslim countries, and hundreds of thousands of Jewish refugees from Europe.

16. Jiryis 1976, Lustick 1980, S. Robinson 2003, Zureik 1979.

17. Beinin and Stein 2006, Collins 2004, Hasso 2005, Peteet 2008, Rosenfeld 2004.

18. Abu Hadba 1990, p. 195.

19. Sa'id 1991, p. 20.

20. Stewart 1996, pp. 37–38.

21. Sumrayn 1993, p. 40.

22. 'Abd al-'Aal says that they were distributed on *kryakat*, which means rakes or hoes (except in the northern Galilee, where it means wheelbarrows).

23. 'Abd al-'Aal 2005, pp. 103–104.

24. 'Abd al-'Aal 2005, p. 26. Interview with Yusif 'Abd al-'Aal, July 29, 2008, Damascus, Syria.

25. Kan'aan 1998, p. 7.

26. Abu Hadba 1990, 207.

27. Most typewritten Arabic words consist of consonants and long vowels. The short vowel markers are generally not used, because most readers know the words, but that leaves the pronunciation of unknown words obscure. For example, *al-maris*, in Arabic, is typed as *al-mar_s; al-shi'b* looks like *al-sh_'_b*, and *al-marah* looks like *al-m_r_h*. A knowledgeable reader could fill in the blank with the correct vowel.

28. It seems that by not putting vowels in the texts the authors are assuming some familiarity with the terms on the part of the readers. My informal and limited experience shows that the younger generations in the diaspora neither know the meaning of the terms nor know how to pronounce them. I also used 'Abd al-Latif al-Barghuti's *al-Qamus al-'Arabi al-Sha'bi al-Filastini* (The Dictionary of Palestinian Colloquial Arabic, 1987) to vowel the words.

29. de Certeau 1984, p. 118.

30. Kana'ana and al-Ka'bi 1987, p. 3.

31. Tall 1993, p. 207.

32. Kana'ana and al-Madani 1987c.

33. Basso 1999, p. 28.

34. Picture #7872, comment number 30998, http://www.palestineremembered.com/haifa/ijzim/picture7872.html. Accessed December 23, 2008.

35. Slyomovics 1998, p. xi.

36. Jayyusi 2007.

37. Davis 2007b.

38. According to Muslim tradition, Sheet was the third son of Adam. There is also a town in Lebanon called al-Nabi Sheet (The Prophet Sheet), and a shrine in Mosul, Iraq, is named for him as well. For religious details about him, see Huart 2009.

39. Shahin 2002, p. 6.

40. Sumrayn 1993, 40.

41. Basso 1999.

42. Abu Khiyara, Fanush, Sulayman, and 'Ashur 1993, p. 76.

43. The issue of poetic form and the pre-1948 Palestinian village is dealt with more fully in Davis 2002; see also Slyomovics 1998 for an excellent discussion of this subject. Thanks to Margaret Larkin for pointing out the *atlal* elements in these poems.

44. Ibrahim Muhawi (2009) remarks on how the poetic lament form was used by Mahmud Darwish to open his poem "The Train Fell Off the Map" (*Saqt al-qitaar 'an al-kharita*), which Darwish published to commemorate the sixtieth anniversary of the *nakba*. The poem was published on p. 12 of the *al-Quds al-Arabi* newspaper on May 15, 2008. Muhawi notes that the opening lines of the poem ("grass, solid air, thorns and cactus") echo the opening of the *atlal* lament and are "exactly what a person encounters at the site of one of these destroyed villages." Even the title of his poem connects to this idea that even the most tangible thing—here it is a train—is lost in the recording of Palestinian history (p. 8).

45. For details on the contents of Jordanian school textbooks, see Katz, n.d.

46. Abu Hadba 1990, p. 178. During the British Mandate, the curriculum of the village schools included classes in agriculture; hence the schools had gardens attached to them. See Tibawi 1956 for more on the subject.

47. 'Imwas was one of the three villages in the Latrun area that were depopulated

and destroyed in 1967 during the Israeli invasion and occupation of the West Bank, Gaza, and the Golan Heights.

48. Abu Ghush 1990, p. 11.

49. Al-'Ali 2002, pp. 278–280.

50. I. Abu-Lughod 1998, L. Abu-Lughod 2007, Amiry 2004, al-Hout 1998, Khasawneh 2001, Said 1999b, Sharabi 1993, Tamari and Hammami 1998.

51. Bardenstein 1998.

52. Bardenstein 2005, Benvenisti 2000, Boyarin 1996, Kanaana 2000.

53. Abu Hadba 1990, p. 392. Ironically, the cactus is a plant indigenous to the Americas and thus was introduced to the Middle East only within the last five hundred years.

54. Abu Hadba 1990, p. 392.

55. W. Khalidi 1992. For more details see Chapter One text and notes.

56. Bardenstein 1998, pp. 9–10.

57. Bardenstein 1998, pp. 9–10.

58. Benvenisti 2000, p. 310.

59. Kana'ana and al-Madani 1987c.

60. Interview with Ghalib Sumrayn, Amman, Jordan, April 30, 2005.

61. Diab and Fahoum 1990, p. 23.

62. Bardenstein 1999; Lynd, Bahour, and Lynd 1994; Parmenter 1994.

63. Dinnematin 1987.

64. For images of Palestinian art used in posters, see Liberation Graphics' extensive Web site of the Palestine Poster Project Archives at http://palestineposterproject.org. Accessed August 21, 2009.

65. Halabi 1999. http://www.art.net/samia/pal/palart/rana/rana.html

66. Benvenisti 2000, Kanaana 2000, W. Khalidi 1992.

67. The Muslim buildings fall under the moribund *waqf* (endowment) administration. See Dumper 1994.

68. Benvenisti 2000, p. 288.

69. Activities that involve visits to the destroyed villages are undertaken by individuals; by Palestinian political movements such as Abna' al-Balad; by individual village organizations (for example, the Abna' Suhmata, http://www.suhmata.com/indexa .php); and by nongovernmental organizations such as the Association for the Defense of the Rights of the Internally Displaced Persons in Israel (*Jama'iyat al-difa' 'an huquq al-muhajjarin*), http://www.ror194.org/index.php?id=250, and the Israeli group Zochrot, http://www.nakbainhebrew.org/index.php?lang=english

70. Benvenisti 2000, pp. 294–295.

71. Benvenisti 2000, pp. 294–296. Pictures of the mosque, the fence (with razor wire), and the rest of the village are available at http://www.palestineremembered.com/Acre/ al-Ghabisiyya/index.html#Pictures. Accessed August 7, 2009.

72. See Benvenisti 2000, especially chapter seven, "Saints, Peasants, and Conquerors," pp. 270–306.

73. Abu El-Haj 2001; Slyomovics 1998, pp. 29–81. Museums have been made out of mosques in Safad and Majdal 'Asqalan, and the mosques in Ayn Hawd and Tiberius are now restaurants. Others are falling into ruin, and some are used as stables or storage facilities. The mosque in 'Ayn Karim is locked up, and political and religious graffiti inside have defaced the interior decoration. Information obtained on personal visits to these locations, 1989–2000.

74. Taufik Canaan, Palestinian physician and folklorist, writes, "The protection exercised by the saint, because of the general respect he enjoys, is another cause for burying the dead close to the *weli*'s [holy man/saint] tomb. This used to be practiced especially by important political families who were continually on bad terms with other families. When a leader died, they buried him near a sacred spot to protect his body from being exhumed by his enemies and thus dishonoured. The 'man of God' is sure to protect every thing put under his care; nobody dares to molest the sanctitiy of a man so buried" (1927, p. 9).

75. Dirbas 1993, p. 40.

76. Shahin 2002, p. 7.

77. Al-Qassam is often credited, through his death, with serving as the impetus for the popular revolt against British colonial rule that began in April 1936 and that also challenged the traditional elite Palestinian leadership. Schleifer 1993, p. 164.

78. Although a number of Palestinian political groups in Israel have formed cleanup crews for the Balad al-Shaykh cemetery and have even replaced al-Qassam's headstone, there is no overarching project—individual, communal, or political—to pay attention to the more than four hundred abandoned cemeteries. The Muslim *waqf* authority, which takes care of cemeteries elsewhere for Muslims, in Israel is appointed by the state and is largely ineffectual.

Chapter 7: Identities and History

1. Abu Sbayh 2001 and W. Khalidi 1992, p. 232, mention 1932. Shurrab 2000, p. 164, says "the director of the school in 1936, Mustafa al-Tahir," renamed the village on the basis of the tomb of the *wali* (holy man) buried there. Al-Lubani 2003, p. 166, says that "the village is on the land of the Canaanite village of Yahud . . . and was known as al-Yahudiyya until the inhabitants changed the name at the end of 1932 to al-'Abbasiyya. The history of the village's name is not mentioned in Barhum and Kharrub 1990, pp. 173–174, or in Abu Mayila, al-Lawh, Sha'th, and Abu Zayid 1998.

2. *The New English Study Bible* 1977, p. 243.

3. W. Khalidi 1992, p. 232.

4. Benvenisti 2000, p. 276.

5. Al-Lubani 2003, p. 166.

6. See the Salama books—Kana'ana and 'Abd al-Hadi 1986 and Dirbas 1993—for the petitions to the Mandate government authorities in which the *mukhtars* list themselves as from al-Yahudiyya (in 1936 and 1940).

7. Anderson 1991, Gellner 1983, and Hobsbawm 1983, among others, specifically theorize on national identity, nations, and nationalism, and many other works apply their theories to specific cases.

8. R. Khalidi 1997, p. 150.

9. Rashid Khalidi discusses this extensively and in detail throughout *Palestinian Identity: The Construction of a Modern National Consciousness* (1997). See in particular chapters one, seven, and eight.

10. Hammer 2005, Hasso 2005, Sayigh 1979, Swedenburg 1995/2003.

11. Hammer 2005, Kanaaneh 2002, R. Khalidi 1997, Peteet 2005, Rosenfeld 2004, Said 1979, Tamari 2009.

12. Of course self-identification, particularly in the case of Palestinians, is not an isolated category. Identification by others has also been a factor because of the absence of a Palestinian role in authoritative, institutional nation-state politics. Thus Israel is predicated as a "Jewish" state, and Israel's establishment and success affect Palestinians' conceptions of themselves as others. Similarly, Palestinian refugees living outside the borders of historic Palestine again find themselves defined against the indigenous populations of the states in which they live. Therefore, as Palestinians self-identify, it is both in concert with and contrapuntal to others' definitions of them.

13. Al-Ashhab 1999; Davis 2004; Jawhariyah 2005; H. Sakakini 1990; K. al-Sakakini 1955, 2003-2010; Segev 2000; Tamari 2009.

14. Kattan 2009, p. xix.

15. Kattan 2009, p. 259.

16. Brubaker and Cooper 2000, p. 1.

17. Brubaker and Cooper 2000, p. 27.

18. Brubaker and Cooper 2000, p. 14.

19. Brubaker and Cooper 2000, p. 14.

20. Brubaker and Cooper 2000, p. 14.

21. Brubaker and Cooper 2000, p. 17.

22. Brubaker and Cooper 2000, p. 18.

23. Brubaker and Cooper 2000, p. 21.

24. Brubaker and Cooper 2000, p. 21.

25. Brubaker and Cooper 2000, p. 15.

26. Brubaker and Cooper 2000, p. 15.

27. Brubaker and Cooper 2000, p. 15–16.

28. Tamari 1982, p. 181.

29. Conversation with Salim Tamari, April 21, 2008.

30. In the modern reconfigurations of these relations, identifications have been built

around political solidarities. Thus help is still offered for the olive harvest, especially by internationals who can help protect Palestinians from armed settler and Israeli army attacks during the harvest. The International Solidarity Movement, the Palestine Monitor (http://www.palestinemonitor.org/spip/spip.php?article166), Birzeit University, and others have, in the past and the present, organized the work of nationals and internationals in this regard.

31. Where the books were published breaks down roughly as follows: Jordan, 45; West Bank and Gaza, 37; Syria, 19; Lebanon, 10; Israel, 2; United States, 2; Egypt, 1; and Cyprus, 1. A number of them have no identifiable place of publication.

32. Alcalay 1993, Boyarin 1996, Shohat 1992.

33. The foreign/Ottoman distinction was relevant because until the late nineteenth century, foreigners were not allowed to own land in the Ottoman Empire.

34. Massad 1996; Shohat 1988, 1992, and 2006. See also Shenhav 2006 and Khazzoom 2003.

35. As quoted in Kanaaneh 2002, p. 157–158.

36. Shohat 1992, p. 28.

37. The film *Forget Baghdad* (Samir 2002) chronicles the experiences of four Iraqi Jewish communists who immigrated to Israel in the 1950s. See also Gil Hochberg's *In Spite of Partition: Jews, Arabs, and the Limits of Separatist Imagination* (2007), which examines literature in order to to challenge the ideologies of separation.

38. Segev 2000, pp. 325–326.

39. Shohat 1988, p. 35.

40. Sulayma 2003, pp. 43–44, 58. The Jewish farm of Sejara, established around 1899, is now called Moshava Ilaniya.

41. Sulayma 2003, p. 145.

42. Sulayma 2003, p. 57. He only mentions this story and does not provide any references or documents.

43. Kanaaneh 2002, p. 159.

44. Kana'ana and 'Abd al-Hadi 1991, p. 28.

45. Kana'ana and 'Abd al-Hadi 1991, p. 29.

46. Kana'ana and 'Abd al-Hadi 1991, p. 28.

47. Kana'ana and 'Abd al-Hadi 1991, p. 29.

48. Interview with a person from 'Ayn Karim (an 'Ikirmawi), Jerusalem, February 5, 1999.

49. Kana'ana and 'Abd al-Hadi 1991, p. 29; al-Yahya 1998, p. 43. The man from Tantoura had come to the village from Ijzim. I neither heard nor found stories of Muslim or Christian women marrying Jewish men.

50. Shahin 2002, p. 20.

51. Dirbas 1993, pp. 65–66; Kana'ana and 'Abd al-Hadi, 1986, pp. 70–73.

52. Kana'ana and 'Abd al-Hadi 1986, p. 70. The three of the four petitions with legible

dates are from 1936, 1940, and 1941. The petition in Hebrew is from the *mukhtars* (*mukhtarim*) and residents of the nearby Jewish settlement of HaTikva, and the ones in Arabic are signed by the *mukhtars* of Salama, Khayriyya, Saqiya, Kafr 'Ana, and al-Yahudiyya, along with around one hundred individuals. Note that in the petition signed by the village of al-Yahudiyya, it is still referred to as such and not as al-'Abbasiyya, although it had changed its name in the 1930s.

53. This petition uses the Arabic word *mukhtar*, but with the Hebrew plural form, *mukhtarim*.

54. Kana'ana and al-Madani n.d., p. 41.

55. Although Kenneth Stein's *The Land Question in Palestine, 1917–1939* (1984) is the most comprehensive account of this subject in English, a number of other authors have now built on his work. According to Amos Nadan (2006, pp. 12–13), the statistics kept by the Jewish Agency between 1890 and 1936 indicated that the following land was purchased by Jews from Arabs: 53.6 percent from owners living outside Palestine, 24.6 percent from noncultivators (not peasants), 9.4 percent from owner-cultivators (peasants), and 13.4 percent from "others." Issa Khalaf (1997, p. 98), in making the argument about the destabilizing effect on Palestinian society of peasants becoming wage laborers, notes, however, that that percentage shifted and "from the early 1930s, many smallholders sold part or all of their land to Jews. Between 1933 and 1942, of 6,207 land transactions, 5,713 (or 92.04 percent) involved sales of less than 100 dunums." As the source of this information he cites Stein 1984, p. 182, table 13.

56. Kana'ana and 'Abd al-Hadi 1990, p. 41.

57. Nadan 2006, p. 22.

58. Gabbay 1959, p. 29.

59. Gabbay 1959, p. 26.

60. Stevens 1971, p. 130.

61. Sulayma 2003, p. 58.

62. Atran 1989, pp. 734–735. Quote is from Morris 1987.

63. W. Khalidi 1992, pp. 193–195.

64. Al-Yahya 1998, p. 121. The village books contain many more stories of attempted deals, requests to end the attacks, and refusals on both sides. One of the factors influencing the appearance of these stories is the reputation of the village and those who have attempted to broker such agreements, not only in the past but also in the present. As it was for some Palestinians who remained in Israel, the fear is that if they are seen as willing to concede and not fight, they might be branded as collaborators or as weak by Palestinian rejectionist fronts in the diaspora.

65. Massad 1996, Shohat 1992.

66. In part, rising Arab nationalism was set against the Ottoman Empire (that Arabs were part of), which by the nineteenth century had a dominant but not overwhelming Turkish character to it. See Hourani 1991 and Rogan 2009.

67. Hourani 1991.

68. Brubaker and Cooper 2000.

69. See Eph'al 1982. See also Shahid 1988 on the presence of the Arab tribes in Palestine and Jordan during Byzantine rule in the area.

70. Bakhtin 1981, p. 137–138.

71. Slyomovics 1998, p. 107.

72. Benvenisti 2000, p. 194.

73. Qatifan and 'Allush 1993.

74. Eph'al 1982.

75. 'Atiya 1991.

76. Abu Khiyara, Fanush, Sulayman, and 'Ashur 1993, p. 77. The origin stories of villages and families, in this and all the other books, do not all conform to some heroic forefather or significant event in the Arab past. But family lineages are part of peopling this claim to the past.

77. The Circassians live in the Caucus mountains, which today is within the Russian Federation. They are predominantly Muslim and their native tongue is Circassian. Many of the Circassian communities currently living in Turkey and the Levant took refuge there during the *Russian conquest of the Caucasus* (1763–1864), but there have long been Circassian communities in these areas due to the Mamluke-era slave practices that trained young men in elite military education to rule (which continued even after the Mamluke empire had faded).

78. Abdullah Abdulal 2001, Agha 2001, Qablawi 2001, and Ahmad Abdulal 2001.

79. Qablawi 2001. The English text I have quoted has been edited for spelling and grammar.

80. Qablawi 2001. English original.

81. Darwish 1998.

82. Kretzmer 1990.

83. Evidence of this land-based national identity of Palestinians is the variety of people who think of themselves as Palestinian: Arabs, Muslims, Christians, the Druze, Jews, Armenians, people of African origin, and so on. Of course certain Islamist movements in recent years want Palestine to be Muslim and define it only as such.

84. Dirbas 1992, p. 5.

85. 'Awadallah 1996, p. 9.

86. Kana'ana and al-Madani 1987a, p. 7.

87. Kana'ana and Ishtayyah 1987, p. 6.

88. Palestinian authors seem to ignore the known details (but not the existence of) the Israelite period of history. This is likely for both ideological reasons (in that they do not want to promote more of the history that is used to disenfranchise them from their rights to their homeland) and practical reasons (in that the majority of village book authors do not read Hebrew or English, the primary languages of publication for Biblical archeology).

89. Malkki 1992, p. 34.

90. Malkki 1995, p. 30.

91. Obtained from Birzeit University CRDPS Web site at http:www.birzeit.edu/crdps /sus@vil.html. Accessed January 2002. No longer available online.

92. Abu el-Haj 2001; Benvenisti 2000; Nassar 2006a, 2006b.

93. This view of Palestinians extended even into popular culture. For example, in an issue of *National Geographic* magazine from 1950, the embroidered scarf of a Palestinian woman is described as follows: "A scarf such as that worn by this young woman may have served Ruth when she gleaned an ephah of barley in the fields of Boaz" (Shaheen 1992, p. 195).

94. Abu El-Haj 2001, p. 3.

95. Discussions about the influence of modern religious desires to reconstruct only certain elements of the past (that is, ancient Israelite kingdoms) are taking place in biblical studies. See Thompson 1998, Whitlam 1996, Provan 2003, and Davies 1992, among others.

96. Thompson 1998, p. 24.

97. Lemche 1991.

98. Abu Khiyara, Fanush, Sulayman, and 'Ashur 1993, p. 83.

99. Benvenisti 2000, p. 262.

100. Benvenisti 2000, p. 34.

101. Benvenisti 2000, p. 34. Other methods included naming places after "biblical characters" or "lyrical phrases from the Bible" (p. 34) as well as translating the meaning of the Arabic name into Hebrew, or naming the village after symbolic characteristics of the new Israeli state (p. 35). Benvenisti cites a study by Nurit Kliot in which "of 770 names of places of Jewish settlements within the pre-June '67 borders of Israel, 350 are names of 'biblical or ancient' places" (p. 34).

102. Joshua 15:1—The allotment for the tribe of Judah, clan by clan, extended down to the territory of Edom, to the Desert of Zin in the extreme south. [...] Joshua 15:11—It went to the northern slope of Ekron, turned toward Shikkeron, passed along to Mount Baalah, and reached Jabneel. The boundary ended at the sea. Joshua 19:32—The sixth lot came out for Naphtali, clan by clan. *33*—Their boundary went from Heleph and the large tree in Zaanannim, passing Adami Nekeb and Jabneel to Lakkum and ending at the Jordan.

103. 2 Chronicles 26:6–7. The Hebrew text says *Aravim*, which has been translated as "Arabs."

104. Ego 2009.

105. Abu Sbayh 2001, p. 25. Al-'Abbasiyya stayed as Yahud (or more precisely al-Yahudiyya) until the 1930s.

106. Al-Lubani 2003, p. 68. Other texts containing this type of information include Abu Mayila, al-Lawh, Sha'th, and Abu Zayid 1998; al-'Alami 1990; 'Arafat 2004a, 2004b; Barhum and Kharrub 1999; Shurrab 2000.

107. Al-Mahsiri 2002, p. 28. Al-Mahsiri's historical timeline is faulty in that the Arab Muslims defeated the Byzantine Empire to take over Palestine in the seventh century CE. The Byzantine Empire was seen as a continuation of the Greek conquest of the region. All over the Mediterranean, people call very old olive trees, which coring has shown can be up to two thousand years old, *Rum* or *Roman* (which in Arabic also means *Byzantine*).

108. Abu Khiyara, Fanush, Sulayman, and ʿAshur 1993, p. 45.

109. http://www.palestineremembered.com/jerusalem/al-walaja/story385.html. Accessed June 20, 2002. English original. I corrected the spelling mistakes in the original text.

110. Abu Hadba 1990, p. 302.

111. Abu Hadba 1990, p. 285.

112. Abu Hadba 1990, p. 285. As narrated by Mahmoud Ikhrayush.

113. Abu Hadba 1990, p. 302.

114. Zerubavel 1995, Abu el-Haj 2001.

115. Hammer 2005, Khalili 2007, Massad 2005, Tibawi 1963.

Chapter 8: Conclusion: Connecting Geographies of Dispossession

1. Al-Qasim 1993. Translation is mine. This six-volume collection of his poetry did not mention either the date or the particular circumstances of the poem's first publication.

2. The most well-known and popular of these musicians and performers is Marcel Khalifa. Others include al-ʿAshiqin Group and Ahmad Qaʿbur. For a discussion of Palestinian music, see Massad 2003 and McDonald (forthcoming). For a discussion of Palestinian poetry from inside Israel during this period, see Kanafani 1966.

3. Sabreen was established in 1980. The song is called "Smoke of the Volcanoes" as well. The band's members are Odeh Turjman, Kamilya Jubran, Said Murad, Samer Musalam, and Issam Murad. See http://www.jerusalemquarterly.org/ViewArticle.aspx?id=271 Accessed September 17, 2009.

4. See her Web site: http://www.rimbanna.com/index.html

5. See her Web site: http://www.dimaorsho.com

6. See his Web site: http://www.myspace.com/ziadelahmadie

7. See Gugelberger and Kearney 1991, Latina Feminist Group 2001, Marin 1991. Some *testimonios* are produced by people who are illiterate, in conjunction with anthropologists, activists, and others.

8. Esber 2008, Morris 1987, Nazzal 1978.

9. Morris 1987, pp. 57–60.

10. Morris 1987, pp. 128–131.

11. UNRWA, "Number of Registered Refugees, as of 30 June (each year)" for 1950, available at http://www.unrwa.org/userfiles/reg-ref%282%29.pdf

12. One of the subjects rarely talked about is the 100,000 Syrian refugees displaced from more than a hundred villages and the city of Quneitra into the rest of Syria when

Israel occupied the Golan Heights in 1967. A completely ignored subject, but one that becomes obvious if one lives in the camps in Syria, is the number of Palestinians who took refuge in the Golan Heights in 1948 and worked and farmed there. They were made refugees for a second time (along with the 100,000 Syrians for the first time) in 1967.

13. Y. Sayigh 1997, pp. 39–42.

14. Peteet 2005 and R. Sayigh 1994.

15. In 2009, UNRWA ran 689 schools with a total of 479,156 students and 21,217 staff. Female students constituted 50 percent of those in attendance. These schools included elementary and preparatory schools, as well as six secondary schools in Lebanon. UNRWA also ran 137 health care facilities, with a combined staff of 4,087, which received 5,477,516 visits in the first six months of 2009. They also treated 263,474 Special Hardship Cases (6 percent of the registered refugee population). UNRWA 2009.

16. http://www.un.org/unrwa/publication/pdf/figures.pdf

17. Lybarger 2007, Milton-Edwards 1996, Robinson 1997, Sayigh 1979.

18. 'Abd al-Rahim 1994.

19. Seikaly 1995, Davis 1999a.

20. Peteet 1995, p. 174; and Peteet 2005.

21. R. Sayigh 1994, pp. 35–36. See also R. Sayigh 1979, p. 37, where Sayigh notes that despite the presence of a large number of Majd al-Krum villagers, "unlike most other camps in Lebanon, where sizeable village quarters were formed, Shateela's small size and fragmented composition prevented such village clustering."

22. Peteet 2005.

23. Slyomovics 1998, p. 137.

24. Slyomovics 1998 details how groups must register in Jordan with the Ministry of the Interior, and that they register as charitable organizations, which allows them to provide scholarships and loans to members, and to rent space for events, and so on (p. 161).

25. At the same time, however, the social upheavals that resulted from the dispossession and impoverishment of the refugees has meant that wealthier families could no longer afford to maintain the guesthouse at the ready alone as they had done before 1948, and the increased opportunities for education and work allowed formerly poor families to take a more active role in hosting. See Slyomovics 1998, pp. 148–168.

26. According to Ylana Miller (1985, p. 55), "According to Ottoman law *mukhtars* and village councils were to be elected by villagers as their representatives. Regulations stipulated that *mukhtars* and elders were to be elected yearly by those over eighteen years of age who paid a specified amount in taxes; the results of this procedure were then to be forwarded to the local government representative."

27. The central authority tried to dissipate the authority of the local families who had grown in power as the central authority of the Ottoman Empire had weakened in the late eighteenth and nineteenth centuries. Some of the smaller families were unrepresented, and therefore could align themselves with whomever they chose.

28. The mukhtar's role in tax collection and allocation existed until 1935 (Miller 1985, p. 58). He was compensated with 2 percent of the tax revenue until 1932, and then 5 percent until 1935. After the job of tax collection was given to official tax collectors, the *mukhtar*s were given a regular annual salary.

29. Miller 1985, pp. 56–57, notes the new role that these duties gave to *mukhtar*s in the 1920s and 1930s, when there was the greatest pressure on Palestinians to sell land to Jewish immigrants and land speculators

30. Miller 1985, p. 62.

31. Miller 1985, p. 55.

32. Both refugees and aid workers have chronicled how a few *mukhtar*s used this new position to gain a little extra money by acquiring supplies or taking a fee to ignore the death of someone getting aid rations. Feldman 2007; Peteet 2005, chapter 3.

33. Peteet 2005, p. 108.

34. See Feldman 2006 for more on the early infiltrations across borders, and Khalili 2007 for more on the military raids.

35. Feldman 2006, p. 40.

36. 'Abd al-Rahim 2005, pp. 256–81.

37. Feldman 2006.

38. 'Abd al-Rahim 2004, pp. 78–84. My translation here is a considerably shortened version of the story.

39. Y. Sayigh 1997, p. ix.

40. R. Sayigh 1979, Peteet 2005, and Khalili 2007 discuss in great detail the transformations of Palestinian camp life in Lebanon due to the rise of the resistance movements.

41. The events that took place in Nahr el-Bared camp in Lebanon in 2007 illustrate the increased violent power of breakaway (and transnational) Islamist groups and the weakness of the PLO. In the camps in Syria, Hamas has the most funds among the political factions and therefore holds many more events for the public (and makes more commemorative posters) than the other groups.

42. Feldman 2006, p. 39.

43. There is an excellent scene in Mourid al-Barghouti's *I Saw Ramallah* (2000, pp. 138–139) in which a bewildered border guard stops him and his family members as they cross between France and Switzerland in two cars, with passports from Jordan, Syria, the United States, Algeria, Britain, and Belize, all with the same last name—Barghouti— on them.

44. Although the land records from the British Mandate list the village as Zanghari-yya, it was not exactly one village; rather, it was a group of four villages of recently settled Bedouin of the Zanghariyya tribe.

45. al-Jam'an 1999, pp. 28–29.

46. al-Jam'an 1999, pp. 34–46.

47. Palestinians also rely on village stereotypes to identify, tease, and insult people:

Ja'unehs from the village of al-Ja'una are stingy, Lubanis from Lubya are elitist. Well-known sayings exist: 'Aashir Nuri wa-la ta'shir Turi (give a place to stay to a gypsy but not to someone from al-Tur village), Shabab al-rayneh, kull 'ashara bil-qutayneh (ten young men of al-Rayneh village are equal to a dried fig).

48. 'Arafat 2004a, 2004b.

49. Al-Maw'id and al-Maw'id 2004; Musa and Isma'il 2001a, 2001b.

50. The most active group in this movement is the Association for the Defense of the Rights of the Internally Displaced in Israel (Jama'iyat al-difa' 'an huquq al-muhajjarin).

51. Newsletter from Adalah: The Legal Center for Minority Rights in Israel. http://www.adalah.org/newsletter/eng/sep08/5.php. Accessed March 30, 2009.

52. This telephone book was published in 2003 by the Iqrit Heritage Society. The villagers of Iqrit, who numbered 491 in 1948, won repeated court cases in the Israeli courts, but on Christmas Day of 1951 the Israeli Defense Forces blew up the village. Still, and despite more court decisions in their favor, they have never been allowed to return or to gain possession of their lands.

53. Al-Ramhi 2004, pp. 265–275. It is not clear why he does not include any of those who graduated with nonscience degrees, or degrees in engineering, or master's degrees in any other fields. Nor do I know why he separated them into lists of women and men.

54. Ben-Ze'ev 2005, p. 13.

55. Interview with Matar 'Abd al-Rahim, June 20, 2005, Damascus, Syria. For two of his memoirs see 'Abd al-Rahim 1995 and 2004.

56. Present absentees are rendered as hadirin gha'ibin in Arabic and nifkadim nokhahim in Hebrew.

57. Breckenridge and Appadurai 1989, quoted in Malkki 1992, p. 38.

58. Some of these institutions—schools, police, and ministries of culture and information—exist under the Palestinian Authority in the West Bank and Gaza (although no longer really in Gaza since the 2007 breakup of the Palestinian government and the boycott and embargo of the Hamas-led government there).

59. Anderson 1991, Gellner 1983.

60. Swedenburg 1995/2003.

61. Among many oral history projects, two comprehensive ones are those posted on PalestineRemembered.com and on nakba-archive.org, which includes interviews with 1948 refugees from every village that has refugees living in Lebanon.

62. Basso 1999, p. 38.

63. Interview with Abu Hussein (Matar 'Abd al-Rahim), 20 June 2005, Damascus, Syria.

64. Interview with Abu Ayham, Yarmouk Camp, Damascus, Summer 2008.

BIBLIOGRAPHY

This list of sources includes a separate list of village books, alphabetized by author's name. Each village book author is also found in the index under the village name. Occasionally a book in the village book list describes a Palestinian village that still exists and is lived in by some of its residents, but the book was written by those who were made refugees in 1948 and are now living in the diaspora, so I included it in this list. Other books about Palestinian villages and cities that are still extant are included in the larger bibliography. In the entries for works published by Birzeit University's Center for Research and Documentation of Palestinian Society (*Markaz Dirasat wa Tawthiq al-Mujtama' al-Filastiniyya*) I have used the English acronym CRDPS. Author's names that begin with *al-*, such as al-Bash, are alphabetized under the letter that follows the *al-*. Thus, al-Bash is found with the Bs.

Village Book Sources

'Abd al-'Aal, Muhammad Hassan. 1999. *Baqiyat ma baqayna: Al-Ghabisiyya, al-Shaykh Daoud, al-Shaykh Danun* [Remnants of what remained of us: Al-Ghabisiyya, al-Shaykh Daoud, al-Shaykh Danun]. Lebanon: Al-Lajna al-Filastiniyya lil-Thaqafa wal-Turath.

'Abd al-'Aal, Yusif 'Ali. 2005. *Judhur wa furu' Filastiniyya min al-Mallaha* [Palestinian roots and branches from Mallaha]. Damascus, Syria: Dar al-Umma lil-Tiba'a wal-Nashr wal-Tawzi'.

'Abeed, 'Ayish Muhammad Ibrahim. 2003. *Burayr fi al-dhakira wa al-tarikh* [Burayr in memory and in history]. Gaza: Al-Markaz al-Qawmi lil-Dirasat.

Abu 'Aal, 'Abd al-'Aziz Muhammad. 2007. *'Iraq al-Manshiyya: Fi dhakirat al-tarikh al-Filastini* [Iraq al-Manshiyya: In memory of Palestinian history]. Amman, Jordan: n.p.

Abu Fadda, Muhammad 'Abd al-Hadi. 1985. *'Ajjur: Ard al-ajdad fi ajnadeen* ['Ajjur: Land of our ancestors in Ajnadeen]. Jordan: Shneller Press.

Abu Ghush, 'Abd al-Majid. 1990. *'Imwas* [Imwas]. West Bank: Matba'at 'Ayn Rafa.

Abu Hadba, 'Abd al-'Aziz. 1990. *Dirasa fi al-mujtama' wal-turath al-sha'bi al-Filastini: Qaryat Dayr Aban* [A study of the society and the popular heritage of Palestine: Dayr Aban village]. Al-Bira, West Bank: Jam'iyyat In'ash al-Usrah.

Abu Hadhud, Yusif. 1994. *Tarikh 'Ayn Karim ma bayn 'amay 1095 ila 1948 miladi 'am 587 hijri* (The history of 'Ayn Karim from 1095 to 1948 CE). Jordan: n.p.

Abu Khiyara, 'Aziz, Salih Fanush, Muhammad Sulayman, and Musa 'Ashur. 1993. *Al-Walaja: Hadara wa tarikh* [Al-Walaja: Culture and history]. Amman, Jordan: Jam'iyyat al-Wajala al-Ta'awaniyya.

Abu Khusa, Ahmad. 1982. *Bi'r al-Sabi' wal-hayat al-badawiyya* [Beersheba and Bedouin life]. Jordan: n.p.

Abu Rashid, 'Abd al-Samad. 1993. *Tirat al-Karmal: Tirat Haifa* [The heights of the Carmel mountains: Tirat Haifa village]. Irbid, Jordan: n.p.

Abu Sbayh, Abdullah Wahba. 2001. *Min dhakirat al-jihad al-Filastini: Baldat al-'Abbasiyya, tarikhuha wa jihaduha* [From the memoirs of a Palestinian struggle: Al-'Abbasiyya, its history and struggle]. Jordan: Matabi' al-Jazira.

Al-'Adarba, Ahmad. 1997. *Qaryat al-Dawayima* [Village of al-Dawayima]. Birzeit, West Bank: Birzeit University, CRDPS.

'Ajaj, Muhammad 'Issa. 2006. *Qaryat Talhum—al-Samakiyya: Dhikrayat hafaraha al-tarikh* [The village of Talhum—al-Samakiyya: Memories etched by history]. Damascus, Syria: n.p.

'Alayan, Ribhi Mustafa. 1988. *Yalu: Al-ard, al-insan, wal-ma'saa* [Yalu: The land, the people, and the tragedy]. Amman, Jordan: Rabita Ahali Yalu.

Al-'Ali, 'Abd al-Majid Fadl. 2002. *Kuwaykat: Ahad sharayin Filastin* [Kuwaykat: An artery of Palestine]. Beirut, Lebanon: n.p.

'Amayri, Khalid Ahmad. 2007. *Al-Ja'una: Qarya bi hajm al-watan* [Al-Ja'una: A village the size of the nation]. Damascus, Syria: Dar al-Shajara.

Al-Amir, Kawthar. 2002. *Likay la tansi hafidati al-Burj* [So my granddaughter doesn't forget al-Burj]. Amman, Jordan: Dar 'Alam al-Thaqafa.

Al-A'raj, Hassan Sa'id. 2004. *Tarbikha fi al-tarikh wal-turath* [Tarbikha: History and heritage]. Beirut, Lebanon: Dar al-Muhajja al-Bayda'.

'Arar, 'Abd al-'Aziz. 1995. *Qaryat Bayt Jibrin* [Bayt Jibrin village]. Birzeit, West Bank: Birzeit University, CRDPS.

'Arisha, 'Abd al-Karim 'Ali. 2002. *Fir'im muhrat kan'an* [Fir'im: The horse of Canaan]. Burj al-Baranjeh, Lebanon: Markaz Jenin.

Ashqar, Muslih. 2008. *Al-Sammu'i: Mudhakkirat qarya Filastiniyya* [Al-Sammu'i: Memoir of a Palestinian village]. Damascus, Syria: Dar al-Shajara lil-Nashr wa Tawzi'.

'Atiya, Ahmad, and Hassan 'Atiya. 1998. *'Alma: Zaytunat bilad safad* ['Alma: The olive tree of Safad]. Lebanon: n.p.

'Atiya, 'Atiya 'Abdallah. 1991. *'Ayn Karim: Al-haqiqa wal-hulm* ['Ayn Karim: The reality and the dream]. Jordan: n.p.

'Awadallah, Ibrahim. 1996. *Suba: Ihda qura Filastin al-mudammara* [Suba: One of Palestine's destroyed villages], 2nd ed. Jordan: Jam'iyyat Suba al-Ta'awuniyya.

Al-Bash, Ahmad Mustafa. 2001. *Tirat Haifa* [Tirat Haifa]. Damascus, Syria: Dar al-Shajara.

Al-Biss, Zakariyya Ahmad. 1990. *Saydun: Qaryat al-ajdad fi Filastin* [Saydun: The ancestors' village in Palestine]. Jordan: n.p.

Dakwar, Mahmud. 2001. *Baqiyat ma baqayna: Qidditha safad, burkan al-jabal* [Remnants of what we remain: Qidditha of Safad, volcano of the mountain]. Beirut, Lebanon: n.p.

Damara, Ibrahim 'Ali. 1993. *Majdal al-Sadiq* [Majdal al-Sadiq]. Jordan: n.p.

Dirbas, Sahira. 1993. *Salama: Watan 'asi 'ala al-nisyan* [Salama: A homeland that refuses to be forgotten]. West Bank: Dar al-Qudsiyya.

———. 1992. *Al-Birwa*. West Bank: n.p.

———. 1991. *Tirat Haifa: Watan 'asi 'ala al-nisyan* [Tirat Haifa: A homeland that refuses to be forgotten]. West Bank: Dar al-Qudsiyya.

Al-Dirbashi, 'Abd al-Mu'ti. 2000. *Summiel al-Khalil: Qaryati* [Summiel of Hebron: My village]. Jordan: Dar al-Yanabi' lil-Nashr wal-Tawzi'.

Al-Fatayani, Muhammad. *Qaryat Sataf bayn al-madi wal-hadir: Dirasa tawthiqiyya min al-'ahd al-'uthmani hata 'am 1900 miladi* [The village of Sataf between the past and the present: A documentary study from the Ottoman era until 1900 CE]. Damascus, Syria: n.p.

Ghanaym, Khalid Isma'il. 2003. *Tall al-Safi: Baldat al-raw'a wal-jamal* [Tall al-Safi: Town of splendor and beauty]. Amman, Jordan: Matba' al-Shadfan.

Al-Habashi, Badr al-Din. 2002. *Safar qaryat al-Kabri: Rawda min riyad Filastin al-mubaraka* [The book of the village al-Kabri: A garden among the meadows of blessed Palestine]. Beirut, Lebanon: n.p.

Haddad, Yusif Ayub. 2002. *Al-Mujtama' wa al-turath fi Filastin: Qaryat al-Bassa* [Society and heritage in Palestine: Al-Bassa village]. n.p.

———. 1984. *'Adat al-khutba wal-zawaj fi Qaryat al-Bassa al-Filastiniyya* [Customs of engagement and marriage in the Palestinian al-Bassa village]. Nicosia, Cyprus: Shu'un Filastiniyya.

Hadeem, Musa 'Abd al-Salam. 1985. *Qaryat al-Dawayima* [Village of al-Dawayima]. Jordan: Dar al-Jalil lil-Nashr.

Hassan, 'Othman Muhammad. 2001. *Qalunya: Bawwabat al-Quds al-gharbiyya* [Qalunya: The western gate to Jerusalem]. Chicago: Qalunya Association.

Al-Hindi, Hani 'Ali. 2006. *Al-Qubab: Min dhakira al-shuyukh ila qulub al-shabab* [Al-Qubab: From memory of the elders to hearts of the youth]. Amman, Jordan: n.p.

Hummayd, Nihad Fawzi. 2000. *Dallata: Ta'ir al-finiq al-Filastini* [Dallata: The Palestinian phoenix]. Damascus, Syria: Dar al-Shajara.

Al-Hurani, 'Abdullah Ahmad. 1988. *Masmiyyat al-Hurani: Min qura Filastin al-mubada*

[Masmiyyat al-Hurani: Among the destroyed Palestinian villages]. Amman, Jordan: Dar al-Karmal.

Husayn, 'Abd al-Rahim Ahmad. *Qissat madinat al-Majdal wa 'Asqalan* [The story of the city of al-Majdal 'Asqalan]. Cairo, Egypt: Al-Munadhdhama al-'Arabiyya lil-Tarbiya wal-Thaqafa wal-'Ulum.

Al-Jam'an, Muqbil. 1999. *Al-Zanghariyya: Ard wa 'ashira* [Al-Zanghariyya: Land and tribe]. Damascus, Syria: Dar al-Shajara.

Jaradat, Idris Muhammad. 2001. *Tariq al-shumukh ila qaryat al-Shuyukh* [The proud road to the village of al-Shuyukh]. Hebron, West Bank: Markaz al-Sanabil lil-Dirasat wal-Tarikh al-Sha'bi.

Jud'an, Muhammad Rajih. 1998. *'Ayn Ghazal: Kifah qarya Filastiniyya* ['Ayn Ghazal: The struggle of a Palestinian village]. Damascus, Syria: Dar al-Shajara.

Kana'ana, Sharif, and Bassam al-Ka'bi. 1991a. *Al-qura al-Filastiniyya al-mudammara: Kafr Saba* [The destroyed Palestinian villages: Kafr Saba]. Birzeit, West Bank: Birzeit University, CRDPS.

———. 1991b. *Al-qura al-Filastiniyya al-mudammara: Miska* [The destroyed Palestinian villages: Miska]. Birzeit, West Bank: Birzeit University, CRDPS.

———. 1987. *Al-qura al-Filastiniyya al-mudammara: 'Ayn Hawd* [The destroyed Palestinian villages: 'Ayn Hawd]. Birzeit, West Bank: Birzeit University, CRDPS.

Kana'ana, Sharif, and Lubna 'Abd al-Hadi. 1991. *Al-qura al-Filastiniyya al-mudammara: Lifta* [The destroyed Palestinian villages: Lifta]. Birzeit, West Bank: Birzeit University, CRDPS.

———. 1990. *Al-qura al-Filastiniyya al-mudammara: Abu Kishk* [The destroyed Palestinian villages: Abu Kishk]. Birzeit, West Bank: Birzeit University, CRDPS.

———. 1986. *Al-qura al-Filastiniyya al-mudammara: Salama* [The destroyed Palestinian villages: Salama]. Birzeit, West Bank: Birzeit University, CRDPS.

Kana'ana, Sharif, and Muhammad Ishtayya. 1991. *Al-qura al-Filastiniyya al-mudammara: Kafr Bir'im* [The destroyed Palestinian villages: Kafr Bir'im]. Birzeit, West Bank: Birzeit University, CRDPS.

———. 1987. *Al-qura al-Filastiniyya al-mudammara: 'Innaba* [The destroyed Palestinian villages: 'Innaba]. Birzeit, West Bank: Birzeit University, CRDPS.

Kana'ana, Sharif, and Rashad al-Madani. 1987a. *Al-qura al-Filastiniyya al-mudammara: Al-Faluja* [The destroyed Palestinian villages: Al-Faluja]. Birzeit, West Bank: Birzeit University, CRDPS.

———. 1987b. *Al-qura al-Filastiniyya al-mudammara: Al-Lujjun* [The destroyed Palestinian villages: Al-Lujjun]. Birzeit, West Bank: Birzeit University, CRDPS.

———. 1987c. *Al-qura al-Filastiniyya al-mudammara: Majdal 'Asqalan* [The destroyed Palestinian villages: Majdal 'Asqalan]. Birzeit, West Bank: Birzeit University, CRDPS.

———. n.d. *Al-qura al-Filastiniyya al-mudammara: Al-Kawfakha* [The destroyed Palestinian villages: Al-Kawfakha]. Birzeit, West Bank: Birzeit University, CRDPS.

Kan'aan, 'Abd al-Rahim. 1998. *Baldat dayr ba'alba* [The village of Dayr Ba'alba]. Damascus, Syria: Matba'at Akrama.

Kan'aan, Deeb Ahmad. 1998. *Ishwa': Qarya Filastiniyya* [Ishwa': A Palestinian village]. Jordan: n.p.

Kansh, Hassan Mahmood Hamoodeh. *Jihad qarya Filastiniyya: Al-'Abbasiyya 1921–1948* [The struggle of a Palestinian village: Al-'Abbasiyya 1921–1948]. Amman, Jordan: n.p.

Khadar, Shafiq 'Eid. 2002. *Qaryat Bir Ma'in: Al-Hilm wal-haqiqa* [Bir Ma'in village: The dream and the reality]. Jordan: n.p.

Khalifa, Ahmad Mohammad Ali. 1988. *Qaryat al-'Ubaydiyya* [The Village of 'Ubaydiyya]. Jordan: Mataba' al-Jazira.

Khatib, 'Alya'. 1987. *'Arab al-Turkuman: Abna' Marj ibn 'Amir* [The Turkmen Arabs: Sons of Marj ibn 'Amir]. Amman, Jordan: Dar al-Jalil lil-Nashr.

Al-Khatib, Fakhri Ahmad. 1999. *Qalunya: Al-Insan, al-ard, al-tarikh* [Qalunya: The people, the land, the history]. Amman, Jordan: n.p.

Lajnat Ahali Qaryat 'Imwas. 1994. *'Imwas: Nashrat li-marra wahida* ['Imwas: One-time publication]. n.p.: Lajnat Ahali Qaryat 'Imwas.

Al-Lubani, Hussein 'Ali. 1999. *Al-Damun: Qarya Filastiniyya fi al-bal* [Al-Damun: A Palestinian village in the mind]. Lebanon: Dar al-'Arabi.

Al-Madi, Marwan. 1994. *Qaryat Ijzim: Al-Hamama al-bayda'* [Ijzim village: The white dove]. Damascus, Syria: Al-Ahali lil-Tiba' wal-Nashir wal-Tawzi'.

Mahjaz, Khadar. 2003. *Al-Jiyya: Dirasat fi al-ard wa al-insan* [Al-Jiyya: Studies of the land and the people]. Gaza: Al-Markaz al-Qawmi lil-Dirasat.

Al-Mahsiri, 'Ali Islim. 2002. *Bayt Mahsir wa madinatuha al-Quds* [Bayt Mahsir village and its city, Jerusalem]. Amman, Jordan: Dar al-Baraka lil-Nashr wal-Tawzi'.

Mar'i, Ibrahim Jamil. 1994. *Qaryat Zir'in* [The village of Zir'in]. Birzeit, West Bank: Birzeit University, CRDPS.

Al-Maw'id, Hisham 'Arif, and Ma'mun Ahmad al-Maw'id. 2004. *Saffuriyya: Jabal al-sindiyan* [Saffuriyya: Mountain of oak]. Damascus, Syria: Dar al-Umma lil-Tiba'a wal-Nashr.

Al-Mudawwar, 'Abd al-Rahim. 1995. *Qaryat Tirat Haifa* [The village of Tirat Haifa]. Birzeit, West Bank: Birzeit University, CRDPS.

———. 1994. *Qaryat Qaqun* [The village of Qaqun]. Birzeit, West Bank: Birzeit University, CRDPS.

Musa, Salih, and Tawfiq Isma'il. 2001a. *Saffuriyya: 'Arus al-Jalil.* [Saffuriyya: The bride of the Galilee]. Part 1. Beirut, Lebanon: Jam'iyyat al-Shajara li-Ihya' al-Dhakira wal-Turath al-Sha'bi al-Filastini.

———. 2001b. *Saffuriyya: Safhat mushriqa min jihadina* [Saffuriyya: Glorious pages from our struggle]. Part 2. Beirut, Lebanon: Jam'iyyat al-Shajara li-Ihya' al-Dhakira wa al-Turath al-Sha'bi al-Filastini.

Nabhan, Yahya. 2001. *Al-Qubayba ta'ud min ard can'aan* [Al-Qubayba goes back to the land of Canaan]. Jordan: Dar Yaffa.

Al-Najjar, 'Atiyah 'Abd al-Hafiz. 1996. *Qaryat Jimzu: Dirasa 'amma al-ard wa-al-sukkan wa-al-turath wa-al-dhakira* [*The village of Jimzu: General study of the land, people, culture and memory*]. Amman, Jordan: Dar al-Jalil lil-Nashr wal-Dirasat wal-Abhath al-Filastiniyya.

Nasir, Muhammad. 2001. *Tarsheeha: Zahra 'ala sidr al-Jalil* [Tarsheeha: A flower on the bosom of the Galilee]. n.p.: Al-Awa'il lil-Nashr wal-Tawzi' wal-Khidmat al-Taba'iyya.

Nassar, Jaber. 1991. *Al-Mujaydil* [Al-Mujaydil]. n.p.: n.p.

Nimr, Mahmud Amin. 2005. *Kharbitha Bani Harith: Bayna al-madi wal-hadir* [Kharbitha Bani Harith: Between the past and present]. n.p.: n.p.

———. 2001. *Qaryat Shilta* [Shilta village]. n.p.: n.p.

'Uthman, Kamal Muhammad Salah. 1997. *Al-Jusayr: Ard wa tarikh* [Al-Jusayr: Land and history]. Jordan: n.p.

Qatifan, Hassan Mahmud, and Musa Ibrahim 'Allush. 1993. *Bayt Nabala* [Bayt Nabala]. Al-Bira, West Bank: Al-Fatayeb.

Al-Qatrawi, Jamal 'Abd al-Rahim. 2000. *Qatra: Al-Huwiya wal-tarikh* [*Qatra: Identity and history*]. Gaza: Al-Markaz al-Qawmi lil-Dirasat.

Rahal, Ahmad Salim. 2001. *'Artuf: Al-'ahd wal-wa'd* ['Artuf: The era and the promise]. Amman, Jordan: n.p.

Al-Ramahi, Qasim Ahmad. 2004. *Al-Muzayri'a: Ihda qura Filastin al-mudammara* [Al-Muzayri'a: One of Palestine's destroyed villages], 2nd ed. Amman, Jordan: n.p.

———. 1991. *Al-Muzayri'a: Ihda qura Filastin al-mudammara* [Al-Muzayri'a: One of Palestine's destroyed villages]. 1st ed. Amman, Jordan: n.p.

Rumman, Muhammad Sa'id Muslih. 2000. *Suba: Qarya maqdisiyya fi al-dhakira* [Suba: A Jerusalem village in memory]. Jerusalem, West Bank: n.p.

Al-Sahli, Nabil Mohammad. 2001. *Qaryat Balad al-Shaykh* [Balad al-Shaykh village]. Damascus, Syria: Dar al-Shajara.

Sa'id, Mahmoud Ahmad. 1991. *Tirat Haifa ma bayn 1900–1948* (Tirat Haifa between 1900–1948]. Irbid, Jordan: Qudsiyya lil-Nashr wal-Tawzi'.

Salih, 'Uthman Muhammad. 1988. *Bayt Mahsir* [Bayt Mahsir]. Al-Baq'a, Jordan: n.p.

Sulayma, Fadi. 2008. *Dayr Yasin: Al-Qarya al-shahida* [Dayr Yasin: The martyred village]. Damascus, Syria: Dar al-Shajara.

———. 2003. *Min qurana al-mudammara fi Filastin: Al-Shajara* [From our destroyed villages in Palestine: Al-Shajara]. Damascus, Syria: Dar al-Shajara.

Saliha, Muhammad. 1999. *Majdal 'Asqalan: Tarikh wa hadara* [Majdal 'Asqalan: History and civilization]. Gaza: n.p.

Saqr, 'Abd al-'Aziz Muhammad. 2004. *Muhadara . . . 'an baldat salama mujtami'an wa mawqi'an wa nidalan* [A lecture on the society, situation, and struggle of the village of Salama]. Amman, Jordan: n.p.

————. 1990. *Salama al-basila: Basalat balda Filastiniyya* [Brave Salama: The heroism of a Palestinian village]. Amman, Jordan: n.p.

Al-Shahabi, Ibrahim Yahya. 1994a. *Lubya: Shawka fi hasirat al-mashuru' al-sahyuni* [Lubya: A thorn in the side of the Zionist project]. Damascus, Syria: Dar al-Shajara.

————. 1994b. *Qaryat Lubya [Lubya village]*. Birzeit, West Bank: Birzeit University, CRDPS.

Shaheen, Iyad. 2002. *Hikayat qarya mudammara: Bashsheet [Stories of a destroyed village: Bashsheet]*. West Bank: Dar 'Allush lil-Nashr wal-Tawzi'.

Al-Shuqayrat, Faysal Ahmad. 1999. *Min shuhada' 'asha'ir 'arab al-Turkuman: Abna' marj ibn 'amir* [Among the martyrs of the Arab Turkmen tribes: The sons of Marj Ibn 'Amir]. Amman, Jordan: n.p.

Al-Shuyukhi, Hammad Mohammad. 1999. *Qaryat al-Shuyukh, muhafizat al-Khalil* [The village of Shuyukh, Hebron district]. Amman, Jordan: Jam'iyyat 'Ummal al-Matabi' al-Ta'awaniyya.

Siyyam, Zakaria. 1996. *Al-Quds madinati wa Lifta qaryati* [Jerusalem is my city and Lifta is my village]. Jordan: Jam'iyyat 'Ummal al-Matabi' al-Ta'awuniyya.

Al-Sufi, 'Abdallah Isma'il. 1993. *'Innaba: Ard al-aba' wa al-ajdad* ['Innaba: The land of parents and ancestors]. Amman, Jordan: n.p.

Suhmata: Zahra min riyad al-Jalil al-a'la [Suhmata: From the gardens of the upper Galilee]. n.d. Israel: n.p.

Sumrayn, Ghalib Muhammad. 1993. *Qaryati . . . Qalunya: Al-ard wa al-judhur* [My village . . . Qalunya: The land and the roots]. Amman, Jordan: Matba'at al-Tawfiq.

'Uthman, Ibrahim Khalil. 2000. *Dayr al-Qasi: Zanbaqa Khalil al-awsat al-gharbi* [Dayr al-Qasi: Lily of mid-western Hebron]. Tyre, Lebanon: n.p.

Al-Waridat, Anwar. 2003. *Al-Zahiriyya [al-Dhahiriyya] goshen bint Filastin* [Al-Zahiriyya, daughter of Palestine]. Al-Zarqa', Jordan: n.p.

Al-Yahya, Yahya Mohammad. 1998. *Al-Tantura* [al-Tantura]. Damascus, Syria: Dar al-Shajara.

Ya'qub, Nasr, and Fahum al-Shalabi. 1995. *Qaryat Abu-Shusha (qada al-Ramla)* [Abu-Shusha village, al-Ramla district]. Birzeit, West Bank: Birzeit University, CRDPS.

Al-Zanghari, Khamis al-Jaradat. 2002. *Al-Judhur al-tarikhiyya lil-Zanghariyya [The historical roots of al-Zanghariyya]*. Damascus, Syria: Dar al-Shajara.

Zina, Jamil. 2004. *Dalil Lifta: 2004* [Guide to Lifta: 2004]. Amman, Jordan: n.p.

Other Sources

Al-'Abadi, Mahmud. 1977. *Safad fi al-tarikh* [Safad throughout history]. Beirut, Lebanon: Jam'iyyat 'Ummal al-Matabi' al-Ta'awuniyya.

Al-'Abbasi, Mustafa Ahmad. 1996. Qura qada' Safad fi 'ahd al-intidab [*Villages in the Safad district during the mandate era*]. Israel: Arab Education Department.

———. 1994. *Al-Jish: Sandiyanat al-diyar al-Safadiya* [Al-Jish: Oak trees of the homes of Safad]. Israel: Matba' al-Jish.

'Abd al-Rahim, Matar. 2004. *Shadhaya min 'umri* (Fragments of my life]. Damascus, Syria: Dar al-Shajara.

———. 1995. *Udfununi hunaka: Sira Filastiniyya yahlum bil-watan* [Bury me there: The story of a Palestinian dreaming of the homeland]. Damascus: Dar al-Shajara.

Abdel Jawad, Saleh. 2006. The Arab and Palestinian narratives of the 1948 war. In *Israeli and Palestinian narratives of conflict: History's double helix*, ed. Robert I. Rotberg, p. 72. Bloomington: Indiana University Press.

Abdulal, Abdullah. 2001. Umm al-Faraj people are from Mamlukes origins. Available from http://www.palestineremembered.com/Acre/Umm-al-Faraj/Story608.html

Abdulal, Ahmad. 2001. We are Palestinians. Available from http://www.palestineremem bered.com/Acre/Umm-al-Faraj/Story614.html

Abi-Mershed, Osama. 2010. *Apostles of modernity: Saint-Simonians and the French civilizing mission in Algeria*. Stanford, CA: Stanford University Press.

Abu El-Haj, Nadia. 2001. *Facts on the ground: Archeological practice and territorial self-fashioning in Israeli society*. Chicago: University of Chicago Press.

Abu Gharbiyya, Bahjat. 1993. *Fi khidamm al-nidal al-'Arabi al-Filastini: Mudhakkirat al-munadil, 1916–1949* [In the midst of the struggle for the Arab Palestinian cause: The memoirs of freedom-fighter Bahjat Abu Gharbiyya, 1916–1949]. Beirut, Lebanon: Mu'assasat al-Dirasat al-Filastiniyya.

Abu-Ghazaleh, Adnan. 1972. Arab cultural nationalism in Palestine during the British mandate. *Journal of Palestine Studies* 1(3): 37–63.

Abu Hanna, Hanna. 1998. Min al-mufakkira (From the diary]. *al-Karmel* 55–56(Spring/Summer): 232–249.

Abu Jarar, Mohammad Hassan. 1999. *Al-Jabarat: Tarikh wa wujud munthu aqdam al-'uhud* [Al-Jabarat: History and presence throughout the ages]. Jordan: n.p.

Abu-Lughod, Ibrahim. 1998. Al-yawm al-akhir qabl suqut Yafa [The last day before the fall of Jaffa]. *Al-Karmel* 55–56(Spring/Summer): 117–129.

Abu-Lughod, Janet. 1971. The demographic transformation of Palestine. In *The transformation of Palestine: Essays on the origin and development of the Arab-Israeli conflict*, ed. Ibrahim A. Abu-Lughod, pp. 139–163. Chicago: Northwestern University Press.

Abu-Lughod, Lila. 2007. Return to half-ruins: Memory, postmemory, and living history in Palestine. In *Nakba: Palestine, 1948, and the claims of memory*, ed. Ahmad Sa'di and Lila Abu-Lughod. New York: Columbia University Press.

———. 1991. Writing against culture. In *Feminist anthropology: A reader*, ed. Ellen Lewin. Hoboken, NJ: Wiley Blackwell.

Abu Mayila, Yusif, Mansur al-Lawh, Maha Sha'th, and Ra'ida Abu Zayid. 1998. *Al-qura al-mudammara fi Filastin hatta 'am 1952* [The destroyed Palestinian villages up to 1952]. Egypt: Al-Jam'iyya al-Jughrafiyya al-Misriyya.

Abu Sitta, Salman. 2004. *Atlas of Palestine, 1948*. London: Palestine Land Society.

———. 1998. *Palestinian right to return: Sacred, legal and possible*. London: Palestinian Return Centre.

Adams, Paul C., Steven D. Hoelscher, and Karen E. Till. 2001. *Textures of place: Exploring humanist geographies*. Minneapolis: University of Minnesota Press.

Agha, Ahmad. The Turks of Umm al-Faraj. 2001. Available from http://www.palestine remembered.com/Acre/Umm-al-Faraj/Story609.html. Accessed May 2, 2002.

Agmon, Iris. 2006. *Family and court: Legal culture and modernity in late Ottoman Palestine*. Syracuse, NY: Syracuse University Press.

Agnew, John A., and James S. Duncan. 1989. *The power of place: Bringing together geographical and sociological imaginations*. Boston: Unwin Hyman.

Ahmed, Leila. 1992. *Women and gender in Islam*. New Haven, CT: Yale University Press.

'Al-Alami, Ahmad. 1990. *Al-Mudun wal-qura al-'Arabiyya al-mudammara wal-manhuba, 1920–1970* [The destroyed and plundered Arab villages and cities]. n.p.: n.p.

'Al-Alami, Musa. 1949. *'Ibrat Filastin* [The lesson of Palestine]. Beirut, Lebanon: Dar al-Kashshaf.

Alcalay, Ammiel. 1993. *After Jews and Arabs: Remaking Levantine culture*. Minneapolis: University of Minnesota Press.

Alexander, Livia. 2005. Is there a Palestinian cinema? The national and transnational in Palestinian film production. In *Palestine, Israel, and the politics of popular culture*, ed. Rebecca L. Stein and Ted Swedenburg, pp. 150–172. Durham, NC: Duke University Press.

———. 2001. *Conflicting images: Palestinian and Israeli cinemas, 1988–1998*. Ph.D. Thesis, New York University.

'Ali, Taha Muhammad. 2006. *So what: New and selected poems, 1971–2005*, trans. Peter Cole, Yahya Hijazi, and Gabriel Levin. Port Townsend, WA: Copper Canyon Press.

Amiry, Suad. 2004. *Sharon and my mother-in-law: Ramallah diaries*. New York: Pantheon.

Amiry, Suad, and Vera Tamari. 1989. *The Palestinian village home*. London: British Museum Publications.

'Amr, Sami, and Kimberly Katz. 2009. *A young Palestinian's diary, 1941–1945: The life of Sami 'Amr*, trans. Kimberly Katz. Austin: University of Texas Press.

Anderson, Benedict. 1991. *Imagined communities: Reflections on the origin and spread of nationalism*. London: Verso.

An-Na'im, Abdullahi, ed. 2002. Islamic family law in a changing world: A global resource book. London: Zed Books.

Antoun, Richard T. 1972. *Arab village: A social structural study of a Transjordanian peasant community*. Bloomington: Indiana University Press.

Arab Higher Committee. 1937. Memorandum submitted by Arab Higher Committee to the Permanent Mandates Commission and the Secretary of State for the colonies, July 23, 1937. Jerusalem: Commercial Press.

'Arafat, Jamil. 2004a. *Qura wa-'asha'ir qada Baysan* [Villages and tribes of the Baysan district]. Damascus: Dar al-Shajara.

———. 2004b. *al-Qura al-Filastiniyya al-muhajjara fi qada Haifa* [Emptied Palestinian villages in the Haifa district]. Damascus: Dar al-Shajara.

Al-'Arif, 'Arif. 1961/1992. *Al-mufassal fi tarikh al-Quds* [A detailed history of Jerusalem]. Jerusalem: Maktabat al-Andalus.

———. 1956/1980. *Nakbat Filastin wal-firdaws al-mafqud* [The catastrophe of Palestine and the lost paradise]. Beirut, Lebanon: Dar al-Huda.

———. 1943. *Tarikh Ghazza* [The history of Gaza]. Jerusalem: Matba'at Dar al-Aytam al-Islamiyya.

———. 1933/2004. *Al-qada' bayna al-Bedu* (Bedouin law]. Beirut, Lebanon: Al-Mu'assasa al-'Arabiya lil-Dirasat wal-Nashr.

'Arraf, Shukri. 1985. *Al-qaryah al-'Arabiyya al-Filastiniyya: Mabna wa-isti'malat aradin* [The Arab Palestinian village: Building and land use]. Jerusalem: Jam'i yat al-Dirasat al-'Arabiyya.

Artz, Donna. 1997. *Refugees into citizens: Palestinians and the end of the Arab-Israeli Conflict.* New York: Council on Foreign Relations.

Asad, Muhammad, trans. 2003. The message of the Qur'an. Bitton, UK: Book Foundation.

Asad, Talal. 1976. Class transformation under the Mandate. *MERIP Reports* (53): 3–8, 23.

———. 1975. Anthropological texts and ideological problems: An analysis of Cohen on Arab villages in Israel. *Economy and Society* 4(3): 251–282.

Al-Ashhab, 'Awda. 1999. *Tadhakkurat 'Awda al-Ashhab: Safahat min al-dhakira al-Filastiniyya* [Memories of 'awda al-ash-hab: Pages from the Palestinian memory]. Birzeit, West Bank: Birzeit University, CRDPS.

Atran, Scott. 1989. The surrogate colonization of Palestine, 1917–1939. *American Ethnologist* 16: 716–744.

———. 1986. Hamula organisation and Masha'a tenure in Palestine. *Man* 21(2): 271–295.

———. 1985. Managing Arab kinship and marriage. *Social Sciences Information* 24: 659–696.

Avneri, Arieh L. 1984. *The claim of dispossession: Jewish land-settlement and the Arabs, 1878–1948*, trans. Kfar-Blum Translation Group. New Brunswick, NJ: Transaction Books.

'Awda, 'Abdallah. 1980. *al-Kababeer . . . Baladi* [al-Kababeer, my land). Shafa 'Amr, Israel: n.p.

Al-'Awdat, Ya'qub. 1992. *Min A'lam al-fikr wal-adab fi Filastin* [Among the luminaries of thought and literature in Palestine]. Jerusalem: Dar al-Isra'.

Axel, Brian, ed. 2002. *From the margins: Historical anthropology and its futures.* Durham, NC: Duke University Press.

Ayalon, Ami. 2004. *Reading Palestine: Printing and literacy, 1900–1948.* Austin: University of Texas Press.

'Aziza, Khalid, and Jamil 'Arafat. 1988. *Dabburiyya: Watan wa judhur* [Dabburiyya: Homeland and roots]. Nazareth, Israel: n.p.

Badran, Margot. 1995. *Feminists, Islam, and nation: Gender and the making of modern Egypt.* Princeton, NJ: Princeton University Press.

Badran, Nabil. 1980. The Means of Survival: Education and the Palestinian Community, 1948–1967. *Journal of Palestine Studies* 9(4): 44–74.

Bahloul, Joëlle. 1996. *The architecture of memory: A Jewish-Muslim household in colonial Algeria, 1937–1962.* New York: Cambridge University Press.

Bakhtin, M. M. 1981. *The dialogic imagination: Four essays,* ed. Michael Holquist. Austin: University of Texas Press.

Bal, Mieke, Jonathan V. Crewe, and Leo Spitzer. 1999. *Acts of memory: Cultural recall in the present.* Hanover, NH: Dartmouth College Press.

Barakat, Halim. 1993. *The Arab world: Society, culture, and state.* Berkeley: University of California Press.

Bardenstein, Carol. 2005. Cross/Cast: Passing in Israeli and Palestinian cinema. In *Palestine, Israel, and the politics of popular culture,* eds. Rebecca L. Stein and Ted Swedenburg, pp. 99–125. Durham, NC: Duke University Press.

———. 1999. Trees, forests, and the shaping of Palestinian and Israeli collective memory. In *Acts of memory: Cultural recall in the present,* ed. Mieke Bal, Jonathan V. Crewe, and Leo Spitzer, pp. 148–168. Hanover, NH: Dartmouth College Press.

———. 1998. Threads of memory and discourses of rootedness: Of trees, oranges and the prickly-pear cactus in Israel-Palestine. *Edebiyat: A Journal of Middle Eastern Literatures* 8(1): 1–36.

Al-Barghouti, Mourid. 2000. *I Saw Ramallah,* trans. Ahdaf Soueif. Cairo, Egypt: American University in Cairo.

Al-Barghuti, 'Abd al-Latif. 1987. *Al-Qamus al-'Arabi al-sha'bi al-Filastini* [The dictionary of Palestinian colloquial Arabic]. Al-Bira, West Bank: Jam'iyat In'ash al-Usrah, Lajnat al-Abhath al-Ijtima'iya wa-al-Turath al-Sha'bi al-Filastini.

Barhum, Mahmud, and Muhammad Kharrub. 1990. *Qamus al-qura al-Filastiniyya ibbana al-intidab al-britani* [Lexicon of Palestinian villages from the British Mandate]. Amman, Jordan: Dar al-Karmal.

Bashir, Nabih. 2004. *Judaizing the place: Misgav regional council in the Galilee.* Haifa, Israel: Mada al-Carmel—Arab Center for Applied Social Research.

Basso, Keith H. 1999. *Wisdom sits in places: Landscape and language among the western Apache.* Albuquerque: University of New Mexico Press.

Bauer, Yehuda. 1982/2001. *A history of the Holocaust.* New York: Franklin Watts.

Baylouny, Anne Marie. 2006. Creating kin: New family associations as welfare providers in liberalizing Jordan. International Journal of Middle East Studies 38: 349–368.

Beinin, Joel, and Rebecca L. Stein, eds. 2006. *The struggle for sovereignty: Palestine and Israel, 1993–2005.* Stanford, CA: Stanford University Press.

Benvenisti, Meron. 2000. *Sacred landscape: The buried history of the holy land since 1948*. Berkeley: University of California Press.

Ben-Ze'ev, Efrat. 2005. Transmission and transformation: The Palestinian second generation and the commemoration of the homeland. In *Homelands and diasporas: Holy lands and other places*, eds. Andre Levy and Alex Weingrod. Stanford, CA: Stanford University Press.

———. 2004. The politics of taste and smell: Palestinian rites of return. In *The politics of food*. Oxford, UK: Berg.

———. 2002. The Palestinian village of Ijzim during the 1948 war: Forming an anthropological history through villagers' accounts and army documents. *History and Anthropology* 13(1): 13–30.

Blecher, Robert. 2005. Citizens without sovereignty: Transfer and ethnic cleansing in Israel. *Comparative Studies in Society and History* 47(3): 725–754.

Bowker, Robert. 2003. *Palestinian refugees: Mythology, identity, and the search for peace*. Boulder, CO: Lynne Rienner.

Boyarin, Jonathan. 1996. *Palestine and Jewish history: Criticism at the borders of ethnography*. Minneapolis: University of Minnesota Press.

———, ed. 1994. *Remapping memory: The politics of timespace*. Minneapolis: University of Minnesota Press.

Boym, Svetlana. 2001. *The future of nostalgia*. New York: Basic Books.

Brand, Laurie. 1988. *Palestinians in the Arab world: Institution building and the search for state*. New York: Columbia University Press.

Brison, Susan J. 1999. Trauma narratives and the remaking of the self. In *Acts of memory: Cultural recall in the present*, ed. Mieke Bal, Jonathan Crewe, and Leo Spitzer, pp. 39–54. Hanover, NH: Dartmouth College Press.

Brockmeier, Jens. 2002. Introduction: Searching for cultural memory. *Culture and Psychology* 8(1): 5–14.

Brubaker, Rogers, and Frederick Cooper. 2000. Beyond "identity." *Theory and Society* 29(1): 1–47.

Bunton, Martin. 2007. *Colonial land policies in Palestine, 1917-1936*. Oxford, UK: Oxford University Press.

Burke, Peter. 2004. *What is cultural history?* Malden, MA: Polity Press.

Canaan, Taufik. 1936. Arabic magic bowls. *Journal of the Palestine Oriental Society* 16: 90-92.

———. 1935. The curse in Palestinian folklore. *Journal of the Palestine Oriental Society* 15: 235-279.

———. 1933. *The Palestinian Arab house: Its architecture and folklore*. Jerusalem: Syrian Orphanage Press.

———. 1927. *Mohammedan saints and sanctuaries in Palestine*. London: Luzac.

Casey, Edward S. 1987. *Remembering: A phenomenological study*. Bloomington: Indiana University Press.

Christelow, Allan. 1994. The art of autobiography in post-independence Algeria. *Maghreb Review* 19(3–4): 257–265.

Clifford, James, and George E. Marcus, eds. 1986. *Writing culture: The poetics and politics of ethnography.* Berkley: University of California Press.

Cobban, Helena. 1984. *The PLO: People, power and politics.* Cambridge: Cambridge University Press.

Cohen, Abner. 1965. *Arab border-villages in Israel: A study of continuity and change in social organization.* Manchester, UK: Manchester University Press.

Cohen, Chester. 1985. *Shtetl finder: Jewish communities in the nineteenth and early twentieth centuries in the pale of settlement of Russia and Poland, and in Lithuania, Latvia, Galicia, and Bukovina, with names of residents.* Los Angeles: Periday.

Cohen, Hillel. 2008. *Army of shadows: Palestinian collaboration with Zionism, 1917–1948.* Berkeley: University of California Press.

Cohen, Ilise. 2007. Kfar Shalem: The village of wholeness is being broken apart." *Sephardic Heritage Update* 290. Available at http://groups.google.com/group/newprofile /browse_thread/thread/c6ab3af959a11bbd?pli=1

Cohen, Shaul Ephraim. 1993. *The politics of planting: Israeli-Palestinian competition for control of land in the Jerusalem periphery.* Chicago: University of Chicago Press.

Collins, John. 2004. *Occupied by memory: The intifada generation and the Palestinian state of emergency.* New York: New York University Press.

Comaroff, John, and Jean Comaroff. 1992. *Ethnography and the historical imagination.* Boulder, CO: Westview Press.

Cooke, Miriam. 1992. Arab women writers. In *The Cambridge history of Arabic literature: Modern Arabic literature,* ed. Muhammad Mustafa Badawi, pp. 443–462. Cambridge, UK: Cambridge University Press.

Creswell, Robyn. 2009. Eloquent phantom: Tayeb Salih's search for an elusive present. *Harper's Magazine* 319(1910): 75–79.

Al-Dabbagh, Mustafa Murad. 1965. *Biladuna Filastin* [Our country Palestine]. Ten volumes. Beirut, Lebanon: Dar al-Tali'ah.

al-Dajjani, Amin Hafiz. 1996. *Jabhat al-tarbiya wal-ta'lim wa nidaluha did al-isti'mar: Al-Baramij wa al-manahij wa al-mu'allimun wa al-tullab 'abr arba'a 'uhud* [The education front and the battle against colonialism: The programs, curricula, instructors, and students over the course of four eras]. West Bank: n.p.

Dalen, B. van, R. S. Humphreys, Manuela Marín, Ann K. S. Lambton, Christine Woodhead, M. Athar Ali, J. O. Hunwick, G.S.P. Freeman-Grenville, I. Proudfoot, and F. C. de Blois. 2009. Ta'rikh. In *Encyclopedia of Islam,* 2nd ed., eds. P. Bearman, T. Bianquis, C. E. Bosworth, E. van Donzel, and W. P. Heinrichs. Brill Online, http://www.brill online.nl/subscriber/entry?entry=islam_COM-1184. Accessed September 2, 2009.

Dalman, Gustaf. 1928–1942. *Arbeit und Sitte in Palästina* [Work and customs in Palestine]. Eight volumes. Gutersloh: C. Bertelsmann.

Al-Damin, Rawan, and Dina al-Damin. 1997. *Al-tahjir fi dhakirat al-tufula: Shahadat Filastiniyya hayya* [The displacement in the memory of childhood: Living Palestinian witnesses]. West Bank: al-Lajna al-Wataniyya al-Filastiniyya lil-Tarbiya wal-Thaqafa wal-'Ulum.

Darwaza, Muhammad 'Izzat. 1993. *Khamsa wa tis'un 'aman fi al-hayat: Mudhakkirat wa tasjilat* (Ninety-five years of life: Memories and recordings]. Jerusalem: Arab Thought Forum.

Darwish, Mahmud. 1998. "The Palestinian people's appeal on the 50th anniversary of the Nakba." Delivered May 14.

———. 1973. *Selected poems of Mahmoud Darwish.* Cheshire, UK: Carcanet Press.

Davies, Philip R. 1992. *In search of "ancient Israel."* Sheffield, UK: JSOT Press.

Davis, Charles, and Henry Louis Gates Jr. 1985. *The slave's narrative.* Oxford, UK: Oxford University Press.

Davis, Rochelle. 2007a. Mapping the past, re-creating the homeland: Memories of village places in pre-1948 Palestine. In *Nakba: Palestine, 1948, and the claims of memory*, eds. Ahmad Sa'di and Lila Abu-Lughod. New York: Columbia University Press.

———. 2007b. al-Kutub al-tidhkariyya al-Filastiniyya wal-siyar al-dhatiyya al-jama'iyya [Palestinian memory books and collective autobiographies]. In *Dirasat fi al-tarikh al-ijtima'i li-bilad al-sham* [Studies in the social history of the Levant], ed. Salim Tamari and Issam Nassar, pp. 153–180. Ramallah, West Bank: Institute of Jerusalem Studies.

———. 2004. Peasant narratives: Memorial book sources for Jerusalem village history. *Jerusalem Quarterly* (20): 62–72.

———. 2002. The attar of history: Palestinian narratives of life before 1948. Ph.D. thesis, University of Michigan.

———. 1999a. The growth of the western communities. In *Jerusalem 1948: The Arab neighbourhoods and their fate in the war*, ed. Salim Tamari, pp. 32–73. Jerusalem: Institute of Jerusalem Studies and Badil Resource Center for Palestinian Residency and Refugee Rights.

———. 1999b. Ottoman Jerusalem. In *Jerusalem 1948: The Arab neighbourhoods and their fate in the war*, ed. Salim Tamari, pp. 10–31. Jerusalem: Institute of Jerusalem Studies and Badil Resource Center for Palestinian Residency and Refugee Rights.

De Certeau, Michel. 1984. *The practice of everyday life.* Berkeley: University of California Press.

De Certeau, Michel, Luce Giard, and Tom Conley. 1997. *Culture in the plural*, trans. Tom Conley, ed. Giard Luce. Minneapolis: University of Minnesota Press.

Deeb, Lara. 2006. *An enchanted modern: Gender and public piety in Shi'i Lebanon.* Princeton, NJ: Princeton University Press.

Diab, Imtiaz, and Ziyad Fahoum. 1990. *Hikayat qarya: Qura Filastin al-mudammara 'am 1948 fi mintaqat al-Quds* [Story of a village: Destroyed Palestinian villages in

1948 in the Jerusalem area]. Beirut, Lebanon: al-Mu'assasa al-'Arabiyya lil-Dirasat wa al-Nashr.

Dinnematin, Gilles (dir.). 1987. *Does the cactus have a soul?* France: La Boîte à images.

Dirks, Nicholas B. 1992. Introduction: Colonialism and culture. In *Colonialism and culture*, ed. Nicholas B. Dirks, pp. 1–26. Ann Arbor: University of Michigan Press.

Dirks, Nicholas B., Geoff Eley, and Sherry B. Ortner. 1994. Introduction. In *Culture/ power/history: A reader in contemporary social theory*, ed. Nicholas B. Dirks, Geoff Eley, and Sherry B. Ortner, pp. 3–47. Princeton, NJ: Princeton University Press.

Doumani, Beshara. 1995. *Rediscovering Palestine: Merchants and peasants in Jabal Nablus, 1700–1900.* Berkeley: University of California Press.

Dumper, Michael. 1997. *The politics of Jerusalem since 1967.* New York: Columbia University Press.

———. 1994. *Islam and Israel: Muslim religious endowments and the Jewish state.* Washington, DC: Institute for Palestine Studies.

Ego, Beate. 2009. Jabne. *Brill's New Pauly*, ed. Hubert Cancik and Helmuth Schneider. Brill Online. Available at http://www.brill.nl/brillsnewpauly

Eickelman, Dale. 1997. Tardjama: In literature. In *Encyclopedia of Islam*, Vol. 9, 2nd ed., ed. H.A.R. Gibb, pp. 224–225. Leiden, Netherlands: E. J. Brill.

Enderwitz, Susanne. 1999. The mission of the Palestinian autobiographer. In *Conscious voices: Concepts of writing in the Middle East: Proceedings of the Berne symposium, July 1997*, ed. Stephan Guth, Priska Furrer, and J. Christoph Bürgel. Beirut, Lebanon: Orient-Institut der Deutschen Morgenländischen Gesellschaft.

Eph'al, Israel. 1982. *The ancient Arabs: Nomads on the borders of the fertile crescent, 9th–5th centuries BC.* Jerusalem: Magnes Press, Hebrew University.

Esber, Rosemarie M. 2008. *Under the cover of war: The Zionist expulsion of the Palestinians.* Alexandria, VA: Arabicus Books & Media.

Esposito, John. 1998. *Islam and politics*, 4th ed. Syracuse, NY: Syracuse University Press.

Evans, Ben. 2007, April 26. Israeli Forest honors Coretta Scott King. Associated Press.

Falah, Ghazi. 1989. *Al-Filastiniyyun al-mansiyyun: 'Arab al-naqab, 1906–1986* [The forgotten Palestinians: Arabs of the Negev, 1906–1986]. al-Tayiba, Israel: Markaz Ihya' al-Turath al-'Arabi.

Farah, Randa. 1998. Dhikrayat tufula fi Haifa [Memories of a childhood in Haifa]. In *Al-Jana al-Arabi*, Vol. 6. Beirut, Lebanon: Arab Resource Center for Popular Arts.

Feldman, Ilana. 2008. *Governing Gaza: Bureaucracy, authority, and the work of rule, 1917–1967.* Durham, NC: Duke University Press.

———. 2007. Difficult distinctions: Refugee law, humanitarian practice, and political identification in Gaza. *Cultural Anthropology* 22(1): 129–169.

———. 2006. Home as a refrain: Remembering and living displacement in Gaza. *History & Memory* 18(2): 10–47.

Felman, Shoshana, and Dori Laub. 1992. *Testimony: Crises of witnessing in literature, psychoanalysis, and history*. New York: Routledge.

Fendel, Hillel. 2007, December 25. Kfar Shalem: Government erred in 1948, residents pay price today. *Arutz Sheva*, http://www.israelnationalnews.com/News/News.aspx/124705

Fentress, James, and Chris Wickham. 1992. *Social memory*. Oxford, UK: Blackwell.

Fields, Karen. 1994. What one cannot remember mistakenly. In *Memory and history: Essays on recalling and interpreting experience*, eds. Jaclyn Jeffrey and Glenace Ecklund Edwall, pp. 89–106. Lanham, MD: University Press of America.

Firestone, Ya'akov. 1990. The land-equalizing *Musha'* Village: A reassessment. In *Ottoman Palestine, 1800–1914*, ed. Gad Gilbar. Leiden, Netherlands: E. J. Brill.

Fischbach, Michael R. 2008. *Jewish property claims against Arab countries*. New York: Columbia University Press.

———. 2003. *Records of dispossession: Palestinian refugee property and the Arab-Israeli conflict*. New York: Columbia University Press.

Fischer, A. 2009. Kahtan. In *Encyclopaedia of Islam*, 2nd ed., ed. P. Bearman, T. Bianquis, C. E. Bosworth, E. van Donzel, and W. P. Heinrichs. Brill Online. Available at http://www.brillonline.nl/subscriber/entry?entry=islam_COM-1184

Fisk, Robert. 2008, November 1. Arabs have to rely on Britain and Israel for their history. *The Independent*. Available at http://www.independent.co.uk/opinion/commentators/fisk/robert-fiskrsquos-world-arabs-have-to-rely-on-britain-and-israel-for-their-history-981765.html

Fleischmann, Ellen. 2003. *The nation and its "new" women: The Palestinian women's movement, 1920–1948*. Berkeley: University of California Press.

———. 1999. Women's movements in the Middle East. In *Social history of women and gender in the modern Middle East*, eds. Margaret Lee Meriwether and Judith E. Tucker, p. 220. Boulder, CO: Westview Press.

———. 1998. Young women in the city: Mandate memories. *Jerusalem Quarterly File* 2: 31–39.

Fluehr-Lobban, Carolyn. 1993. Toward a theory of Arab-Muslim women as activists and scholars in secular and religious movements. *Arab Studies Quarterly* 15: 87–107.

Forman, Geremy. 2002. Settlement of the title in the Galilee: Dowson's colonial guiding principles. *Israel Studies* 7(3): 61–83.

Forty, Adrian, and Susanne Küchler. 1999. *The art of forgetting*. Oxford, UK: Berg.

Foucault, Michel. 1984. What is an author? In *The Foucault reader*, ed. Michel Foucault and Paul Rainbow. New York: Pantheon Books.

———. 1980. *Power/knowledge: Selected interviews and other writings, 1972–1977*, ed. and trans. Colin Gordon. New York: Pantheon.

———. 1978. History of sexuality, Vol. 1, trans. Michael Hurley. New York: Pantheon.

Freij, Jamileh. 1993. Growing up in Jerusalem. *Middle East Report* 182(May-June): 15–17.

Frisch, Michael H. 1994. American history and the structures of collective memory: A modest exercise in empirical iconography. In *Memory and history: Essays on recalling and interpreting experience*, ed. Jaclyn Jeffrey and Glenace Edwall, pp. 33–60. Lanham, MD: University Press of America.

Furlonge, Geoffrey Warren, Sir. 1969. *Palestine is my country: The story of Musa Alami*. New York: Praeger.

Gabbay, Rony E. 1959. *A political study of the Arab-Jewish conflict: The Arab refugee problem, a case study*. Geneva, Switzerland: E. Droz.

Geertz, Clifford. 1983. *Local knowledge: Further essays in interpretive anthropology*. New York: Basic Books.

———. 1973/2000. *The interpretation of cultures: Selected essays*. New York: Basic Books.

Gellner, Ernest. 1983. *Nations and nationalism*. Oxford, UK: Blackwell.

General Union of Palestinian Women. The national strategy for the advancement of Palestinian women: 3. In the legal realm. Available from http://www.gupw.net/pub lications/st5.htm

Ghosheh, Subhi. 1988. *Shamsuna lan taghib* [Our sun will not set]. Kuwait: n.p.

Ghuri, Imil. 1972. *Filastin 'abra sittin 'aman* [Palestine over sixty years]. Beirut, Lebanon: Dar al-Nahar, 1972.

———. 1959. *15 Ayyar 1948: Dirasa siyasiyya 'ilmiyya murakkaza 'an al-asbab al-haqiqiyya li-nakbat Filastin* [15 May 1948: A scientific political study focused on the true reasons for the Nakba in Palestine]. Beirut, Lebanon: Dar al-Nashr al-'Arabiyya, 1959.

Glavanis, Kathy, and Pandeli Glavanis, eds. 1989. *The rural Middle East: Peasant lives and modes of production*. London: Zed Books.

Gluck, Sherna. 1977. What's so special about women? Women's oral history. *Frontiers: A Journal of Women Studies* 2(2): 3–17.

Gluck, Sherna Berger, and Daphne Patai, eds. 1991. *Women's words: The feminist practice of oral history*. New York: Chapman and Hall.

Golan, Arnon. 1997. The transformation of abandoned Arab rural areas. *Israel Studies* 2(1): 94–110.

Gordon, Edmund W., Faynesse Miller, and David Rollock. 1990. *Educational Researcher* 19(3): 14–19.

Gorkin, Michael, and Rafiqa Othman. 1996. *Three mothers, three daughters: Palestinian women's stories*. Berkeley: University of California Press.

Graham-Brown, Sarah. 1989. Agriculture and labour transformation in Palestine. In *The rural Middle East: Peasant lives and modes of production*, ed. Kathy and Pandeli Glavanis, pp. 53–69. London: Zed Books.

Granqvist, Hilma. 1947/1975. *Birth and childhood among the Arabs: Studies in a Muhammadan village in Palestine*. New York: AMS Press.

———. 1931–1935/1975. *Marriage conditions in a Palestinian village*. New York: AMS Press.

Green, Arnold H. 1997. Family trees and archival documents: A case study of Jerusalem's

Bayt al-Dajani. In *Arab and Islamic studies: In honor of Marsden Jones*, eds. Thabet Abdullah, Bernard O'Kane, Hamdi Sakkut, and Muhammad Serag, pp. 95–110. Cairo, Egypt: American University in Cairo Press.

Greenberg, Ela. 2004. Educating Muslim girls in Mandatory Jerusalem. *International Journal of Middle East Studies* 36(1): 1–19.

Groiss, Arnon, and Yohanan Manor. 2001. *Jews, Israel and peace in Palestinian school textbooks: A survey of the textbooks published by the Palestinian National Authority in the years 2000-2001*. Israel: Center for Monitoring the Impact of Peace. Available at http://www.impact-se.org/docs/reports/PA/PA2001.pdf

Gugelberger, Georg, and Michael Kearney. 1991. Voices for the voiceless: Testimonial literature in Latin America. *Latin American Perspectives* 18(3): 3–14.

Gusdorf, Georges. 1980. Conditions and limits of autobiography. In *Autobiography: Essays theoretical and critical*, ed. James Olney, p. 360. Princeton, NJ: Princeton University Press.

Habash, Dalia, and Terry Rempel. 1999. Assessing Palestinian property in the city. In *Jerusalem 1948: The Arab neighbourhoods and their fate in the war*, ed. Salim Tamari. Jerusalem: Institute of Jerusalem Studies and BADIL Resource Center.

Habib, Jasmin. 2007. "We were living in a different country": Palestinian nostalgia and the future past. In *Mixed towns, trapped communities: Historical narratives, spatial dynamics, gender relations and cultural encounters in Palestinian-Israeli towns*, eds. Daniel Monterescu and Dan Rabinowitz, pp. 65–83. Burlington, VT: Ashgate.

Habiby, Emile. 1989. *The secret life of Saeed, the ill-fated pessoptimist: A Palestinian who became a citizen of Israel*. London: Readers International.

Hadawi, Sami. 1970. *Village statistics, 1945: A classification of land and area ownership in Palestine*. Beirut, Lebanon: Palestine Liberation Organization Research Center.

———. 1957. *Land ownership in Palestine*. New York: Palestine Arab Refugee Office.

Hadawi, Sami, and A. A. Kubursi. 1998. *Palestinian rights and losses in 1948: A comprehensive study*. London: Saqi Books.

Al-Haj, Majid. 1988. The changing Arab kinship structure: The effect of modernization in an urban community. *Economic Development and Cultural Change* 36(2): 237–258.

Hajjar, Lisa. 2001. Human rights in Israel/Palestine: The history and politics of a movement. *Journal of Palestine Studies* 30(4): 21–38.

Halabi, Awad. 2006. The transformation of the prophet Moses festival in Jerusalem, 1917–1937: From local and Islamic to modern and nationalist celebration. Ph.D. Dissertation, University of Toronto.

Halabi, Osama. 1993. *Baladiyyat al-Quds al-'Arabiyya* [Jerusalem Arab municipality]. Jerusalem: Palestinian Academic Society for the Study of International Affairs.

Halaby, Samia A. 1999. "Rana Bishara in Tarsheeha." Available at http://www.art.net/samia/pal/palart/rana/rana.html. Accessed August 7, 2009.

Halbwachs, Maurice. 1992. *On collective memory*. Chicago: University of Chicago Press.

Hamadina, Muhammad Sa'id Sabir. 1998. 'Asira al-Shamaliyya . . . Turath wa 'amal ['Asira al-Shamaliyya . . . Heritage and hope]. Amman, Jordan: n.p.

Hammer, Juliane. 2005. *Palestinians born in exile: Diaspora and the search for a homeland.* Austin: University of Texas Press.

———. 2001. Homeland Palestine: Lost in the catastrophe of 1948 and recreated in memories and art. In *Crisis and memory in Islamic societies: Proceedings of the third summer academy of the working group modernity and Islam held at the Orient Institute of the German Oriental Society in Beirut,* ed. Angelika Neuwirth and Andreas Pflitsch, pp. 453–482. Würzburg, Germany: Ergon Verlag.

Hammond, Marle. 2001. Review of *The object of memory: Arab and Jew narrate the Palestinian village* by Susan Sloymovics. *Journal of Palestine Studies* 31(1): 87.

Al-Hanna, Nizar. 2000. The cleansing of al Bassa. Available from http://www.palestineremembered.com/Acre/al-Bassa/Story103.html

Hannun, Sara. 1998. *Tadhakkurat al-marhuma Sara Hannun* [Memoir of Sara Hannun]. Birzeit, West Bank: CRDPS Birzeit University.

Al-Hardan, Anaheed. 2008. Remembering the catastrophe: Uprooted histories and the grandchildren of the *Nakba.* In *Auto/biography Yearbook,* ed. Andrew Sparkes. Oxford, UK: Clio Press.

Hart, Janet. 1996. *New voices in the nation: Women and the Greek resistance, 1941–1964.* Ithaca, NY: Cornell University Press.

Hasso, Frances. 2005. *Resistance, repression, and gender politics in occupied Palestine and Jordan.* Syracuse, NY: Syracuse University Press.

———. 2000. Modernity and gender in Arab accounts of the 1948 and 1967 defeats. *International Journal of Middle Eastern Studies* 32(4): 491–510.

Hay'at al-Mawsu'ah al-Filastiniyya 1984. *Al-Mawsu'a al-Filastiniyya* [The Palestinian encyclopedia]. Damascus, Syria: Hay'at al-Mawsu'a al-Filastiniyya.

Hayden, Dolores. 1995. *The power of place: Urban landscapes as public history.* Cambridge, MA: MIT Press.

Haykal, Yusif. 1989. *Rabi' al-hayat* [Springtime of life]. Amman, Jordan: Dar al-Jalil.

———. 1988. *Ayyam al-siba: Suwar min al-hayat wa safahat min al-tarikh* [Days of youth: Snapshots of life and pages from history]. Amman, Jordan: Dar al-Jalil.

Hirsch, Marianne. 2002. Marked by memory: Feminist reflections on trauma and transmission. In *Extremities: Trauma, testimony, and community,* ed. Nancy K. Miller and Jason Daniel Tougaw. Champaign: University of Illinois Press.

Hobsbawm, Eric. 1983. Introduction: Inventing traditions. In *The invention of tradition,* ed. Eric Hobsbawm and Terrence Ranger. Cambridge, UK: Cambridge University Press.

Hochberg, Gil. 2007. *In spite of partition: Jews, Arabs, and the limits of separatist imagination.* Princeton, NJ: Princeton University Press.

Hoffman, Adina. 2009. *My happiness bears no relation to happiness: A poet's life in the Palestinian century.* New Haven: Yale University Press.

Hourani, Albert. 1991. *A history of the Arab peoples.* Cambridge, MA: Belknap Press.

———. 1968. Ottoman reform and the politics of the notables. In *Conference on the beginnings of modernization in the Middle East in the nineteenth century,* ed. William Roe Polk and Richard L. Chambers, p. 427. Chicago: University of Chicago Press.

Al-Hout, Shafiq. 1998. Yafa: Madinat al-'inad [Jaffa: The city of stubbornness]. *Al-Karmel* 55–56: 130–139.

Hoyland, Robert G. 2001. *Arabia and the Arabs: From the bronze age to the coming of Islam.* New York: Routledge.

Huart, Clement. 2009. Shith [Sheeth]. In *Encyclopedia of Islam,* Vol. 9, 2nd ed., ed. C. E. Bosworth. Leiden, Netherlands: E. J. Brill.

Humphreys, R. Stephen. 1991. *Islamic history: A framework for inquiry,* rev. ed. Princeton, NJ: Princeton University Press.

Humphries, Isabelle. 2008a. Listening to the displaced narrative: Politics, power and grassroots communication amongst Palestinians inside Israel. *Middle East Journal of Culture and Communication* 1(2): 180.

———. 2008b. The dust and stones of al-Birweh. *Washington Report on Middle East Affairs* 27(8): 17–18.

———. 2007. Looking back to look forward: A call for international commemoration of Nakba 60. *Washington Report on Middle East Affairs* 26(1): 18.

Hurani, Faysal. 1998. Harb al-layl wal-nahar [War of day and night]. *Al-Karmel* 55–56: 149–161.

Husseini, Mohammed Amin. 1937. *Memorandum submitted by the Arab higher committee to the permanent mandates commission and the secretary of state for the colonies, dated July 23d 1937.* Jerusalem: Commercial Press.

Hutchinson, John. 1987. *The dynamics of cultural nationalism: The Gaelic revival and the creation of the Irish nation state.* London: Allen & Unwin.

Hutton, Patrick H. 1993. *History as an art of memory.* Lebanon, NH: University Press of New England.

Huzayin, Salah. 1998. al-Balda allati lam azurha [The town that I never visited]. *Al-Karmel* 55–56.

Ibn Rabi'ah, Labid. 1974. *The golden ode,* trans. William Polk. Chicago: University of Chicago Press.

Idris, Kirsten. 1998. *Ma alladhi taghayyar? mulahazat awwaliyya hawl al-tarikh al-shafawi li-dhakirat al-iqtila' al-Filastini fi al-'am 1948* [What has changed? Initial impressions about oral history in recalling the Palestinian removal of 1948]. Al-Jana al-Arabi. Beirut, Lebanon: Arab Resource Center for Popular Arts.

Irshaid, Alex A. Ala. Al-charcha ya Walagia ala al-charcha [To the charcha, you Walaji, to the charcha]. 2001. Available from http://www.palestineremembered.com/Jerusalem/al-Walaja/Story385.html. Accessed June 2002.

Issa, Mahmoud. 1997. Decoding the silencing process in modern Palestinian historiography. Paper presented at Worlds & Visions, Perspectives on the Middle East Today conference, December 5–7, 1997, Aarhus University,Aarhus, Denmark.

'Issa, Mahmoud. 1996. Filastiniyyun fi al-shatat: Tajarib wa shahadat [Palestinians in the diaspora: Experiences and testimonies]. *Samid al-Iqtisadi* (105).

Jabra, Jabra Ibrahim. 1995. *The first well: A Bethlehem boyhood*, trans. Issa Boullata. Fayetteville: University of Arkansas Press.

———. 1993. *Al-bi'r al-ula* [The first well]. Beirut, Lebanon: Mu'assasa al-'Arabiyya lil-Dirasat wal-Nashr.

Jackson, Peter. 1989. *Maps of meaning: An introduction to cultural geography*. Boston: Unwin Hyman.

Jawhariyya, Wasif. 2005. *Al-Quds al-intidabiyya fi al-mudhakkarat al-Jawhariyya* [British mandate Jerusalem in the Jawharieh memoirs], Vol. 2, ed. 'Issam Nassar and Salim Tamari. Jerusalem: Institute for Palestine Studies.

Jayyusi, Lena. 2007. Iterability, cumulativity, and presence: The relational figures of Palestinian memory. In *Nakba: Palestine, 1948, and the claims of memory*, ed. Ahmad Sa'di and Lila Abu-Lughod. New York: Columbia University Press.

Jayyusi, Salma Khadra, ed. 1992. *Anthology of modern Palestinian literature*. New York: Columbia University Press.

Jeffrey, Jaclyn, and Glenace Edwall, eds. 1994. *Memory and history: Essays on recalling and interpreting experience*. Lanham, MD: University Press of America.

Jewish Agency for Palestine. 1947. *The Jewish case before the Anglo-American committee of inquiry on Palestine: Statements and memoranda*. Jerusalem: Jewish Agency for Palestine.

Jiryis, Sabri. 1976. *The Arabs in Israel*. New York: Monthly Review Press.

———. 1973. The legal structure for the expropriation and absorption of Arab lands in Israel. *Journal of Palestine Studies* 2(4): 82–104.

Jones, Christina. 1975. *The untempered wind: Forty years in Palestine*. London: Longman.

Kabha, Mustafa. 2007. *The Palestinian press as shaper of public opinion: 1929–1939*. London: Vallentine Mitchell.

———, ed. 2006. *Nahu siyaghat riwaya tarikhiyya lil-nakba: Ishkaliyyat wa tahadiyyat* [Toward a historical narrative of the *nakba*: Complexities and challenges]. Haifa, Israel: Mada al-Carmel.

Kamal, Hatim. 1995. *Tadhakkurat* [Memoir]. Birzeit,West Bank: Birzeit University,CRDPS.

Kamen, Charles. 2005. *The 2008 Israel integrated census of population and housing: Basic conception and procedure*. Jerusalem: Central Bureau of Statistics. Available at http://www.cbs.gov.il/mifkad/census2008_e.pdf. Accessed September 17, 2009.

Kanaana, Sharif. 2000. *Still on vacation! The eviction of the Palestinian in 1948*. Jerusalem: SHAML: Palestinian Diaspora and Refugee Centre.

Kanaaneh, Rhoda Ann. 2002. *Birthing the nation: Strategies of Palestinian women in Israel*. Berkeley: University of California Press.

Kanafani, Ghassan. 1987. *'A'id ila Haifa* [Return to Haifa]. Beirut, Lebanon: La Fondation Culturelle Ghassan Kanafani.

———. 1980. *Thawrat 36–39 fi Filastin: Khalfiyya wa tafasil wa tahlil* [The revolution of 36–39 in Palestine: Background, details, and analysis]. Jerusalem, West Bank: Wikalat Abu 'Arafa lil-Sihafa.

———. 1966. *Adab al-muqawama fi Filastin al-muhtalla, 1948–1966* [Literature of resistance in occupied Palestine, 1948–1966]. Beirut, Lebanon: Dar al-Adab.

Kark, Ruth, and Dov Gavish. 1993. The cadastral mapping of Palestine, 1858–1928. *The Geographical Journal* 159(1): 70–80.

Karmi, Ghada. 1999. After the nakba: An experience of exile in England. *Journal of Palestine Studies* 28(3): 52–63.

———. 1998, April 25. Leaving the lemon tree. *The Tablet*. Available from http://www.thetablet.co.uk/article/6619. Accessed June 3, 1999.

———. 1994. The 1948 exodus: A family story. *Journal of Palestine Studies* 23(2): 31–40.

Kattan, Victor. 2009. *International law and the origins of the Arab-Israeli conflict 1891–1949.* New York: Pluto Press.

Katz, Kimberly. 2005. *Jordanian Jerusalem: Holy places and national spaces.* Gainesville: University Press of Florida.

———. 1998. *School books and tourism brochures: Constructions of identity in Jordan.* Unpublished paper delivered at Middle East Studies Association Annual Meeting, Chicago.

Kayyal, Mahmoud. 2001. Tas-hih ba'd al-ma'lumat al-warida 'an al-Birwa [Corrections to some of the information about al-Birwa]. Available from http://www.palestineremembered.com/Acre/al-Birwa/Story667.html

Kayyali, A. W. 1978. *Palestine: A modern history.* London: Croom Helm.

Al-Kayyali, 'Abd al-Wahhab. 1981. *Tarikh Filastin al-hadith* [Modern Palestinian history], 8th ed. Beirut, Lebanon: Al-Mu'assasa al-'Arabiyya lil-Dirasat wa al-Nashr.

Kenny, Michael G. 1999. A place for memory: The interface between individual and collective history. *Comparative Studies in Society and History* 41(3): 420–437.

Khader, Hassan. 1997. Confessions of a Palestinian returnee. *Journal of Palestine Studies* 27(1): 85–95.

Khalaf, Issa. 1997. The Effect of Socioeconomic Change on Arab Societal Collapse in Mandate Palestine. *International Journal of Middle East Studies* 29(1): 93–112.

———. 1991. *Politics in Palestine: Arab factionalism and social disintegration, 1939–1948.* Albany: State University of New York Press.

Al-Khalidi, 'Anbara Salaam. 1997. *Jawla fi al-dhikrayat bayn Lubnan wa Filastin* [A trip in memory between Lebanon and Palestine], 2nd ed. Beirut, Lebanon: Dar al-Nahar.

Khalidi, Rashid. 2009. *Sowing crisis: The cold war and American dominance in the Middle East.* Boston: Beacon Press.

———. 2006, October 1. Unwritten history: The challenges of writing Palestinian history reflect the larger challenges facing the Palestinians' quest for statehood. *The Boston Globe*, p. D-1.

———. 2001. The Palestinians and 1948: The underlying causes of failure. In *The war for Palestine: Rewriting the history of 1948*, ed. Eugene L. Rogan and Avi Shlaim, pp. 12–36. New York: Cambridge University Press.

———. 1997. *Palestinian identity: The construction of modern national consciousness.* New York: Columbia University Press.

Khalidi, Tarif. 1981. Palestinian historiography: 1900–1948. *Journal of Palestine Studies* 10(3): 59–76.

Khalidi, Walid. 1993. Benny Morris and before their diaspora. *Journal of Palestine Studies* 22(3): 106–119.

———, ed. 1992. *All that remains: The Palestinian villages occupied and depopulated by Israel in 1948.* Washington, DC: Institute for Palestine Studies.

———, ed. 1984. *Before their diaspora: A photographic history of the Palestinians, 1876–1948.* Washington, DC: Institute for Palestine Studies.

———. 1971. *From haven to conquest.* Washington, DC: Institute for Palestine Studies.

———. 1961. Plan Dalet: The Zionist master plan for the conquest of Palestine. *Middle East Forum* 37(9): 22–28.

Al-Khalidi, Walid Raghib. 1992a. Al-Kulliya al-ʿArabiyya fi al-Quds: Jiʾna lak ya Sharq al-ʾUrdunn jiʾna lak [The Arab college in Jerusalem: We came to you, oh East Jordan, we came to you]. *al-Quds al-Sharif* 87: 44–53.

———. 1992b. Al-Kulliya al-ʿArabiyya fi al-Quds: Sana ula intermediat [The Arab College in Jerusalem: First year intermediate]. *al-Quds al-Sharif* 86: 39–49.

———. 1991. Al-Kulliya al-ʿArabiyya fi al-Quds [The Arab College in Jerusalem]. *al-Quds al-Sharif* 78: 40–52.

Khalili, Laleh. 2007. *Heroes and martyrs of Palestine: The politics of national commemoration.* New York: Cambridge University Press.

———. 2005. Virtual nation: Palestinian cyberculture in Lebanese camps. In *Palestine, Israel, and the politics of popular culture*, ed. Rebecca L. Stein and Ted Swedenburg, pp. 126–149. Durham, NC: Duke University Press.

———. 2004. Grassroots commemorations: Remembering the land in the camps of Lebanon, *Journal of Palestine Studies* 34(1): 5–22.

Khasawneh, Diala. 2001. *Memoirs engraved in stone: Palestinian urban mansions.* Ramallah, West Bank: Riwaq-Centre for Architectural Conservation and the Institute of Jerusalem Studies.

Khashan, Matar. 2002. *Kafr Kanna: Al-Jalil bayn al-madi wa al-hadir* [Kafr Kanna: The Galilee between the past and the present]. Damascus, Syria: Dar al-Shajara.

Khazzoom, Loolwa, ed. 2003. *The flying camel: Essays on identity by women of North African and Middle Eastern Jewish heritage.* New York: Seal Press.

Khleifi, Michel, dir. 1985. *Ma'loul celebrates its destruction* [*Ma'loul tahtafil bidimariha*]. Brussels, Belgium: Marisa Films.

Khouri, Yusef. 1976. *Al-Sahafa al-'Arabiyya fi Filastin: 1876–1948* [The Arabic press in Palestine: 1876–1948]. Beirut, Lebanon: Institute for Palestine Studies.

Khoury, Elias. 1998. *Bab al-shams* [Gate of the sun]. Beirut, Lebanon: Dar al-Adab.

Kilpatrick, Hilary. 1991. Autobiography and classical Arabic literature. *Journal of Arabic Literature* 22(1): 1–20.

Klaus, Dorothee. 2003. *Palestinian refugees in Lebanon—Where to belong?* Berlin: Klaus Schwarz Verlag.

Klein, Kerwin Lee. 1995. In search of narrative mastery: Postmodernism and the people without history. *History and Theory* 34(4): 275–298.

Kluitenberg, Eric. 1999, July 21. Politics of cultural memory: Identity, belonging and necessity. Available at http://www.nettime.org/Lists-Archives/nettime-l-9907/msg000 83.html. Accessed May 4, 2002.

Knapp, Steven. 1989. Collective memory and the actual past. *Representations* 26: 123–149.

Kotre, John N. 1996. *White gloves: How we create ourselves through memory.* New York: Norton.

Kretzmer, David. 1990. *The legal status of the Arabs in Israel.* Boulder, CO: Westview Press.

Krystall, Nathan. 1999. The fall of the new city. In *Jerusalem 1948: The Arab neighbourhoods and their fate in the war*, ed. Salim Tamari. Jerusalem: Institute of Jerusalem Studies and Badil Resource Center.

———. 1998. The de-Arabization of west Jerusalem 1947–1950. *Journal of Palestine Studies* 27(2): 5–22.

Kubursi, A. A. 1996. *Palestinian losses in 1948: The quest for precision.* Washington, DC: Center for Policy Analysis on Palestine.

Kugelmass, Jack, and Jonathan Boyarin. 1998. *From a ruined garden: The memorial books of Polish Jewry*, 2nd ed. Bloomington: Indiana University Press.

Al-Lajna al-'Arabiyya al-'Ulya, Great Britain, and Palestine Royal Commission. 1937. A memorandum submitted by the Arab Higher Committee to the Royal Commission on January 11, 1937. Jerusalem: Modern Press.

Langellier, Kristin, and Eric Peterson. 1993. Family storytelling as a strategy of social control. In *Narrative and social control: Critical perspectives*, ed. Dennis K. Mumby. Newbury Park, CA: Sage.

Latina Feminist Group. 2001. *Telling to live: Latina feminist testimonios.* Durham, NC: Duke University Press.

Lejeune, Philippe, and Paul John Eakin. 1988. *On autobiography.* Minneapolis: University of Minnesota Press.

Lemche, Niels Peter. 1991. *The Canaanites and their land: The tradition of the Canaanites.* Sheffield, UK: JSOT Press.

LeVine, Mark. 2005. The Palestinian press in Mandatory Jaffa: Advertising, nationalism, and the public sphere. In *Palestine, Israel, and the politics of popular culture*, ed. Rebecca L. Stein and Ted Swedenburg, pp. 51–76. Durham, NC: Duke University Press.

Lockman, Zachary. 2004. *Contending visions of the Middle East: The history and politics of orientalism*. Cambridge, UK: Cambridge University Press.

———. 1996. *Comrades and enemies: Arab and Jewish workers in Palestine, 1906–1948*. Berkeley: University of California Press.

Lowenthal, David. 1985. *The past is a foreign country*. New York: Cambridge University Press.

Al-Lubani, Hussein 'Ali. 2003. *Mu'jam asma' al-mudun wal-qura al-Filastiniyya wa tafseer ma'aniha* [Lexicon of Palestinian city and village names and explanations of their meanings]. Beirut, Lebanon: Markaz Bahith lil-Dirasat.

Lustick, Ian. 1980. *Arabs in the Jewish state: Israel's control of a national minority*. Austin: University of Texas Press.

Lutfiyya, Abdulla M. 1966. *Baytin, a Jordanian village: A study of social institutions and social change in a folk community*. London: Mouton.

Lybarger, Loren. 2007. *Identity and religion in Palestine: The struggle between Islamism and secularism in the occupied territories*. Princeton, NJ: Princeton University Press.

Lynd, Staughton, Sam Bahour, and Alice Lynd. 1994. *Homeland: Oral histories of Palestine and Palestinians*. New York: Olive Branch Press.

Maddox, Gregory H., and Ernest M. Kongola. 2006. *Practicing history in central Tanzania: Writing, memory and performance*. Portsmouth, NH: Heinemann.

Mahmood, Saba. 2005. *Politics of piety: The Islamic revival and the feminist subject*. Princeton, NJ: Princeton University Press.

Makdisi, George. 1990. *The rise of humanism in classical Islam and the Christian West: With special reference to scholasticism*. Edinburgh, Scotland: Edinburgh University Press.

Malkki, Liisa H. 1995. *Purity and exile: Violence, memory, and national cosmology among Hutu refugees in Tanzania*. Chicago: University of Chicago Press.

———. 1992. National geographic: The rooting of peoples and the territorialization of national identity among scholars and refugees. *Cultural Anthropology* 7(1): 24–44.

Marin, Lynda. 1991. Speaking out together: Testimonials of Latin American women. *Latin American Perspectives* 18(3): 51–68.

Masalha, Nur. 1992. *Expulsion of the Palestinians: The concept of "transfer" in Zionist political thought, 1882–1948*. Washington, DC: Institute for Palestine Studies.

Al-Masri, Zaki Hasan. 1994. *Hadith al-dhikrayat: Fusul wa tarjama dhatiya mundhu 'am 1936–1994* [Narrative of memories: Chapters in an autobiography from 1936–1994]. Ramallah, West Bank: n.p.

Massad, Joseph. 2005. Liberating songs: Palestine put to music. In *Palestine, Israel, and the politics of popular culture*, ed. Rebecca L. Stein and Ted Swedenburg, pp. 175–201. Durham, NC: Duke University Press.

————. 2003. Liberating songs: Palestine put to music. *Journal of Palestine Studies* 32(3): 21–38.

————. 1997. Review: Reviving the discredited. *Journal of Palestine Studies* 27(1): 103–106.

————. 1996. Zionism's internal others: Israel and the oriental Jews. *Journal of Palestine Studies* 25(4): 53–68.

Mast, Edward. 2000. Sahmatah: Awakening history. *The Drama Review* 44(3): 113–130.

Al-Mawed, Hamad Said. 1999. *The Palestinian refugees in Syria: Their past, present and future.* Ottawa, Ontario: International Development Research Centre.

Al-Maw'id, Hamad. 1998. Khamsun 'aman min al-luju': al-Mukhayyam wal-huwiyya al-Filastiniyya [Fifty years of refuge: The camp and Palestinian identity]. *Samid al-Iqtisadi* (113).

McCarthy, Justin. 1990. *The population of Palestine: Population history and statistics of the late Ottoman period and the mandate.* New York: Columbia University Press.

McDonald, David. Forthcoming. *My voice is my weapon: Music, nationalism, and the poetics of Palestinian resistance.* Durham, NC: Duke University Press.

Miller, Ylana N. 1985. *Government and society in rural Palestine, 1920–1948.* Austin: University of Texas Press.

Milton-Edwards, Beverly. 1996. *Islamic politics in Palestine.* London: Tauris.

Mitchell, Timothy. 2002. *Rule of experts: Egypt, techno-politics, modernity.* Berkeley: University of California Press.

————. 2000. Introduction. In *Questions of modernity,* ed. Timothy Mitchell, pp. xi–xxvii. Minneapolis: University of Minnesota Press.

————. 1988. *Colonising Egypt.* Cambridge, UK: Cambridge University Press.

Mittwoch, E. 1999. Ayyam al-'Arab [Days of the Arabs]. In *Encyclopaedia of Islam,* Vol. 1, 2nd ed., ed. H.A.R. Gibb. Leiden, the Netherlands: E. J. Brill.

Monterescu, Daniel, and Dan Rabinowitz, eds. 2007. *Mixed towns, trapped communities: Historical narratives, spatial dynamics, gender relations and cultural encounters in Palestinian-Israeli towns.* Hampshire, UK: Ashgate.

Moors, Annelies. 2001. Presenting Palestine's population premonitions of the Nakba. *MIT Electronic Journal of Middle East Studies* 1.

————. 1995. *Women, property, and Islam: Palestinian experience, 1920–1990.* New York: Cambridge University Press.

————. 1994. Women and dower property in twentieth-century Palestine: The case of Jabal Nablus. *Islamic Law and Society* 1(3): 301–331.

Moors, Annelies, and Steven Machlin. 1987. Postcards of Palestine: Interpreting Images. *Critique of Anthropology* 7(2): 61–77.

Morris, Benny. 1987. *The birth of the Palestinian refugee problem, 1947–1949.* Cambridge, UK: Cambridge University Press.

Morrow, Phyllis. 1995. On shaky ground: Folklore, collaboration, and problematic outcomes. In *When our words return: Writing, hearing, and remembering oral traditions of Alaska and the Yukon*, ed. Phyllis Morrow and William S. Schneider, pp. 27–51. Logan: Utah State University Press.

Moughrabi, Fouad. 2001, October 1. Battle of the books in Palestine. *The Nation*. Available at http://www.thenation.com/article/battle-books-palestine

Al-Mudawwar, 'Abd al-Rahim, ed. 1999. Muqaddima (Introduction). In *Tadhakkurat 'Awda al-Ashhab: Safahat min al-dhakira al-Filastiniyya* (Memories of 'Awda al-Ashhab: Pages from Palestinian memory). Birzeit, West Bank: Birzeit University, CRDPS.

Muhawi, Ibrahim. 2009. *Contexts of language in Mahmoud Darwish*. Occasional papers. Washington, DC: Center for Contemporary Arab Studies.

Nadan, Amos. 2006. *The Palestinian peasant economy under the Mandate: A story of colonial bungling*. Cambridge, MA: Harvard University Press.

Najjar, Orayb Aref, and Kitty Warnock. 1992. *Portraits of Palestinian women*. Salt Lake City: University of Utah Press.

al-Nammari, Muhammad. 2000. A Jerusalemite story. Available from http://www.jerusalemites.org/memoirs/men/8.htm. Accessed February 27, 2000.

al-Nammari, Tahir Hashim. 1995. *Hayy al-Namamra fi al-Baq'a* [The Namamra neighborhood in Baq'a]. Jerusalem, West Bank: n.p.

Nassar, Issam. 2006a. *European portrayals of Jerusalem: Religious fascinations and colonialist imaginations*. Lewiston, NY: Edwin Mellen Press.

———. 2006b. 'Biblification' in the service of colonialism: Jerusalem in nineteenth-century photography. *Third Text* 20(3): 317–326.

———. 2002. Reflections on the writing of Palestinian identity. *Palestine-Israel Journal of Politics, Economics & Culture* 8/9(1): 24–37.

———. 1997. *Photographing Jerusalem: The image of the city in nineteenth-century photography*. Boulder: East European Monographs.

Nazzal, Nafez. 1978. *The Palestinian exodus from Galilee, 1948*. Beirut, Lebanon: Institute for Palestine Studies.

Neihardt, John Gneiseau. 1996. *Black Elk speaks*. Woodstock, IL: Dramatic Publishing.

New English Study Bible, The. 1977. Oxford Study Edition. New York: Cambridge University Press.

Al-Nimr, Ihsan. 1936–1961. *Tarikh Jabal Nablus wal-Balqa (History of Jabal Nablus and al-Balqa)*. 4 vols. Nablus. n.p.: n.p.

Nofal, Mamdouh, Fawaz Turki, Haidar Abdel Shafi, Inea Bushnaq, Yezid Sayigh, Shafiq al-Hout, Salma Khadra Jayyusi, and Musa Budeiri. 1998. Reflections on al-Nakba. *Journal of Palestine Studies* 28(1): 5–35.

Nora, Pierre. 1996. General introduction: Between memory and history. In *Realms of memory: Rethinking the French past*, Vol. 1: Conflicts and Divisions, ed. Pierre Nora and Lawrence D. Kritzman. New York: Columbia University Press.

———. 1989. Between memory and history: Les lieux de mémoire. *Representations* 26: 7–24.

Obenzinger, Hilton. 1999. *American Palestine: Melville, Twain, and the Holy Land mania.* Princeton, NJ: Princeton University Press.

Ochs, Elinor, and Lisa Capps. 1996. Narrating the self. *Annual Review of Anthropology* 25: 19–43.

Odeh, Nadja. 1998. Coded emotions: The description of nature in Arab women's autobiographies. In *Writing the self: Autobiographical writing in modern Arabic literature,* ed. Robin Ostle, Ed de Moor, and Stefan Wild. London: Saqi Books.

Ohnuki-Tierney, Emiko. 1990. *Culture through time: Anthropological approaches.* Stanford, CA: Stanford University Press.

Olney, James. 1985. "I was born": Slave narratives, their status as autobiography and as literature. In *The slave's narrative,* ed. Charles Davis and Henry Louis Gates Jr. Oxford, UK: Oxford University Press.

———. 1980. Autobiography and the cultural moment: A thematic, historical, and bibliographical introduction. In *Autobiography: Essays theoretical and critical,* ed. James Olney. Princeton, NJ: Princeton University Press.

Ong, Walter J. 1982. *Orality and literacy: The technologizing of the word.* New York: Methuen.

Ortner, Sherry B. 1989. *High religion: A cultural and political history of Sherpa Buddhism.* Princeton, NJ: Princeton University Press.

———. 1984. Theory in anthropology since the sixties. *Comparative Studies in Society and History* 26(1): 122–166.

Owen, Roger, ed. 1982. *Studies in the economic and social history of Palestine in the nineteenth and twentieth centuries.* Edwardsville: Southern Illinois University Press.

Ozick, Cynthia. 1989. *Metaphor and memory: Essays.* New York: Vintage International.

Palestine Government. 1945–1946/1991. *A survey of Palestine: Prepared in December 1945 and January 1946 for the information of the Anglo-American Committee of Inquiry.* Reprint. Vols. I, II, and Supplement. Beirut, Lebanon: Institute for Palestine Studies.

Papailias, Penelope. 2005. *Genres of recollection: Archival poetics and modern Greece,* ed. Ann Stoler and John L. Comaroff. New York: Palgrave Macmillian.

Pappé, Ilan. 2006. *The ethnic cleansing of Palestine.* Oxford, UK: Oneworld.

———. 2005. Post-Zionism and its popular cultures. In *Palestine, Israel, and the politics of popular culture,* ed. Rebecca L. Stein and Ted Swedenburg, pp. 77–95. Durham, NC: Duke University Press.

———. 2001. The Tantura case in Israel: The Katz research and trial. *Journal of Palestine Studies* 30(3): 19–39.

———. 1999. Were they expelled? The history, historiography and relevance of the Palestinian refugee problem. In *The Palestinian exodus, 1948–1998,* ed. Ghada Karmi and Eugene Cotran, pp. 37–62. Reading, UK: Garnet.

Parmenter, Barbara M. 1994. *Giving voice to stones: Place and identity in Palestinian literature.* Austin: University of Texas Press.

Passerini, Luisa. 1988. *Fascism in popular memory: The cultural experience of the Turin working class.* Cambridge, UK: Cambridge University Press.

Peteet, Julie. 2008, Fall. Stealing time. *Middle East Report Online* (248). Available at http://www.merip.org/mer/mer248/peteet.html. Accessed September 4, 2009.

———. 2005. *Landscape of hope and despair: Palestinian refugee camps.* Philadelphia: University of Pennsylvania Press.

———. 1999. Gender and sexuality: Belonging to the national and moral order. In *Hermeneutics and honor: Negotiating female "public" space in Islamic/ate societies*, ed. Asma Afsaruddin, pp. 70–88. Cambridge, MA: Harvard University Press.

———. 1995. Transforming trust: Dispossession and empowerment among Palestinian refugees. In *Mistrusting refugees*, ed. E. Valentine Daniel and John Chr Knudsen, pp. 168–186. Berkeley: University of California Press.

———. 1991. *Gender in crisis: Women and the Palestinian resistance movement.* New York: Columbia University Press.

Peters, Joan. 1984. *From time immemorial: The origins of the Arab-Jewish conflict over Palestine.* New York: Harper & Row.

Pollock, Della. 1998. Making history go. In *Exceptional spaces: Essays in performance and history*, ed. Della Pollock, p. 394. Chapel Hill: University of North Carolina Press.

Portelli, Alessandro. 1997. *The battle of Valle Giulia: Oral history and the art of dialogue.* Madison: University of Wisconsin Press.

———. 1991. *The death of Luigi Trastulli and other stories: Form and meaning in oral history.* Albany: State University of New York Press.

Porteous, J. Douglas. 1990. *Landscapes of the mind: Worlds of sense and metaphor.* Toronto: University of Toronto Press.

Provan, Iain W., V. Philips Long, and Tremper Longman. 2003. *A biblical history of Israel.* Louisville, KY: Westminster John Knox Press.

Qablawi, Sami. 2001. Who are the people of the Acre district? Available from http://www.palestineremembered.com/Acre/Umm-al-Faraj/Story610.html. Accessed May 2, 2002.

Al-Qasim, Samih. 1993. *Al-A'mal al-kamila lil-sha'ir Samih al-Qasim* [The complete works of the poet Samih al-Qasim], Vols. 1–6. Kuwait: Dar Su'ad al-Sabah.

Qasimiyya, Khayriyya. 2007. al-Mudhakarat wal-siyar al-dhatiyya masdaran li tarikh Filastin fi al-qarn al-'ashrin [Memoirs and autobiographies serving as sources of history of Palestine in the twentieth century]. In *Dirasat fi al-tarikh al-ijtima'i li-bilad al-sham* [Studies in the social history of the Levant], ed. Salim Tamari and Issam Nassar, pp. 153–180. Ramallah, West Bank: Institute of Jerusalem Studies.

Quandt, William, Fuad Jabber, and Ann Lesch. 1973. *The politics of Palestinian nationalism.* Berkeley: University of California Press.

Rabinowitz, Dan. 2007. 'The Arabs just left': Othering and the construction of self amongst Jews in Haifa before and after 1948. In *Mixed towns, trapped communities: Historical narratives, spatial dynamics, gender relations and cultural encounters in Palestinian-Israeli towns*, ed. Dan Rabinowitz and Daniel Monterescu, pp. 51–64. Burlington, VT: Ashgate.

Rapoport, Meron. 2008, March 6. Demolition Derby. *Ha'aretz*. Available at http://www .haaretz.com/print-edition/features/jerusalem-s-demolition-derby-1.247050

———. 2007a, December 25. Police finish evacuation of Kfar Shalem residents in south Tel Aviv. *Haaretz*. Available at http://www.haaretz.com/news/police-finish-evacuation -of-kfar-shalem-residents-in-south-t-a-1.235892

———. 2007b, July 15. Suddenly they are called "squatters." *Ha'aretz*. Available at http:// www.haaretz.com/print-edition/features/suddenly-they-are-called-squatters-1.225574

Raymond, André. 2002. *Arab cities in the Ottoman period: Cairo, Syria, and the Maghreb*. Aldershot, UK: Ashgate.

Reiker, Martina. 1992. Constructing Palestinian subalternity in the Galilee: Reflections on representations of the Palestinian peasant. *Inscriptions* 6. Available from http:// www2.ucsc.edu/culturalstudies/PUBS/Inscriptions/vol_6/Reiker.html

Rempel, Terry. 1999. Dispossession and restitution. In *Jerusalem 1948: The Arab neigh-bourhoods and their fate in the war*, ed. Salim Tamari, pp. 189–237. Jerusalem: Insti-tute of Jerusalem Studies and Badil Resource Center for Palestinian Residency and Refugee Rights.

Reynolds, Dwight, ed. 2001. *Interpreting the self: Autobiography in the Arabic literary tra-dition*. Berkeley: University of California Press.

Riessman, Catherine Kohler. 1993. *Narrative analysis*. Newbury Park, CA: Sage.

Al-Rimawi, Mahmud. 1998. Thaqafat al-samt [Culture of silence]. *Al-Karmel* 55–56: 227–231.

Rippin, Andrew. 2009. Shuayb. In *Encyclopedia of Islam*, 2nd ed., ed. P. Bearman, T. Bian-quis, C. E. Bosworth, E. van Donzel, and W. P. Heinrichs. Brill Online.

———. 1993. *Muslims: Their religious beliefs and practices*. Vol. 2: *The contemporary period*. New York: Routledge.

Robinson, Glenn. 1997. *Building a Palestinian state: The incomplete revolution*. Bloom-ington: Indiana University Press.

Robinson, Shira. 2003. Local struggle, national struggle: Palestinian responses to the Kafr Qasim massacre and its aftermath, 1956–1966. *International Journal of Middle East Studies* 35(3): 393–416.

Robson, J. 1999. Hadith [Narrative]. In *Encyclopedia of Islam*, Vol. 3, 2nd ed., ed. H. A. R. Gibb. Leiden, the Netherlands: E. J. Brill.

Rogan, Eugene. 2009. *The Arabs: A history*. London: Allen Lane.

Rogan, Eugene, and Avi Shlaim, eds. 2001. *The war for Palestine: Rewriting the history of 1948*. Cambridge, UK: Cambridge University Press.

Rogers, Mary Eliza. 1862. *Domestic life in Palestine*. London: Bell and Daldy.

Rooke, Tetz. 1997. *In my childhood: A study of Arabic autobiography*. Stockholm: Almqvist & Wiksell International.

Rosaldo, Renato. 1989. Imperialist nostalgia. *Representations* 26: 107–122.

———. 1980. *Ilongot headhunting, 1883–1974: A study in society and history.* Stanford, CA: Stanford University Press.

Rose, John H. Melkon. 1993. *Armenians of Jerusalem: Memories of life in Palestine.* New York: St. Martin's Press.

Rosenfeld, Maya. 2004. *Confronting the occupation: Work, education, and political activism of Palestinian families in a refugee camp.* Stanford, CA: Stanford University Press.

Rosenthal, Franz, trans. 1988. *The history of al-Tabari.* Vol. 1: *General introduction and from the creation to the flood.* Albany: State University of New York Press.

Roth, Michael S. 1989. Remembering forgetting: Maladies de la mémoire in nineteenth-century France. *Representations* 26: 49–68.

Rothenberg, Celia E. 2004. *Spirits of Palestine: Gender, society, and the stories of the Jinn.* Lanham, MD: Lexington Books.

———. 1998–1999. A review of the anthropological literature in English on the Palestinian Hamula and the status of women. *Journal of Arabic and Islamic Studies* 2. Available at http://www.uib.no/jais/v002ht/02-024-048Rothen1.htm. Accessed August 18, 2009).

Rowan, Yorke, and Uzi Baram, eds. 2004. *Marketing heritage: Archaeology and the consumption of the past.* New York: Altamira Press.

Rubenberg, Cheryl. 1983. *The Palestine Liberation Organization: Its institutional infrastructure.* Belmont, MA: Institute of Arab Studies.

Rubinstein, Danny. 1991. *The people of nowhere: The Palestinian vision of home,* trans. Ina Friedman. New York: Times Books.

Rushdie, Salman. 1991. *Imaginary homelands: Essays and criticism, 1981–1991.* London: Granta Books.

Safieh, Afif. 2007, February 16. We Palestinians will honor our word. Jewish Daily *Forward.*

Sahlins, Marshall David. 2004. *Apologies to Thucydides: understanding history as culture and vice versa.* Chicago: University of Chicago Press.

Said, Edward. 2001. Afterword: The consequences of 1948. In *The war for Palestine: Rewriting the history of 1948,* ed. Eugene L. Rogan and Avi Shlaim. Cambridge, UK: Cambridge University Press.

———. 1999a, December 2–8. The hazards of publishing a memoir. *Al-Ahram Weekly.*

———. 1999b. *Out of place: A memoir.* New York: Knopf.

———. 1979. *The question of Palestine.* New York: Vintage Books.

———. 1978. *Orientalism.* New York: Pantheon Books.

Sakakini, Hala. 1990. *Jerusalem and I: A personal record.* Amman, Jordan: Economic Press.

al-Sakakini, Khalil. 2003–2010. *Yawmiyat Khalil al-Sakakini* [Diary of Khalil al-Sakakini], Vols. 1–9. Ramallah, West Bank: Markaz Khalil al-Sakakini al-Thaqafi.

———. 1955. *Kadha ana ya dunya: Yawmiyyat* [Such am I, world: A diary]. Jerusalem: Al-Matba'a al-Tijariyya.

———. 1925. *Filastin ba'd al-harb al-kubra: al-Juz' al-awwal* [Palestine after the Great War: Part one]. Jerusalem: Bayt al-Maqdis.

Salah, Yusra A. 1992. *Tadhakkurat: Safahat min al-dhakira al-Filastiniyya* [Memoir: Pages from the Palestinian memory]. Birzeit, West Bank: Birzeit University, CRDPS.

Samilanski, Yazhar. 1988. *Khirbat khaz'a: Qarya 'Arabiyya fi Filastin lam ya'ud laha wujud* [Khirbat Khaz'a: An Arab village in Palestine that no longer exists]. Beirut, Lebanon: Dar al-Kama lil-Nashr.

Samir (dir.). 2002. *Forget Baghdad: Jews and Arabs—The Iraqi connection.* Zurich, Switzerland: Dschoint Ventschr Filmproduktion AG.

Samuel, Herbert. 1945. *Memoirs by the Rt. Hon. Viscount Samuel.* London: Cresset Press.

Samuel, Raphael. 1994. *Theatres of memory.* London: Verso.

Samuel, Raphael, and Paul Thompson. 1990. Introduction. In *The myths we live by*, ed. Raphael Samuel and Paul Thompson, pp. 1–22. London: Routledge.

Sanbar, Elias. 2004. *Les palestiniens: La photographie d'une terre et de son peuple de 1839 à nos jours.* [The Palestinians: Photography of a land and its people from 1839 to the present]. Paris: Hazan.

Sayigh, Rosemary. 1998. Palestinian camp women as tellers of history. *Journal of Palestinian Studies* 27(2): 42–58.

———. 1994. *Too many enemies.* London: Zed Books.

———. 1979. *Palestinians: From peasants to revolutionaries—A people's history.* London: Zed Press.

Sayigh, Yezid. 1997. *Armed struggle and the search for state: The Palestinian national movement 1949–1993.* Oxford: Oxford University Press.

Sbaiti, Nadya. 2008. Lessons in history: Education and the formation of national society in Beirut, Lebanon, 1920s-1960s. Ph.D. dissertation, Georgetown University.

Schama, Simon. 1995. *Landscape and memory.* New York: Knopf.

Scheper-Hughes, Nancy. 1992. *Death without weeping: The violence of everyday life in Brazil.* Berkeley: University of California Press.

Schleifer, Abdullah. 1993. 'Izz al-din al-Qassam: Preacher and mujahid. In *Struggle and survival in the modern Middle East*, ed. Edmund Burke. New York: IB Tauris.

Schmelz, U. O. 1987. *Modern Jerusalem's demographic evolution.* Jerusalem: Institute of Contemporary Jewry, Hebrew University of Jerusalem, and Jerusalem Institute for Israel Studies.

———. 1981. Notes on the demography of Jews, Muslims, and Christians in Jerusalem. *Middle East Review of International Affairs* 13(3/4): 62–69.

Schrager, Samuel. 1983. What is social in oral history? *International Journal of Oral History* 4(2): 76–98.

Schulz, Helena Lindholm, and Juliane Hammer. 2003. *The Palestinian diaspora: Formation of identities and politics of homeland.* New York: Routledge.

Scott, James C. 1992. *Domination and the arts of resistance: Hidden transcripts.* New Haven, CT: Yale University Press.

———. 1985. *Weapons of the weak: Everyday forms of peasant resistance.* New Haven, CT: Yale University Press.

Scott, Joan W. 1991. The evidence of experience. *Critical Inquiry* 17(4): 773–797.

———. 1986. Gender: A useful category of historical analysis. *American Historical Review* 91(5): 1053–1075.

Segev, Tom. 2000. *One Palestine, complete: Jews and Arabs under the mandate.* New York: Metropolitan Books.

Seikaly, May. 1995. *Haifa: Transformation of an Arab society 1918–1939.* London: I. B. Taurus.

Shafir, Gershon. 1989. *Land, labor, and the origins of the Israeli-Palestinian conflict, 1882–1914.* Cambridge, UK: Cambridge University Press.

Shaheen, Naseeb. 1992. *A pictorial history of Ramallah.* Beirut, Lebanon: Arab Institute for Research and Publishing.

Shahid, Irfan. 1988. *Byzantium and the Semitic Orient before the rise of Islam.* London: Variorum Reprints.

Shahid, Serene al-Husseini. 2000. *Jerusalem memories.* Beirut, Lebanon: Naufal.

Shai, Aron. 2006. The fate of abandoned Arab villages in Israel, 1965–1969. *History & Memory* 18(2): 86– 106.

Shammas, Anton. 1997, August 23. Al-Falafal: Tabaq Isra'il al-qawmi [Falafel, Israel's national dish]. *Al-Nahar,* Cultural Supplement.

———. 1988. The retreat from Galilee. *Granta* 23: 44–68.

Shanna'a, Tal'at. 1993. *Ayyam zaman: al-Tarikh al-shafawi lil-'Urdunn wa Filastin* [Days of old: The oral history of Jordan and Palestine]. Amman, Jordan: Al-ahliya lil-Nashr wal-Tawzi'a.

Shapiro, S. 1973. Planning Jerusalem: The first generation, 1917–1968. In *Urban geography of Jerusalem: A companion volume to the atlas of Jerusalem,* ed. David H. K. Amiran and Arie Shachar, p. 173. New York: W. De Gruyeter.

Sharabi, Hisham. 1993. *Suwar al-madi: Sira dhatiyya* [Pictures of the past: An autobiography]. Beirut, Lebanon: Dar Nilsun.

Shenhav, Yehouda. 2006. *The Arab Jews: A postcolonial reading of nationalism, religion, and ethnicity.* Stanford, CA: Stanford University Press.

Shepherd, Naomi. 1999. *Ploughing sand: British rule in Palestine, 1917–1948.* London: John Murray.

Shlaim, Avi. 2000. *The iron wall: Israel and the Arab world.* New York: Norton.

Shohat, Ella. 2006. *Taboo memories, diasporic voices.* Durham, NC: Duke University Press.

———. 1997. The Narrative of the nation and the discourse of modernization: The Case of the Mizrahim. *Critique* 10: 3–18.

———. 1992. Rethinking Jews and Muslims: Quincentennial reflections. *Middle East Report* 178: 25–29.

———. 1988. Sephardim in Israel: Zionism from the standpoint of its Jewish victims. *Social Text* 19/20: 1–35.

Shoman, Abdulhameed. 1984. *The indomitable Arab: The life and times of Abdulhameed Shoman (1890–1974), founder of the Arab Bank*. London: Third World Centre.

Shqayr, Mahmoud. 1998. *Dhul akhir lil-madina* [Another shadow of the city]. Jerusalem: Dar al-Quds lil-Nashr wal-Tawziʻ.

Shryock, Andrew. 1997. *Nationalism and the genealogical imagination: Oral history and textual authority in tribal Jordan*. Berkeley: University of California Press.

Shurmer-Smith, Pamela, and Kevin Hannam. 1994. *Worlds of desire, realms of power: A cultural geography*. New York: Routledge, Chapman, and Hall.

Shurrab, Muhammad Hasan. 2000. *Muʻjam asmaʼ al-mudun wal-qura al-Filastiniyya* [Dictionary of Palestinian city and village names]. Amman, Jordan: al-Ahliya lil-Nashr wal-Tawziʻ.

Sibley, David. 1995. *Geographies of exclusion: Society and difference in the West*. New York: Routledge.

Sider, Gerald. 2005. Anthropology and history: Opening points for a new synthesis. In *Critical junctions: Anthropology and history beyond the cultural turn*, ed. Don Kalb and Herman Tak. New York: Berghan Books.

Sidqi, Najati, and Abu Hanna Hanna. 2001. *Mudhakkarat najati sidqi* [Memoir of Najati Sidqi]. Beirut, Lebanon: Muʼassasat al-Dirasat al-Filastiniyya.

Silberman, Neil Asher. 1989. *Between past and present: Archaeology, ideology, and nationalism in the modern Middle East*. New York: Holt.

Sirhan, Nimr. 1989. *al-Mabani al-kanʻaniyya fi Filastin* [The Canaanite structures in Palestine]. Amman, Jordan: Dar al-Karmal al-Samid.

———. 1977. *Mawsuʻat al-fulklur al-Filastini* [Encyclopedia of Palestinian folklore]. Amman, Jordan: Maktabat Rami.

Sirhan, Nimr, and Mustafa Kabha. 2000a. *ʻAbd al-Rahim al-Hajj Muhammad: Al-Qaʼid al-ʻaam li-thawrat 1936–1939* [ʻAbd al-Rahim al-Hajj Muhammad: The general leader of the 1936–1939 revolt]. Ramallah, West Bank: n.p.

———. 2000b. *Bashir Ibrahim: al-Qadi wal-thaʼir fi thawrat 1936–1939* [Bashir Ibrahim: Judge and fighter in the 1936–1939 revolt]. Ramallah, West Bank: n.p.

Slyomovics, Susan. 1998. *The object of memory: Arab and Jew narrate the Palestinian village*. Philadelphia: University of Pennsylvania Press.

———. 1994. The memory of place: Rebuilding the pre-1948 Palestinian village. *Diaspora* 3(2): 156–168.

———. 1993. Discourses on the pre-1948 Palestinian village: The case of Ein Hod/Ein Houd. *Traditional Dwellings and Settlements Review* 4(2): 27–37.

Smith, Anthony. 1989. The origins of nations. *Ethnic and Racial Studies* 12(3): 348–356.

Snobar, Ibrahim. 1992. *Tadhakkurat* [Memoir]. Birzeit, West Bank: Birzeit University, CRDPS.

Somers, Margaret R. 1994. The narrative constitution of identity: A relational and network approach. *Theory and Society* 23(5): 605–649.

Spiegel, Gabrielle M. 2005. *Practicing history: New directions in historical writing after the linguistic turn*, ed. Gabrielle M. Spiegel. New York: Routledge.

State of Israel, Central Bureau of Statistics. 2009. *Israel in Statistics, 1948–2007*. Jerusalem: Central Bureau of Statistics. http://www1.cbs.gov.il/statistical/statistical60_eng .pdf. Accessed September 17, 2009.

Stein, Kenneth W. 1991. A historiographic review of literature on the origins of the Arab-Israeli conflict. *American Historical Review* 96(5): 1450–1465.

———. 1984. *The land question in Palestine, 1917–1939*. Chapel Hill: University of North Carolina Press.

Stevens, Richard. 1971. Zionism as a phase of western imperialism. In *Transformation of Palestine*, ed. Ibrahim Abu Lughod. Evanston, IL: Northwestern University Press.

Stewart, Kathleen. 1996. *A space on the side of the road: Cultural poetics in an "other" America*. Princeton, NJ: Princeton University Press.

———. 1988. Nostalgia—A polemic. *Cultural Anthropology* 3(3): 227–241.

Stillman, Norman. 1991. *The Jews of Arab lands in modern times*. Philadelphia: Jewish Publication Society.

Stoler, Ann Laura. 1995. *Race and the education of desire: Foucault's history of sexuality and the colonial order of things*. Durham, NC: Duke University Press.

Sturken, Marita. 1999. Narratives of recovery: Repressed memory as cultural memory. In *Acts of memory: Cultural recall in the present*, ed. Mieke Bal, Jonathan V. Crewe, and Leo Spitzer, pp. 231–248. Hanover, NH: University Press of New England.

Sufian, Sandy. 2007. *Healing the land and the nation: Malaria and the Zionist Project in Palestine, 1920–1947*. Chicago: University of Chicago Press.

Swedenburg, Ted. 1992. Seeing double: Palestinian/American histories of the Kufiya. *Michigan Quarterly Review* 31(4): 557–577.

———. 1995/2003. *Memories of revolt: The 1936–1939 rebellion and the struggle for a Palestinian national past*. Austin: University of Texas Press.

———. 1990. The Palestinian peasant as national signifier. *Anthropological Quarterly* 63(1): 18–30.

Tall, Deborah. 1993. *From where we stand: Recovering a sense of place*. Baltimore, MD: Johns Hopkins University Press.

Tamari, Salim. 2009. *Mountain against the sea: Essays on Palestinian society and culture*. Berkeley: University of California Press.

———. 2005a. Wasif Jawhariyyeh, popular music, and early modernity in Jerusalem. In *Palestine, Israel, and the politics of popular culture*, ed. Rebecca L. Stein and Ted Swedenburg, 27–50. Durham, NC: Duke University Press.

———. 2005b. "Bourgeois nostalgia and the abandoned city." *Comparative Studies of South Asia, Africa, and the Middle East* 23(1–2): 173–180.

———. 2001. The enigmatic Jerusalem Bolshevik. *Jerusalem Quarterly File* 14: 49–55.

———. 1999. al-Dhakira al-mu'adhdhaba [Tormented memory]. *al-Karmel* 54.

————, ed. 1999. *Jerusalem 1948: The Arab neighbourhoods and their fate in the war*. Jerusalem: Institute of Jerusalem Studies.

————. 1989. From the fruits of their labour: The persistence of sharetenancy in the Palestinian agrarian economy. In *The rural Middle East: Peasant lives and modes of production*, ed. Kathy and Pandeli Glavanis, 70–94. London: Zed Books.

————. 1982. Factionalism and class formation in recent Palestinian history. In *Studies in the economic and social history of Palestine in the nineteenth and twentieth centuries*, ed. Roger Owen. Carbondale: Southern Illinois University Press.

Tamari, Salim, and Issam Nassar, eds. 2007. *Dirasat fi al-tarikh al-ijtima'i li-bilad al-sham* [Studies in the social history of the Levant]. Ramallah, West Bank: Institute of Jerusalem Studies.

Tamari, Salim, and Rema Hammami. 1998. Virtual returns to Jaffa. *Journal of Palestine Studies* 27(4): 65–79.

Tannous, Izzat. 1975–1985. *Failures of the United Nations in the Palestine tragedy*. New York: Palestine Arab Refugee Office.

Tannous, Izzat. 1988. *The Palestinians: A detailed documented eyewitness history of Palestine under British mandate*. New York: I.G.T.

Tessler, Mark A. 1994. *A history of the Israeli-Palestinian conflict*. Bloomington: Indiana University Press.

Thompson, Paul. 1994. Believe it or not: Rethinking the historical interpretation of memory. In *Memory and history: Essays on recalling and interpreting experience*, ed. Jaclyn Jeffrey and Glenace Edwall, pp. 1–16. Lanham, MD: University Press of America.

Thompson, Thomas. 1998. Hidden histories and the problem of ethnicity in Palestine. In *Western scholarship and the history of Palestine*, ed. Michael Prior, p. 111. London: Melisende.

Tibawi, Abdul Latif. 1972. *Islamic education: Its traditions and modernization into the Arab national systems*. London: Luzac.

————. 1963. Visions of the return: The Palestine Arab refugees in Arabic poetry and art. *Middle East Journal* 17(5): 507–526.

————. 1956. *Arab education in mandatory Palestine: A study of three decades of British administration*. London: Luzac.

Tleel, John. 2000. *I am Jerusalem*. Jerusalem: n.p.

Tonkin, Elizabeth. 1992. *Narrating our pasts: The social construction of oral history*. Cambridge, UK: Cambridge University Press.

Toubbeh, Jamil I. 1998. *Day of the long night: A Palestinian refugee remembers the Nakba*. Jefferson, NC: McFarland.

Trouillot, Michel-Rolph. 1995. *Silencing the past: Power and the production of history*. Boston, MA: Beacon Press.

Tuan, Yi-fu. 1996. *Cosmos and hearth: A cosmopolite's viewpoint*. Minneapolis: University of Minnesota Press.

Tucker, Judith E. 1998. *In the house of the law: Gender and Islamic law in Ottoman Syria and Palestine*. Berkeley: University of California Press.

Tuqan, Fadwa. 1990. *A mountainous journey: An autobiography* [*Rihla jabaliyya, rihla sa'ba*]. Trans. Olive Kenny and Naomi Shihab Nye, ed. Salma Khadra Jayyusi. St. Paul, Minnesota: Graywolf Press.

Turan, Zeynep. 2004. Personal objects from the homeland: Reconstructing cultural and personal identities. *International Journal of Humanities* 1: 465–480.

Tyler, Warwick P. N. 2001. *State lands and rural development in mandatory Palestine, 1920–1948*. Brighton, UK: Sussex Academic Press.

United Nations Relief and Works Administration. 2009. UNRWA in figures. Gaza: UNRWA Headquarters, Public Information Office. Available at http://www.unrwa.org/userfiles/uif-june09.pdf

United Nations Special Committee on Palestine. 1947. Report on Palestine: Report to the general assembly by the United Nations Special Committee on Palestine. Foreword by Senator Robert F. Wagner. New York: Somerset Books.

United States Holocaust Memorial Museum. 1996. *Historical Atlas of the Holocaust*. New York: Macmillan.

Van Oord, Lodewijk. 2008. The making of primitive Palestine: Intellectual origins of the Palestine-Israel conflict. *History and Anthropology* 19(3): 209–228.

Vansina, Jan. 1985. *Oral tradition as history*. Madison: University of Wisconsin Press.

Wakim, Wakim, and Riad Beidas. 2001. The "internally displaced": Seeking return within one's own land. *Journal of Palestine Studies* 31(1): 32–38.

Wasserstein, Bernard. 1991. *The British in Palestine: The mandatory government and the Arab-Jewish conflict, 1917–1929*, 2nd ed. Cambridge, MA: Basil Blackwell.

Weir, Shelagh. 1989. *Palestinian costume*. London: British Museum Publications.

White, Hayden. 1980. *The value of narrativity in the representation of reality. Critical Inquiry* 7(1): 5–27.

Whitlam, Keith. 1996. *The invention of ancient Israel: The silencing of Palestinian history*. London: Routledge.

Wood, Denis. 1992. *The power of maps*. New York: Guilford Press.

Al-Wuhush, Mohammad Shahda Mustafa. 1990. *Halhul: Ard wa sha'b* [Halul: Land and people]. Jordan: n.p.

Yaghi, Abdelrahman. 1968. *Hayat al-adab al-Filastini al-hadith: Min awwal al-nahda hatta al-nakba* [The life of modern Palestinian literature from the beginning of the renaissance to the catastrophe]. Beirut, Lebanon: al-Maktab al-Tijari.

Yahya, Adel. 1999. *The Palestinian refugees: 1948–1998: An oral history*. Ramallah, West Bank: Palestinian Association for Cultural Exchange.

Yow, Valerie. 1994. *Recording oral history: A practical guide for social scientists*. Thousand Oaks, CA: Sage Publications.

Zemon Davis, Natalie, and Randolph Starn. 1989. Introduction. *Representations* 26: 1–6.

Zerubavel, Yael. 1995. *Recovered roots: Collective memory and the making of Israeli national tradition.* Chicago: University of Chicago Press.

Zionist Organization of America. 1998. Deir Yassin: History of a lie. Available from http://www.zoa.org/pubs/deiryassin.html

Zurayk, Constantine. 1956. *The meaning of the disaster*, trans. R. Bayly Winder. Beirut, Lebanon: Khayat's College Book Cooperative.

Zurayq, Qustantin. 1948. *Ma'na al-nakba* [The meaning of the catastrophe]. Beirut, Lebanon: Dar al-'Ilm lil-Malayin.

Zureik, Elia. 1979. *The Palestinians in Israel: A study in internal colonialism.* London: Routledge & Kegan Paul.

Interviews

'Abd al-'Aal, Yusif ' Ali. July 29, 2008. Damascus, Syria.

'Abd al-Rahim, Matar. June 30, 2005, Damascus, Syria.

'Abdel Jawad, Saleh. July 3, 2008, al-Bira, West Bank.

Abu Hadba, 'Abd al-'Aziz. July 25, 2005, al-Bira, West Bank.

Abu Sbayh, 'Abdallah Wahba. May 26, 2005, Amman, Jordan.

Al-'Ali, 'Abd al-Majid Fadl. January 7, 2005, Beirut, Lebanon.

Al-Amir, Kawthar. June 22, 2005, Amman, Jordan.

'Atiya, 'Atiya 'Abdallah. April 24, 2005, Amman, Jordan.

'Awadallah, Ibrahim. June 4, 2005, Amman, Jordan.

Barakat, Wajih. April 15, 1999, Amman, Jordan.

Ghosha, Yusuf. August 23, 1999, Amman, Jordan.

Al-Hashwa, Zuhdi. November 2, 1998, Jerusalem, West Bank.

Kan'aan, Deeb. 16 July 2005. Amman, Jordan.

Al-Lubani, Hussein. June 6, 2005, Tripoli, Lebanon.

Al-Nammari, Muhammad Zuhayr. July 6, 1999, Amman, Jordan.

Al-Najjar, 'Atiya. July 18, 2005, al-Zarqa, Jordan.

Rahil, Yusif. February 5, 1999, Jerusalem, West Bank.

Al-Ramahi, Qasim. July 21, 2005, Amman, Jordan.

Al-Sahli, Nabil. May 8, 2005, Damascus, Syria.

Saqr, Abd al-'Aziz. June 1, 2005, Amman, Jordan.

Shihabi, Ghassan. July 6, 2005, Damascus, Syria

Siyyam, Zakaria. June 22, 2005, Amman, Jordan.

Al-Sufi, 'Abdallah Isma'il. June 8, 2005, Amman, Jordan.

Sulayma, Fadi. July 6, 2005, Damascus, Syria.

Sulayman, Mahmud. May 3, 2005, Amman, Jordan.

Sumrayn, Ghalib Muhammad. April 30, 2005, Amman, Jordan.

INDEX

Stanford Studies in Middle Eastern and Islamic Societies and Cultures

Joel Beinin, *Stanford University*

Juan R.I. Cole, *University of Michigan*

Haggai Ram, *Iranophobia: The Logic of an Israeli Obsession*
2009

John Chalcraft, *The Invisible Cage: Syrian Migrant Workers in Lebanon*
2008

Rhoda Kanaaneh, *Surrounded: Palestinian Soldiers in the Israeli Military*
2008

Asef Bayat, *Making Islam Democratic: Social Movements and the Post-Islamist Turn*
2007

Robert Vitalis, *America's Kingdom: Mythmaking on the Saudi Oil Frontier*
2006

Jessica Winegar, *Creative Reckonings: The Politics of Art and Culture in Contemporary Egypt*
2006

Joel Beinin and Rebecca L. Stein, editors, *The Struggle for Sovereignty: Palestine and Israel, 1993-2005*
2006